D1631429

STORMING ST NAZAIRE

STORMING ST NAZAIRE

The Gripping Story of the Dock-Busting Raid
March, 1942

by

JAMES DORRIAN

LEO COOPER
LONDON

First published in Great Britain in 1998 by
LEO COOPER
190 Shaftesbury Avenue, London WC2H 8JL
an imprint of
Pen & Sword Books Ltd,
47 Church Street,
Barnsley, South Yorkshire, S70 2AS

ISBN 0 85052 419 9

A CIP record for this book is
available from the British Library

Typeset by Phoenix Typesetting, Ilkley, West Yorkshire.

Printed in England by Redwood Books Ltd, Trowbridge, Wilts.

FOR
SANDIE

Contents

Maps and Diagrams

A Veteran Returns to Europe

Is this defenceless port the place
That once I came to wreck?
Is nothing manned at my approach,
And no one armed on deck?

No, nothing now's afloat to sink,
Nor on the shore to invade.
These by the coach are teachers.
These in the boat want trade.

And over old unhappy things
Pacific ledgers mount,
Deals must have duplicates, and lives,
That had no copies, count,

And children come with flowers
To place where teachers bid,
Who never heard of Goering,
Or ask what Goebbels did . . .

O glittering wings, so suddenly
High in the vacant blue,
Stay, till to-day dies normally,
And normal nights ensue!

Never again the premature,
Never again the pain.
And a rose for those who went in first,
And where they fall, remain.

Michael Burn, 1997

Introduction and Acknowledgements

As the 20th century draws to an uncertain close with emergencies and minor wars an everyday component of the news, it is almost impossible to conceive of a military reality which would fail to recognize the capabilities of special fighting forces such as the Commandos, the SAS and the SBS.

And yet, little more than half a century ago, at a time when Britain stood in mortal peril, the diversion of talent away from mainstream formations was seen as little less than a disruptive madness by the many who believed that victory was a prize far beyond the grasp of any but the big battalions.

Against a background of such easy prejudice and deprived as they were of materiel, cooperation, even a clear and certain rôle, the newly formed Army Commandos struggled to take the fight to the enemy, engineering a series of attacks against the enemy coast of which the Combined Ops raid on the heavily defended port of St Nazaire was by far the most hazardous yet.

Representing, as it did, both the best and worst of all that Britain had to offer at that time – the best in respect of the quality and enthusiasm of the young men who could not wait to sail for France; the worst in respect of the muddle and parsimony that saw them face the enemy with no weapon more potent than their absolute determination to win regardless of the cost – the story of this particular operation is a poignant memoir both of a great adventure stained by pain and loss, and of an era whose attitudes and aspirations were soon to change forever.

In attempting to make a record of their sacrifice, truthfully and with conviction, I have been fortunate indeed in securing the wholehearted support of the committee and membership of the St Nazaire Society, whose soldier and sailor veterans have displayed considerable patience in the face of my many enquiries. I list the names of all those who contributed, alphabetically, as any attempt to establish an order of precedence must fall foul of the fact that each contributed as best he could. Most were interviewed on tape while others completed questionnaires, submitted written accounts or allowed me to quote from as yet unpublished memoirs. In the interests of brevity, I have excluded decorations from the list.

F.W.M. Arkle; H.W. Arnold; A. Ashcroft; J. Aspden; F.R. Axford; L.H. Ball; R.J. Barron; P.St G. Barry; Cdr M.J. Blake; H. Bracewell; R. Bradley; F. Brown; L.W. Brown; R.F. Brown; C.W.S. Burkimsher; M. Burn; R.H. Butler; F.A. Carr; F.H.C. Catton; E.L.D. Chappell; W.C. Clibborn; R.E. Collinson; D.K. Croft; J. Cudby; G. Davidson; S.B.E. Davis; L. Denison; H.R. Dyer; D.G. Edwards; P.C. Ellingham; Col. W.W. Etches; F. Folkard; J.A. Gardner; A.R. Green; T.G. Hannan; J. Hayhurst; S. Hinks; W.A. Holland; R. Hoyle; W.J. Johnson; A.W. King; J.H. Laurie; W.H. Lawson; F. Lemon; H.C. Lloyd; J. May; T. Milner; R.E. Mitchell; Lt-Col. R.K. Montgomery; H.H. Morgan; N.R. Nock; Dr D. Paton; A.W. Peacock; F.A. Penfold; A. Porter; F.E. Pritchard; G.J. Pryde; Maj-Gen. C.W.B. Purdon; J. Rafferty; W.E. Rainbird; D.C. Randall; E.C.A. Roberts; Dr J.M. Roderick; J.G. Rogers; G. Salisbury; A.C. Searson; Col. T. Sherman; H.J. Shipton; Revd C.A. Simister; F.A. Smith; D.R. Steele, Cdr W.L. Stephens; S.G. Stevenson; E.D. Stogdon; Lt-Cdr W. Wallach; Dr W.H. Watson; J. Webb; G.R. Wheeler; F.W. Wherrell; C.E. Whittle; A.F. Woodiwiss; Dr R.T.C. Worsley; R.E. Wright.

In the case of participants who have not survived to the present day I have been helped considerably by family members whose contributions include such invaluable documents as Major Copland's detailed account of his activities at St Nazaire, and Lt-Col. Newman's comprehensive report written while still a POW. Of particular importance were the many documents relating to the organization and execution of the raid collected by Cdr Ryder and made available to me by his son, the Revd Canon Lisle Ryder. Mrs Elmslie Henderson was kind enough to provide me with a body of material relating to Lt Nigel Tibbits RN; and Mrs Caroline Carr gave me free access to the archive which she created in memory of her great uncle, Able Seaman William Savage, VC. The full list of family contributors is as follows: Mr and Mrs P. Andrews; Mrs Cecilie Birney; Mrs B. and Mr T.W. Boyd; Mrs E. Copland; Mrs P. Curtis; Mr W.McM. Ferguson; Ms M. Harrison; Mrs L. Holman; Mr J. Maclagan; Mrs J. Westcott and others of Col. Newman's family; the Revd Canon L. Ryder; Mrs C. Carr; Mrs A.P. Inman; Mrs E. Henderson.

As the raid had a significant impact upon the lives of the inhabitants of St Nazaire I have sought to include a number of reminiscences collected by organizations based in and around the port. For their permission to make use of these I am indebted to Mme Michèle Mahé, Vice President of the Association Préhistorique et Historique de la Région Nazairienne, for making available to me the story of Alain Bizard, and to M. Thomas, Secretary of the Memoire et Savoir Nazariens, for arranging the use of material contained in *Souvenance* booklets 1 and 2. Both Mme Mahe and M. Thomas were of tremendous assistance when it came to establishing how St Nazaire looked before it was largely destroyed by allied bombs. Further adding to my store of information was material made available by the French President of the St Nazaire Society, M. Alfred Hemery, Chevalier de la Légion d'Honneur. As most of these documents required translation I owe a great debt to Ms Sharon Greig, Ms Nina Narayan and Ms Kirsty Hewson for completing a mass of work with speed and accuracy.

Although it was impossible to explore the German side of 'Chariot' in any depth, I am grateful to *Kapitänleutnant* Gerd Kelbling, the CO of *U-593* for supplying me with a new perspective on the meeting between his boat and the destroyers *Atherstone* and *Tynedale*. Among the last of the sightseers to leave the hulk of *Campbeltown* prior to her demise, Seamen Heinz Grossmann and Heinz Hunke, of Minesweeper 1601 both submitted accounts which, along with other German papers, were translated by Mrs Lesley Rollason and Mr Peter Collinson. For my description of the participation of other German combatants I must credit the archive of the St Nazaire Society, and particularly the Honorary Secretary Eric de la Torre, MBE. Forever patient and helpful, it is Eric who is to be thanked for providing membership lists, photographs and newsletters.

Perhaps surprisingly only a few accounts of the raid have been published by the 'Charioteers' themselves. Cdr Ryder's book *The Attack on St Nazaire* is acknowledged in the bibliography, otherwise I am indebted to John Murray (Publishers) Ltd for allowing me to quote selectively from Stuart Chant-Sempill's *St Nazaire Commando*, and to Greystone Books for allowing me to quote freely from Corran Purdon's *List the Bugle*.

As a newcomer to the world of Coastal Forces, my research into the operation of MLs, MGBs and MTBs was facilitated by the help I received from L.C. Reynolds and G.M. Hudson of the Coastal Forces Veterans' Association, and from the encyclopaedic John Lambert.

In respect of the actions of naval vessels on the night, the Imperial War Museum were able to furnish me with an impressive body of Crown Copyright material which, in addition to operational instructions and orders and a copy of Lt-Cdr Beattie's excellent narrative, includes post-action reports submitted by Sub-Lts Machin and Wynn and Lts Wallis, Burt, Irwin, Platt, Boyd, Horlock, Curtis and Fenton.

The staff of the museum of the Royal Corps of Signals are to be thanked for supplying me with technical information relating to radios, as is Mr A.P. Powell for allowing me to make use of his excellent list of participating soldiers and sailors. For their help in piecing together the story of the RAF's contribution I am particularly grateful to Eddie Shine, Brian Nation, Walter Ollerhead, C.B. Brinkley, Ray Sermon, R.C. Hogg, L.E. Norris, Vin Crook, Doug Ratcliffe, Group Captain W.S.O. Randle, Wing Commander A.N. Hulme, Wing Commander R.M. Pinkham, and Mrs H. Reeder (for material relating to H.D. Reeder).

Eric de la Torre, John Roderick, John May, Corran Purdon and Michael Burn were kind enough to read and comment on the manuscript, as were the current General Secretary of the Commando Association, Mr Ron Youngman, (who also supplied much useful information relating to the foundation of individual Commando units), and his predecessor, Henry Brown. For the typing of several drafts and for sacrificing much to make possible the writing of this book I am indebted to my wife Sandie, who as the work progressed came to have a deep respect for the individuals who are the subjects of this exercise.

The members of the Society were kind enough to entrust to my care many treasured photographs which are individually acknowledged elsewhere, and the Committee are to be thanked for allowing me to select freely from their archive of images. John Lambert and Al Ross have supplied a number of excellent prints of *Campbeltown* and other vessels; and Mrs S. Walton of the Air Photo Library at Keele University supplied a number of excellent aerial photographs of the target areas. Particularly in the case of photographs I have made every effort to acknowledge contributions and to identify the holders of original copyright. Bearing in mind the age of the images and the fact that many have passed through several hands before reaching my own, this has, however, not been an easy task and if I have infringed any copyright or, as with the body of the text, neglected to name a contributor, the omission is unintended and I apologize for it.

Finally I must express my gratitude to Leo Cooper for his tolerance during the lengthy period of research and writing.

James G. Dorrian

The author and publishers are grateful to the following for the generous loan of, and kind permission to publish, the photographs in this book:

John Lambert and Vosper Thorneycroft (UK) Ltd, 1; E.D. Stogdon, 2, 6, 18; Al Ross II, 3; Canon Lisle Ryder, 4, 5, 28; The St Nazaire Society, 7, 8, 10, 11, 12, 13; Harry James and Mrs Caroline Carr, 9, 29; Lt-Col R.K. Montgomery, 14; Reg Durrant, 15; Des Chappell, 16; Mrs Kate Roach, 17; Michael Burn, 19; T.W. Boyd, 20; Dr W.H. Watson, 21; Mrs Elmslie Henderson, 22; Mrs Ethel Copland, 23, 40; AF Woodiwiss, 24; Major-General Corran Purdon, 25, 43; Mrs C.M.R. Birney, 26; Mrs P. Curtiss, 27; Dr David Paton, 30; Mrs Molly Harrison, 31; L.H. Ball, 32; F.A. Carr, 33; Tom Milner, 34; P.C. Ellingham, 35; F. Pritchard, 36; Mr Roderick Roy, 37; Jim Hayhurst, 38; F.W.M. Arkle, 39; Mrs P. Beattie, 41; Jack Webb, 42.

The maps and diagrams were drawn by the author.

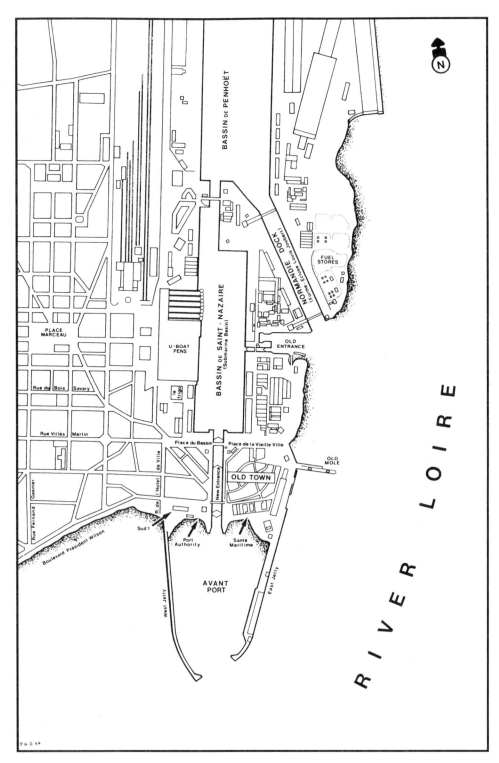

The Port of St Nazaire, March, 1942

1

'Big Trouble! – Tommies Kommen!'

When Adolf Hitler issued his War Directive No. 40 on 23 March, 1942, he could hardly have imagined just how timely was its warning of imminent British strikes against the exposed and vulnerable coastline of the new Reich.

More often than not an albatross around the necks of his many more gifted subordinates, the Führer and Supreme Commander was nevertheless capable of acting from time to time with uncanny prescience; and on this occasion his prediction was so accurate that he might almost have been able to see inside the mind of Admiral Lord Louis Mountbatten, the determined and charismatic adversary charged with delivering to Adolf just such unwelcome surprises.

The thrust of his warning was that, however unlikely such adventures might seem from a purely military standpoint, the desperate British must eventually be driven by political and propaganda considerations alone to mount a strong attack somewhere along the borders of the Reich. Yes, they were woefully short of men and materiel; and, yes, their hard-pressed armies were retreating almost everywhere: however, their attacks at Vaagso and in the Lofotens during 1941, and their recent assault on the radar site at Bruneval, had proved they could still lash out from behind the shelter of Churchill's bombastic oratory.

In an absolute sense such escapades posed little threat to the overall security of the Reich; however, they most certainly could – as Hitler feared and Mountbatten fully intended – force a withdrawal of vital resources from other theatres in order to mount a comprehensive defence.

With such an extended seaboard to protect, stretching from the North Cape to the Franco-Spanish frontier, it was all but impossible to define with any certainty even the general area against which such a strike might be launched. Past experience, fuelled by Hitler's personal conviction that the British would eventually attempt a full-scale invasion in the north, would seem to place Norway at the top of any list of potential targets; however, no one could be sure, so his warning was issued to all commanders of strong points and Coastal Defence Sectors, each of whom must gauge its import on the basis of how vulnerable he believed his own particular charge to be.

Of all the potential targets, temptingly close to England though its channel coast might be, Occupied France must surely be considered far too hard a nut to crack, unless an attacking force was prepared to risk being mauled by coastal artillery and the Luftwaffe.

Perhaps the most secure of all were the chain of heavily fortified western seaports, the glittering prizes of Brest, Lorient, St Nazaire, La Pallice and La Rochelle, which gave the German navy direct access to the Atlantic from France's Biscay coast; and of these the defenders of St Nazaire had particular cause to feel smug, for in addition to the multiplicity of cannon that surrounded it, the benign hand of mother nature had rendered this important port and submarine base all but unapproachable by stealth.

Situated six miles from the open sea, tucked deep inside the throat of the yawning estuary of the River Loire, St Nazaire was protected by shoals and mudflats so extensive as to restrict ships of any substance to a narrow, twisting and easily defended deep-water channel. No enemy warship could pass along this channel and survive the guns which lined the estuary shores, this almost certain guarantee of her destruction greatly easing the mind of the commander of the port, the Sea Commandant Loire, *Kapitän zur See* Zuckschwerdt.

Apparently inviolate, it was small wonder, therefore, that when the air-raid sirens wailed out at 2320 on the night of 27th March no significance was attached to the event beyond the expectation of yet another pounding from the bombers of the RAF.

As the progress of the lumbering Whitleys and Wellingtons was carefully monitored by radar, the defenders of St Nazaire rushed to their action stations at searchlight batteries and coastal artillery emplacements, as well as at the light and heavy flak positions infesting the port itself and the area immediately surrounding it.

As the gun crews and garrison troops tumbled from their shelters, most of the townspeople, whose support for the RAF did not render them immune from the blast of the coming bombs, hurried to their favoured places of safety. In what was becoming an all-too-depressing routine they took up their suitcases and valuables and helped the children and those of the elderly and the infirm who could be moved down to the shelters they were coming to know so well. All but forgotten in the cruel equation of war, they had only themselves to rely on: themselves, that is, and the courageous personnel of the *Défense Passive*, whose ambulances, first-aid posts and volunteer groups were spread across the waiting city.

One such group quickly came together in the cellar of the Santé Maritime building, situated in the 'Little Morocco' district of the Old Town, on its seaward edge and with a perfect view along both river and estuary. Old St Nazaire was the original seaport, built long before the town of the Second Empire which sprawled across the countryside to the west of the great north-south basins which effectively cut the community in two. A tightly packed muddle of buildings, alleyways and crooked streets, it was virtually an island in its own right. Flanked by the estuary to east and south, its western edge was defined by the long, straight moat of the New Entrance, the lock that gave access directly from the tidal estuary to the Bassin de St Nazaire, while to the north it looked out across the empty expanse of the Place de la Vieille Ville, to the disparate clutter of dockyard sheds and workshops which harsh experience would all too soon prove to be the perfect infantry 'killing ground'.

Dr Bizard, who was in charge of the Santé Maritime as well as the Municipal Laboratory, had control of the aid post, which was equipped for the primary care of the injured and burned. In addition to nurses and other medical personnel, he was joined there by his son Alain, his son's friend Gilles Chapelan, and Gérard Pelou.

They did not have long to wait before the bombers arrived overhead. Alain, Gilles and Gérard, who would also act as stretcher-bearers should the need arise, set off to tour the houses and shelters of their district. Distinctively clad in navy-blue greatcoats and white helmets, wearing red-cross arm bands and with whistles at the ready to catch the attention of the careless or the tardy, their first jobs were to see that all the people were safe and that the blackout was being fully observed. They hurried through the twisted network of streets and alleys, accompanied by the crack of anti-aircraft guns from rooftops, from bunkers and flak towers, even from the warships tied up in the basins.

Although most of the Nazairiens in the threatened area had quickly gone to ground, not everyone had been quite so prudent in respect of their personal safety. Nineteen-year-old Jean Bouillant, with his mother and his aunt, all of whom lived at No. 32 Grande Rue, just a few streets north of the Santé Maritime, preferred to die at home in their beds. Though most of the buildings were quickly vacated, one or two other hardy souls remained to face the music, such as old mother Filipon, who lived just opposite the Bouillants, and who was too unwell to be moved. Her two daughters, Germaine and Louise, would stay by her side throughout.

As he waited in vain for the first bombs to drop, Jean became increasingly concerned by the apparent impotence of the aircraft overhead and eventually concluded that, if it was not bombs they had brought to St Nazaire, then it must be parachutists. This was a new and dangerous development which he thought must surely bring fighting to the streets, with the possibility that none of them might survive to greet the dawn. To be suitably attired to meet St Peter they put on their smartest clothes, after which they sat down to have what might well turn out to be their own 'last supper'.

As the time dragged by and neither bombs nor parachutists put in an appearance, the family decided to go down to their cellar after all. Like so many of the houses in the Old Town, this gave on to a little courtyard which was joined to the street by a path. Jean heard whispering behind the door and slowly opened it, to find himself confronted by the members of a nervous German patrol, looking for a place in which to keep their heads down till the worst of the danger had passed. The officer gave Jean a German cigarette and then they all settled down to wait in the gloom and cold of the cellar.

Similarly cavalier in his response to the aircraft, Pierre Brosseau, also nineteen, who lived with his grandparents on the Boulevard Président Wilson, had chosen to hide where his view of the aerial fireworks display would not be obstructed. His refuge was the open drain that ran down to the beach at the bottom of the Rue Fernand Gasnier. It was hardly ideal, as it was sometimes used as a toilet and so one had to take care in the dark. But it afforded a wonderful view of both the sky above and the leaden waters of the estuary. He watched the searchlights and the waving fronds of flak; he heard the restless droning of the aircraft circling high above; and, like so many others in the threatened town, he puzzled at the strangeness of an air raid in which the bombers seemed prepared to risk the German fire and yet do nothing that might justify the effort that had brought them here.

Much closer to the centre of the town and denied Pierre's grandstand view of the developing situation in the estuary, Serge Potet waited patiently with the other members of his team, close by the indoor market.

A fireman by profession, Serge and the others had left headquarters at the first sound of the alert and stationed their ambulance and fire-engine opposite the Rue du Bois Savary. The streets nearby appeared deserted; however, other eyes peering anxiously from the tops of cellar stairways joined his own in scanning the riven sky. What was happening just did not make any sense. The bombers were coming over much more frequently these days, to the extent that people in the town could speak with authority on both their intentions and technique. They were after the docks, of course, and the U-boats and the fourteen huge pens built to keep them safe that were even now close to completion. In the twisted logic of war the planes had stayed away in the early days of their construction. They could have destroyed them then. Now they could not, for their bombs were no better than firecrackers tossed against the burster slab atop the massive roof. It was the town that suffered more: the homes, the shops, the innocents who could only hide and hope. They had come over four times already during March. Just this past Wednesday a raid had hit the Rue de la Paix, killing ten and injuring more. Always they had dropped their bombs; so why not tonight?

Ground down by tiredness and fear, vulnerable, confused, their children fractious at being forced to swap the warmth of their beds for the gloom and chill of the shelters, men and women all across the town wondered just what it was the Tommies were up to this time. Some said the pilots could not see their targets, others that only a single British aircraft was circling high above.

As the seconds stretched to minutes that seemed disinclined to end, the cold seeped through their clothes and they prayed to hear the sounding of the 'all clear'. For most of them the only missiles heard to fall were metal fragments from the bursting anti-aircraft shells, which showered the city. Eventually the droning faded and their spirits leapt as it was slowly swallowed by the distance. Those who could see through windows or doors, and the few brave souls who climbed up through the buildings for a better view, saw the searchlights flick off one by one, and heard golden silence almost instantly replace the shattering cannonade. The Tommies had gone at last, but still no 'all clear'. Then the lights came on again, and then the guns rang out again, more of them this time, firing not into the sky as before, but in glowing curves towards the waters of the estuary and river.

Alarming in itself, this new twist to an already eccentric plot-line was made doubly strange by what had happened earlier. It kept the prudent in their shelters and filled their ears with mews and wails not heard before. In an effort to explain it the invention of the very best was strained beyond the limits of reality, consideration even being given to the thought that, since no bombs had dropped, perhaps the whole thing was no more than an elaborate concoction of the Germans – an exercise designed to test the port's defences whilst darkness shielded their activities from prying eyes.

Hiding in his ditch by the Boulevard, Pierre Brosseau was one who laboured under no such happy illusion, as the wondrous but distant display of the mystery air raid was suddenly replaced by a living nightmare, the fearsome sights and sounds of which were all around him.

There had been an all-too-brief hiatus after the last drone of engines had faded into the night, before Pierre's attention was caught and held by lights reflecting out upon the waters of the estuary. At the eastern end of the beach the powerful searchlights on the east and west jetties of the Avant Port flicked on again as the Germans, clearly nervous about something, swept their beams across the surface of the sea. Suddenly there was an exploratory crack of cannon fire. Another precious nugget of silence. Then the guns all round the port and estuary really began to thunder, spitting out shell after shell into a dark void out of which came returning streams of fire of new and different colours. There was barely time to register surprise when a group of German soldiers ran out of 'Sud 1', the slab-sided blockhouse on the seafront between Pierre's position and the Avant Port. Pierre was used to meeting them; however, on this occasion they were not at all inclined to be friendly.

'Big trouble!' they yelled out. 'Tommies kommen!'

They demanded that Pierre get out and join the other civilians in the blockhouse. They even threatened to toss a grenade if he didn't move quickly. But Pierre was far from persuaded of the safety of the German structure which would surely become a target, if indeed the Tommies were 'kommen', and so he scrambled instead across the Boulevard to where his own home was, keeping low to avoid the steadily increasing fire.

Outside the house he met and stopped his frightened young cousin, who was running away. Not thinking clearly, he put her inside an empty rainwater barrel as though its flimsy construction might somehow protect her from the rain of bullets. After a time he plucked her out again and carried her instead to the basement of the bakery where, among the kneading machines, many of the district's inhabitants, perhaps thirty or forty, were already sheltering. Not content to remain with the others, he climbed back up again to where he could peer out from the porch. A boat was on fire out in the river. The cries of those on board could clearly be heard. But there was nothing Pierre could do for them and he watched with growing anguish as the grim spectacle of the developing English attack unfolded on the water before him.

Over on the far side of the Avant Port, in Old St Nazaire itself, the men of the *Défense Passive* were similarly caught out by these new and sinister developments.

Alain Bizard and his friend Gilles, acting together as a team, had gone as far as the Place de la Vieille Eglise, right at the north-east corner of the Old Town, by the time the ineffectual air raid spluttered to a close. Returning to their post along the rue de l'Ecluse, which runs beside the New Entrance, they saw ahead what appeared to be an exchange of signals between the observation post atop the Port Authority Office and an unidentified ship out in the roadstead. Clearly illuminated by a searchlight, it looked very much like one of the German boats that had sailed from the port the evening before, perhaps returning early to its berth.

Gérard Pelou, watching the same scene from close by the Santé Maritime, also thought the ship was German until the gun batteries over at Villès-Martin, followed by those atop the 'Frigorifique' building and on the bunker adjacent to the aid-post, opened up on her. The response was swift and punishing, and very soon a furious exchange of fire was taking place, reverberating through the streets as well as through the minds of the dazed spectators.

Alain and Gilles hurried to rejoin the others in the aid-post, who had already been told of what was happening by the incredulous Pelou. The Santé Maritime, because of its proximity to the gun position at the base of the East Jetty, was already being peppered with 'misses'. Gérard, who was concerned for the safety of his parents, set off through the old town to warn his father, who was leader of a block on the corner of the Place de la Vieille Eglise. Once the Hôtel Blanconnier, the building was now home to nine families. The offices of the 'Loire Fluviale' occupied the ground floor, and the family Pelou the third. Always when there was an air raid, the families gathered together in the cellar. Gérard found them there now. In a tearing hurry to get on, he had time only to call to them through the door, 'The English are landing! Do not move!' And then he was gone again, back through the hazard of the twisting streets.

There were Tommies in the Place itself. Gérard had seen them clearly. A little further on he spied a cluster of Germans in position to fire. The normally peaceful port had been transformed into a madhouse. Blades of brilliant light stabbed through the darkness of the estuary occasionally fixing in their glare grey, elusive shapes.

German sailors, armed and helmeted, had already entered the Old Town from the direction of the Port Authority Office. They were even now feeling their way round either side of the Santé Maritime, prior to moving north towards the enemy. All across the town, and in the countryside around it, the German defence plan was being enacted just as quickly as units could be mobilized and despatched to their emergency positions. Reinforcements were summoned from outlying bodies of infantry. Everyone who could carry a weapon was being given a part to play in hurling the Tommies back into the sea.

But why had the Tommies come at all? What had driven them to accept the risks involved in such a crazy, costly enterprise? There were the shipyards of course, plenty of targets there, though few that could not be more safely bombarded from the air. And then there were the massive bunkers of the U-boat base, far and away the most visible manifestation of German presence within the town. With nine out of fourteen pens already built, the base had long been home to the boats of the U-flotillas. Largely immune from the bombs of the RAF, it would when complete be a fortress in its own right, sporting flak towers, strong steel doors and embrasures for ground defence. Bearing in mind the awful loss of merchant tonnage being suffered by the British, perhaps they had sent their soldiers to accomplish what their air force clearly could not.

This was the target most obviously worth the heavy loss of life an attack must surely incur. But as the events of the night would all too quickly show, its disruption was merely a consolation prize.

It was not for fear of U-boats that so many young men would fight and die this night, but of the awful potential of a German warship far away in northern waters, so strong and swift that British guns and bombs alone were not a match for her.

2

Cat and Mouse
in Northern Waters

As far as the German Navy was concerned, the Second World War began several years too soon. Having just proposed a major programme of construction which by 1944 would have given it the power to dispute Britain's domination of the high seas, the Kriegsmarine instead found itself embroiled in an unwanted war, with a mere two capital ships to pit against its adversary's fifteen.

Immediately blockaded by the Royal Navy, Germany had no alternative but to use her ships as raiders, sneaking them singly, or in small groups, through the encircling cordon to do such damage as they could to Britain's convoy lifelines. Free to roam the high seas, they were able to strike at will, their destructive potential more than making up for their lack of numbers. Echoing down through the years, the names of such vessels as the pocket-battleship *Admiral Graf Spee* and the battle cruisers *Scharnhorst* and *Gneisenau* still retain a mystique born of the very real threat they posed at a time when Britain's ability to maintain a long war effort was far from assured. So successful were they in carrying the German flag across the oceans of the world that the then Commander-in-Chief Home Fleet, Admiral Sir Charles Forbes, had no option but to disperse his own core forces in penny packets just to seek them out, such a negative policy teaching the hard-pressed Admiralty a lesson it would well remember in the years to come.

During the early months of 1941, at which time the principle of surface raiding was reaching its zenith, Grand Admiral Raeder attempted to build on the successes of his other ships by unleashing upon the harried Royal Navy the new and immensely powerful battleship *Bismarck*.

Faster, heavier and better armed than almost any British ship she might be called upon to fight, *Bismarck* slipped away from Gotenhafen on 18 May, sailing in the company of the heavy cruiser *Prinz Eugen*. Making for the northern exits from the North Sea, the two were intercepted by a powerful British squadron built around the old battle cruiser *Hood* and the brand new battleship *Prince of Wales*. Fire was opened at 0553 hours on the morning of 24 May and in a chilling demonstration of the vulnerability of Britain's older ships, *Hood* blew up at 0600 hours, following which tragic reverse the damaged *Prince of Wales* was forced to turn away.

Pulling out all the stops to revenge itself upon the German ships, the Royal Navy finally brought *Bismarck* to book on the morning of the 27th when, trailing a slick of oil from a minor hit, she sought to make port in western France. But such was her strength that, even after being mercilessly pounded by heavy guns, it took multiple torpedo strikes to finally send her to the bottom. On the face of it it was over, but in actual fact so great had been the effort expended to deal with just this one great ship that her spectre would remain to haunt the British for as long as any of her kind remained afloat.

Whatever Raeder's hopes for *Bismarck* might have been, her destruction only served to accelerate Hitler's loss of interest in a navy which was swallowing scarce resources he now needed to drive forward his ambitions in the east. Vastly expensive to build and man, the construction of capital ships was therefore discouraged in favour of the cheaper and more lethal U-boats. All of which meant that, with *Bismarck* gone, only one of her kind remained afloat: her sister ship and last of the breed, her twin in almost every detail, particularly in respect of the threat she would continue to pose to British sea-power – the *Tirpitz*.

Declared operational in January, 1942, this ship, unknown to British strategists, was to face a catalogue of restrictions which would deny her much of the freedom of movement enjoyed by her predecessors.

Chief amongst Raeder's concerns was the fact that the French Atlantic bases were not living up to their promise as bolt-holes from which warships might sally forth at will, for the predations of the RAF were steadily turning them into traps from which a full withdrawal of surface ships might have to be considered. Indeed, such were the risks involved that to add *Tirpitz* to the list of ships already under threat there would be to throw away any such advantage as might yet be salvaged from Germany's huge investment in her.

Oil, too, was becoming a determining factor, more likely to humble

Tirpitz than any guns or bombs of the British; for the great battle waggons were voracious consumers of fuel oil, demands for the everyday use of which now regularly exceeded supply. Bound by treaty to meet the needs of their Italian allies, the situation by the end of 1941 had become so grave that when *Tirpitz* finally left her Baltic training ground there were simply not the supplies available to make full use of her.

Then there was the question of German prestige, which would certainly suffer were her last great battleship to go the way of the first. Raeder might wish to use her aggressively; but Hitler decided instead that her power should be employed at minimum cost and hazard to deter what he believed were British ambitions in the north. Certain that Churchill would eventually try to wrest Norway from the Reich, Hitler saw his capital ships as no more than the key to that country's defence. Station *Tirpitz* in the relative security of the fjords, and the British would not dare to put their ships and men at risk. Station her there and she could menace the convoys to Russia. Keep her where she could not be touched and, by the very fact of her existence as a 'fleet in being', she would force the British to keep their best ships tied to Scapa Flow.

Taken together, all these factors served to draw much of *Tirpitz*'s sting, and so it was that, when she finally sailed, as far as Hitler at least was concerned, she was bound not for glory but for life at the end of a leash within the prison of the North Sea.

While seen from the German side such a guarded move might have been judged both prudent and logical, to the British it was the glory option of which they were most immediately afraid. Unaware of the extent to which factors such as Hitler's fixation with Norway were constricting her, there was an alarming sense of *déjà vu* in the way she moved to the north. Would she come out? Was the whole sorry affair of *Bismarck* to be gone through yet again? Would *Tirpitz* even try to link up with other German ships in Brest, as the lynchpin of a German Atlantic Fleet? These were the developments that fear and vulnerability had long conditioned them to expect and no one doubted they must at all costs be obstructed or delayed.

The subject of a long dispute with Churchill, who was anxious to divert warships to the Far East, the Admiralty's concern with *Tirpitz* was demonstrated by their policy of retaining their three most modern battleships in home waters, just in case.

This was not a strategy with which the belligerent Churchill agreed; first, because he fully understood that the threat posed by *Tirpitz* was so effective in itself that the Germans would hardly be so foolish as to give up their advantage by risking her at sea; and, second, because he knew full well how the cryptanalytical miracle that was 'Ultra' was allowing his side to break and read most of the signals communicated to her by radio. In fact it was Ultra which betrayed the first manoeuvrings of *Tirpitz* as she prepared to leave the Baltic during the first few days of January, 1942. And it was Ultra which warned that she would be operational by the 10th, that she had sailed from Gdynia on the 11th, and that she had reached Wilhelmshaven on the 14th. She sailed again that night and arrived with her destroyer escort in Trondheimsfjord on the 16th, a fact that Ultra confirmed the following day.

Moored ultimately in Foettenfjord, a distant arm of the much larger Trondheimsfjord, *Tirpitz*'s intentions became rather less clear, as she was now able to communicate by secure teleprinter land-line. Her destroyers, however, having returned to Germany on the 19th, she clearly had no intention of moving anywhere in the short term.

Having been immune from attack in the Baltic, *Tirpitz*, now in the North Sea, was marginally more vulnerable, a fact which prompted Churchill, who knew that his own best ships would not be released until such time as the threat she posed was erased, to minute the Chiefs-of-Staff Committee, on 25 January. The gist of his message was that *Tirpitz*'s neutralization was now of paramount importance in respect of the many benefits it would bring to naval strategy worldwide.

While this was a laudable objective, there was simply no way of achieving it with the means at hand, for, snug in her fjord, *Tirpitz* could not be reached by either surface ships or conventional submarines; nor did the RAF seem capable of dealing her a decisive blow: all of which left the strategists and tacticians casting around for some means by which the range of options open to her could at least be limited.

So long as *Tirpitz* lurked in the fjords, little could be done to prevent her dominating the North Sea; however, strenuous efforts could be made to bar her from the wider oceans. Such an approach would do nothing for Churchill's ambitions in the Far East, as the blocking force of battleships would have to remain. But it would preserve the safety of the lumbering merchantmen hauling supplies in from the Americas, which would have no answer to her awesome destructive power.

Ironically, it was *Tirpitz* herself who held the key to such an embargo, for there were only a handful of dry docks worldwide that were large enough to accommodate her huge bulk, and only one that could be accessed directly from the Atlantic. Trailing her slick of oil, *Bismarck* had been making for its shelter when she was caught and sunk. Destroy this great dock and, should she be damaged in battle on the high seas, *Tirpitz* would be forced to return to Germany for repairs, running the gauntlet of British forces. Destroy the

Forme-Ecluse Louis-Joubert, built to house the giant liner *Normandie*, in the French Atlantic port of St Nazaire and this might be enough to persuade her masters not to set her free.

During a meeting on 26 January with the First Sea Lord, Admiral of the Fleet Sir Dudley Pound, Churchill explored this option futher. Certainly the alternatives seemed quite straightforward, in that, for so long as the 'Normandie' dock existed, the possibility of a sortie would continue to hang over them. While if they could somehow deny the Germans its use then the already considerable risks to their last great ship which were inherent in such a perilous expedition would be so greatly magnified that they might well be considered not worth taking at all.

Far from being an original proposal, this was an idea which had taxed the minds of planners for many months already, its endless catalogue of difficulties having thus far always overwhelmed the search for a solution. Admiral of the Fleet Sir Charles Forbes, who, having by this time lost his command of the Home Fleet, was now Commander-in-Chief Plymouth, had been asked by the Admiralty the previous August to study the scheme in conjunction with the then Director of Combined Operations, Admiral of the Fleet Sir Roger Keyes. They had not succeeded in producing a workable plan at that time, nor had they some weeks later when they looked at it again.

At the end of September, 1941, by which time Keyes was on the way to being replaced by Lord Louis Mountbatten, a further review led to the problem being passed across to the Special Operations Executive; however, SOE were far too weakly represented in France even to consider the covert collection and placing of the huge quantity of explosives which would be required to blow a lock of such proportions.

At 350 metres long by fifty metres wide, and a full sixteen metres deep, the Forme-Ecluse Louis-Joubert, named after the President of the St Nazaire Chamber of Commerce, was indeed a mammoth target. Specially constructed to house the 80, 000-ton *Normandie* which had been built in the Penhoët shipyard and launched in 1932, it was now the primary means of access from the River Loire to the man-made inner basins of the port. Capable of being used as either a dry or wet dock, its ends were capped by giant hollow gates, or 'caissons', each nine metres wide, which could be wound into 'cambers' on the dock's west side by machinery contained in 'winding huts' placed at the end of each camber. Also to be found on the west side was the impressive pumping-house, by means of which the lock could be either drained or filled – an arduous process which took all of 14 hours.

To demolish such a facility, or at least render it unusable for a significant period, would certainly involve the movement of hundreds of men, carrying tons of explosives, all the way through the Bay of Biscay, then disembarking them onto landing craft light enough to pass across the shallows; after which they would have to travel six miles up the estuary of the Loire, force a landing against heavy opposition, blow up their targets, re-embark, and then withdraw past the waiting guns of the estuary defences. In the light of conventional thinking, and no matter how desirable the end result might be, such an expedition, were it ever to be launched, would quite clearly be heading for disaster.

It was against this background that on 27 January Mountbatten was asked to look again for a solution, this time by his friend Captain Charles Lambe, the Deputy Director of the Plans Division at the Admiralty. With *Tirpitz* pawing at the door to the Atlantic, it was quite clear that something would have to be done, and quickly; and as that something must almost inevitably involve a seaborne assault on the enemy shore, it would be the responsibility of Mountbatten's highly specialized raiding organization to find some way of making it work.

Neither a new service in its own right, nor able to command those on whose good offices it would depend for most of its resources and expertise, Combined Ops had at first struggled to find its feet under the ambitious tutelage of Keyes. During a term in office of some fifteen months, this officer's aggressive plans for operations against the enemy had outstripped both scarce material means and the fragile tolerance of the many traditionalists whose feathers had been ruffled by the sudden appearance of such an irregular body. Beset by sustained disinterest and often outright hostility, he had eventually been pushed aside to make way for Mountbatten who, with the title 'Adviser', brought to Combined Ops both the energy of youth and the political skills required to win acceptance for his new charge.

A cousin of the King and blessed with both good looks and potent charm, Mountbatten was a mover and shaker who immediately applied himself to the task of cultivating the cooperation which had always eluded Keyes. He had at his disposal the Army Commandos of the Special Service Brigade, a unique body of troops whose commitment and expertise would soon make them the most effective light fighting force in Europe; however, both ships and aircraft had to be begged and borrowed from a Navy and Air Force not enamoured of any new body which promised to usurp their roles and employ their resources, but over whose actions they could not exercise complete control. It was a situation which could only be made to work by a leader with the determination of a lion, the patience of a saint, and the skills of an accomplished politician; such a leader Mountbatten proved himself to be, forging Combined Ops into a thoroughly professional organization within which the representatives of all three services cooperated for the purpose of hitting the enemy as hard and as often as the country's resources would allow.

Now headquartered at Richmond Terrace in London, at its heart were the Intelligence and Planning staffs, the former providing the latter with raw materials which, when fashioned into plans, were 'sold' to the Chiefs-of-Staff, without whose approval nothing of substance could be done.

The Intelligence staff, under Wing-Commander the Marquis de Casa Maury, liaised with the Special Operations Executive, the two organizations exchanging information on the subjects of arms and explosives, specialist equipment, and raiding techniques. In respect of producing the finished product, the Planning staff was constructed around the representatives of the primary services, each of whom acted as an Adviser to Combined Ops HQ. The Naval Adviser was Captain John Hughes-Hallett, the Air Adviser Group Captain A.H. Willetts and the Military Adviser Brigadier J.C. Haydon. Together with their staffs, these men combined when necessary into 'Inter-Service' committees tasked with producing 'Preliminary' plans in respect of any given target or objective. Following Mountbatten's approval, an outline plan would then be produced for authorization by the Chiefs-of-Staff Committee, at which time the scheme either would, or would not, take on the life that would see it through to its conclusion.

On his return from the meeting with Lambe, this was the machinery into which Mountbatten fed the Admiralty's request for a fresh look at St Nazaire, and with rather speedier results than he might have anticipated, for his own staff had already come up with a new twist which at least held out the prospect of a successful attack on the port.

It was all to do with tides, or, more specifically, the extraordinarily high spring tides which would wash across the estuary in just two months' time, covering the shoals with just sufficient water to allow the passage of vessels of particularly shallow draft. It was a narrow window of opportunity which would not come again until the autumn. Further research might prove it to be a mare's nest; however, it was at least a potentially exploitable chink in the port's otherwise impenetrable armour.

Excited by the prospect of unconventionality winning the day, Mountbatten instructed his staff to go into every detail of how it might be done, with the object of producing preliminary proposals. They had at their disposal a veritable mine of intelligence material gathered by the services and others in respect of their own particular interests in the port. This included

SOE data originating from within St Nazaire itself, as well as target information gathered by the RAF, who just happened to have constructed an intricate model of the harbour. Perhaps most fortunate of all was the discovery that two sapper officers, pursuing a private interest in the nascent science of port destruction, had already produced plans for the demolition of many of the targets in which COHQ was now showing such an interest.

The two young officers concerned, Captains Bill Pritchard, twenty-eight, and Bob Montgomery, twenty-one, had both come out of France in 1940 with the retreating BEF. A territorial officer of the Royal Engineers, Bill Pritchard had been brought out through Dunkirk and had been awarded the Military Cross for his demolition of a bridge whilst under enemy fire. An RE regular who had still been at Woolwich when war broke out, the tall and forceful Montgomery had returned to British shores from St Nazaire itself.

It was during their postings as instructors to Aldershot that the two had become friends and, ultimately, fellow conspirators in Pritchard's chosen field. A Welshman by birth, the tall, dark, highly motivated Pritchard had derived his interest in docks both from his father's position as Dock Master in Cardiff and from time spent as an engineering apprentice in the dockyards of the Great Western Railway. Very well aware of the offensive and defensive importance of these complex facilities in a modern war, he was convinced by his superior knowledge as well as by personal observation of the failure of German air raids on Cardiff docks that the machinery crucial to their operation could only be put out of action by precisely placing charges where they could be guaranteed to have the maximum destructive effect.

Keen to spread the gospel, Pritchard took his ideas to the RE Transportation Directorate, who responded by giving him the plans of an unnamed dock and requesting that he go away and work out the details of how best it could be denied to an enemy. On his return to Aldershot he and Montgomery set to work immediately, the result of their considerable labours then being passed back to the Directorate. Neither man was to know it at the time, but they had just spent the better part of two months working out how best to lay waste to the dockyards at St Nazaire.

Following this phase in their activities, Pritchard was moved to the Directorate so that he could pass on his theories and expertise to others, while Montgomery in the fullness of time was posted to a Field Company. The two were not parted for long, however, for as soon as Pritchard became an integral part of COHQ's St Nazaire planning exercise he called for Montgomery to join him.

Having met with Haydon and agreed to become a member of the team,

Montgomery travelled down to Southampton with Pritchard to examine the facilities of the King George V dock. Particularly in respect of the massive caissons which secured the open ends of the dry dock, the two facilities were almost identical, those at Southampton having been constructed after study of the ones at St Nazaire. In the absence of the real thing, it would prove to be the perfect training ground for both this and subsequent phases of the developing project.

Using to the full all the material and specialist advice that was to hand, the Inter-Service Planning Committee set up for the purpose and chaired by Hughes-Hallett, as Naval Adviser, produced within ten days of Lambe's request a simple and effective set of proposals for Mountbatten to consider.

Taking into account the distance to be travelled through waters regularly observed by the enemy, the configuration of the estuary to be penetrated and the strength of the port's defences, it was clear from the outset that success was going to have to depend to an extraordinary degree on the ability to take the enemy completely by surprise.

As a first priority, the attacking force must not be identifiable as such to the Germans, which meant that it must not contain any of the landing ships customarily used by the Commandos; second, to give it the best chance of approaching unobserved up part at least of the estuary, it would have to be light enough to traverse the treacherous shoals; and, third, it must be strong enough to carry both the men and the large quantity of explosives needed to do the job.

In settling on specially lightened destroyers, Hughes-Hallett and the others achieved the perfect compromise between speed, strength, anonymity and shallow draft. They proposed that two units be used, one with explosives packed in her bows to ram the outer caisson of the dry dock, after which the charge – and, of course, the destroyer – would be set to blow up on a time fuse; the second to act as an escort on the way in, and then evacuate the crew of the first ship as well as the Commandos she would disgorge after ramming, for demolition duties on shore. Having successfully blown up the outer gate, a specially adapted motor torpedo boat would then sail through the breach and fire delayed-action torpedoes at the inner caisson, hopefully destroying it as well.

To ensure a sufficient depth of water, the operation would be carried out at the time of the highest spring tides, in just seven weeks' time, at which period a moon would also be present. To confuse the enemy's radar and ensure that his dual-purpose cannon were pointed skywards and not at the estuary, a programmed series of air raids was planned to coincide with all the critical phases of the attack.

It was an audacious plan for a surgically efficient strike, which offered the maximum return in exchange for only a very minor investment in ships and men. Hughes-Hallett presented it to Mountbatten on 6 February, and Mountbatten put it up to the Vice-Chief of Naval Staff on the 7th. On the face of it the Admiralty now had precisely what they had always asked for, a means of slamming the door to the Atlantic in *Tirpitz*'s face, and yet their response was an obdurate refusal to supply even one of their own destroyers. In the light of available knowledge it was clearly a *non sequitur*. On the one hand the Admiralty were seeking to bar from the Atlantic a ship whose presence there would certainly require the diversion of many British capital ships to seek her out, and could also easily force a suspension of the vital convoys, and yet the certain loss of one old destroyer, allied to the risk of losing a second, was considered too high a price to pay.

Of course the strategic situation on the high seas was very much a chess game, with pieces moving to and fro about the board, changing the balance of advantage and constantly effecting the degree of threat as the Admiralty would have seen it.

COHQ's plan went up to the Admiralty just a handful of days before a major event took place, as a result of which the advantage took a sudden and unexpected lurch in Britain's favour. Warned during the latter part of January by its own Operational Intelligence Centre that activity on the part of the battle cruisers *Scharnhorst* and *Gneisenau*, which for many months had been stationed in Brest, now pointed towards a break for Germany, preparations were made, throughout the period when Hughes-Hallett was concentrating on St Nazaire, to give them a very warm welcome should they choose to attempt a passage of the Channel. The break was confidently expected to take place at night, but it did not, this being only one of a number of miscalculations and mistakes which allowed these ships and others to pass successfully through Britain's back yard in broad daylight during the course of 12 February, 1942.

Loudly decried as a humiliating fiasco, the passage of the German squadron removed from the doorstep of the Atlantic Germany's most powerful ships next to *Tirpitz*. Having striven for so long to maintain both its Atlantic bases and its dream of one day combining all its major warships into an Atlantic fleet, the German Navy was now retreating from both. In line with the move of *Tirpitz* to Trondheim, the Brest squadron was being called home to buttress the new Norwegian fleet Hitler was creating, due to his fear of Churchill's ambitions in the north.

Ultra had played its part by contributing to the build-up of information which pointed to the move from Brest. Now it was to strike a far more crucial blow, by directing Bomber Command to lay mines in the predicted paths of the eastward-moving ships. So precisely were they placed that, at the very height of their triumph, both big ships struck. *Scharnhorst* was put out of action for six months and *Gneisenau* would later be bombed while under repair and so badly damaged that she would play no further part in the war.

At a stroke the threat of *Tirpitz* combining with other ships had therefore ceased to be a concern to the hard-pressed Admiralty. And on 17 February, just two days prior to a conference critical to the very future of the St Nazaire enterprise, Churchill felt able to reassure President Roosevelt that the situation in the North Atlantic had been eased considerably, at least for several months, by which time both their fleets would be much stronger.

3

'Hell's Glen' and Beyond

While the Navy's initial response to the Hughes-Hallett proposals might have been far from confidence-inspiring, Combined Operations had no need to be concerned about the enthusiasm of its own immensely capable striking force, the men of the Army Commandos.

Shamefully under-used since their formation in 1940, few of the men belonging to the British-based units of the Special Service Brigade had ever seen action, even though it was the prospect of getting quickly to grips with the enemy that had prompted them to volunteer for 'Special Service' in the first place. Some had been in Norway with the Independent Companies before the Commandos were thought of; others had been involved in the later adventures at Vaagso and in the Lofotens, or in one of the handful of tiny nuisance raids launched across the Channel; but most had trained to distraction for the better part of a year and a half, and were beginning to wonder if they were not fated to become the best-trained troops in the time of a 'hot' war never to have fired a shot in anger.

By February, 1942, most were gathered in south-western Scotland, on the face of it a very long way indeed from the war they had rushed to join; however, though they were not to know it quite yet, redemption was almost at hand, for no fewer than eight Commando units were destined to play some part in the proposed attack on St Nazaire. Shouldering the burden of the many and varied demolition tasks to be carried out on the night would be teams of specialists drawn from numbers 1, 3, 4, 5, 6, 9 and 12 Commandos, while Lieutenant-Colonel Charles Newman's 2 Commando, presently carrying out landing exercises in the Outer Hebrides, would, upon return to its base in Ayr, be instructed to provide the 'fighting' troops, whose job it would be to overwhelm the local German defences.

Arising out of the ashes of the defeat in France, and with the backing of Churchill, the idea behind the Commandos had been to wound the enemy with a series of stinging attacks on his infrastructure, delivered by an élite force of men whose sole function would be to knock him off his guard, encourage him to spread his forces far and wide and gradually wear down his morale.

Though destined for individual fame, the Commandos had at first been obliged to share their irregular status with a formation of a slightly earlier vintage, called the Independent Companies. Created in April, 1940, at a time when most regular units were in France, and formed primarily of volunteers from the home-based territorial divisions, these units had fulfilled a need for a mobile, self-contained force capable of fighting behind enemy lines in Norway; but with the collapse of that campaign, they had been left to wither on the vine throughout the summer of 1940, dispersed about the UK on garrison or anti-invasion duties, or simply training.

In October, 1940, an attempt was made to reorganize both these and the fledgling Commandos into new formations known as Special Service Battalions, within a Special Service Brigade, commanded by Brigadier J.C. Haydon. Unfortunately, however, these large and unwieldy battalions proved less than successful and they were soon disbanded in favour of reconstituted Commando units which, now containing volunteers from both original sources, would remain within Haydon's Brigade. In the particular case of 2 Commando, which unit was to contribute by far the greatest number of men to the coming attack, its ranks consisted primarily of men who had served with the Independent Companies and who had been incorporated into the 1st SS Battalion the previous autumn. It therefore had a distinctly territorial flavour to it, deriving from units such as The Royal Fusiliers, The Queen's Westminster Rifles and the London Scottish, in which clusters of officers and men had sometimes served together for many years.

As finally established, each Commando was a fighting unit in the purest sense of the word, consisting of an HQ plus six rifle troops each commanded by a captain. Within the troop were two subalterns each ideally commanding a section of thirty men. A troop sergeant-major supported the troop commander, while each section officer could rely on his own section sergeant. Within a section were two sub-sections, each made up of a lance-sergeant, a corporal, two lance-corporals and ten private soldiers. The troop therefore consisted of three officers and sixty-two men, just enough to fit in two landing craft.

Unlike regular army units, the Commandos were almost entirely self-sufficient, with no administrative tail and no barracks to house the men. In effect the Commando soldier lived out, being dismissed at the end of his day to retire to his personal billet for the night. Both officers and men provided for themselves out of a daily living allowance of thirteen shillings and four pence (67p) for an officer and half that amount for the men. They found their own billets within the area designated for each troop and often established close relationships with the families who looked after them. Sometimes the relationships were inherently profitable, if most of their allowance could be retained in cases where only a small charge was made for the billet; sometimes they took on the more permanent form of romantic liaisons with the daughters of the billeting families.

Mobility was the watchword of the Commandos, their organization allowing for the unit as a whole, or for any troop or section within it, to come and go without notice, and in the majority of cases without transport either. A troop being moved from point X to point Y would simply be dismissed at X and ordered to parade again at Y, on a given day and at a given time. Whilst fostering the initiative of the individual soldier, this system also allowed units to disappear without trace and reappear without notice, a useful device indeed at a time when secrecy was paramount.

Whilst encouraged by their officers to exercise freedom of thought, the discipline of Commando soldiers was second to none, and all the more effective because so much of it was self-imposed, a function of pride in themselves and their officers, pride in their unit, and the absolute conviction that they were the best. As Acting Lance-Corporal John Webb, the medical orderly attached to 2 Troop of 2 Commando has put it: 'Individually and collectively we were smart. Colonel Newman required us to turn out on parade looking like guardsmen. All webbing equipment had to be scrubbed to creamy whiteness, brasses polished and boots mirror-like. We were smart on and off parade and we knew it! On training schemes webbing had to be camouflaged with mud or other suitable colouring, yet, the next day on parade it had to be "white" again, and *not* whitened by the use of blanco. Yes, we knew we were smart and we were proud of it, and therefore proud of our unit, and therefore well-disciplined.'

All the men were volunteers, chosen because they possessed the special combination of physical ability and quickness of mind, allied to a strong desire to get on with winning the war that was demanded of all would-be Commandos. Although the media have fostered an image of the Commandos as tall, strong, physically dominant individuals, inches and pounds were in fact no measure of the courage and toughness of spirit that would see the men through some of the most gruelling exercises yet devised. To men who were expected to be able to fight when others had long since passed the limits of their physical and mental endurance, the normal standards of performance and expectation did not apply. Each man was 'on loan' from his parent unit and could be swiftly returned to it if he did not measure up, the disgrace of his exclusion from the élite being the ultimate punishment the Commando soldier could receive.

'We knew we were in it for the future of our country, for the future peace of the world, and for the future children of the world, ' recalls John Webb. 'We talked of this – we believed it. We were uplifted by the belief that we were a special kind of soldier, ranking with the very best in the world, if not the best.'

With such high quality men in the ranks, the Commandos were doubly blessed in respect of their officers who, as well as inspiring their subordinates, were often able to enjoy with them a far more intimate relationship than traditionalists might have believed possible or advisable. Indeed so close could this relationship become that there were times when it transcended the mere requirements of training together to fight a war.

In Captain Michael Burn's 6 Troop of 2 Commando there were, for instance, a number of men with whom he had been soldiering ever since joining the Queen's Westminster Rifles in 1937. They had gone to war together, volunteered for No. 5 Independent Company together, and now shared both the hardships and rewards of Commando life. Micky had seen these men and others grow in confidence, ability and self-assurance under the rigorous régime of training and, concerned that this enhancement of personal gifts should not be wasted in peacetime, had even dared to put a paper up to Haydon's HQ which argued that everyone would benefit were it to be fostered for use in future years.

Tall, good-looking and immensely charming, Micky had taken his first step along a lengthy and distinguished literary career by writing a biography of Sir Henry Birkin, after dropping out of New College, Oxford, without completing his studies. Then in 1936 he joined *The Times* and travelled the world as a foreign correspondent, before leaving to join his unit on the day that war was declared. Following service with No. 5 Independent Company in Norway, Micky was put in charge of the 'resistance' in East Anglia – the Auxiliary Units designed to fight on should Britain be overwhelmed. But he was not content simply to wait around for action and joined the Commandos, having at one point even toyed with the idea of being dropped into France with SOE. No more military-minded than most of the boys in his troop, who were every bit as individualistic as he, Micky's intense personal concern for their well-being would be powerfully demonstrated in the aftermath of the coming action when, in an effort to trace survivors, he wrote to his parents from France, to plead, 'Can you move heaven and earth to send me news of them? ... I can't really bear to think of them as killed. I had built my whole life around them for the last year, and we were all such friends.'

To the many within the military hierarchy, who were neither so liberally inclined, nor so egalitarian, such familiarity as this was seen to diminish rather than enhance the discipline which in so many units was more a function of enforcement than of encouragement and empathy. Certainly the whole notion of a Commando élite had many detractors at all levels, from Battalion HQs up to the War Office itself. At a time of great crisis in the nation as a whole, it was seen as foolish and foolhardy to strip the regular units of their best and most valued men. That Churchill keenly supported the idea mattered not a jot to those who stood firmly in the opposition camp, casting jaundiced eyes over the behaviour of this upstart élite, in search of proof that their scepticism had all along been justified.

As the months passed by in continued training, with only a small return apparent for all this investment in time and talent, the Commandos themselves, through accident or over-exuberance, sometimes managed to earn publicity that was far from helpful to their cause.

One such incident, recalled by Micky Burn, involved a brother officer, Lieutenant Philip Walton of 1 Troop, a schoolteacher in civilian life, who was 'rather given to putting excessive charges on things!' It was all to do with a prank designed to frighten, just a little, the well-off guests in the Redcliffs Hotel in Paignton, who had taken refuge there for the duration. The intention had been to set off a minor charge; however, the resulting explosion turned out to be anything but minor and blew in all the windows, terrifying the residents and causing a general alarm. 'Next morning, ' recalls Micky, 'Tom [Peyton] and I thought we should apologize to the lady who managed the hotel and bought her a big bunch of lilies. That's enough, we thought, it'll be forgotten. It was not forgotten. The rocket went slowly but surely from Western Command to London, and from London to Scottish Command, where we then were. I was sent for to Brigade HQ and I thought, I'm going to be court-martialled. However, when I got to the bit about the lilies, I realized that our Brigadier, Charles Haydon, at heart thought it rather funny and was trying not to laugh.'

Bearing in mind that these highly motivated young men were preparing to become involved in the most intensive kind of fighting, while still being distributed among the civilian population, such incidents were inevitable.

While particular locations existed at which specialized training could take place well away from public view, much of the basic endurance training was carried out at unit level in and around the Commandos' own billeting areas. Particularly in Scotland, civilians therefore became used to the presence of these earnest young men.

To learn about boats, explosives, fieldcraft, weapons technique, unarmed combat and the like, a series of special training centres was set up in western Scotland, at locations such as Inveraray, for boat work, and Inverailort and Achnacarry Castles, this last the ancestral home of the Camerons of Lochiel. Of these primary locations, the name of Achnacarry, which would ultimately become the Commando Basic Training Centre, has best stood the test of time; however, before this was established in February, 1942, it was the Irregular Warfare School at Inverailort Castle, Lochailort, which had served both Commandos and Independent Companies with great distinction, establishing the pattern of training that Achnacarry was later to perfect.

To poor mortals experiencing for the first time the intensive training that was so crucial to the success of all special forces, the extreme demands it could impose upon both body and mind usually came as quite a shock. Recalling his arrival at Inverlochy Castle in the summer of 1940, for service with No. 5 Independent Company, Second Lieutenant Bill Watson, of 1 Troop 2 Commando, affirms that the weeding-out process began the very moment he and his fellow victims stepped down from the truck. Bearing in mind that they had just endured a long journey by rail to nearby Fort William, he writes that it was no pleasure to hear

'that we would now take a little exercise after being cooped up in the train all that time. Anybody who fell out or who drank the burn water, which would incidentally cause severe stomach cramps, would be returned to his unit.

'We were then marched at a cracking pace to the foot of the nearest mountain and led straight up it. Perhaps "led" is the wrong word. Our escorts, like sheep-dogs, drove us up. It was hell. We were out of condition, short of sleep and unused to such steep slopes. The instructors barked at our heels. Mercifully we were not burdened with ammunition, or we might have been tempted to use it on our tormentors, if we had had the strength, that is. Half blinded by sweat, it became a personal struggle for each of us to get his breath and keep his aching legs moving.

'As we lay there, an old shepherd strolled by serenely smoking his pipe. He looked down at the exhausted soldiery sprawled out any which way and shook his head pityingly. He passed on, climbing easily, his dogs at his heels. No doubt he thought us mad and we were ready to agree with him.'

Of Inverlochy's 'companion in torment', Lochailort, less has been recorded in print, although 'Hell's Glen', as it was dubbed by some, engendered a not-to-be-forgotten mixture of respect and awe in the minds of those who were committed to its tender mercies.

Situated on the western coast of Scotland, on the 'Road to the Isles', between Fort William and Mallaig, Lochailort was in that part of the country north of the Caledonian Canal to which access was severely restricted. Commanded by Lieutenant-Colonel 'Hughie' Stockwell, Lochailort housed a collection of experts and eccentrics without equal in respect of the range of talents upon which they could draw. Surgeon-Commander Murray Levick, RN, who introduced the men, with only partial success it must be admitted, to the delights of 'Pemmican', had been in the Antarctic with Scott before the First World War and Major Jim Gavin had been to Everest. Lord Lovat's Scouts taught the men how to live off the land and Messrs Sykes and Fairbairn instructed them in how to kill or maim each other in many more subtle ways than simply pulling a trigger. Both were ex-members of the Shanghai Police Force and they served Combined Operations as well as SOE, imparting their lethal skills to Commando soldiers and secret agents alike.

Lieutenant Corran Purdon of 12 Commando has summed up both the hardships of Lochailort and the perverse pleasures of having passed through all that could be thrown at its students in his book *List the Bugle*, in which he writes;

'We fired every type of infantry weapon including the Boyes anti-tank rifle standing, and the two-inch mortar from the hip. We had been told terrible tales about what happened to those who fired these last two weapons – shattered shoulders, broken hips, etc – But I reckoned if we were invited to shoot them it must be safe.

'Led by Colonel Stockwell, we splashed through hip-high freezing sea-loch estuaries, forded icy torrents holding boulders to combat the force of the rushing spate, climbed seemingly interminably high mountains and ran down steep scree slopes. We were carefully instructed in the science of demolitions by Jim Gavin and his fellow sapper Captain Gabriel.

'Fairbairn and Sykes, looking like two benevolent square-shaped padres, took us close-combat shooting in their sandbagged basement range where moving targets suddenly materialized from the gloom. We were taught how to live off the land by Lovat Scouts and on one exercise we had to kill, skin, cook and eat some unfortunate sheep.

'We ended our course with a splendid exercise during part of which I remember following a track, white in the moonlight, round the side of Loch Morar, and wondering if we would see its monster in the glittering water! First light found us seated on the platform of a railway halt, the seats of our battledress trousers seemingly stuck to the ground by frost. And how marvellous that hot, sweet porridge tasted, which was brought out on the trucks which came to take us back to camp!'

Many of the Commandos attended courses at Lochailort more than once, and during the early part of February, 1942, a number of groups from the various units returned for yet another bruising stint, completely unaware that this time their arrival in the wilds of Arisaig promised much more than just another step along the apparently endless road to technical and physical perfection.

Along with a group of NCOs and men from 5 Commando, the dark and mischievous Lieutenant Stuart Whitemore Chant, a blue button on the London Stock Exchange prior to the war, who had come to Special Service from the Gordon Highlanders, was 'once again deposited on the platform of that remote station and made to run the two miles all the way to Inverailort Castle . . . But this time there was a difference: instead of the physical training and tests of endurance, we were now being initiated into the handling of more sophisticated explosives and destruction than hitherto. We enjoyed blowing up dead trees and large slabs of mountainside, but it did not cross our minds that this portended our being earmarked for duties of a different kind.'

Nevertheless, earmarked they indeed had been and, along with other groups training on Highland hills and lochs, and on the rock faces of Cumbria and Glencoe, or simply waiting in their coastal bases, they would very soon be called from their wilderness of preparation and propelled into the great adventure which for most would become the defining moment of their young lives.

4

Men of War

On 19 February representatives of the Admiralty visited COHQ with the aim of hammering out a compromise plan of attack, such as would bring about the destruction of the 'Normandie' dock for the least possible cost to themselves in scarce resources.

With no British destroyers on offer, they suggested instead that a Free-French boat, the *Ouragan*, be used as the ramming ship and that she be supported not by a second destroyer but by a small fleet of 'B'-class motor launches. As a solution it favoured the Navy, in that they were able to side-step the issue of putting one of their own valuable escorts up for sacrifice, but it ran right across the grain of Hughes-Hallett's original proposal, first by involving the French and second by increasing the numerical size of the attacking force while at the same time reducing its ability to engage the enemy effectively.

Currently the *Ouragan* was being used as a depot ship in Portsmouth. In order to secure her release the cooperation of De Gaulle's Free French would have to be solicited, at an additional risk to security which it was suggested could be overcome by misinforming their allies as to the exact time and place of her immolation. As the price of their participation they would also have to be represented in the accompanying force of MLs (motor launches), with four French boats supporting a British contingent of eight, ready to disembark their crews and Commandos should any be lost.

Drawn from the various coastal forces flotillas, these 65-ton wooden-hulled launches were normally used for patrol, escort or anti-submarine duties and were entirely unsuited to the role of assault ships; but they did

28

have the particular advantage of being cheap to build and man, and therefore also cheap to lose.

Designed by the Fairmile Construction Company, the 'Bs' measured a mere 112 feet in length by 18 feet across the beam. In normal service they carried a crew of sixteen officers and men; however, for this attack that number would effectively be doubled by the inclusion of extra officers and ratings, as well as by squads of up to fifteen Commandos. Fuelled by petrol, they were already substantially at risk from fire; yet if they were to make it to St Nazaire and back extra tanks would have to be installed on deck to extend their range. Barely able to defend themselves, their existing obsolescent 3-pounder guns could be replaced by much more modern and effective Oerlikon cannon; but as these fired only 20mm explosive bullets, they would still be no stronger than the weakest of the German guns they could expect to be ranged against them. To rely on such ships was to accept as inevitable the loss of a significant portion of the fleet; however, as the two-destroyer scenario was wholly unacceptable to the Navy, the best would have to be made of them, come what may.

Mountbatten having accepted the compromise, and with time very much of the essence, it was now vital that formal approval be obtained as speedily as possible. Hughes-Hallett was therefore instructed to set the details down in the form of an Outline Plan which, when it went up to the Chiefs-of-Staff, described the attacking force as consisting of the French destroyer and MLs, the British MLs, the specially equipped MTB 74 and an additional two RN destroyers, whose role would be to meet the retiring launches and cover their journey home. It would carry 200 officers and men drawn from the Special Service Brigade, whose demolition tasks in order of priority were to be the twin caissons of the 'Normandie' dock, such other lock gates elsewhere in the port whose loss would render the docking basins tidal, ancillary targets such as pumping equipment and munition stores, and any U-boats unfortunate enough to be caught up in the attack. In the final stages of its approach the force was to be protected by a heavy, diversionary air-raid, initially on the dockyard itself but switching later to nearby portions of the town.

As to how the various elements should come together on the night, the Outline stated that:

'The troops will be divided roughly equally between the destroyer and the MLs, approximately fifteen men going in each ML. The whole force will proceed in company so as to approach St Nazaire after dark on a moonlit night. The destroyer will be lightened sufficiently to enable her to pass over

29

the shoal water in the estuary, thus obviating the need to follow the buoyed channel. On arrival the destroyer will ram the outer gate of the big lock, and the troops on board will disembark over her bows, then proceeding to carry out their demolition tasks. The remainder of the force will disembark from their MLs at selected points in the dockyard area. While the demolition parties are at work, the steaming party on board the old destroyer will place a considerable explosive charge as close to the point of contact between the ship and the lock gate as possible; they will then abandon ship and fire the charge. By this means the destroyer will be sunk just outside the entrance to the lock, and it is hoped that sufficient damage will be done to the lock gate to enable MTB 74 to pass through and attack the inner gate. (Should this not be so, MTB 74 will be employed in attacking the outer gates of one of the smaller locks).'

It was anticipated that the actions on shore would be completed within a maximum of two hours, after which the waiting MLs would take the survivors off and carry them to safety.

Set down in this very simplistic way, Hughes-Hallett's statement of intent would be enough to win from the Chiefs-of-Staff their conditional seal of approval. However, nothing was settled yet, and there would be much dispute and amendment before the final plan emerged which would spawn the feat of arms known to the world as Operation Chariot.

With the game now under way, the focus of attention switched from the manoeuvrings at 'head office' to the fighting men whose job it would be to subdue the port's defences and wreak havoc throughout the dockyard. By this time the decision had already been made that Lieutenant-Colonel Charles Newman's 2 Commando would bear the brunt of the assault and clear the way for the teams of explosives specialists. In fact Newman himself was to be in overall control of the ground attack, with the title of Military Force Commander.

As he brought his boys back home upon completion of their landing exercises, Newman knew nothing of this. In fact when 2 Commando returned to Ayr on Sunday the 22nd, he was, so he later recorded, looking forward to 'the dismal outlook of yet another long period of waiting for a job'. Hastily summoned to a Brigadier's Conference at Irvine, he initially had to listen with a sinking heart to the recitation of orders for what looked like being yet another summer of training. Only later, when he had received instructions to leave that very night for Mountbatten's HQ, did he begin to hope that he and his soldiers might at last be in the way of a job that was worthy of their skill and daring.

Having passed on to his immensely capable second-in-command, Major Bill Copland, Haydon's orders that 100 of their best men be trained in the art of street fighting by night, Newman left for London. 'Speculation and excitement ran high in the Orderly Room, ' he records, 'as to the possibilities of something really coming of it.'

Reporting at Richmond Terrace early the following day, he waited with a growing sense of excitement for Brigadier Haydon to arrive. Though he still knew absolutely nothing about the coming job, it had to be something big, for several members of Mountbatten's staff could not help but make veiled remarks about how lucky he was to be in on it. When Haydon finally appeared he briefly outlined the task ahead and then left Newman to spend the remainder of that day zealously perusing a fat intelligence file, replete with a thousand details relating to the structure and operation of the great dock and the specialized machinery that served it. After all the long months of waiting, here at last was a job that was more than just a gesture. This was designed to be a dagger-thrust right at the heart of the enemy and Newman's boys would be the steel from which that dagger's blade was forged.

With his staff in Ayr pushing rapidly ahead with the preparation of 2 Commando, the second piece of the jigsaw fell into place when the various teams of explosives specialists arrived in the small Scottish port of Burntisland.

Totalling some eighty officers and men, the teams from the various Commandos arrived at their temporary home on the northern shore of the Firth of Forth, believing that this was just another in the sequence of courses that were such an important element of their training. Many already knew each other, having shared the hardships of other schemes designed to improve their knowledge and efficiency, most recently at Lochailort just a handful of weeks before. Whatever the private suspicions of those who wondered what it was really all about, the official line adhered to by Pritchard, who here would reign supreme, was that they were being transformed into experts in the science of dockyard demolitions, specifically so they might destroy such British docks as the enemy might seek to use in the event of a German invasion.

Thus began several days of intensive training during which they learned all about locks and dry docks, caissons and gates, pumping and winding machinery, power production and distribution, cranes and gantries, various formats of moving bridges, and the particular configuration of the charges the destruction of each would require. In Burntisland itself, in the secure Naval dockyard at Rosyth, even on the great Forth Bridge, they practised to the point where they could give a good account of themselves in any dockyard in the world. From Pritchard, who was a born leader of men, they drew both skill and a sense of mission, responding so well to his expert and vibrant tutelage that they would soon be ready to move on to the dockyards at Cardiff and Southampton, there to rehearse the very routines they would be called upon to carry out for real, alone in the darkness and danger of St Nazaire.

With the training well under way and Newman deeply absorbed in knitting together the myriad details of his complex attack plan, the next step was to appoint his Naval opposite number. At this critical juncture, however, the Chiefs-of-Staff set everything back by approving the Outline Plan, but without the involvement of the French. The *Ouragan* was therefore out, and it was now the responsibility of the Admiralty to provide a British ship: but this they were no more keen to do now than when first petitioned; all of which meant that, when the newly appointed Naval Force Commander first arrived upon the scene with only a month to go, he was to find the whole affair bedevilled by an atmosphere of uncertainty.

In requesting that an officer be made available, Hughes-Hallett made it clear to the Admiralty that the appointee would almost certainly win a Victoria Cross, should the operation prove to be a success. The Admiralty, however, did not have an endless supply of suitably qualified candidates and in choosing Commander Robert Edward Dudley Ryder RN for the job they were recommending to work alongside Newman an officer who was very much an unknown quantity. In fact, as Ryder himself was to find out some years later, and much to his amusement, his appointment was due more to the fact that he was the only Commander available than to any special qualities it was thought he might bring to the job.

Under something of a cloud as a result of having lost his last ship to a collision in fog, Ryder was languishing in Wilton House, near Salisbury, when on 25 February the signal arrived which was to restore him to the command of men and ships on the high seas.

Having celebrated his thirty-fourth birthday ten days before, Ryder was already able to look back on a naval career which had been nothing if not eventful. He had been introduced to the service as a cadet on board the training ship HMS *Thunderer*, before serving as a midshipman on HMS *Ramillies*, following which he had returned to Britain to complete his sub's courses. After these, he had decided to serve in submarines, joining the *Olympus* and sailing with her to the China Station. Here there occurred a defining moment in Ryder's life when he joined with four other officers in a project to build, and sail to Britain whilst on extended leave, a 30-ton ketch called *Tai Mo Shan*. The voyage, which was begun in 1933, proved an unforgettable experience, honing skills, both technical and intellectual, which would come to serve him well in later years.

Dark-haired, strong-chinned and very determined, Ryder's outward show was of serious resolve; yet this belied the fact that he was at heart a romantic, who shied away from the rigidity of service in the big ships of the fleet, preferring instead to live by his own wits, free from the dead hand of official control. Possessed of a dry sense of humour and a fine appreciation of beauty, his writings are full of the elemental satisfaction he obtained from the joys and perils of adventure. He was always at his happiest with an independent command, in the company of trusted companions, with a strong and certain purpose, and the freedom of deep water beneath his keel. Very much a convert to the relatively new sport of ocean yacht racing, he was particularly in his element on the deck of a living ship, powered by the wind and directed by the ageless skills of the navigator and master mariner.

Having tasted such freedom with the *Tai Mo Shan*, Ryder had not been in a hurry to return to regular service and therefore considered himself fortunate indeed, at the age of only twenty-six, to have been offered the command of the research ship *Penola*, soon to depart on a three-year voyage to the Antarctic. A three-masted topsail schooner, *Penola* was to transport and succour the expedition of the Australian explorer John Rymill. Sailing with his brother Lisle as second mate, the voyage only served to confirm Ryder in his love of sail, which made it all the harder to bear when, on his return to Britain in August 1937, the Navy saw fit temporarily to clip his wings by transferring him to the armoured deck of HMS *Warspite*, the flagship of the Mediterranean Fleet.

Finally relieved from the tedium of this appointment by the outbreak of war, Ryder had returned to independent command as Captain of a Q-ship, the 5000-ton converted Cardiff tramp, the *Willamette Valley*. Commissioned in February, 1940, she had sailed in search of U-boats as far as Bermuda and the River Plate, before being torpedoed and sunk on 28 June, 200 miles west of Mizen Head. Adrift on a scrap of wreckage, Ryder had been obliged to spend four days in the water before being rescued by the *Inverliffy*, a vessel from the last convoy to be routed through these waters.

Following a short period in command of the frigate *Fleetwood*, Ryder had moved on, early in 1941, to the Captaincy of the *Prince Philippe*, with the rank of Commander. A Belgian cross-channel steamer which was fitting out as a Commando ship, the *Prince Philippe* had commissioned on 14 June, only to be sunk one month later when she collided in thick fog with the steamship *Empire Wave*. Ryder was not held directly responsible for the loss; however, having been sunk twice in one year, he was sent 'for a rest cure with the Army, ' as Naval Liaison Officer to the HQ of Southern Command, at Wilton House.

While at Wilton, he received a letter from the Admiralty informing him that he had 'incurred their Lordships' displeasure, ' against which rather unfair decision he had penned a lengthy rebuttal. No doubt, in the fullness of time, their Lordships' response would be made known to him.

At Wilton Ryder's job was to advise Southern Command on the various aspects concerning a possible invasion along their particular stretch of coastline. It was no place for a man of his experience and ability, and from its pleasant but stultifying anonymity the signal requiring his presence at COHQ, at 1500 hours on the following day came as a welcome if wholly unexpected release.

The COHQ meeting of 26 February began promptly at 3 o'clock, by which time Ryder had not arrived. Included amongst the twenty-two senior officers present were Lord Mountbatten, who was in the chair, and Admiral of the Fleet Sir Charles Forbes, the Commander-in-Chief Plymouth, who, as the force was to assemble at a port within his command, was now the naval 'Patron' of the operation.

The discussion of the various agenda items was already well under way when, a full fifteen minutes late, Ryder was shown into the room. He still had absolutely no idea why he had been summoned and was feeling rather embarrassed as he took in the array of Admirals, Brigadiers, Commodores, Captains and the like. A model of some unidentified dockyard was on the table, which must be the objective under consideration. An agenda was thrust into his hand. Ryder was 'just getting the gist of what it was all about, when Mountbatten said, "We now come to item 5. Commander Ryder has been appointed to command the Navy Forces, under the Commander-in-Chief, Plymouth." He looked up. "Is that all right, Ryder?" I managed to gulp out a fairly prompt "Yes Sir." And the discussion moved on to the next item.'

Having received no prior briefing and Mountbatten having already outlined the plan prior to Ryder's arrival, the new Naval Force Commander was obliged to sit through the remainder of the meeting with no idea which port it was they were planning to attack. Item by item an agenda was slowly completed which encompassed such diverse topics as concealment of the force from aerial observation, the enhancement of the MLs' meagre armament, the despatch of the Commandos from Ayr on board the assault ship *Princess Josephine Charlotte*, which was to be their floating home, and liaison with Bomber and Fighter Commands regarding air support. Falmouth was identified as the port at which the various elements of the force would come together; and while there, the security cover for the MLs was to be that of extended anti-submarine patrols. Inevitably the dispute between COHQ and the Admiralty regarding provision of a ramming ship rumbled on and on, the latest suggestion being that a submarine be substituted for the destroyer.

Only upon the conclusion of all these discussions was Ryder at last able to meet his Commando opposite number and he remembers 'drawing him to one side and saying, "Where the hell is this place?"' Newman laughed. 'Oh, didn't they tell you? – well, it's St Nazaire.' And that was how Ryder came into it.

Plucked from the obscurity of Southern Command, he was flattered indeed by his selection, but the task ahead was nothing if not formidable. Unlike Newman, he had no support of any kind: no staff, no office, no phone, no car, no ships, and a mere four weeks in which to plan and organize a major operation of war. However, with the experience of the *Tai Mo Shan* and *Penola* expeditions behind him, he did not doubt his ability to carry it off. In fact he felt as though everything he had done before had led him to this particular point in time. Writing later of his feelings, he records that 'at a stroke my morale which had been languishing after the loss of *Prince Philippe*, soared into top gear. I felt this was something I fully understood and knew just how to tackle. It was as if I had been waiting for it.'

Having been given no clue beforehand that he was to be appointed to command such a complex and urgent naval operation, Ryder had not come prepared to spend the night, and so he was obliged to return almost immediately to Wilton. Explaining the situation to the Brigadier to whose staff he was attached, he packed that night and was back in London the following day, after visiting *en route* two MLs which were fitting out in Southampton.

In company with Newman again, the two were at last able to begin work on the detailed plan, which they would shortly have to present at yet another meeting at Richmond Terrace. A room at COHQ had been set aside for their use, and taking pride of place within it was the RAF's model of the docks at St Nazaire. The two men sized each other up and were not disappointed. Indeed, despite obvious differences in character and attitude, they were quickly able to establish a working relationship, the closeness and amicability of which greatly enhanced their ability to meet the very tight deadlines imposed upon them.

At thirty-seven 'Colonel Charles', as Newman was affectionately known, was three years older than Ryder. Both were married, although while Ryder's liaison with Hilaré was relatively recent, the avuncular Newman already had four children and his wife, Audrey, was soon to give birth to a fifth. In spite of hailing from an Army family, Ryder was a Navy man through and through, who had always believed that 'there is no better way of serving one's country than in the armed forces of the Crown'. Newman on the other hand, was a civil engineering contractor, most of his military training having been gained during his sixteen years as a Territorial Officer with the 4th Battalion, the Essex Regiment. Straightforward and honest to the point of vulnerability, the very private Ryder concealed his inner self behind a rather dour façade, while the pipe-smoking Newman greeted the world with a calm and reflective geniality. And yet, in spite of these superficial differences, both were very much alike where it counted most, each demanding of their men the highest possible standards of performance. As leaders they shared in equal measure the qualities of courage, determination and absolute reliability, which would soon be reflected in their victories over the very many difficulties that lay ahead.

Newman had commanded No.3 Independent Company during the Norwegian campaign of 1940. On the demise of the Independent Companies, he had been appointed second-in-command to Lieutenant-Colonel Glendinning, the Commanding Officer of No.1 Special Service Battalion, and when the SS Battalions had ceased in their turn to exist, he was promoted to Lieutenant-Colonel and given command of the newly formed 2 Commando. A talented pianist, and keen and successful sportsman, who played both rugby and golf and had been a gifted light middleweight amateur boxer, Newman brought to 2 Commando a philosophy of performance based on choosing the right men and then encouraging them to do their jobs to the very best of their ability. By exercising effective control without rigidity or force, he won the respect and affection of everyone, while at the same time establishing 2 Commando as one of the best led and trained units in Haydon's Brigade.

To new officers arriving from more conventional military backgrounds, his quiet, encouraging approach came as something of a surprise. Second Lieutenant Bill Watson certainly found it so when he arrived in Ayr to take command of a section within No.1 Troop, the original officer of which, Lieutenant Johnny Roderick, had recently been promoted to the command of 3 Troop.

Prior to the war Watson had been a Territorial with the London Scottish. He had first been introduced to Special Service by Lieutenant Tom Peyton of the Rifle Brigade, who recruited him into No. 5 Independent Company, a unit with which he was to serve until commissioned into the Black Watch. Keen to return to Special Service, however, he had later renewed his contact with Peyton who, as he himself was by this time serving with 6 Troop of 2 Commando, had been in a position to advise his protégé of the vacancy.

Only twenty years old at the time, Watson had duly presented himself at 2 Commando HQ, and was taken into Newman's office by the Adjutant, Captain Stanley Day. His reception was not at all what he expected and in describing it some years later, he wrote,

'Newman sat behind his desk in a blue haze of tobacco smoke. He was an inveterate pipe-smoker. A large man, his face strongly reminded me of a benign elephant. This was due to the downward curve of his prominent broken nose, above a small moustache, and a pair of large cauliflower ears. These were the badges of his previous enthusiasm for amateur boxing.

'I gave him a crashing salute. He winced slightly and motioned me to a chair. Gingerly sitting to attention on the chair edge, I answered his questions in a respectfully staccato military manner. After a time he sighed. "This won't do, " he murmured. "We'd better have a drink." He took up his bonnet and led me out to the nearest pub.

'I was astounded. I had never been asked to have a drink with my commanding officer before. After the second pint I began to relax. "What's your first name?" the Colonel asked. "Bill, sir, " I replied. The Colonel wrinkled his forehead. "Oh dear, that won't do at all. We have two Bills already. We'll have to call you something else".'

The two Bills Newman referred to were his Second-in-Command, Major Copland, and Lieutenant Bill Clibborn, a section officer in David Birney's 2 Troop. An altogether more aggressive soubriquet was waiting in the wings for Bill number three, who with Newman's encouragement began to talk more about himself. Suddenly Newman thought of just the thing. 'I've got it! You have a grin just like Tiger Tim's. I'm going to call you "Tiger", and see that you live up to it.'

The 'Tiger Tim' referred to was the hero of a popular children's comic who, to Watson's mind, looked rather more like a striped Cheshire cat than a tiger; however, the decision had been made and 'Tiger' he would remain, his new name an ever-present reminder of his introduction to a very different kind of military organization, every corner of which was permeated by the benevolent philosophy of its very exceptional CO.

5

Old Dog: New Trick

Coming together with only one month to go, the first priority for the Force Commanders was to try to resolve the vexed question of the ramming ship.

Having been told to look at the idea of using a submarine, Ryder and Newman were quick to dismiss such a notion as impracticable, as she would be too small and slow, and a question mark would hang over the condition of any troops forced to spend many hours crammed inside her narrow hull. This took them right back to square one, so Ryder appealed both to Hughes-Hallett and, to the Admiralty, but, as he was later to write, 'Having approved the plan, no one seemed to be interested in getting me what I wanted. All I could find was an antagonistic atmosphere between the Admiralty and Combined Ops, and time was vital.'

Rather than risk outright cancellation, the two commanders therefore pressed ahead with developing their own plan, which would rely on an augmented force of small boats alone. By ruling out the use of any large ship, they felt they could by-pass the Admiralty road-block and get on with the job in hand. Having detailed the necessary additional MLs, MTBs and MGBs, they were quite prepared to run with it. However, Hughes-Hallett had constructed his original proposal around the use of a destroyer and he was not prepared to compromise, arguing that by themselves the small boats would be far too vulnerable to enemy fire. With time running out, they therefore let it be known to the Admiralty that a suitable ship must be allocated, and that if one was not provided by 3 March at the latest, then the whole operation would have to be cancelled.

Faced with this ultimatum the Admiralty at last conceded defeat. It was the acid test of their resolve to see the 'Normandie' dock destroyed. They offered the 'Chariot' team the old destroyer *Campbeltown*, one of the fifty superannuated American boats provided by President Roosevelt in exchange for the lease of British bases. Originally named the USS *Buchanan*, she was a flush-decked four-stacker built in the Bath Iron Works and launched in 1919. Having spent most of her service life in reserve, she had been rescued from oblivion by Britain's desperate need for convoy escorts. A relic of the previous war, she was a weary old dog by 1942, to whom fate was about to give one last chance for glory.

With the centrepiece finally in place, Ryder and Newman were free at last to deliver a fully structured plan of attack to the COHQ meeting of 3 March. Among the many topics considered were questions relating to German recognition procedures, the possible, though unlikely, provision of additional MGBs, the positioning of a submarine off the entrance to the Loire to act as a navigational beacon and the choice of Falmouth as the best site in which to carry out final training. The decision was taken that *Campbeltown* should be refitted at Devonport and news was released of the appointment of Lieutenant Nigel Tibbits, RN, as the officer to head the Naval Demolition Party and take responsibility, with the help of Pritchard, for transforming *Campbeltown* into a floating bomb. Of potentially greatest significance to the final result was the clear indication from the RAF representatives that Bomber Command's commitment to the raid was dwindling. At this stage it was Newman's request for low-flying aircraft that was meeting resistance. Other more fundamental reservations were destined to surface later.

Following the meeting, which cleared them to push ahead with drawing up their detailed orders, the two Force Commanders could be reasonably satisfied that, provided work on *Campbeltown* could begin without delay, all the ships and men should be ready to sail on the appointed day, 27 March.

Setting aside their growing doubts about the RAF, they could take comfort from the fact that the naval force was steadily coming together, and that the training of Newman's men continued apace, with the demolition parties having already left Burntisland for the docks of Cardiff and Southampton.

Split now into two halves, these teams were directed and supervised in Cardiff's Barry Docks by Pritchard, while in Southampton Bob Montgomery trained them to the pitch of Olympic athletes as time and time again they 'destroyed' the giant King George V dock, so close in scale to their target in St Nazaire. Operating both in daylight and in darkness, on their own objectives and on those of other teams, the men steadily trimmed their times and honed their skills to the point where their actions became automatic and their performance could be predicted with certainty.

Towards the end of the first week in March most of the parties would swap between the two sets of docks to complete the process of preparation, struggling always to excel while weighed down by packs containing sixty or more pounds of explosives, fuses, detonators, incendiaries and the like. Because they had not been told yet what all the work was for, the constant repetition did take its toll on morale, but security was paramount, and anyway they would come to know the reason for it soon enough.

Accompanied by Constructor-Commander Merrington, Ryder and Newman set off to visit *Campbeltown*, then lying at Portsmouth. Merrington had been with Ryder in *Warspite* and was to prove a valuable ally when it came to steering a straight course through the complex relationship which existed between the Admiralty and the dockyards.

'Merrington's advice,' wrote Ryder, 'was to get the ship sailed without delay to Devonport. Only Devonport dockyard, he maintained, could get the extensive alterations completed in the three weeks left. They still prided themselves on having fitted out the battle cruisers in time for the victorious battle of the Falkland Islands in 1914.'

They arrived in Portsmouth having made a short detour to witness a demonstration of flame-throwers, ready to set the wheels officially in motion which would transform the old ship into their principal weapon. At more than 95 metres long, by almost 10 metres across the beam, she was a very slim craft indeed, her flush-deck and four tall funnels giving her an instantly recognizable silhouette. She displaced almost 1200 tons and at her best, with steam in all four boilers, was capable of making a good 35 knots. Her draught, which was a primary consideration throughout, was listed at just below 3 metres, although her loading, and the fact that she squatted by the stern at speed, brought this figure to more than the maximum depth of water she could expect to find covering the shoals. Her slow-speed manoeuvrability posed a potential problem because her large turning circle, and the fact that she tended to skid in the turn, could well compromise her ability to answer the helm quickly during the final stages of her approach. As she was not fitted with rolling chocks she was liable, in the words of her Ordnance Artificer, Frank Wherrell, to 'roll on wet grass,' a feature which, if the weather did not cooperate, might seriously impair the fighting ability of her complement of troops.

In converting her it would be necessary always to think of how her draught would be affected by every pound of armour and explosives brought on board. Indeed, to be sure of getting her safely across the mudbanks she would have to be lightened to the extent that, even when the work was completed, her draught would be less than it was at present. Her primary armament of three 4" guns would have to be sacrificed, as would her torpedo tubes, her depth-charges and their throwers. The light 12-pounder gun normally mounted on the aft deckhouse could be moved to the fo'c'sle and mounted in place of the forward 4" gun. And for close fire support eight 20 mm Oerlikon cannons could be installed on her upperworks – two on the aft deckhouse, two above the main deck and four on the midships gun platform. Both bridge and wheelhouse would need to be protected by armour plate and, to give a modicum of shelter to the commandos during the final approach, it would be necessary to bolt four low armoured screens along most of the length of the main deck. As to the explosive charge itself, it was at this stage envisaged that three tons of explosives in the form of fifty-pound charges would be carried forward immediately after ramming, placed at the point of impact and then fused. To stiffen the forward part of the ship the suggestion was made that one of the bow compartments be filled with cement. However, Merrington was concerned about the potential effects of the added weight and undertook to check its ramifications with the Chief Constructor at Devonport.

Returning immediately to London, such was the pressure to get things done quickly that Ryder and Newman took less than an hour to complete a list of all the additions and alterations they felt would be required. While the lengthy signal requesting this work was being drafted, they shot off another to ask that the *Campbeltown* be sailed to Devonport as soon as possible.

Having reached the limit of his effectiveness in London, Ryder was now free to move to Devonport. Newman, however, would remain behind to complete the military details with the assistance of his Adjutant, Captain Stanley Day, who had been called down from 2 Commando HQ in Ayr. A great deal remained to be done. The orders for each individual party had to be set down in intricate detail. All sorts of items of equipment had to be tested and either accepted or rejected. As the attacking forces would inevitably come into contact with French civilians, Newman was called upon to interview a number of French personnel for possible inclusion in the force. A row erupted with the Ministry of Information over the degree to which the press should be represented on the raid, with the Ministry of Information wanting a full squad to be carried along, and Newman arguing that all available places were needed for fighting troops. In the end it was agreed that only one reporter would go, though in fact two actually joined the force, Gordon Holman and Edward Gilling, both of the *Exchange Telegraph*.

Constant demands were made of the Naval and Combined Ops intelligence organizations for up-to-date aerial photographs. At the end of the week, just at the time when the Cardiff and Southampton demolition teams were switching places to begin the last few days of their training, a recent set arrived which showed new gun positions, to deal with which an additional thirty fighting troops were allocated at Newman's and Haydon's insistence.

Ryder, meanwhile had arrived in Plymouth on Friday the 6th. He reported to Forbes, whose attitude towards 'Chariot' was far more constructive than had been the Admiralty's. 'Mountbatten was critical of Forbes, ' records Ryder, 'but no one could have been nicer to me. "I'm here to get what you want, " he replied in answer to my pleas for help, and he was as good as his word. "Not much use being a Commander-in-Chief if you can't get what you need."' It was a refreshingly different approach to getting the job done and it helped greatly to put Ryder at his ease.

In spite of having requested *Campbeltown*'s urgent dispatch from Portsmouth, Ryder was dismayed to find that his signal to sail her 'as soon as possible' had been interpreted to mean 'by the next convoy', which was not due to leave the port for several days. He therefore enlisted the help of Forbes' Chief of Staff, who telephoned Portsmouth and arranged for her to sail in the small hours of the following morning. She arrived in thick fog later that day and as soon as she berthed a small dockside conference, held under the auspices of the Admiral Superintendent, settled the details of her conversion programme. Ryder already knew Mr Grant, who was to be the Senior Constructor in charge of the work, having met him before in Hong Kong, and did not doubt that the ship was now in the best possible hands.

Of crucial importance at this stage were decisions concerning the fixing and fusing of *Campbeltown*'s main explosive charge. Turning the ship into a bomb was not a difficult problem in itself; however, placing the charge where it would do the most damage, when it was not known how deformed the bows would be by their impact with the caisson, was rather more problematical, as was exploding the charge at the most advantageous moment. The original plan had called for the charge to be brought forward after impact and fused on site, after which there would be a fifteen-minute delay before it went up: but Newman was very unhappy at the prospect of such a violent explosion taking place while his demolition teams were still working in the area. He tried to persuade Ryder of the virtues of a two-to three-hour delay; however, Ryder was concerned that, should the fuses fail, such a lengthy delay would present the ship to the enemy.

Cutting right through to the heart of the problem, Lieutenant Nigel Tibbits, RN, the newly appointed officer in charge of *Campbeltown*'s demolition, proposed that the ship be scuttled immediately after ramming and that her charge be exploded while she rested on the bottom, several hours after the force had cleared the area. The charge would be fixed in place before sailing, fused *en route* and completely sealed to guard against interference. Tibbits produced a type of fuse that would work under water and convinced the interested parties of its reliability, although as a final safeguard against damage from shell and shot, Ryder insisted that a number of long-delay time-fuses be fitted right inside the collection of twenty-four watertight 400-pound depth charges which would now make up her lethal cargo. To conceal the charge and at the same time afford it the greatest possible degree of protection from the impact, it would be hidden within a special compartment built on top of the fuel tanks, immediately abaft the forward gun support, beyond which point the structure of the ship was not expected to sustain significant damage. Their problem apparently solved to the satisfaction of everyone, the Force Commanders then left Tibbits to get on with the work, subject only to stringent testing of the fusing mechanisms. An utterly dependable regular officer of twenty-eight, who had been a torpedo specialist at HMS *Vernon* since December 1939, Tibbits could be relied upon to address the problem with his customary diligence, his strength of intellect and tireless attention to detail, guaranteeing that absolutely nothing would be left to chance.

With the alterations at last in hand, Ryder let Lord Teynham, the Captain of the *Campbeltown*, and coincidentally a cousin of Hilaré's, into the secret, and asked him if he would like to come on the raid. However, as Teynham was an older man who had returned to the service from retirement, Forbes instead required that an active-service CO with destroyer experience be appointed, as a consequence of which Lieutenant-Commander S.H. Beattie was sent down, much to Ryder's delight. 'We had in fact joined the Navy at the same time, ' he writes, 'and so we had been in the training ship together, and had also done our course together. I could wish for no one better.'

As far as his remaining personnel needs were concerned, Ryder's requirement for a qualified navigator was met by the appointment of Lieutenant A.R. Green, RN, who would act as his personal Chief-of-Staff. Also added to the team were Sub-Lieutenant O'Rourke, RCNVR, as Signals Officer, and Lieutenant R.E.A. Verity, RNVR, as Beachmaster.

With these key posts filled, Ryder was able to return briefly to London to review progress with Newman, following which the two men travelled back to Plymouth by train. As time was so very short, they took every opportunity they could to go over the many details still requiring attention. For this they required absolute privacy, a condition not easy to find on wartime trains. 'To facilitate this, ' recalls Ryder, 'Charles used to reserve a first-class compartment to ourselves. This was not popular on crowded trains, with people standing in the corridors. One indignant man protested, "Why can't we be allowed to occupy those seats?" "My friend, " replied Charles, indicating me, "is infectious". "Infectious, " retorted the man. "What's wrong with him?" "Well, you've probably already got VD, so I suppose there's nothing against you sharing – but don't say I haven't warned you." That fooled him.'

In Plymouth for the purpose of a final review before the elements of the 'Chariot' force began to assemble at the port of departure, Ryder and Newman attended a meeting at Forbes' HQ on Tuesday, 10 March. Present at the meeting, which was very much a naval affair, were Green and O'Rourke, as well as Beattie, who was being initiated into the plan. Tibbits and Pritchard were attending, both to explain their demolition plan for *Campbeltown* and to have it formally accepted. Lieutenant-Commander Billie Stephens, RNVR, was there in his capacity as CO of the 20th ML Flotilla, as well as Senior Officer of the whole ML force. Also present were Lieutenant-Commander Wood, the CO of the 28th ML Flotilla; Lieutenant Dunstan Curtis, RNVR, the Captain of the headquarters ship, MGB 314; and Sub-Lieutenant Micky Wynn, who commanded the specially modified MTB 74.

'At our conference, ' writes Ryder, 'the explosion plan designed by Tibbits, and all our other plans based on it were formally accepted. After this the route out was discussed. In this the chief consideration was to avoid being spotted by enemy reconnaissance patrols. We were told that the only regular one was the Paris Zenit [enemy meteorological flight] which passed over the Scilly Isles at 0800 each morning. So our time of sailing had to be after that. Then there was the question of how far we were to pass off Ushant. Were we to go inside or outside our own minefield which lay some sixty miles off? The original plan was to go outside, but that meant longer at sea, and the Commander-in-Chief, after weighing up the possibilities, decided to route us inside. The minefield was due to sink the day we passed, but we couldn't chance that.'

Having also looked into the training programme, the security arrangements and the dates at which all leave could be stopped without giving rise to comment, the meeting went on to consider a mock attack which was planned to take place on the night of the 21st. The 'target' was to be

Devonport dockyard itself, and to conceal its true purpose it was to be dressed up as a test of the defences of both dockyard and town, about the details of which all interested parties would be warned in advance. Newman's soldiers would be landed from Ryder's MLs, with both commanders letting it be known beforehand how little they appreciated the diversion of their men and ships from other, more important, tasks. *Campbeltown* would not be involved as it was considered prudent to keep her out of sight. As the format of the exercise would cause the men themselves to speculate, this was considered the most appropriate time to stop all leave and begin the process of letting them in on the secret.

At the conclusion of the meeting Ryder moved on to Falmouth to await the arrival of Stephens' and Wood's flotillas, while Newman returned briefly to London to conclude his business with COHQ. All the wheels were at last in motion, and on the face of it their enterprise appeared unstoppable; however, as they went about their business none of the major players had any way of knowing just how close recent events in the northern seas had come to snatching their prize away. For even while they had been preparing to meet with Forbes, Ultra had handed the Navy *Tirpitz* on a plate, and had a better job been made of attacking her the future might have been very different indeed.

It had begun on Thursday the 5th when, far away in Arctic waters, a German aircraft sighted the Murmansk-bound convoy PQ 12 and, on receipt of her report, *Tirpitz* was ordered to intercept the ships and destroy them. She sailed from Trondheimsfjord on the 6th, only to search in vain for the convoy, pursued by a powerful British squadron under the command of Admiral Sir John Tovey, who was receiving constant inputs of intelligence. Finally warned of Tovey's presence, *Tirpitz* decided, on the evening of the 8th, to run for home. Guided by Ultra intercepts, Tovey chased her until, on the morning of the 9th, the carrier *Victorious* was close enough to launch an air strike, flying off a squadron of Albacore torpedo bombers. It was an ideal situation and the only time *Tirpitz* would ever be brought to action at sea: but the attack was bungled and in the event she managed to avoid every single torpedo.

For the Germans it was a wasteful and humbling adventure, which had cost 8, 000 tons of fuel and shown just how vulnerable their last great ship was to carrier-borne aircraft. And for the Royal Navy it was an opportunity missed that would not come again. However, for Operation 'Chariot', which could hardly have survived the loss of the ship whose threat had given it birth, it finally sealed the fates of the many young soldiers and sailors who, in just two weeks' time, would sail to St Nazaire, never to return.

6

A Pride of 'Tigers'

When Ryder arrived in Falmouth his first priority was to find some way of operating freely in a port where gossip and speculation were the order of the day. To explain away his own presence, along with that of the MLs with their extra fuel tanks and Oerlikons, he set about establishing a wholly fictitious organization known as the Tenth Anti-Submarine Striking Force, with himself as Senior Officer. 'To cover our activities both ashore and afloat, ' he explains, 'I let it be known with all due secrecy that our striking force was going to carry out extended sweeps to the south and west of the Scilly Isles in the hope of intercepting enemy U-boats returning to France. The force was specially fitted with additional tanks to give it the necessary endurance, and was re-armed to beat off air attack.'

Thus established, Ryder was able to set up an operations centre in the conservatory of 'Tregwynt', the seafront hotel that was being used as the headquarters of the Naval Officer in Charge. To help him maintain a close and confidential contact with the commanding officers of all the small boats, he was assisted both by Green and by Sub-Lieutenant Christopher Worsley, RNVR, who was added to the team shortly after Ryder's arrival. As one of the very few officers who had been let fully into the secret behind Ryder's spurious command, Green's primary responsibility was that of accurately navigating the force to St Nazaire. Worsley, on the other hand, knew nothing of the affair. Until recently the First Lieutenant of a new C-class gunboat operating out of Great Yarmouth, he had been posted to Falmouth simply as 'additional for duties', which duties required him, among other things, to personally hand over all signals and messages to the COs of the various boats under Ryder's command.

The fictitious 'striking force' officially came into being on the 12th, which day also saw the demolition teams come together at Cardiff before entraining for Falmouth, the *Princess Josephine Charlotte* leave Ayr with the majority of the fighting troops on board and Stephens' and Wood's flotillas arrive at the port that would be their home and training ground for the next two weeks.

The arrival of the MLs marked the beginning of an intensive period of training, the purpose of which was to get their officers and crews used to manoeuvring in a much larger formation than was the norm in Coastal Forces. The majority of boats arriving belonged to Wood's flotilla, the newly-formed 28th, whose eight MLs had not had an opportunity to train together as a unit. 'At the first opportunity I took Wood's flotilla to sea, ' writes Ryder, 'and in fact we had, as far as possible, MLs to sea every day and night, and even when they didn't go out for the night they were made to shift berth in the narrow waters of Falmouth harbour on the darkest of nights. As soon as Stephens arrived, I put him in charge of all the MLs and he put them through the most rigorous training, altering course wildly without signal to try and shake off those who were not keeping their wits about them. Then, on return to harbour, he would make them berth along-side, and cast off and berth alongside again, until they were as good as could be wished for.'

MLs 298, 306, 307, 341, 443, 446, 447, and 457, all of which were rela-tively new boats, made up Wood's flotilla. MLs 298 and 306 had arrived in Falmouth, which, coincidentally, was their base, at the end of January, oper-ating together as 'chummy' ships, until Wood arrived with the remaining boats in time for 'Chariot'. Their respective companies having had time to become acquainted, Sub-Lieutenant Bob Nock, RNVR, the twenty-one-year-old commander of ML 298, had become friends both with Lieutenant Ian Henderson, the thirty-year-old skipper of ML 306, and with Henderson's 'Jimmy the One', Sub-Lieutenant Philip Dark, also RNVR. Nock had worked in a bank before volunteering at the age of nineteen, while Henderson had been an underwriting member of Lloyds before the war, with plenty of good yachting experience in local waters. All three officers were married, though while Henderson already had a family, both Nock and Dark were newly-weds. Lieutenant Norman Wallis, RANVR, an officer from the Australian reserve, commanded ML 307; Lieutenant Douglas Briault, RNVR, had charge of ML 341; and ML 443, which would bear the formation number 13 throughout the attack, was in the capable hands of the ex-merchant service officer Lieutenant T.D.L. Platt, RNR, yet another newly-wed, having married a Wren in Clovelly only a few months before. ML 446 was skippered by Lieutenant Dick Falconar, RNVR, and ML 457 had as her captain the courageous Lieutenant Tom Collier, RNVR, a Scot who was also known for his yachting ability. Completing the eight was Lieutenant-Commander Wood's own boat, the flotilla leader, ML 447.

Responsible for all the MLs in the 'Chariot' force was the leader of the 20th flotilla, the thirty-year-old Ulsterman Lieutenant-Commander Billie Stephens, RNVR, in ML 192. Completing his contingent of four Fairmiles were ML 262, commanded by Lieutenant Ted Burt, RNVR, a Metropolitan police officer who was married with one daughter, ML 267 which was the boat of the solicitor, Lieutenant E.H. Beart, RNVR, and Lieutenant Bill Tillie's ML 268.

In these dozen boats, as was the case throughout Coastal Forces, there was a preponderance of 'Wavy Navy' officers, and 'Hostilities Only' ratings. Thrown together in very close proximity, they shared the tedium of patrol and escort duties that were only very occasionally relieved by bursts of action. In the majority of cases wardroom and messdeck had a closer and friendlier relationship than would have been possible on big ships. Discipline was more democratic, people got to know each others' little ways and in a well-run boat a 'family' atmosphere could exist which enhanced rather than diminished the overall effectiveness of the crew.

For the men themselves, the primary living and sleeping space was the messdeck, a large compartment with six folding bunks along each side, which occupied most of the forward third of the hull. Immediately aft of the messdeck was the messdeck lobby, a small open space approximately amidships, which contained the main access to the upper deck. Opening off the lobby were four small compartments; on the port side the Petty Officers' cabin and wc, the spaces reserved for the coxswain and engine-room chief, and, on the starboard side, the radio room and galley. Aft of these compartments was the engine-room, containing two American 600 horse-power V12 Hall-Scott 'Defender' marine engines, which could power the boat to a little over twenty knots. This particular compartment, which had the petrol tanks immediately behind it, was sealed off from the interior of the boat and could only be accessed from the deck above. Right behind the petrol tanks, and occupying much of the after portion of the boat, were the officers' quarters, comprising a small wardroom and officers' pantry and wc. This portion of the hull was accessed from the upper deck by its own companionway. Right at the stern were a number of small storage spaces, the after magazine and the steering gear.

The main deck itself was flat and open, forward and aft of the low superstructure which occupied the middle third of the space. The superstructure did not extend right across the full width of the deck, leaving walkways along either side which, for the purposes of 'Chariot', were used as the mounting sites for rectangular auxiliary fuel tanks. The foremost portion of the super-structure contained the enclosed wheelhouse, behind and slightly above which was the open bridge. Immediately abaft the bridge, the deck was only slightly raised, this lowest portion of the superstructure containing the companionway to the messdeck lobby, the stubby funnel and the engine-room ventilators.

As modified for 'Chariot' the foredeck housed the bandstand mounting for the forward 20mm Oerlikon cannon, as well as its ready-use ammunition lockers, while the after portion of the deck housed the second Oerlikon mounting, the depth-charges, where fitted, and the apparatus for making smoke, which was situated right at the stern. In addition to the Oerlikons, some bridge-wings were fitted with studs on which could be mounted stripped-Lewis guns. Additional Lewis mountings, for anti-aircraft use, were to be found on the after part of the superstructure, or on the after-deck. The boats were fitted with, and used generally at their peril, a device called a Holman Projector, the purpose of which was to toss Mills bombs into the path of low-flying aircraft. Most crews found potatoes and beer cans to be rather safer projectiles to fire from it.

Of round-bilge construction, the Fairmile 'B's were capable of standing up to very severe sea conditions, although in certain circumstances they could roll and corkscrew mercilessly, as Newman's Commandos were soon to discover for themselves. Consigned to a dusty and forgotten corner of the Navy, the 'B's lived a solitary existence, seen by many only as a wartime necessity; coastal forces vessels were tolerated – no more. They were never taken as seriously as steel-hulled ships: however, as 'Chariot' would show, their crews – who, unlike Newman's Commandos, were not given the option of volunteering for the job – would behave under fire in such a manner as to prove themselves more than worthy custodians of the very best traditions of the Senior Service.

The boats of the two flotillas having immediately embarked upon their exhaustive programme of training, the next major piece of the 'Chariot' jigsaw fell into place when the *PJC*, or, less politely, *Charlotte the Harlot*, arrived in Falmouth on Friday the 13th with the bulk of Newman's fighting troops on board. Consisting of the majority of the officers and the very best of the NCOs and men of 2 Commando, this select contingent had trained to the very peak of perfection in the art of street fighting by night, under the demanding gaze of Newman's Second-in-Command, Major William Oranmore Copland.

Known to the troops as Major Bill, this tall, steely-eyed veteran of the

First War would prove to be one of the dominant figures of 'Chariot', his fearless disdain of enemy fire a feature of every phase of the attack. At forty-four, he was considerably older than the general run of Commando soldiers, although neither his age nor the fact that he had been gassed at Passchendaele had prevented him from overcoming the many hardships of Commando life. During the mid-1930s, while part of the management team of Rylands Bros. in Warrington, he had returned to the colours as a Territorial officer with the South Lancashire Regiment. He had served since the outbreak of war with No. 4 Independent Company and No. 1 Special Service Battalion, before joining Newman in 2 Commando. Together they made the perfect team, Newman's affability concealing an iron resolve, and Copland's air of austerity masking a warmth of emotion not normally betrayed to those under his command who failed to meet his exacting standards of discipline and performance.

For most of her stay in Falmouth the *PJC* would be anchored out in the roadstead, well away from the MLs; however, on first arriving she tied up at the quayside for the purpose of taking on quantities of stores, weapons and ammunition. To add to the press of bodies already on board, the demolition teams under Pritchard and Montgomery arrived and sought sleeping space wherever it could be found.

Friday the 13th was also the date upon which Newman finally concluded his business in London. As he was leaving COHQ to motor down to Falmouth he was called back by Mountbatten and treated to what he has described as an 'inspiring interview' on the steps of the Richmond Terrace building. Mountbatten was anxious to emphasize the strategic importance of 'Chariot', which he described as not just an ordinary raid, but rather 'an important operation of war, ' from which few could expect to return. This being the case, Newman was encouraged to impress the risks upon the men and to offer those who had worries, or family ties, a chance to remain behind without detriment to their standing amongst their peers.

After obtaining the very latest reconnaissance photos of his target, which showed a large armed raider in the 'Normandie' dock, Newman spent the night in Tavistock before joining his men on board the *PJC* on the 14th. They were all, as he was later to write, 'in fine fettle, and bursting to know what it was all about'; however, an explanation would have to wait until the formal briefings scheduled to take place in just four days' time. Meanwhile a thousand and one details remained to be sorted out with Ryder, while all the time maintaining the pretence that neither their presence in the port nor the activities of their respective commands were in the slightest way related.

While the ship was still attached to the dockside, Pritchard and Montgomery took their demolition teams ashore to pack their individual rucksacks from the consignment of specially prepared charges which, having arrived by rail, were now stored under guard in a Nissen hut.

The charges, which mostly consisted of varying weights and formats of 'plastic' explosive, had been specially designed by Major David Wyatt of the Special Operations Executive, according to target specifications supplied by the Commandos. They consisted of 'sausage' charges for cutting gun-barrels and pipes and for wrapping around key pieces of machinery, 'opportunity' charges to allow the men some latitude in dealing with the unexpected, and the special packages of explosives developed to ensure the destruction of both great caissons – the eighteen-pound charges to be hung in the water close to their outside faces, and the 'wreaths' of connected charges which must be placed inside for the purpose of blowing both their inner faces and their numerous internal walls. Weighing some two and a half tons all told, these beautifully prepared charges were, along with magnetic clams and limpets, distributed among the men in relation to the targets they would be expected to attack, and packed complete with the necessary safety and instant fuses, igniters, detonators and all the rest.

Too dangerous to store on board ship, it was planned that the packs would remain in the hut until much closer to the time of departure. On completion of the exercise, therefore, they were left behind while the men returned to the quayside to find the *PJC* already in the process of moving to her isolated anchorage. Boarding last of all and with the gangplank already removed, Pritchard and Montgomery were hoisted on to the deck, one at a time, standing in the hook of a crane. Later that night the two sapper officers returned to the hut to check that all was well and that the guard had been fed. It was quite a chilly night and, when Montgomery opened the door, he found to his disbelief that in the midst of all the packs the stove was burning fiercely. Considering the quantity of explosives stored within, it was not hard to imagine the size of the bang that would have resulted from any mishap. However, in the event the only explosion to rend the night air was Montgomery's own, when he delivered himself of a few well-chosen words of rebuke.

Since arriving in Falmouth Ryder's primary concern had been to divert attention away from his notional Striking Force; however, his efforts were rather undermined by the arrival, on the same day as Newman, of the very distinctive MTB 74. She sailed into port, he recalls, 'with every form of insurmountable defect and painted in such a dazzling style that even the cows in the fields paused in their endless task of converting grass into milk, and looked down on her with astonishment as she passed. What could be done to account for her presence in my force?'

A very odd-looking bird indeed, MTB 74 was a one-off adaptation of the Vosper 70′ design, specially fitted out to attack the German battle cruisers in Brest. At the suggestion of her CO, Sub-Lieutenant R.C.M.V. Micky Wynn, RNVR, she had been fitted with 18 inch tubes mounted right forward on the fo'c'sle, where their height would allow them to fire two unpowered torpedoes over the nets protecting the ships. These special projectiles, each containing 1800 pounds of explosives and known as 'Wynn's Weapons', would then sink beneath the target ships and explode after MTB 74 had used her great speed to escape – or so at least was the theory. In the event it was never put to the test, leaving this wondrous 'toy' without a purpose. This was the point at which the COHQ planners had brought her into the 'Chariot' fold, the idea being to employ the special torpedoes against the dry-dock caissons instead.

Small and cramped by comparison with the Fairmiles, MTB 74 had been built for speed and dash. Her three main V12 supercharged Packard engines, each delivering 1,250 horse-power, gave her a sustainable velocity of some 35 knots, and could power her at close to 40 knots when necessary. At the other end of the speed scale she could employ her two Ford V8 auxiliary motors for slow-speed manoeuvring and silent running at up to 6 knots. In between these two extremes her behaviour could become erratic, and because of her inability to easily maintain the steady 7 to 15 knot plod of the remainder of the 'Chariot' force, she would be stationed at the very rear of the formation where her surging progress would least disrupt the other boats.

As a first precaution Ryder ordered Wynn to paint the heads of his special torpedoes red, to make them look like practice units. Then he incorporated the MTB in a series of supposedly secret signals designed to steer speculation about the purpose of his force well away from the truth, these hinting strongly that the future duties of his boats lay overseas.

How successful these efforts to muddy the waters were it was difficult to quantify, although the arrival of tropical kit did divert the thoughts of some among the boats' crews, not all of whom had fallen for the 'Striking Force' subterfuge. Nevertheless, as a policy, the process of carefully disseminating misleading information would have to continue right up to the time of departure. With respect to the Commandos on *PJC*, the story was put about that they were to be the attacking force in the upcoming test of Devonport's defences, and Ryder let it be known that he was not happy at having to disrupt his own formation's training programme in order to have his boats used as ferries for the 'Pongos'. Having established his irritation at being in any way involved with Newman and his men, it was a relatively simple matter to extend this display of pique to cover another joint exercise planned for the 16th and 17th, with the presence of Commandos on board Ryder's MLs for an extended sweep out into the Atlantic being explained away as a necessary prelude to the Devonport exercise.

As the planning for 'Chariot' itself progressed, it became abundantly clear that the force would require some teeth if it was to have enough offensive ability to deal with enemy vessels encountered *en route*, or during the final approach to the port. MGBs and MTBs would have been ideal for the purpose; however, the official response in London was that no extra craft were available. It was yet another example of the authorities in the capital failing to come up with the goods and so Ryder again turned to Forbes for help, on which he commented that, 'down in Plymouth, however, the atmosphere was quite different, and we soon found that everyone was all out to help us. Four more launches were at once allocated to us and a search was made for the necessary tanks, and although they joined our force rather late, they were completed and most welcome.'

The launches concerned, MLs 156, 160, 177 and 270, were Fairmile 'B' Torpedo Boats belonging to the 7th ML Flotilla in Dartmouth. In most respects they were identical to the boats of Stephens' and Wood's flotillas; however, they had been fitted with two torpedo tubes, mounted on either side of the funnel and angled outwards so that their bases rested on the after portion of the coach deck. The balance of the boats was not enhanced by the additional topweight, and there was some concern that their stability in heavy seas might be severely compromised if deck-mounted petrol tanks were to be fitted as well: but their 'fish' were badly needed and so the risk was deemed acceptable. They would sail to Falmouth after having the tanks installed at Devonport. Unfortunately there would not be time to fit them with Oerlikons and they would be forced to rely upon the firepower of their antiquated Hotchkiss 3-pounders.

ML 156 was under the command of Lieutenant Leslie Fenton, RNVR, a film actor just turned 40, who was married to the beautiful actress Ann Dvorak; Lieutenant Thomas Wilson 'Nero' Boyd, RNVR, twenty-seven years old, also married, and the son of a Hull trawler owner, was the strong-willed skipper of ML 160. ML 177 was the boat of Sub-Lieutenant Mark Rodier, RNVR, and ML 270 had, as her CO the Senior Officer of the 7th Flotilla, the ex-Merchant Service Lieutenant C.S.B. Irwin, RNR.

Having been assigned to the force so late in the day, the Dartmouth boats did not receive a mention in the Combined Plan issued by COHQ on 16 March. Prepared by the COHQ planning staff in conjunction with Forbes

53

and the Force Commanders, this document listed the other participating vessels and gave Newman's force as consisting of 245 officers and men in all, of whom 161 were drawn from his own Commando. By far the most detailed statement yet of the means by which the aims of 'Chariot' could be achieved, it included a draft of the orders for the submarine *Sturgeon*, which was to act as a final positioning beacon, a statement of the course and speed to be followed and an outline of the military assault plan, in which the fighting troops were now broken down by function into 'assault' parties, whose job it would be to overwhelm the defences, and 'protection' parties, which would give close support to the 'demolition' teams. Despite doubts about Bomber Command's commitment to the operation, it also detailed the various phases of the bombing support, which was regarded as crucial to success, with aircraft over the target two hours before zero time, which was 0130 BST, and support continuing throughout the hours of darkness. All activity on shore was to cease on time for an 0330 withdrawal, except in cases where major demolitions had not yet been completed.

On the same day the plan was issued, Newman's Commandos boarded Ryder's MLs for the thirty-six-hour sweep into deep water to get the Commando parties attuned to travelling on board the boats. With the gunboat not yet available, Ryder and Newman were making the trip on board Billie Stephens' ML 192.

As the little fleet rounded the Lizard the weather began to deteriorate and soon the boats were running into heavy seas stirred and churned by gale-force winds. Ryder was assured by Stephens that the boats could stand the battering, but what really worried him was the thought of what might happen during the hours of darkness, with the boats being tossed this way and that and their officers unused to travelling in large formations. The plan had called for them to remain at sea all night, but Ryder decided instead to shelter in the Scilly Isles until the morning. 'As it was, ' he writes, 'we didn't miss much, as we weighed from Crow Sound the next morning and spent the whole day manoeuvring by signal, until we ran into thick fog. We were able in this way to try out our two intended cruising orders – the extended anti-submarine sweep which we initiated as our day formation, and our close formation by night or in thick weather.'

Much more a trial than an exercise, the whole affair was particularly horrible for many of the Commandos, who were effectively disabled by such a violent passage. All in all it was a chastening experience for the Force Commanders, which showed how easily their carefully laid plans could be undermined by factors far beyond their control. As nauseated Commandos would not get the job done, then, perhaps, in line with all their other precautions, a prayer or two in favour of a calm crossing would not go amiss.

The MLs returned to Falmouth on Tuesday the 17th, the same day that MGB 314 arrived in Plymouth prior to being towed to join the main force on the Wednesday. Under normal circumstances it would have been both logical and in keeping with tradition for Ryder and Newman to have established their headquarters for the raid itself in *Campbeltown*: but as there was a very real danger of this ship grounding, the decision was taken to use something smaller and more manoeuvrable instead. MGB 314, of the 14th MGB Flotilla, fitted the bill quite nicely, because in addition to being faster and better armed than the MLs, she was also equipped with radar and an echo sounder, both of which would be invaluable aids in guiding the remainder of the fleet safely through the perils of the estuary.

MGB 314 was a Fairmile 'C'-class gunboat. Slightly shorter and narrower than the 'B'-type, her three supercharged Hall-Scott engines could power her to a sustainable 23 knots and a maximum speed of 26.5 knots. Wooden-hulled as were the 'B's, she was of hard chine construction, with her officers' accommodation forward of the crew spaces, and most of the after portion of her hull taken up by the engines and their petrol tanks. She was quite heavily armed, with a Vickers 2-pounder pom-pom forward, and a Rolls Royce 2-pounder semi-automatic cannon aft. Amidships on either side of the deck twin .5" machine guns were mounted in power-operated turrets and on the bridge there were .303 machine guns.

As far as her suitability for 'Chariot' was concerned, the only note of caution concerned her very limited range, which was a considerable worry for Ryder. With her standard fuel load she had not enough range to make it to St Nazaire, let alone get back, and so in deciding to use her Ryder was accepting the possibility that she might have to be towed both ways. As this was hardly ideal, her charming and incisive captain, the thirty-one-year-old Lieutenant Dunstan Curtis, RNVR, set out to obtain two of the 500-gallon deck tanks that had been fitted to the MLs, and in doing so wandered into the crossfire between those in Falmouth, who wanted to help, and the Admiralty, who could only seem to put obstacles in their way. Writing of the affair, Ryder records that, 'The ML base at Falmouth arranged with Messrs Fairmile to send the tanks as soon as possible, while at the same time we made a signal asking for them to be hastened. The reply came, as we were busily having the tanks screwed down, "No tanks available". This was amusing, but when it was followed by a further signal from the Admiralty, "Tanks are not to be fitted", we were very incensed. This was deliberate obstruction, and to this day I am surprised by it.'

Her involvement with 'Chariot' was quite a departure for the gunboat as, for most of her operational career, she had inhabited the shadowy world of intelligence, ferrying agents to and from the enemy shore and returning to bases such as Dartmouth and the Hamble River. However, as fate would have it, she was to lead a charmed life during the coming action, losing only two members of her crew, the chain of events encompassing whose deaths began at the very moment she tied up to the Plymouth quayside.

Her forward Vickers pom-pom had a crew of two, with Able Seaman Frank Smith, only just turned nineteen, as 'trainer', and Able Seaman Bill Savage, twenty-nine, as 'layer'. Born in Smethwick in 1912, the youngest of the twenty-two children born to James and Kitty Savage, Bill was a 'Brummie' through and through. A product of the Cape Hill School, he had left at fourteen to follow his father into work with Mitchell and Butler's Brewery. Keen on sports, he was both introspective and possessed of all the Savage family's stubbornness. Married, on 27 March, to Doris Hobbs, Bill was destined to celebrate his fifth wedding anniversary whilst cruising through the Bay of Biscay. Straight as a die, he was not at all the sort of man to be swayed from a commitment, even to the extent of having grown a rather splendid beard simply because he had told his pal Bill Whittle that he would if Whittle started his. Described by a shipmate as the biggest man on board, and with the biggest heart, Bill did have one misfortune, which was that, try as he might, he could not seem to persuade Lady Luck to remain by his side for long and this failure was aptly demonstrated by the manner of his arrival in Devonport when, while attempting to take a forward line ashore, he injured a knee and was obliged to take to his bunk.

As he was unable to carry out his duties, Curtis brought on board, as a replacement for Bill, the extremely competent 'regular' gunnery rating, Able Seaman 'Lofty' Stephens. Although he had been relieved by Stephens, Bill remained on board and, when he was sufficiently recovered, returned to his post on the pom-pom, in his turn displacing Stephens. The new man should, by rights, have left at this point; however, with 'Chariot' coming up Curtis was loathe to part with such a valuable rating and so Stephens remained with the crew. Ironically, and each man having had legitimate excuses to be else-where, it was these two who were destined to die within feet of one another, right at the fag end of the action and with the gunboat almost within sight of the open sea and home.

7

Hostages to Fortune

The gunboat arrived in Falmouth on the 18th, the same day *Sturgeon* reported to Plymouth. An important date in the chronology of the raid, the 18th also saw the arrival of the Dartmouth boats, to bring the total number of 'B's up to sixteen, and the first disclosure of the plan of attack to Commando officers, thirty-nine of whom were brought together behind locked doors in the wardroom of the *PJC*.

In an atmosphere that was heady with excitement, they paid rapt attention to Colonel Charles, who told them that their target was to be a port, as yet unnamed, somewhere on the coast of France. It was displayed to them in the dual forms of a map drawn on a blackboard and the model which Newman had brought down with him from London.

Describing the whole affair as 'the sauciest thing since Drake', he explained that, having rammed the outer caisson of the port's great dry dock, several parties under Major Copland's command would scramble over the destroyer's bows to secure the immediate area and wreck the dock's pumping and winding machinery. While this was being done, troops would be landed at two other points, to assist in forming a defensible bridgehead and to carry out a number of subsidiary demolitions. These troops were to be landed from the same small launches in which they had made their unpleasant excursion to the Scillies. On fulfilment of all the tasks ashore, the men would gather at a single re-embarkation point, from which surviving MLs would seek to carry them home again.

The most southerly of all the landing points was to be the Old Mole, a narrow stone structure standing high above the waters of the Loire, about 500 metres south of the dry dock. Landing at the slipway on its northern face, several groups of men under the overall command of Captain Bertie Hodgson, the fearless CO of Newman's 1 Troop, would secure the south-eastern portion of the dockyard and isolate it from the town by blowing both bridges across the New Entrance. With the area cleared of Germans, Hodgson's demolition teams could then destroy a number of important dockyard facilities, such as the boiler house and the hydraulic power station. High on their list of priorities would be the several sets of lock gates in the New Entrance itself, which, if destroyed, would contribute significantly to making the Submarine Basin tidal.

Between the Mole and the dry-dock entrance was the third of the landing points, a deep indentation known as the Old Entrance, which contained a second, smaller lock permitting access to the Submarine Basin directly from the Loire. If the gates of this lock were destroyed in conjunction with those of the New Entrance, then the Submarine Basin would fill and drain with the tide and the hours during which the U-boats could come and go would be dramatically reduced – even if only in the short term. Landing here would be a contingent of troops under Captain Micky Burn, whose task, in addition to destroying the lock gates, would be to secure the northern portion of the bridgehead against penetration from the town by blowing the bridge at the northernmost end of the Submarine Basin. Two flak towers in the immediate area of the bridge would also be destroyed and a protective block would be formed and maintained until such time as the general with-drawal was signalled. Landing with this body of troops would be special assault teams which, having overwhelmed the defences in the area between the Mole and the Old Entrance, would join Newman and come into HQ reserve.

Hodgson's group would be designated 'Group One', Micky Burn's con-tingent at the Old Entrance, 'Group Two' and Copland's squads on the *Campbeltown* 'Group Three'. All groups were to be led in by assault teams of about a dozen men, whose job it would be to quell the defences and block the approach of reinforcements. Immediately behind them would be small demolition squads of about five men, including an officer, who would be given close cover by similarly-sized protection squads. The assault and protection squads, to be drawn from Newman's 2 Commando, would be relatively heavily armed. By contrast, the demolition teams, which would be weighed down by heavy packs of explosives, would carry only pistols, which meant that they would be of very limited effectiveness in a fighting role, once their jobs were done. Bob Montgomery, travelling with Copland on board *Campbeltown*, would oversee the demolitions in the area of the dry dock. Bill Pritchard, travelling in an ML, and landing with the

Old Mole group, would oversee all the subsidiary demolitions.

As the men listened intently, the more experienced among them perhaps a little surprised by the role assigned to the flimsy launches, as well as by the magnitude of the tasks entrusted to such tiny groups of men, the general reaction was one of barely suppressed elation in spite of the obvious risks. Sitting right next to Micky Burn, Lieutenant Tom Peyton, who was one of his 6 Troop section officers, gasped with excitement, his reaction exemplifying the longing of them all to be in the coming action; and yet, along with so many others in the crowded, smoky room, he would all too soon be dead. Tiger Watson was also on the edge of his seat, fearful that he might not be cast to play a role in the unfolding drama which Newman was identifying by the code name 'Chariot': 'We listened with straining attention, ' he recalls, 'as the Colonel outlined the role of each individual officer. My heart was in my mouth. I was terrified ... of being left behind. But I breathed again with exultant relief when I heard that I was to be in charge of one of the protection parties.'

As set out by Newman, 'Chariot' was to be an enormously complex affair in which speed and split-second timing would be crucial to success. Surprise was to be their primary weapon, enhanced by a heavy diversionary air raid and by the use of deception. On the way to France the force would allay suspicion by adopting the formation of an anti-submarine sweep. The presence of Commandos on the *Campbeltown*'s deck, and on the decks of the MLs, would be strictly controlled so that no hint would be given to inquisitive enemy aircraft that the ships were carrying troops. The German flag was to be used whenever appropriate and in the run-up to the target itself the enemy would be confused both by the use of his own supposedly secret recognition devices and by the fact that the old destroyer would be disguised to look like one of his large torpedo boats.

The noise from the bombers would hopefully mask the many ships' engines as they entered the estuary, while at the same time the pattern of the developing air raid should divert the enemy gunners' attention away from the sea. The initial phase of the bombing was to include the Commandos' targets, right up to the point of landing, after which the bomb-aimers' attention would switch to adjacent areas. Sorties would continue throughout the hours of darkness to support the Commandos, both while they were on shore and during their eventual withdrawal to the open sea. Because of the entrapping configuration of the estuary, the extent of its 'impassable' shoals and the strength of the seaport's gun defences, it was believed that the enemy effectively considered himself immune, and in this complacency might just lie the key to Operation 'Chariot's' success.

Command of the operation was being shared between Army and Navy. The HQ ship would be the gunboat, although as she would need to be towed for much of the way, both Ryder and Newman would travel as far as the enemy coast in the towing destroyer HMS *Atherstone*. Having satisfied themselves that *Campbeltown* was in place, Newman and his small staff would be landed in the Old Entrance, with Ryder remaining on the gunboat, the two communicating thereafter by radio. Once ashore, Newman was to establish his HQ in a building close by the Old Entrance lock, where he would later be joined by the men of his pitifully small reserve.

If all went to plan, the withdrawal would be signalled by Newman no later than 0330 BST, at which time the parties would disengage, reform under the Colonel's direct command and make their way to the re-embarkation point at the Old Mole, where a naval Beachmaster would allocate them to waiting MLs. To minimize the risk of casualties from 'friendly' fire, various recognition devices were to be employed, ranging from blue pinpoint torches, through the use of officers' names, to a code-phrase developed by Newman which would be difficult for Germans to pronounce, this being 'War Weapons Week', with the countersign 'Weymouth'. Webbing was to be whitened for added visibility, rubber-soled boots were to be worn, and faces were to be left undarkened – though restrictions on shaving during much of the passage over would leave many faces darkened by stubble anyway.

The men were to be briefed the following day, after which the parties could plan and rehearse to the point where each individual would be able to fight on alone – whatever the conditions on the ground, whatever the losses around him and with or without the guidance and instruction of officers.

As put to the assembled company, 'Chariot' was an operation of great strategic importance, towards which the Colonel himself displayed an infectious enthusiasm. But it was also clearly a suicide job and at the conclusion of the briefing, none could doubt that behind the grand words, behind the hopes expressed, behind the banter and the smiling faces, lay the awareness that success would demand a heavy price indeed, and that for many of them that price would be the sacrifice of all their future years.

The details of the raid were made known to the men on the 19th, which was the day the conversion work on *Campbeltown* was completed. Gathered on the messdeck of the *PJC*, they listened to Newman with barely suppressed excitement as he confirmed that they were indeed going to bloody the nose of the enemy. No disappointment this time, no last-minute word from on high that all their work and all their hopes had been for nought. In explaining the task ahead, he was careful to re-emphasize that if any man felt un-comfortable about taking part he would be allowed to stand down without fear of criticism, such an offer in itself speaking volumes about their chances of survival. However, it would have taken tremendous courage to desert one's friends, and no one did, in spite of the fear felt by many that they might never see their loved ones again.

One soldier for whom Newman's offer opened a doorway through which his conscience would not allow him to pass was Lance-Corporal Edward Bryan of 4 Troop 2 Commando. Ted was married and a proud new father to boot. Following the briefing he took his concerns to his Troop Sergeant-Major who, typically of so many at this time, was brimming with confidence, especially as they had been to Vaagso at Christmas and come back all right. 'I've got this opportunity to withdraw; I don't know whether to back out or not. What do you think Sar'nt Major?' was the question. To which the reply was, 'Oh it's going to be a piece of cake, Ted. Don't worry. We'll all come back.' It was an expression of optimism which, sadly, would not long survive the opening salvoes of the German guns.

With the Commando briefings over, the intensive party-by-party instruc-tion began, with every man being given an opportunity to study the model. Lance-Corporal Stanley Stevenson of 2 Troop, 2 Commando, who would sail on board ML 156 as part of Captain 'Higgledy Piggledy' Hooper's assault team, was mightily 'impressed with the meticulous detail that went into the plan, and the care that went into ensuring that every Commando knew and understood what was expected of him.' As with all the others, he was encouraged to search for ways of improving his own performance on the night, such enhancement in his case taking the form of a Lewis light machine gun, fitted with a sling and fired from the hip, which he determined to carry in addition to his Tommy gun.

Having familiarized the men with essential particulars of 'Chariot', the time had come to send them off on exercise 'Vivid', the dress rehearsal that was being publicly billed as a test of the defences of Plymouth and Devonport. For security reasons *Campbeltown* herself would not be involved, and so all the participating Commandos would approach the port on board Ryder's MLs. With the defences forewarned as part of the policy of deflecting suspicion by being as open-handed as possible, it was hoped to provoke a lively response such as would prepare the men for what was to come and at the same time throw up possible flaws within the plan of attack itself. As this would be the last opportunity to try the equipment out under near-operational conditions, 'Vivid' would also be used as a test of the vital radio links connecting the Force Commanders with various other stations on shore and on the boats, the mechanics of which had already been a considerable source of anxiety to Newman's signals Sergeant, the twenty-four-year-old Londoner and trainee chartered surveyor, Ronald Steele.

So often the Achilles heel of operations such as this, the signals side of 'Chariot' had received an early blow when it was decided that, because of the press of numbers, Ron would be the only member of the 2 Commando signals section to be involved in the raid in the capacity for which he had been trained. His section officer, Lieutenant Neil Oughtred, would be present in a fighting capacity, with Captain Bertie Hodgson's assault group and Ron would be accompanied as far as Falmouth by his instrument mechanic, Lance-Corporal Jock Fyfe, but otherwise the remaining trained personnel would remain behind in Ayr.

A highly proficient signaller, who had begun learning his craft while with the OTC at Haberdashers' School, Ron had been called up to the Royal Corps of Signals in 1940 and posted to the 18th Division, before volunteering for the Independent Companies. Upon the demise of these he had moved on to No. 1 SS Battalion, before eventually joining 2 Commando with the rank of Signalman.

On arriving in Falmouth, he was surprised to learn that, in addition to being expected to work with personnel he did not know, he would also have to incorporate in the signals plan a new type of lightweight radio only then coming in to general use. He and Jock were familiar with the older and much bulkier 18 set, a number of examples of which they had brought to Falmouth with them. Weighing 34 lbs and backpacked on a rudimentary carrying frame, this unit was capable of both Morse and R/T transmissions, in contrast to the new and lighter 38 set, which could operate on R/T only, by means of a throat microphone. Destined to take pride of place in 'Chariot', this equipment was much more portable, the radio and separate battery unit weighing just 7 and 6 lbs respectively.

When it came to the checking of the 38 sets, faults were found, the tracing and repair of which ate up valuable time. They were eventually located in the battery charging units and corrected, but only after having returned the sets to the manufacturer.

With the equipment functioning correctly at last, Ron's next tasks were to train the naval personnel who would be required to operate the other sets in the net and to ensure that all units were tuned to the same frequency as his own HQ set and locked. In this latter task he was assisted by Sub-Lieutenant Chris Worsley, and by Lieutenant Verity who, as beachmaster, was to have his own 18 set positioned close by the re-embarkation point. Verity had some knowledge of what was required, but Chris had none at all, despite which he recalls that, following Ron's instructions, 'We took our places at widely separated points around Falmouth and, after a tedious afternoon and evening's work, managed to get all the sets tuned to work on the same frequency.' It was as a consequence of this very limited practical experience that Chris was later roped into the 'Vivid' experiment to help test the sets under conditions more likely to reflect those they would meet on the raid itself. He was therefore temporarily assigned to the gunboat as Third Officer and ordered to take a set on board, land with it in Devonport and attempt to establish contact with Commando HQ.

With the gunboat leading them in and Haydon on board as observer, the attacking force arrived off Plymouth late on the evening of Saturday the 21st to be quickly illuminated by searchlights, the number and brilliance of which made it almost impossible for the skippers to identify and reach their landing places. From this point onwards the whole affair was pretty much a shambles, the totality of which served to warn the commanders of what might well be waiting for them in the estuary of the Loire, where they would be met by defences considerably more lethal than the water hoses and potatoes with which they were bombarded at Plymouth.

'Frankly, ' writes Ryder, 'we found it difficult. The dazzling effect of the searchlights not only confused us but made us feel most uncomfortably conspicuous, and finally, although we led the force to the right place in the dockyard more by luck than anything else, a large liner was berthed just where we didn't expect her, and half the MLs overshot the mark. Altogether there was a good deal of confusion and we all came back feeling that it was much more difficult than we had supposed. The Commander-in-Chief watched our arrival from the top of a shed and was most scornful of our efforts when I next saw him. He did in fact suggest our having another rehearsal, but there was no more time for it and I assured him that we had learned more by our failures than we should have had all gone well.'

For the Commandos themselves their 'assault' reflected the muddle and confusion of events in the harbour, as they were landed late or in the wrong places by ML skippers struggling to find their bearings in the unremitting glare of the lights. As for Chris Worsley, he did finally make it ashore when Curtis, who he already knew from his time in the 14th MGB Flotilla, took the gunboat alongside in a sheltered area of the docks. As instructed, he attempted to raise Commando HQ on his radio, but to no effect. 'No matter how I tried, ' he recalls 'and even after I had performed every manoeuvre Sergeant Steele had taught me, I was unable to get any response to my repeated calls. Eventually concluding that I could do nothing more . . . I got back aboard pretty smartly. As I thought it was important to report that I had been unable to establish contact with the Commandos, I went up to the bridge, and just as I reached the top of the steps I heard the last few words of a conversation between Dunstan and Commander Ryder. At that moment Commander Ryder was saying, "But I don't suppose it will be quite so bad on the night!" Not very much later, and under very different circumstances, the significance of the thought behind those words was borne in on me.'

Following the chaos that was 'Vivid' nothing appears to have been done to improve the chances of the all-important communications net working more effectively on the night. To decrease the reliance on Steele's HQ set, and to provide a spare in case the Sergeant was wounded or killed, the decision was taken to add Lance-Corporal Fyfe to the strength, give him his own 38 set, and attach him to Copland's party on board the *Campbeltown*. But, apart from Fyfe, no new signals personnel were added, and the operation of the tricky sets remained the responsibility of the marginally trained naval personnel on board the boats. At this very early stage in the history of wireless at war, even the most modern sets were both weak and unreliable – all too easy to knock off frequency and liable to have their signals disrupted where buildings and other obstacles existed between stations. Despite the very best efforts of all concerned, they had remained mute during 'Vivid' and, unfortunately for the men seeking to escape the trap of the dockyard, they would prove no less quiet during the mayhem of St Nazaire itself.

The chastened assault force returned to Falmouth on Sunday the 22nd, their adventure having given them little cause for optimism. They were into the final countdown now and had only a handful of days remaining in which to make everything work. Friday the 27th had been determined as the departure date most likely to put them over the estuary shoals at the highest point of the spring tides; however, as they moved further into a period of weather so benign as to offer them an easy passage of the Bay of Biscay, Ryder would find himself increasingly tempted to take advantage of it by moving the start date forward.

As Falmouth was a busy port with its own coastal forces base, great care had been taken since the arrival of Ryder's flotillas to maintain a pretence of operational normality and, in support of this, the decision had been taken not to let the Navy into the secret until the last possible moment because, once briefed, the sailors would have to be restricted to their boats – a move which, if it was made too soon, would certainly give rise to suspicions that an 'event' was in the offing. Now that they had been involved in 'Vivid', however, the men would inevitably speculate about its relevance to their future, so Ryder decided this was the most appropriate time to stop all shore leave and move the boats out into the estuary. Upon their return from Plymouth, therefore, the MLs were ordered to refuel, top up with water, anchor out in Carrick Roads and hold themselves available at immediate notice.

Already worn down by the efforts of the night, the crews then found themselves saddled with the extra burden of a re-paint, the purpose of which was to reduce their reflectivity when caught by searchlights. During 'Vivid' many of the boats had sported a striking livery, composed of stripes and rays of pale blue, pale green and white, designed to help them merge with the sea mists, which in the glare of the brilliant beams had instead made them shine like stars. Now all were to be garbed alike in a drab and uniform shade of mauve, known as 'Plymouth Pink', as were all the other Navy ships then operating in the channel.

While the MLs busied themselves with putting on their new and sombre faces, the gunboat, minus Chris Worsley, who had returned to his duties on Ryder's staff, remained alongside to complete the fitting of her deck tanks, against the stated wishes of the Admiralty. By dint of hard work she would be ready to sail on time; however, the same could not be said of Wynn's MTB, which came limping back from Plymouth in need of an engine change. As the Falmouth base was not equipped to service this kind of boat, the case for her continued participation in 'Chariot' at first looked hopeless; but neither Wynn nor his Chief Motor Mechanic, Bill Lovegrove, were the kind of men to be put off their stride by such an apparently insuperable difficulty, and so, with Lovegrove assuring him that its installation could be completed in time for them to participate, Wynn set out at once to obtain a replacement.

For the Commandos the return to the *PJC* was in effect the end of the beginning. Morale was just about as high as it could be and no one doubted that with just a little bit of luck they would successfully carry out the many tasks assigned to them.

Having been fully briefed, they would now be restricted to the ship herself, the days of route marches and pistol and grenade practice ashore being replaced by a minute examination of their tasks and kit. If they were to succeed at St Nazaire nothing must be forgotten and nothing left to chance. Target recognition was critical, as each and every soldier must know his area of the dockyard so intimately that he would be able to find his way and do his job in spite of pain and fear, regardless of the fate of those around him. Weapons drill was important too, as was lightening the load where possible. The demolition teams got to know their protection squads and men in general continued to question and suggest, until such time as the plan they had to follow was as good as human will could make it. Stores continued to come aboard, which would be transferred to the ships of the fleet under cover of darkness during the last nights before departure. Out of fear for the safety of the ship, these did not include the explosive-filled packs, which would remain under guard in their Nissen hut until the last possible moment. As storm troops, the Commandos would carry with them all their arms and ammunition, their armoury including fighting knives, grenades, Colt .45 pistols, .303 rifles, .45 Thompson sub-machine-guns, .55 Boyes anti-tank rifles, and 2" mortars. As they would be entirely reliant on what they could carry, they would somehow have to bring along sufficient ammunition to keep these weapons firing, creatively tailoring their battledress and webbing to hold the extra stores. Should the action prove as hot as was expected they could find their lives hanging on such extra rounds or bombs as they could somehow manage to cram about their persons.

On Monday the 23rd the fleet was reinforced by the arrival of the passage escorts, the Hunt-class destroyers *Tynedale* and *Atherstone*, the latter already known to crew of the gunboat, having acted as their parent ship during previous cross-channel escapades. Berthed well away from the other ships, their appearance in the busy port was at this stage of significance only to Ryder, who was at last able to quit his conservatory in Tregwynt and establish along with Green a fully staffed and equipped HQ afloat. 'I transferred my headquarters to the *Atherstone*, ' he writes, 'where Lieutenant-Commander Jenks, her Captain, afforded me every comfort and every facility. In my opinion more was done to put our force in order in these last two days than we could have hoped to do in two weeks without these resources.'

Monday the 23rd also saw the issue of Forbes' own operational orders, specifying the various positions through which the force should pass on its way to and from St Nazaire. Of particular importance was their warning of the presence of five German torpedo boats, roughly equivalent in tonnage and armament to Hunt-class destroyers, somewhere on the French west coast. The Commander-in-Chief undertook to keep Ryder apprised of current enemy movements and dispositions, allowing him considerable freedom for the exercise of initiative in response to unforseen circumstances, up to and including abandonment of the operation. Bearing in mind that the start date was but days away, it is amusing to think that these orders bore the same date of issue as Hitler's Directive, warning against just such a madcap enterprise.

As promised by Wynn, the replacement engine for MTB 74 arrived on the Monday evening. The crew were very much on their own when it came to installing the heavy Packard; nevertheless, under Lovegrove's direction, they buckled to and somehow hoisted it into place in the narrow engine-room. Improvising all the way, the indefatigable Chief Motor Mechanic somehow had it ready for a trial run by the evening of Tuesday the 24th. With time so short, he would still be working on final adjustments even while the boat was gliding through the Bay of Biscay on the end of *Campbeltown*'s tow.

While Lovegrove laboured to meet his self-imposed deadline of being ready for sea by the Wednesday, Ryder began the process of briefing his skippers and First Officers on board the *PJC*. They were introduced to 'Chariot' in small groups, with Ryder talking them through the plans and photographs, and lighting the model by torchlight so as to give an impression of what the dockyard's silhouette would look like illuminated only by the moon. He then issued them with his personal version of the orders, which was a very much shorter document than Newman's offering, practically demonstrating his commitment to flexibility and the exercise of initiative. Newman would have to intimately control a complex set-piece attack, hence his reliance on detail, whereas Ryder and his crews, once the action began, would pretty much have to make it up as they went along, relying on signalling to communicate instructions and intent.

As with the Commandos, the name of the target was withheld; however, as with the Commandos, its location was instantly recognized by the handful of men who knew of the port or had been fortunate enough to visit it. One of the officers of 2 Commando, Lieutenant Bill Clibborn of 2 Troop, had known as soon as he saw the photographs that it was the 'Normandie' dock, because he knew the ship and they showed her sitting right in it. Now the same discovery was to be made by Sub-Lieutenant John May, the 'Jimmy' of Falconar's ML 446, who had been on the London staff of an American newspaper before joining up, and was leaving behind his wife, Joy, and their four year-old daughter. In the summer of 1930, as a boy of 16, John had spent the long hols as a deckhand on a ship delivering coal from Cardiff to Nantes. 'So before they told us where we were going, ' he recalls, 'and showed us a model of the place we were to attack, I knew exactly where it was. And I also knew that either the Chiefs-of-Staff had gone crazy, or the situation in the Atlantic was a great deal more desperate than we imagined.'

On the *PJC* the sense of excitement was steadily building, though for many it was moderated by the realization that they might well not return. In a last letter to his father, written on the 24th, Lance-Sergeant Bill Gibson of 6 Troop encapsulated the feelings of those who believed they would not survive, but were determined nonetheless to see the job through to the end.

Writing in the realization that his words would be read only in the event of his death, he told his dad that, even though they knew the job was 'virtually suicide', he and his great pal, Lance-Sergeant Peter Harkness, realized their sacrifice would be for a worthwhile cause. He wrote:

'Peter and I will be together; our task is very important and just a wee bit dangerous, but if we can hold Jerry off it will mean the saving of the lives of a lot of our pals.

'It seems peculiar to be writing this, we've just finished tea and God's lovely sunshine is streaming through the portholes. We've been on deck sunbathing all day. Peter is very red, as am I. It all seems so far removed from the job ahead of us. Spring is in the air and everything looks so beautiful.

'Well, dad, dearest, I will close now, don't be too unhappy, remember what you always told me, keep your chin up. I'll have done what chance has made my duty and I can only hope that by laying down my life the generations to come might in some way remember us and benefit by what we have done.'

In the days before their departure Bill, despite being supposedly locked away in the *PJC*, had somehow managed to get ashore in the company of Sergeant Stanley Rodd and have a last drink. He had been sure of what was to come and in his certainty and acceptance had joined an illustrious band of comrades and friends, all of whom had foreseen and come to terms with their fates.

During an idyllic afternoon ashore, the only 4 Commando officer present on the raid, Lieutenant Harry Pennington, had remarked to Corran Purdon that he believed England worth dying for. Lieutenant Tom Peyton, the Old Etonian whom Micky Burn records as having 'gasped with excitement' during the briefing, solemnly took his leave of Newman before joining his ML, as did Captain Bertie Hodgson, the commander of 1 Troop, described by Tiger Watson as 'charming and unflappable'.

Tiger himself recalls being approached by two of the men from 1 Troop, who asked him to make sure that their letters were delivered to their families in the event they did not return. 'But I'm going too!' protested Watson. 'Ah, but *you* won't killed, ' was their confident reply. 'Sadly, ' as Tiger records, 'my two companions' premonitions proved accurate also. Both were killed.'

On the naval side, while there were those such as Sub-Lieutenant Mark Rodier, the skipper of ML 177, whose misgivings would not be voiced until the latter stages of the voyage across, others knew very early on that this adventure might well be their last.

Petty Officer Sam Wallace was one of the team from Billie Stephens' base staff at Weymouth, who had moved to Falmouth with the flotilla. Along with his long-standing friend, Chief Petty Officer John Rafferty, and the Flotilla Engineer Officer, Sub-Lieutenant Toy, he was to accompany the MLs to St Nazaire, with a roving commission to assist wherever in the fleet mechanical repairs were needed. Sam had had a premonition about the raid and made his concerns known to Chief Petty Officer Rafferty, who could have detailed another Chief Petty Officer mechanic in his place. A substitute was in fact available and raring to go; he was most disappointed when Rafferty made light of Sam's fears.

Also confiding his growing certainty that he would not return was the gifted Nigel Tibbits, who during *Campbeltown*'s conversion had been staying, along with his wife, Elmslie, in the Grand Hotel, Plymouth.

Nigel and Elmslie, who were of an age, had known each other for many years, having first met in their early teens when he was called upon to partner her in tennis. They had not at first got on; however, when they met again by chance some four years later, their reactions to each other could hardly have been more changed, time, allied to the spice of experience, having done much to develop Nigel's character and abilities. Then he had been young and diffident, only newly entered into Dartmouth Naval College; now he was the Robert Roxborough prizewinner, having passed out top cadet and with a glittering career at his feet. Then they had shared a mutual indifference; now they were set to embark upon a relationship characterized by deep and unwavering affection, which would ultimately lead to their marriage in Shanghai Cathedral in 1937, during Nigel's period of service on the China Station.

Such had been the burdens on his mind that, during their private times together in the hotel, Nigel had been restless and ill-at-ease. Eventually, during a picnic out on Dartmoor, he had told her of the raid and of his growing conviction that he would not survive it. Thus it was that when *Campbeltown* finally sailed for Falmouth with Nigel on board, Elmslie, watching the ship's departure from the Hoe, could not dispel the dread feeling that they would never meet again. She prayed fervently for a storm to force the cancellation of the raid, but in the event, the weather could hardly have been kinder to the Gods of war.

Arriving in Falmouth on Wednesday the 25th *Campbeltown* anchored out in Cross Roads. In addition to all the alterations previously specified, her after pair of tall, slender funnels had been removed and the forward pair cut at a slant to give her the silhouette of the German Möwe class boats then known to be active along the Biscay coast. There had been some difficulty in obtaining a German Naval Ensign for her to fly as part of the deception plan, but one had at last been made available, which Ryder handed over to Beattie shortly after her arrival. Looking at the lines of their stripped-down explosive-filled hybrid, an American ship, in British service, about to try to pass herself off as a German, neither man could suppress a smile.

She had been successfully trimmed so that her stern would draw a mere eleven feet when travelling at 10 knots, which should allow her to pass safely over the shoals. It had already been agreed with Newman that, as the most important unit in the fleet, she was to be given maximum support right up until the moment of her ramming, whatever the sacrifice involved. By dint of great effort, Ryder's staff had managed to supply her Oerlikons with a full outfit of shells, amounting to some 1800 rounds per gun. However, as Ryder records, 'among the MLs our supply was pathetic. We continued our attempts to get more Oerlikon ammunition for our guns but with little success. Jenks (in *Atherstone*) most nobly said, "You can have half of mine," and this, together with a few small additions that were sent to us, enabled us to make a general distribution, so that we had about 800 rounds per gun. How many of our countrymen realized, I wonder, that we were setting out to make a frontal attack on one of the most heavily defended enemy bases with only half our allowance of ammunition.'

With the last of the MLs due to come alongside *PJC* that night to take on stores and water, Ryder turned his mind to the fine weather and the advisability of sailing while it still held, even though this would put *Campbeltown* over the shoals before the spring tides were quite at their highest. In early spring it was fairly common for spells of bright sunny weather to set in, which warmed the sea and could cause a useful haze to lie off the west coast of France. Such a spell having begun some five days earlier, Ryder decided not to risk losing it and, with Newman having confirmed that he was ready for anything, he therefore telephoned Forbes' Staff Officer Plans, Commander Pat McCrum, RN, and obtained permission to have everything moved forward by twenty-four hours. They would now depart the very next day, with *Campbeltown* due to ram her caisson at 0130 hours BST on the morning of Saturday the 28th.

On board the *PJC*, in an atmosphere charged with anticipation, the men completed their personal preparations. Pay-book wills were organized, some pals bequeathing their worldly goods to one another. All identifying badges save those of rank were removed and Newman ordered that all should wash and don clean underclothes so as to prevent fabric carried into wounds from promoting infection. Kit was checked and double-checked. Daggers were honed and weapons cleaned to perfection.

For many of those who hailed from Scottish units the thought of presenting themselves to the enemy in any dress which did not include a kilt was pure anathema, although, as Tiger Watson of the Black Watch recalls, the sentiment was not universally observed. 'Donald Roy, ' he writes, 'that fanatical Highlander, was insistent that I should wear my kilt as he and his [No. 5] troop intended. But I was not prepared to put my precious and much coveted pre-war kilt to such risk. In any case, with my grenades, spare magazines of .45 ammunition for my Tommy gun and Colt, plus a Very pistol and its signalling cartridges, a fighting knife, etc, I thought that my heavy pockletless kilt would merely prove a further encumbrance. If cast into the water it was imperative to divest oneself of one's harness hung with all this ironmongery before sinking irrevocably to the bottom.'

As the time for departure neared, Newman's numbers continued to grow as deficiencies in certain areas were made good, and individuals not originally included in the 'fighting force' successfully lobbied their Colonel to have their names added to the list. The original selection, which had been cut to the bone because of limitations of space, had already been swollen by the arrival of the French liaison officers, Captain Vicomte Peter de Jonghe and Second Lieutenant W.G. Lee, whose task it would be to bridge the gap between the Commandos and civilians, and by the pressmen Gordon Holman and Edward Gilling. A rather low-key addition to Newman's headquarter's group, from the murky world of intelligence, was Captain Anthony Terry, a fluent German and French speaker. Jock Fyfe, with his spare 38 set, had already been added to the strength; now he was joined by Armourer Sergeant Gerry Taylor, RQMS 'Sandy' Seaton and Corporal Crippin, all of 2 Commando HQ Troop. As Ronnie Mitchell, the Administrative Officer who had done so much to prepare the Commando for departure and would be waiting in Plymouth for its return, records, the latter two 'were definitely not supposed to go. They were on my staff and I needed them.'

Also wending his way toward Falmouth was Acting Lance-Corporal John Webb, RAMC, the Medical Orderly of 2 Troop, who had left Ayr with a party of three in tow, after being called to HQ and asked if he would like to join the rest of the unit.

Having received his travel instructions, John had returned to his billet to organize his own gear and see to the belongings of his pal and billet-mate, Guardsman Bob Grose, who had marched out with the first selection in February. John had been deputed to write to four of Bob's many girlfriends, recording that, 'These were his special ones. The list of addresses of all his amorata includes just about every place he had ever been stationed. He was a good-looking chap and very likeable.'

From Glasgow the party's paper-chase of travel documents was to take them through London, Exeter and Truro. Such were the delays involved in their circumnavigation of the stressed and crowded wartime railway system that they would not arrive in Falmouth until the Thursday morning, with barely time to board the readying fleet and none at all in which to learn the details of their great adventure.

On board the *PJC* Newman's men were being given some very basic instruction on escape and evasion techniques by Squadron Leader Evans, who had made a name for himself as an escaper in the previous war; but it was all rather incomplete and half-hearted, a fact that the men put down to an official acceptance of losses so great that there would be few men left to capture anyway. As part of their training, the Commandos had learned a little astral navigation which might be of use, but they were given none of the escape aids which might have helped them make their way to Spain and safety. Sapper Corporal Bob Wright, of 12 Commando, scheduled to land from *Campbeltown* with Lieutenant Brett's small demolition party, recalls being told that it was better to be caught in Vichy France, and that, in extremis, one could always approach a Catholic priest for help. Lieutenant Bill Clibborn, of 2 Troop, remembers being given a code by means of which information might be transmitted in normal letter mail. And Corporal George Wheeler, of 1 Troop, whose very recent marriage would spur him to evade the German net, was surprised to be told that a contact could be found in the town of Blain, about thirty miles north-east of St Nazaire. The contact was not identified, this omission promoting visions of dozens of burly 'escaping' Commandos sidling up to doors in the town and demanding of the occupants, 'Are you the contact?'

To bring the last full day to a close, Newman gathered the men together and told them what they had long been waiting to hear, that their mystery target was in fact the important sea port of St Nazaire. It was a pearl of information that would not be made known to their naval comrades until the boats sailed out of harbour. 'The announcement was greeted by a cheer which nearly lifted the messdeck, ' writes Major Bill Copland. 'Confidence lay behind that cheer. We had trained hard, we knew our jobs and we felt equal to any demand.'

With everything so nearly buttoned up, the Force Commanders might reasonably have expected to enter the day of their departure on as positive a note as that sounded by Newman's young fire-eaters. However, the gremlins that lurk in the shadows of all such enterprises finally made their presence known later that evening in the form of a summons from Ryder for Newman, with magnifying glass, to visit him on *Atherstone* right away. In the privacy of the Captain's cabin, Newman then had the 'nasty shock' of viewing a beautifully clear set of aerial photographs taken at 1030 that morning which showed the ships of *Korvettenkapitän* Moritz Schmidt's 5th Torpedo Boat Destroyer Flotilla – the ships of whose presence on the Biscay Coast Forbes had warned earlier – moored along the eastern side of the Submarine Basin, right in the heart of the target area. It was dreadfully bad luck that, of all the ports along the coast, they should have chosen this moment to tie up in St Nazaire; however, there was nothing to be done about them in the short term, and so the 'Chariot' force must sail in the hope that, by the time *Campbeltown* was ready to lead her frail brood into the estuary, they might have moved on. In case they had not, Newman rather hopefully suggested that he attack and capture them with his minuscule 'reserve'.

In order to enlist the help of the Commander-in-Chief, Ryder went ashore first thing on Thursday morning and rang through to McCrum in Plymouth, who promised to ask Forbes for two additional destroyers to reinforce the fleet during its return voyage. Meanwhile the attack would have to proceed with the forces presently available, which would have their work cut out should they meet Schmidt's flotilla *en route* to St Nazaire, or in the area of the estuary itself. On the face of it Ryder and Newman were being forced by circumstance to rely on luck to a degree that was neither desirable nor advisable; but, unknown to either, forces were at work on their behalf which, primarily by means of signals intelligence, would monitor the movements of the German boats and see that they were quickly informed of any change in the degree of threat.

At 0930 hours on the 26th, with the receipt of the signal 'preparative "Chariot"' from Forbes, the sequence of events officially began which would see the force leave Falmouth early that afternoon. John Webb and his small command, having only just made it to the port, found the *PJC* bustling with activity as the men prepared to leave for their passage boats. No one had time to tell them what was going on, but RSM Moss saw to it that they were issued with .45 Colts, following which John was allocated to ML 341, along with Private Tom Everitt, RAMC, and Captain Mike Barling, who was one of the two Commando doctors, the other being Captain David Paton on ML 307.

Also joining his boat at this late stage was Sub-Lieutenant Chris Worsley, who had been ordered that very morning to join MGB 314 as her Third Officer. He recalls that he was on his way to board her 'when somebody whispered that the force was about to sail for St Nazaire, to attack the submarines there. I paid no attention to what I considered was a bit of hearsay, and as I considered it unlikely that anybody would even contemplate such an operation, I did not think the statement was based on truth.'

MGB 314 herself was not to be allowed to leave without a scare, as the dreaded gremlins struck again, this time in the guise of a rope which wrapped itself round one of the gunboat's propellers. As she limped alongside *Atherstone*, Ryder records that 'I rushed to the Chief-of-Staff and said, "for God's sake get me a diver!" Fortunately this was possible and all was well again, and I wondered what other last-minute catastrophe would occur.'

For Newman the final morning brought from COHQ a clear response to concerns that had been growing within him of late, regarding target priority in case the operation could not be carried out as planned. It was in the form of a letter which, while it precisely stated what was required of Newman, would seem to cast doubt, at this late stage, on the overriding importance of the destruction of the dry dock. Should *Campbeltown* ground or be sunk, Newman wanted to know whether the MLs should proceed to destroy their assigned targets, leaving the dry dock intact; or whether this last target was of such importance that he should attempt to attack it with the MLs only. 'It was a great relief to me, ' he writes, 'to get a letter from Brigadier Haydon just before sailing, making the point absolutely clear. The destruction of the dry dock was the main task. If this alone was carried out the operation would be considered successful, but if anything happened to the destroyer, concentration was to be made on the second task only and the completion of this was to be effected before any effort to transfer to the dry dock destruction was to be made.'

While this assuaged Newman's doubts, it was in strategic terms a bit of a fudge, since it confirmed at one and the same time that the destruction of the great dock was – and was not – the primary purpose of the raid. Should *Campbeltown* be prevented from reaching the dock, then Wynn's torpedo boat might or might not be able to target the caisson. Irrespective of whether she could or not, the operation of the dock could still be severely impeded were only its pumping and winding facilities to be blown up. If, by the end of March, the dock was still believed to be just as important strategically as had been the case when *Tirpitz* first moved to Trondheim, then surely Newman would have been instructed to target these facilities first, whether *Campbeltown*'s parties made it ashore or not. The fact that he was not so instructed, allied to the Admiralty's failure to cooperate with Ryder, would seem to indicate that, by the time the force departed, the threat of *Tirpitz* ever needing to use the dock had been seen to have substantially diminished.

While being grateful for this clarification, Newman would not have been so pleased to learn that their bombing support was to be but a shadow of that originally requested. In the first flush of planning, it had been proposed that a force of 350 bombers be allocated to 'Chariot'. Now, however, RAF interest had dwindled to the point where its support would also transpire to be a fudge. Under its new chief, Arthur Harris, Bomber Command was being forged into a war-winning weapon in its own right, with little time to spare for sideshows such as Commando raids, which meant that in the event a mere sixty-two planes were allocated to the raid, even though its stated purpose was to materially affect the balance of sea-power in the North Atlantic. A measure of the RAF's priorities can be gained from the fact that, not long after Ryder's fleet was engaged by the German defences, more than 200 aircraft took off to devastate the medieval town of Lübeck, a town chosen as a test of the new fire-storm theory, because it was easy to find and its ancient wooden buildings would burn well.

Such was the concern at COHQ that serious consideration was given to cancelling the operation altogether should the bombing support fail to materialize; but the fact was that it would have taken a great deal more than this to rein in the enthusiasm of Ryder and Newman.

Earlier that morning Copland had sent Lieutenant Johnny Proctor, of 5 Troop, across to *Campbeltown* to allocate quarters in advance of the movement of troops from the *PJC* to their passage boats shortly before noon. This was the time when it was safe at last to move the explosive-filled packs from their hut in the dockyard and place them by party in the MLs and *Campbeltown*. The order to disembark the troops was made shortly after 1100 hours, following which the men were dispatched in full battle order from the ship they had come to know as home. Micky Burn remembers one of his troop subalterns, Lieutenant Morgan Jenkins, who had been raised from the ranks, going over the side to his boat from the *PJC* and saluting and saying to Micky, 'Goodbye. Thanks for all you've done.' 'I hadn't done anything except get him a commission, ' recalls Micky, 'and he was dead soon after.'

Copland was last to leave the *PJC*. With him were his batman, Private Tom Hannan, Newman's Adjutant, Captain Stanley Day, and Lance-Corporal Harrington, also of the Colonel's HQ party. Boarding their water-taxi, Day was transferred to the *Atherstone* and Harrington put on board the gunboat. Copland and Hannan were then taken to the *Campbeltown*, where they would remain throughout the voyage. Within minutes of boarding and making the signal to *Atherstone*, 'All troops embarked, ' the force was ready to get under way.

The MLs sailed first, to be followed at two o'clock by the three destroyers. Absent from the roll was Lieutenant-Commander Wood, due to command the MLs of the port column, who had gone sick just fifteen minutes before the off. Ryder's gremlins hadn't finished yet. A great deal had depended on Wood's expertise and knowledge, this officer having been one of Ryder's principal collaborators. His loss was a heavy blow. It was far too late to replace him so close to the time of departure and so the port column sailed with no one in command. Later in the day Lieutenant Platt, who was next senior, would be transferred to Wood's boat, his own place on board ML 443 being taken by the spare CO, Lieutenant Horlock, RNVR. It was a far from ideal solution, as it would mean two crews sailing into action under the command of strange COs, in addition to which Platt had not been so intimately involved in the planning as had Wood; however, it was the best that could be made, in the circumstances, of a very bad job.

Off 'D' buoy, the elements of the force formed up into a modified version of Ryder's Night Cruising Order, in three parallel columns with the destroyers in line, flanked on either side by the MLs. *Atherstone*, with Ryder and Newman on board and the gunboat in tow, led the force: *Tynedale* was next in line, followed by *Campbeltown* with the MTB in tow. Together for the first time as a single unit, the twenty-one vessels set off on the first leg of their outward track, sailing a south-westerly course towards position 'A' at 13 knots.

In stark contrast to the trials of the last days and hours, the weather could not have been kinder or more auspicious, with a warm spring sun and light easterlies breathing a fine haze over the lazy swell of the sea. Surrounded by such beauty and secure in the company of one's friends and comrades, it was hard to think of war and to come to terms with the notion that drifting out of sight of the fading coastline was a phase of existence the memory of whose sights, sounds and faces might soon be extinguished for ever. Lest any forget their deadly purpose, however, the roar of the solitary Hurricane fighter which swept in to patrol the skies above the fleet would be an ever-present reminder of the fact that they were now embarked upon a path laid out for them by fate, which they would have to follow come what may, hostages to fortune all.

8

Target Timbuktu

As they sailed steadily towards the open sea the force changed formation into Cruising Order No. 1, which was their simulation of an anti-submarine sweep. On *Atherstone*'s signal, the longitudinal columns to port and starboard of the destroyers opened out from the rear until they were disposed in the form of a broad, open arrowhead, four cables behind the tip of which steamed *Atherstone*. In the open spaces to the rear of each 'wing' steamed *Campbeltown*, still with the MTB in tow, and *Tynedale*.

Remembering that fine first day, Newman, who with his staff was being made very comfortable on board the *Atherstone*, writes that 'the thrill of the voyage was upon me – the study of the navigational course with the Navy – the continuous lookout for enemy aircraft – the preparation of one's own personal kit to land in – and the deciphering and reading of W/T messages from the Commander-in-Chief made night fall on us in no time.'

Across in *Campbeltown*, Copland and the eighty-odd men of his Group Three parties were being made just as welcome by the truncated crew of the old destroyer. 'There was little to do' he remembers; 'all our preparations had been made on *PJC* and it only remained to arrange our tours of duty for AA Defence, rehearse "Action Stations" and wait. Troops and sailors were very quickly "buddies", and as no khaki was allowed to be seen on deck the limited number who were allowed up . . . appeared in motley naval garb, anything from oilskins to duffle coats, not forgetting Lieutenant Burtinshaw who discovered one of Beattie's old naval caps and wore it during the whole voyage. During this first day too, we allocated all our landing ladders and ropes in places on deck where we thought they would be most wanted. Gough [Lieutenant Gough, RN, Beattie's No. 1] was to be in charge of all tying-up and ladder control and his help in the allocation was invaluable.'

In the MLs also the pattern of ready camaraderie between 'pongos' and 'matelots' was quickly established, the representatives of the two services managing to live cheek-by-jowl in the crowded living spaces without dispute. Feeding more than twice the normal complement of men from the limited resources of the tiny midships galley was something of a problem for the designated cook, although in the early stages of the voyage seasickness, or the fear of it, robbed more than a few Commandos of their appetites. Tough as they might have been on dry land, some Commandos had nonetheless blanched at the mere thought of doing battle with the fearsome Bay of Biscay; typical of these was Bombardier 'Jumbo' Reeves, of Brett's demolition party for the inner dry-dock caisson. A member of 12 Commando who had volunteered from the Royal Artillery, Jumbo was a qualified pilot whose aerial ambitions had been dashed as the result of an extreme susceptibility to airsickness. As one of those unfortunates whose stomach tended to come up with the anchor cable, he had had pronounced misgivings about setting off from Falmouth. For Jumbo, as for many others, the unexpected quiescence of the sea came, therefore, as a gift from God.

In the crowded messdecks as the sailors came and went with the changing of the watches, the Commandos talked and smoked, dozed on the matelots' bunks, played cards and checked and re-checked their equipment. Proud of their hard-won skills, they were happy to demonstrate their prowess to their hosts, such as the nineteen-year-old Ordinary Seaman Sam Hinks, the forward Oerlikon gunner on ML 443, who had gone so far as to change his name so that his parents couldn't stop him from joining up. As with so many of the other young sailors, who, unlike their thoroughly briefed Commando brothers, were only now being made aware of their target's identity, Sam was still coming to terms with the fact that they were really on their way to attack a distant foreign port. In keeping with the times when foreign travel was still the exclusive preserve of the monied classes, Sam knew little of France and nothing at all of this place called St Nazaire: in fact, when first hearing the name during a conversation with a Commando by the forward gun, he recalls that, 'St Nazaire meant as much to me as if you were going to Timbuktu!'

Having opened their sealed orders once clear of land, the reaction of the officers to the revelation of their target's identity had generally been that this was a port into which no one with any common sense would wish to sail without benefit of armour plate and heavy guns.

Across on the starboard wing of the formation, 'Temporary Acting' Sub-

Lieutenant Frank Arkle, the twenty-year-old First Officer of ML 177, who before the war had been a clerk in the offices of W.D. and H.O. Wills, greeted the news with 'some uncertainty and a sort of cold resignation'. Behind him in England were his family, his friends, and his childhood sweetheart, Meg; ahead lay a task of prodigious difficulty from which none could confidently expect to return. It was a prospect about which he and many others found it was best not to think too deeply. Better by far to focus on not letting the side down and leave all the rest to fate.

On board the gunboat, which was swinging like a pendulum at the end of *Atherstone*'s tow, Curtis had briefed his crew shortly after the force adopted its cruising formation, prompting Chris Worsley to conclude that they were all embarked upon a very ambitious and dangerous enterprise. Strangely, though, considering all the circumstances, he neither thought of, nor worried about, survival, as it simply never struck him that he might be killed.

Closer to the centre point of the formation, Lieutenant Tom Boyd, RNVR, the skipper of the torpedo-armed ML 160, was concerned about how well the force would perform in action, bearing in mind its poor overall standard of training. There simply hadn't been time to school the crews properly in working as a cohesive unit; as evidence of their lack of preparedness he could cite the same poor standards of station-keeping that were worring Ryder himself. Indeed, during the course of this first day Ryder would make no less than fifty signals to boats, instructing them to close up.

Standing on the bridge of Billie Stephens' ML 192 Leading Telegraphist Jim Laurie, from Coldstream in Scotland, learned of his fate from the skipper himself. A regular, who had joined the Navy in 1936 at the age of only sixteen, Jim had led something of a charmed life, having survived the sinking of the destroyer *Delight*, as well as the loss to a mine of ML 144, while he was fortunate enough to be on leave. Looking back at the fast-disappearing coastline, Stephens said to him, 'Do you think if you jumped overboard you could swim back to Falmouth?' Replying in the negative, Jim was then told, 'Right. You can go in the wheelhouse and study the maps and you'll see just where we're going.' For Jim, as for all the sailors, there was never a question of choice. The highly trained Commandos had been offered a get out, while the much less experienced sailors had not; yet, once they were under the German guns, the risk for all would be the same.

Standing as an example of so many of the sailors, who, on hearing for the first time what was expected of them, rapidly concluded that someone, somewhere must have a screw loose, was Stoker Len Ball of Ted Burt's ML 262. A twenty-five-year-old process chemical worker from Barking in Essex, Len could not believe that they really intended to sail right through

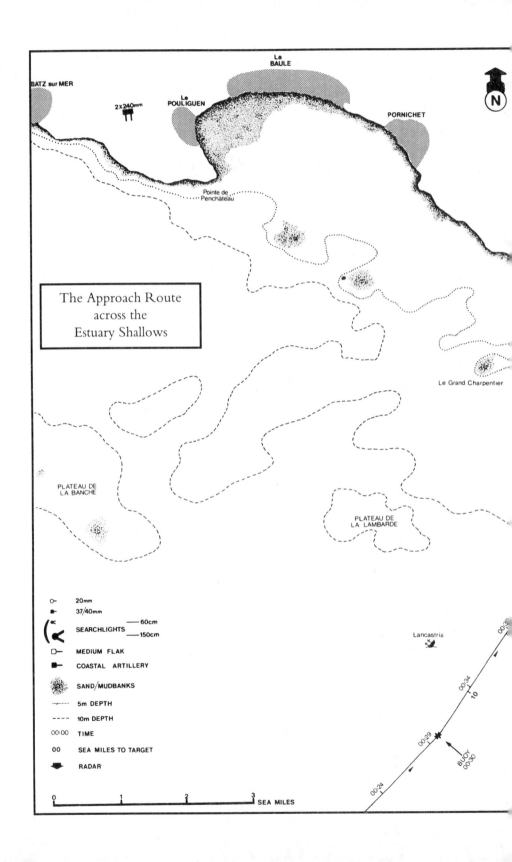

BATZ sur MER

2 x 240mm

Le
POULIGUEN

La
BAULE

PORNICHET

N

Pointe de
Penchâteau

The Approach Route
across the
Estuary Shallows

Le Grand Charpentier

PLATEAU DE
LA BANCHE

PLATEAU DE
LA LAMBARDE

o—	20mm
•	37/40mm
	SEARCHLIGHTS —— 60cm
	—— 150cm
□—	MEDIUM FLAK
■—	COASTAL ARTILLERY
	SAND/MUDBANKS
....	5m DEPTH
- - - -	10m DEPTH
00:00	TIME
00	SEA MILES TO TARGET
⬇	RADAR

Lancastria

00:35

00:34

10

00:29

BUOY
00:30

00:24

0   1   2   3
                            SEA MILES

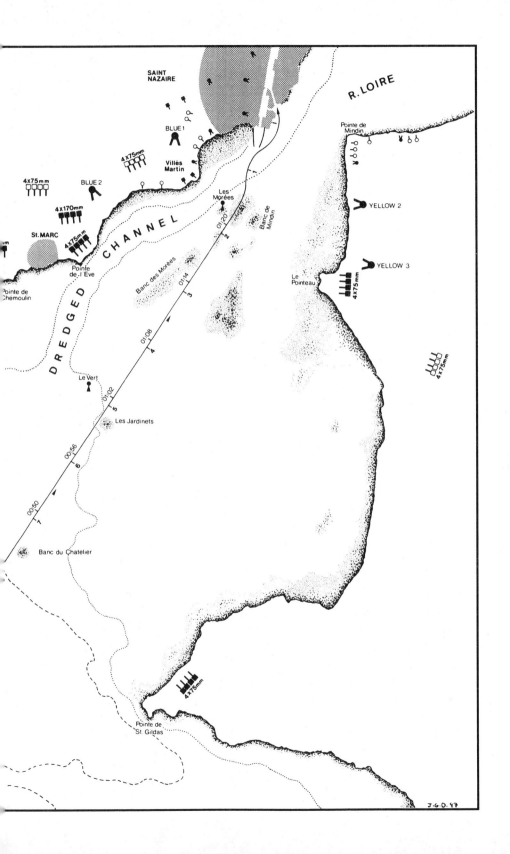

SAINT NAZAIRE

R. LOIRE

Pointe de Mindin

BLUE 1

4 x 75mm

Villès Martin

BLUE 2

4x75mm

Les Morées

4x170mm

YELLOW 2

Banc de Mindin

4x75mm

St.MARC

Pointe de l'Eve

C H A N N E L

Banc des Morées

Le Pointeau

YELLOW 3

4x75mm

Pointe de Chemoulin

D R E D G E D

01:20

2

01:14

3

01:08

4

4x75mm

Le Vert

01:02

5

Les Jardinets

00:56

6

00:50

7

Banc du Chatelier

4x75mm

Pointe de St Gildas

J.G.D. 97

the front door of such a heavily defended base in boats that were little better than tinder boxes. After the briefing he returned to the engine room and thought about it all; the more he thought about it, the more impossible it seemed. He was no more privy than were his pals to all the details of the German guns that lay in wait to greet them, but he knew that, provided the Jerry gunners did their jobs right, there were more than enough of them to cause very substantial damage indeed.

Waiting for Len and the other 'Charioteers', along either bank of the estuary as well as in and around the port itself, were some seventy pieces of ordnance, varying in calibre from 20mm quick-firing cannon all the way up to the huge 240mm railway guns of Battery Batz, a little way west of La Baule.

Under the overall command of the *See Kommandant* Loire, *Kapitän zur See* Zuckschwerdt, who was headquartered in La Baule itself, these consisted of two main classes of weapon, each designed to fulfil a specific purpose. Emplaced so as to defend the approaches to the estuary were the heavy batteries of *Korvettenkapitän* Edo Dieckmann's 280th Naval Artillery Battalion, with Dieckmann himself headquartered close by the gun battery and Naval Radar Station on Chémoulin Point. While for the dual-purpose defence of the port itself there were waiting the three battalions of the 22nd Naval Flak Brigade, commanded by *Kapitän zur See* Mecke, whose own headquarters were situated close to Dieckmann's at St Marc.

Ranging in calibre through 75, 150, 170 and 240mm, Dieckmann's coastal guns were arranged in battery positions, primarily along the northern shore of the estuary, close to which lay the deep-water channel which any ship of substance must use in order to reach the port. These fixed emplacements began at the estuary mouth, and ran eastwards as far as the Villès-Martin – Le Pointeau narrows, at which point the sea-space was reduced to a mere 2.25 sea miles, and beyond which lay the province of Mecke's Flak Brigade.

Approaching the estuary mouth in their attack formation of two long parallel columns extending over almost 2, 000 metres of sea, with the gunboat in the van, and *Campbeltown* steaming between the leading troop-carrying MLs, the 'Chariot' force would find itself entering into a perfect trap from which it would be the very devil to escape. On their starboard beam and guarding the southern extremity of the estuary shore would be the 75mm guns of Battery St Gildas; while to port, and guarding the north, there would be railway guns just inland from the Pointe de Penchâteau. Fine on their starboard bow, as they approached across the shallows, would be the guns of Battery le Pointeau, backed by the 150cm searchlight 'Yellow 3';

fine to port would be the cluster of batteries comprising the 150mm guns of Battery Chémoulin and the 75mm and 170mm cannon of the cliff-top position close by the Pointe de l'Eve. Backing the cliff-top emplacements was the 150cm searchlight 'Blue 2'.

It was to divert the attention of these defences that the diversionary air raid had been proposed, for without it the 'Charioteers' would be forced to rely on luck, their low silhouettes, their unexpected line of approach and such devices as Ryder believed might confuse the enemy into mistaking them for a friendly force. Either way, with or without the bombers, this passage of the outer portion of the estuary would be fraught with danger, including that from mines, patrol vessels and possibly even Schmidt's destroyers; every sea-mile gained towards the target without the alarm being raised would be a triumph.

Assuming they made it to the narrows, they would then be passing into the restricted throat of the estuary, less than two sea-miles from their target, but with the full weight of Mecke's three flak battalions ranged close by them on either hand. These lighter, dual-purpose weapons of the 703rd, 705th and 809th Battalions, primarily 20 and 40mm, but with a sprinkling of 37s, would be able to switch quickly from air to surface targets, and COHQ's original concept of an approach by stealth had been constructed around the premise that their crews must be far too busy firing skywards to worry about the seaward approaches to the town.

Running past *Korvettenkapitän* Thiessen's 703rd Battalion, backed by the large searchlight 'Blue 1', they would come within easy range of the defences both of the outer harbour and of the Pointe de Mindin on their starboard beam, where were mounted the searchlights and 20mm cannon of *Korvettenkapitän* Burhenne's 809th Battalion. At this point, with the range so short, the 'Charioteers' would at least be able to reply in kind; however, they would also be at their most vulnerable, which is why the air plan had been designed to reach its crescendo during this period. Should the diversion succeed, then the force just might reach the dockyard intact, at which point, while *Campbeltown* raced for her caisson, the columns of MLs would break to port and make for their own two landing points.

As leader of the formation, the gunboat, carrying Ryder, Newman, Day, Terry, Holman and a handful of the HQ party, would circle to starboard and support *Campbeltown* as she made her final dash. Only after she was in place would Curtis put Newman's party ashore in the Old Entrance. To observe and record the gunboat's subsequent peregrinations, Holman would remain on board with Ryder.

In company with Curtis, and positioned at the head of either column, the

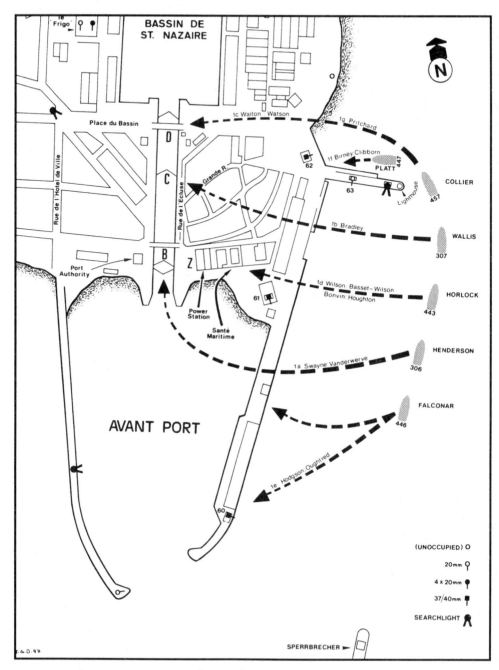

Group One Targets
showing revised landing sequence

non-troop-carrying torpedo MLs, 160 and 270, were to make up a small forward striking force on the way in, should enemy patrol craft be encountered. While the landings were taking place, their job would also be to draw fire and protect their fellow 'B's from interference.

Following ML 270 would be the troop-carrying MLs of the port column, scheduled to land against the slipway on the northern face of the Old Mole. Drawn from Wood's 28th Flotilla, these were now under the direct command of Platt in ML 447. As for the starboard column, sailing in behind ML 160, Stephens' ML 192 and the remaining three troop-carriers of his own 20th Flotilla would lead the second pair of 7th Flotilla boats. Being torpedo-armed, the latter two would have the secondary role of protecting the force from rearward attack. All six boats in this column were to pass under *Campbeltown*'s stern and put their men ashore in the Old Entrance.

Destined to play a crucial role in the coming action, both as a primary landing point and as the position from which all retiring soldiers were to attempt to withdraw, the Old Mole jutted some 130 metres into the waters of the Loire. Standing twenty feet above the decks of the MLs, even at the full height of the tide, it represented an obstacle which was almost medieval in character – a fortress wall rising sheer from the water, which must somehow be scaled, but from the top of which its defenders would prove almost impossible to dislodge.

Strongly fortified by the Germans, its upper surface was crowned by two substantial concrete emplacements, each more than a match for the puny shells with which the 'Chariot' force would be obliged to attack them. At its seaward end, a little to the rear of the lighthouse which marked its furthest extension, was searchlight emplacement LS 21; about one third of the way along was the 20mm gun position number 63, firing through embrasures and all but impervious to attack. Not on the Mole itself, but situated close by its landward end, and positioned so as to control the approaches to its northern face, was the 40mm gun position number 62.

Protected by shallow water where it joined the quayside, the Mole could be effectively attacked only by means of the long slipway running up its northern face. At its tip, and giving access to the lighthouse, were tight, narrow steps up which men might possibly scramble; however, they would then be faced with a frontal attack on position 63. Placing scaling ladders against its sheer stone face at some other point was always a possibility, but, with the defenders able to direct fire downwards on to the decks of the boats, this would surely be a tactic of last resort.

Always assuming they survived for long enough to reach the Mole, a total of six MLs were briefed to put their Commando parties ashore at the slipway,

85

following each other in quick succession and then hauling off to act in accordance with the orders of the Naval Piermaster, Lieutenant Verity, RNVR. Designated Group One, and under the overall command of Captain Bertie Hodgson, these parties, numbering a mere eighty-nine men, had the job of overwhelming all the German defences in and around the Old Town and sealing the area off by blowing up those bridges and lock-gates across the New Entrance by means of which the Germans would surely seek to mount a counter-attack. Should the Commandos succeed in this, then the Old Town area would be protected by water on three sides, and by the Commandos of neighbouring groups on the fourth, making it a secure base from which a successful withdrawal might later be made.

Landing from Platt's ML 447, the first party ashore was to be Captain David Birney's Assault Group '1F', a heavily-armed fourteen-man squad whose primary task was to capture and clear the Mole and establish a bridgehead at its landward end. From this commanding position they could then protect the remaining five MLs, initially as they came in to effect their landings, and later as they sought to re-embark troops and return with them to England. A small but important subsidiary task would involve clearing the building containing gun position 62, so that it could be used as an RAP by the two Commando doctors scheduled to land a short time later.

Following close upon the heels of Platt should be the ML of Lieutenant Douglas Briault, carrying Assault Party '1E', a second fourteen-man unit, this time under the command of Bertie Hodgson himself. Also landing would be Captain Mike Barling, the first of the Commando doctors, and two Medical Orderlies, whose job it was to prepare to receive and treat the wounded. Hodgson was to pass through Birney's bridgehead and move south to capture and secure the long East Jetty of the Avant Port, whose two gun positions, M60 and M61, were able to fire into the flanks of any vessels approaching or leaving the Mole. With the Avant Port secured, his party was then to picket and patrol the built-up area of the Old Town itself.

The way having hopefully been cleared by the assault parties, it would then be the turn of the demolition teams to land. First to come ashore would be Group '1C', landing from Collier's ML 457 and consisting of Lieutenant Philip Walton's demolition team and their five-man protection squad under Tiger Watson. Their job was to move quickly west towards target group 'D' at the northern end of the New Entrance, where Walton and his party of four would prepare the lifting bridge and lock-gate for demolition, while Watson and his men watched over them like mother hens. In this exposed position the men would be open to attack from several different quarters, despite which demolition could not take place until all the other crossings had been similarly prepared, as all the explosives were to be interconnected and fired simultaneously. In overall charge of the demolitions within this sector was Captain Bill Pritchard who, along with his small Control Party, would land with Walton and Watson.

Next in line, and briefed to demolish the central lock-gate, designated target 'C', would be the seven-man team of Captain Bradley, landing from Wallis's ML 307. This team would operate without a protection squad and was to withdraw to the Mole immediately its work was done. Landing with them would be Captain David Paton, the second of the Commando doctors staffing the RAP; recording every detail for the Exchange Telegraph would be Edward Gilling.

Fifth to land, and carried on board ML 443, should be a cluster of demolition parties charged with destroying the group of buildings comprising target group 'Z'. Consisting of three small teams under Lieutenants Wilson and Bonvin, and Second-Lieutenant Paul Basset-Wilson, they would blow the Boilerhouse, Impounding Station and Hydraulic Power Station. Landing with them would be their protection party under Lieutenant Joe Houghton. Upon completion of the work all three demolition parties were to withdraw to the protection of Birney's bridgehead.

Last of the troop-carrying boats of the port column, Lieutenant Ian Henderson's ML 306 would put ashore the third of the demolition teams targeting the New Entrance crossings. Consisting of eight other ranks commanded by Lieutenant Ronnie Swayne, and protected by Lieutenant Vanderwerve's small squad, this team would aim to destroy the lock-gates and swing-bridge comprising target group 'B', and thus complete the isolation of the Old Town area. Generally speaking, all demolition parties were supposed to withdraw in the company of their protection squads; however, in the case of the New Entrance targets, in recognition of the fact that their very substantial construction might prevent their total destruction, it was decided that the protection squads of Watson and Vanderwerve should remain in place until the final stages of the withdrawal, to prevent German infiltration across what might be left of the structures.

As a final precaution, and irrespective of any other tasks they might have, all parties were warned of the absolute necessity of capturing and clearing the Mole. Should Birney fail for any reason to land, the first responsibility of any and all parties following behind was therefore to complete this one essential task.

As with so much of the overall plan, the assault on this all-important structure was a complex pattern of interdependencies, likely to succeed only if the majority of the parties actually landed, and in the order specified.

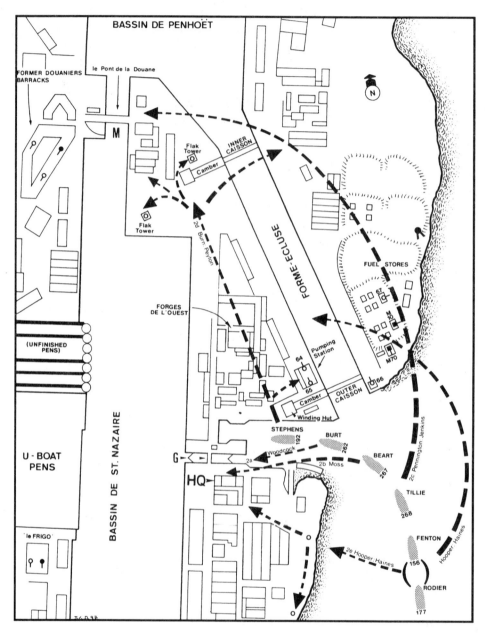

BASSIN DE PENHOËT

FORMER DOUANIERS BARRACKS

le Pont de la Douane

M

Flak Tower

Camber

INNER CAISSON

N

Flak Tower

2d Burt, Peyton

FORGES DE L'OUEST

FORME-ECLUSE

FUEL STORES

67

M

M70

Pumping Station

64

65

66

Camber

OUTER CAISSON

Winding Hut

(UNFINISHED PENS)

STEPHENS

192

BURT

262

2c Pennington-Jenkins

BEART

267

U - BOAT PENS

BASSIN DE ST. NAZAIRE

G

2a

Woodcock

2b Moss

TILLIE

268

HQ

FENTON

156

Hooper-Haines

2e Hooper-Haines

RODIER

177

le FRIGO

Group Two Targets

88

Should this not be the case, then the chances of capturing the position were effectively almost nil. As the final assembly point for all retiring parties, its subjugation was critical to a successful withdrawal. And yet the most powerful weapons at hand to secure its defeat were the dash and élan of the men sent against it, allied to more good luck than any such lightly armed force had a right to expect.

While the boats of the port column were thus occupied, those of Billie Stephens' column were to make straight for the Old Entrance and put the Group 2 Commandos ashore. There was a slight possibility that their forward progress might at this point be impeded by a boom. However, if it was not, then they would be free to select their own landing points, based on the degree to which enemy vessels already moored within the narrow cleft of water obstructed their access to the quaysides.

On landing, the Group Two parties were briefed to operate both north and south of the Old Entrance, combining with *Campbeltown*'s parties to dominate the vital triangle of land between the dry dock and the Bassin de St Nazaire, and working their way southwards through the warehouse area towards Bertie Hodgson's domain. They would, with luck, complete the isolation of the whole zone within which the night's demolitions were to be carried out and thus provide a secure haven through which a phased and orderly withdrawal of the northern parties might later take place.

First to storm ashore from Stephens' own ML 192 was to be assault party '2D', headed by the Group Two commander, Captain Micky Burn. Ultimately aiming to operate against targets on the neck of land which separated the Bassin de St Nazaire from the Bassin de Penhoët, Micky was first charged with ensuring that *Campbeltown*'s landings were not being impeded by the guns atop the pump-house. If these positions, numbers 64 and 65, were in the process of being dealt with by the Group Three parties, all well and good. If not, then Micky was required to subdue them before moving on. Within their own target area, his men were to knock out two wooden flak towers, as well as a possible gun position close by the Pont de la Douane. They would also be required to establish a blocking position at the eastern end of the inner caisson, to protect against attacks mounted from the area north of the oil-storage tanks.

Next in line should be Lieutenant Ted Burt's ML 262, carrying the nine-man demolition party of Lieutenant Mark Woodcock, and the five-man protection squad of Lieutenant Dick Morgan. Woodcock's job, in an area likely to come under fire from vessels in the Bassin, was to wire up the Old Entrance lock-gates and swing-bridge ready for demolition. Should the bridge be in place and crossable, then the lock-gates could be blown first, followed later by the bridge, once all the parties to the north had withdrawn across it. Should the bridge be swung back, however, then it was Woodcock's job to open it to traffic. In the event that the bridge could not be moved, then it was to be demolished in place and the lock-gates retained intact until such time as all the Commandos heading for re-embarkation at the Mole had safely withdrawn across them.

Following close behind ML 262, Lieutenant Eric Beart's ML 267 was scheduled to put ashore RSM Alan Moss and the remaining members of Newman's small though invaluable reserve. While remaining at their Colonel's immediate disposal, they were to engage enemy vessels in the nearby Bassin, as well as such U-boats as were not fully protected by their shelters' massive concrete walls.

Fourth in line was to be Lieutenant Bill Tillie's ML 268, carrying the five-man demolition team of Lieutenant Harry Pennington, their similarly sized protection squad under the command of Lieutenant Morgan Jenkins and a small addition to Newman's reserve. With the party designation '2C', Pennington's and Jenkins' Commandos were to move swiftly to Micky Burn's position, destroy the Pont de la Douane and thus prevent the Germans from counter-attacking across it. Dominating the bridge and inner caisson area would be the cluster of guns atop the old Douaniers' building. Should these be in action, then Pennington had the additional task of setting fire to the structure with incendiaries. Upon completion of all his tasks, he was then to withdraw, leaving Jenkins' team to thwart any German moves to cross from the west bank.

Bringing up the tail of the column, the remaining torpedo MLs, Fenton's 156 and Rodier's 177, were to carry between them the twenty-eight men of Captain Hooper's special assault party '2E'. Briefed to operate both north and south of the Old Entrance, they were to silence two gun positions right on the foreshore, which might or might not be in use on the night, and deal with any enemy vessels unfortunate enough to be trapped within the dry dock. Upon completion of these tasks, Hooper was to place his team at Newman's disposal at the earliest possible moment.

As all three landings were designed to take place within the same slim envelope of time, the activities of Micky Burn's group should neatly dove-tail with those of Major Copland's parties, landing from the *Campbeltown* on to the caisson itself. Of course this assumed that the old destroyer would make it as far as the dockyard, something no one dared predict with certainty, first because she would attract the fullest weight of fire from the German defences, and second because she might well run aground, especially with the operation having been initiated some days before the fullest height of the tides. Should she be damaged or become stuck, MLs 160, 270, 298 and 446 had been detailed to carry off her personnel and take her troops ashore. In this worst-case scenario, her charges were to be set to blow up some time after the last of the small boats had withdrawn. In her absence the attack on the caisson itself would be carried out with MTB 74's special torpedoes.

Supposing *Campbeltown* did make it through, however, there would then be the problem of the caisson itself, which might or might not be closed on the night. If closed, it was to be rammed at speed so that the destroyer's bows might ride over the top and provide a platform from which her troops could rapidly disembark. If open, then Beattie was to lay his ship alongside the dry-dock wall, port-side to, and scuttle her abreast the caisson sill, so as to gain the maximum effect from her eventual explosion. Should the dock be clear and the inner caisson closed, then Wynn was to pass by the destroyer and lay his special torpedoes against it.

In the event that the gods were riding with *Campbeltown* and that Beattie was able to ram the caisson as planned, then the disembarkation of her Group Three Commandos must be carried out in a blur of activity, before the stunned defenders could effectively respond.

During the run-in most of her demolition parties would be tucked away below deck, while the remainder, along with the protection parties and Roderick's and Roy's assault troops, would be sheltering behind the screens abaft the superstructure. While it was the job of the demolition and protection parties to hold themselves in readiness for their attacks on shore, the assault parties were under orders to supplement the naval fire-plan by firing on German positions as they came in to ram. For this purpose a 3" mortar had been installed on either side of the deck just forward of the bridge, the fire from which tubes, when added to that of Oerlikon, Bren and Tommy gun, would hopefully allow the destroyer to lay down an effective counter-barrage.

On ramming, it was the assault troops who were to disembark first, with the object of overrunning the defences in the immediate area of the caisson. Quickly clambering over the starboard bow, the fourteen-man team of Lieutenant Johnny Roderick was tasked with knocking out a cluster of gun positions, numbers 66, M70, M10 and 67, the first of which was in a sand-bagged emplacement close by. Having cleared these and secured the right flank of the attack, he was then to establish a block with the object of preventing a counter-attack across the caisson. Should there be the opportunity to do so without weakening the block, his men had been instructed to attack the oil-fuel stores with incendiaries.

While Roderick was thus occupied, his opposite number, Captain Donald

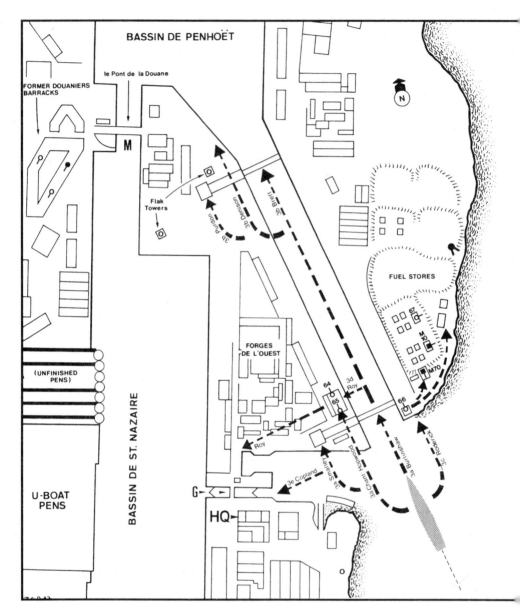

BASSIN DE PENHOËT

FORMER DOUANIERS
BARRACKS

le Pont de la Douane

M

Flak
Towers

3b Purdon

3b Denison

3b Brett

BASSIN DE ST. NAZAIRE

(UNFINISHED
PENS)

FORGES
DE L'OUEST

U-BOAT
PENS

FUEL STORES

67

68M

M70

66

64
65

3d
Roy

Roy

3a Burtinshaw

3c Roderick

G

3e Copland

3a Smalley

3a Chant Hopwood

HQ

N

O

Group Three Targets

92

Roy, would be landing with his own fourteen-man team from the destroyer's port bow. Roy's primary target was the pair of guns emplaced atop the pump-house. High above the quayside, these would have a clear and unobstructed view along the full length of *Campbeltown*'s deck. Roy had arranged to attack them with scaling ladders and grenades, and, during the detailed planning stages on board the *PJC*, had called for a volunteer to accompany him as he attempted to storm the roof, a potentially lethal enterprise for which Sergeant Don Randall had offered himself. Having overrun these positions, Roy was then to move on to bridge 'G' and there form a bridgehead through which the northern parties could later withdraw.

In the wake of the assault teams, it would then be the turn of the demolition parties to disembark. The first of these, party '3A', had the task of destroying a cluster of targets in the immediate area of the ramming point. Should *Campbeltown* not be positioned so as to ensure destruction of the caisson, then the team of Lieutenant 'Burlington Bertie' Burtinshaw was to attack it with man-packed explosives. To make doubly sure of putting it out of action, Lieutenant Chris Smalley's team were meanwhile briefed to destroy the nearby winding house. As the dock could not operate without the means of pumping in and extracting a huge volume of water, the pump-house was a target of critical importance, whose destruction was entrusted to the five-man team of Lieutenant Stuart Chant. Entering the structure which housed the facility's great electric motors, Chant was to descend into the depths where, some forty feet below ground, he would destroy the pumps themselves. Of all the targets to be demolished on the night, these were perhaps the most important as they contained special castings which the Germans could not easily replace. Protecting these teams, Roy's troops having by this time moved off to form their bridgehead at 'G', would be the five men of Lieutenant Hopwood's party.

In conjunction with these teams, the men of party '3B', protected by Lieutenant Denison's small squad, were to destroy the inner caisson and winding house. Lieutenant Gerard Brett and his team of six were to lay charges both outside and inside the caisson, entering the hollow structure by means of manholes in its upper surface; while close by Lieutenant Corran Purdon's team of five were to destroy the winding house. In overall control of the Group Three demolitions was Captain Bob Montgomery, his deputy, Lieutenant Bill Etches, having a special responsibility for these '3B' targets. Last to leave the *Campbeltown* would be Copland himself, who, with his own small party, was to move swiftly via Newman's HQ to the Old Mole where, in conjunction with the Naval Piermaster, he would organize the withdrawal. On completion of their tasks on board ship, the destroyer's crew were to disembark on to the quayside and wait to be taken off by MLs operating in the vicinity of the Old Entrance. Should this option be denied them, they were to make their way to the Mole and be put on board the MLs there.

'Zero hour', the time at which *Campbeltown* was due to strike the caisson, was set for 0130 hours on the morning of Saturday the 28th. The absolute maximum time-on-shore allowed for was a mere two hours, with the last ML due to be clear of the Mole and starting its long voyage home by 0330 hours. In the case of an uncompleted major demolition, this deadline might be exceeded; however, Newman had made sure everyone understood the very real correlation between early withdrawal and their chances of making it back alive.

For those who made it safely through the maelstrom, seconds indeed would be the currency of survival, for the initial advantage won by the shock of their assault would quickly erode as resistance stiffened and the German forces manoeuvred to hurl the tiny assault parties back into the sea.

Immediately available to oppose them, in addition to Zuckschwerdt's own Naval troops, would be a motley collection of units cobbled together from guard companies and ships' crews, as well as technicians and workers operating in their secondary role as infantry. These would be equipped to hold the line until such time as heavily armed Wehrmacht units could rush to the port and mount a formal assault on the tenuous Commando perimeter.

Because of the ongoing work on the submarine pens and port defences, a contingent of workers from the Todt Organization were in place, who would fight if required. The Naval technicians of Nos. 2 and 4 Works Companies also had an infantry role and would be committed early on to help stem the tide of the Commando advance. The crews of the many ships in harbour would supplement the defence both by manning their vessels' weapons and by contributing parties to help with counter-attacks on shore. For safety's sake the highly prized U-boat crews were billeted out of harm's way in La Baule; however, the support staff of the 6th and 7th U-Flotillas would defend their boats against attack, even to the point of destroying them should it prove necessary. Also under Zuckschwerdt's control, as the officer commanding all the defences of both port and estuary, were the guard companies and harbour-defence vessels of the Harbour Commander. And lastly, anchored right in the fairway east of the Avant Port, was the stoutly built and well-armed *Sperrbrecher* 137, a ship of similar tonnage to *Campbeltown* herself, which the 'Chariot' force would have to pass *en route* to the landing places.

Packing a more professional punch were the soldiers of the 333rd Infantry Division, a brigade of whom were stationed just inland of the port. Much more heavily armed than the Commandos, this unit was capable of mounting and sustaining an attack which it must eventually win, unless the Commandos acted with such speed and resolve that their withdrawal could begin before the German unit was in position.

Regarding the withdrawal itself, this was planned to take place in four stages, the first pulling back all the demolition parties, except Woodcock's by bridge 'G', and subsequent stages gradually shrinking the defended perimeter back to Birney's bridgehead. Lieutenant Verity was to be in charge of filling the MLs with up to forty men each and sending them on their way, independently and at maximum speed, towards the point at which they might expect to rendezvous with *Atherstone* and *Tynedale*. After initial treatment at the RAP, wounded were to be transferred to the two MLs which had embarked the doctors at Falmouth. These, when full, would follow the rest. MLs too damaged to complete the return trip were to be scuttled at sea and those which survived the coastal guns were to form themselves into the semblance of a fleet, returning to Britain by the reverse of their outward route.

In the case of an emergency requiring the immediate evacuation of the force, the men would be recalled visually by the firing together of 35-star red and green rockets, and audibly, both by the sounding of the MLs' klaxons and by the use of loud-hailers to pass on the code-word 'Ramrod'. Any or all of these signals would prompt the immediate withdrawal of all ranks to the Mole, always assuming, of course, that someone had managed to take and hold it in the first place!

In essence this was the plan as it was to be carried out on the night, always providing that fate and the German defenders cooperated fully. It was a plan of rather alarming complexity which would certainly be judged audacious were it to succeed, and foolhardy were it to fail to achieve its targets. It pitted flimsy ships and tiny groups of men against the massed defences of one of the Reich's most valued bases, whose five thousand-plus sailors and naval and army troops could be relied upon to mount a swift and punishing response. It depended to an inordinate degree on surprise and luck and was so susceptible to losses that the failure of even a handful of parties could seriously undermine the efforts and success of the whole. Apart from Moss's tiny squad, there was no reserve to speak of, and therefore no means by which such failures could be made good.

Having grown from a clinical attack on the 'Normandie' dock to encompass a number of targets entirely unrelated to the threat posed by *Tirpitz*, the force contained rather more demolition troops than was perhaps wise, and rather fewer assault troops than it might reasonably expect to need. Indeed, the plan had evolved to become nothing less than a broad-spectrum raid, whose confused priorities had in the end prompted Newman to write to Haydon for clarification. Amidst the transparent enthusiasm of the under-used Commandos to get to grips with the enemy at last, an objective assessment of the risks of such a complex distribution of parties seems to have occupied only second place. The plan in fact displayed a heady optimism more suited to a raid on a rival school than to a potentially lethal assault on such a gun-rich enemy stronghold.

But orders were orders: they had been set down and they could not now be changed. A few of the men might have harboured doubts or worries, but as they sailed southwards to the first of the staging points laid out for them by Forbes the spirit of most was held high by an all-pervading sense of mission. The Commandos had worked long and hard to be worthy of the trust placed in them this day, and they were not about to be turned aside by the kind of thinking that would make a present of that spirit to the enemy.

9

Whispers of Glory

At 1911 hours on the evening of the 26th the fleet reached position 'A' and set off on the second leg of the long left hook that was to take them deep into the Bay of Biscay, before beginning their final run to the Loire. The specifics of their course had been worked out by the Admiralty, on the basis of Luftwaffe reconnaissance information supplied by Air Intelligence and Ultra decrypts covering German minefields and recognition signals. It would carry them well to the west of Ushant and allow them to pass by the north-west coast of Brittany under cover of darkness.

With nightfall fast approaching, their fighter escort bade them farewell and flew northwards into the gathering mist. As the roar of its powerful engine faded into nothing, its loss only served to emphasize their solitude and vulnerability as they penetrated ever deeper into waters dominated by the enemy.

Having maintained its anti-submarine pretence throughout the daylight hours, the fleet now adopted its night-cruising order of parallel columns of MLs stationed either side of the three destroyers in line. To guard against strays, the MLs were instructed to watch for sudden changes of course initiated by the formation leader without signal. As there was little danger of being seen, speed was increased to 14 knots so that a corresponding reduction could be made on the morrow, the better to reduce their wakes and therefore their chances of being spotted from the air.

At around 2300 hours they reached point 'B' and changed course slightly to east of south, aiming for the place at which they would begin their slow turn towards the hostile coast. On the vessels of the fleet the Commandos shared the sailors' watches, peering into the dark void beyond the muted

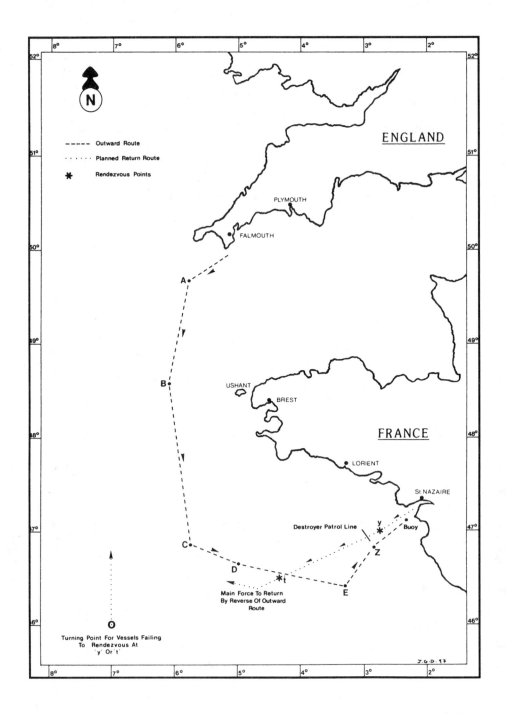

N

- - - - - Outward Route
· · · · · · Planned Return Route
✳ Rendezvous Points

ENGLAND

PLYMOUTH

FALMOUTH

A

B

USHANT

BREST

FRANCE

LORIENT

St NAZAIRE

C

D

E

Z

y

Destroyer Patrol Line

Buoy

Main Force To Return
By Reverse Of Outward
Route

O

Turning Point For Vessels Failing
To Rendezvous At
'y' Or 't'

J.G.D. 97

98

drone of their motors. Those who could snatched their last night's sleep before the fun began, while others sipped their mugs of thick, sweet, scalding 'Pusser's Kye' (naval cocoa), against the chill of the still night air.

Remembering those hours, Copland writes, 'We slept, ate, visited our men, did our tours of duty on deck ... sampled *Campbeltown*'s excellent sherry and waited. The troops ate and ate and ate – no stores to come back, no records to be kept – battle tomorrow, so – eat! Eggs, sausages, ham, chocolate. I issued only one "internal embargo" – rum permitted on the 26th but no rum ration on the 27th.'

Refusing to quit his engine-room, Chief Motor Mechanic Bill Lovegrove, who with his men had worked ceaselessly to tune and ready the torpedo boat's new wing engine, finally allowed himself the luxury of a few hours' fitful sleep. In other engine-rooms throughout the small-boat fleet, hands whose bunks had been commandeered by their soldier guests did likewise, settling down between the pristine Hall-Scott motors.

At first light the fleet awoke to a cloudless sky. This perfect visibility was very bad news indeed for Ryder, who had hoped for some haze, to move the odds some way in their favour. In accordance with Forbes' instructions, the three destroyers hoisted German ensigns. At this early stage, the small boats displayed no flags at all.

Throughout the fleet the ships' crews slipped with practised ease into the day's routine. They were disparate groups of men, bonded into temporary families by the exigencies of war – families such as that described by Able Seaman Donald Croft, RANR, whose ML 307 carried Captain Bradley's demolition party.

'Arising early in anxious anticipation of what was to follow, our captain, Lieutenant Norman Wallis, was on the bridge with our Number One, Sub-Lieutenant Leo Clegg from Glasgow, and Sub-Lieutenant John Williamson, who came aboard especially for the raid. The Coxswain Peter Warrick was getting things organized for the day, with lookouts, deckhands, etc, allocated to the sailors. In the engine-room were Motor Mechanic Murdo Macrae, Leading Stoker Glen Jones and Stoker 'Geordie' Allen. Pat Barry, the wireless operator was in his cabin attending the communication equipment, while in the galley, Ron 'Slosh' Mawson was preparing food for all the hungry men. Being the submarine detector rating I was operating the Asdic equipment, while taking my turn steering. Stan Roberts, Wilfred Jameson, Ron Mawson and Fred Woodward were our four capable gunners, with our only three-stripe Able Seaman, Bert Butterworth [who] with many years of service behind him, was the real teacher of the art of seamanship to all of us.'

As with ML 307, so it was on board every other vessel in the fleet, as the 'Chariot' force settled to the business of the day. At 0700 hours the formation resumed its simulation of an anti-submarine sweep. Having passed through position 'C', a turn to port was made, their new course of 112° carrying them towards the coast of France, now at a much reduced speed of only 8 knots.

Beneath the empty vault of the sky, the sailors and Commandos might well have imagined themselves the only living things loose upon the whole grey surface of the sea; however, at that very moment they were being keenly scanned by lookouts on board the surfaced, but as yet unseen, *U-593*, who sought to divine their identity and purpose in waters regarded by the Germans as their own.

Running damaged for St Nazaire, *U-593* was a new boat, the first operational command of *Kapitänleutnant* Gerd Kelbling, an officer who had captained a minesweeper before transferring to the submarine service. Having left Kiel on 2 March for a war patrol around the northern coasts of the British Isles, she had passed through the Shetland-Faeroes gap during the night of 9/10 March, and sighted a convoy on the 11th, only to be depth-charged by its escorts, on this occasion escaping any damage. On 18 March she had been in action again, this time with three destroyers, which together rained down upon her a total of 136 depth-charges, causing sufficient damage to make a run for base inevitable. With her electrical control system impaired, *U-593* found it hard to steer under water, her hydroplanes and rudder now having to be worked slowly by hand. There were leaks in her high-pressure air system and her outer hull was damaged, though no one could tell how badly. Surfacing when it was safe to do so, she had been instructed by radio to make for St Nazaire at her best speed, following the course which had brought her precisely to the position where she could now play a vital, if unwitting, role in promoting the success of 'Chariot'.

Watching from her conning tower, Kelbling was far from certain whether or not the force in sight was a friendly one. He could not identify the three destroyers accompanying what he took to be MTBs. In this particular stretch of sea they were most unlikely to be British, which therefore raised the possibility that they might be Dutch or Norwegian ships taken into German service. Not unduly worried by their presence, he continued moving east towards the coast, but keeping a careful eye on the distant warships just in case.

Only a matter of minutes after the 'Chariot' force had passed through 'C', *Tynedale* spotted a distant object on a bearing of 037°, at a range of 7 miles. She reported the sighting to Ryder in *Atherstone*, who immediately ordered her to close with the object and identify it. Detaching herself from the force, *Tynedale* raced off towards the north-east at a speed approaching 27 knots. With all eyes trained on the distant object, it was quickly identified as a surfaced U-boat, making for the French coast at an estimated speed of 12 knots.

At such a critical point in their passage to St Nazaire, the last thing Ryder needed was for the U-boat to get off a sighting report and initiate a response from the German Navy or Luftwaffe. It was critically important, therefore, either to sink her, or at the very least force her to dive before she could radio their identity to the shore. Slipping the gunboat's tow at 0736 hours, Ryder ordered *Atherstone* to join the hunt, leaving Beattie in charge of the remaining boats. As she sped after the receding *Tynedale*, *Atherstone* was accompanied by the two spare Fairmiles, ML 298, commanded by Sub-Lieutenant Nock, and ML 446, skippered by Lieutenant Falconar.

Racing towards the U-boat's position, Ryder could now see that two fishing boats were present in her immediate area. As it was possible they might be planning to rendezvous with the German vessel, he directed Jenks, in *Atherstone*, to make for them instead, leaving the U-boat to Lieutenant-Commander Tweedie in *Tynedale*. The problem with fishing boats, of which there were all too many off the Biscay coast, was that the odd one might be carrying a radio and German observer. Considering this whilst still in Falmouth, Ryder had therefore determined that Spanish and neutral trawlers were to be boarded and sent in with an armed guard, and French boats were to be sunk after their crews had been taken off.

Watching the progress towards him of the first destroyer, Kelbling was initially reassured by the sight of her German ensign. He continued to move away at his best speed of 12 to 13 knots, and when the range had closed to six miles put up the appropriate recognition signal, a pyrotechnic device bursting into five silver stars. The mystery vessel did not reply, her silence serving to heighten Kelbling's suspicions. At a range of three and a half miles he put up the signal again, this time prompting a response of five long flashes on *Tynedale*'s Aldis, a lucky guess on Tweedie's part, as it was accepted practice in the German Navy to give long flashes of the lamp if it was not possible to return a recognition signal.

Having thus far managed to forestall any action by Kelbling, *Tynedale* was rapidly approaching the point at which she would have to fire her main armament or miss the chance because the forward twin 4" AA mounting would become 'wooded' by the bow. In the Director Tower, above and behind the open bridge, the Gunnery Control Officer, Sub-Lieutenant David Stogdon, RNVR, had been keeping a careful watch on the U-boat through powerful glasses kept on target by the Director Layer and Trainer.

Very well aware that there was a limit beyond which his guns would not depress and that at this speed the ship's bow was raised above the norm, he had had the stops watched all the way in, so as to let him get as close to his target as was possible. At 0745 hours, when the range was 5600 yards, *Tynedale* ran up the White Ensign and fired, Stogdon's first two shells straddling *U-593*. As the heads in the U-boat's conning tower began to disappear one by one, *Tynedale* swung some 25° to starboard to open up her guns' arc of fire, and with the ship suffering some 'snatch' from her stabilizers in the turn, a further two salvoes were fired, the last shells splashing right on the position where *U-593* had crash-dived.

Resuming her course towards the U-boat's position, *Tynedale* was rewarded with the sighting of *U-593*'s periscope, because Kelbling, having recovered from the initial shock of seeing the White Ensign run up, had decided to mount an attack himself, using his stern torpedo tube. After his earlier experiences by the North Channel, he was fairly confident of taking on this single ship and quickly produced the figures for firing his torpedo. As the trim of his boat was particularly critical at periscope depth, it would be necessary to flood an after-trim tank with a weight of water equivalent to that of the torpedo immediately the order to discharge it was given. The tank was flooded, but unfortunately the torpedo refused to fire, its tube having been damaged in the earlier attack. This left the boat stern-heavy, sure now to shoot to the surface unless Kelbling took rapid action. Fearing that his boat might be rammed by the approaching destroyer, he ordered his crew to rush to the bow compartment to make the boat heavy at the forward end. But he was too late to prevent her surging to the surface.

David Stogdon writes:

'To our amazement the U-boat surfaced slowly, stern first and lay stopped beam-on to *Tynedale* and ahead of her bow. It would have taken only a couple of minutes full ahead to ram her (a solution which would have so damaged *Tynedale* that she would effectively have been lost to the force). Instead we stopped quite close with the U-boat on our port bow and under fire from the pom-pom and small arms. She was too close for the main armament to bear. The U-boat's stern rose up to an angle of 45°, her propeller turning slowly, and remained at this angle as she slid beneath the surface.

'On the surface, *Tynedale* was so near the submarine that she could not drop a full pattern of depth-charges without causing herself serious damage. She may have fired two depth-charges from her side traps over the disturbed water where the U-boat had dived, but the destroyer would not have been doing more than about 10 knots. It was then that I think the Asdic was damaged.

Tynedale then turned away from where the U-boat had dived to work up to a safe speed to fire a full pattern of depth-charges, returning at about 20 knots when a full pattern . . . were dropped on an estimated position for the U-boat, without help from the damaged Asdic.'

The rain of missiles was clearly heard by the U-boat's crew as they at last felt their boat start to go down, slowly at first and then very fast, at an angle of 45°. Undamaged by either guns or depth-charges, however, Kelbling brought her out of her dive at 150 metres and found a trim. Steering with difficulty, he decided to stay down, rigging the boat for silent routine and making little more than one knot through the water. Above could be heard a confusion of sounds which eventually, thankfully, died away into silence.

Deciding at last that the trawlers were French and posed no threat, Ryder ordered Jenks to join Tweedie in his search for the U-boat. As the two MLs could serve no useful purpose, he packed them off to rejoin the main force. On reaching *Tynedale*'s position and having her Asdic failure reported to him, he then ordered Tweedie to clear the area, so that *Atherstone* could initiate her own search, which was made without success.

The fishing boats having very wisely made off, and with no further sign of the U-boat, Ryder became impatient at the cost in time. He was anxious to rejoin Beattie, but anxious also that the U-boat should not infer a threat to the coast from any observation of their return course. Tweedie considered it unlikely that the small boats had been seen and gave it as his opinion that the destroyers would probably be judged to have been on passage to Gibraltar, a conclusion with which Ryder agreed. At 0930 hours, therefore, the search was broken off and *Tynedale* and *Atherstone* set course to the southwest, just in case they were being observed – which they were not – aiming to return to the main force by a circuitous route. There was always the possibility that the U-boat *might* have got off a signal earlier, in which case the attentions of the Luftwaffe could be expected soon. But as there was no evidence of this having been done, and with the sky at last beginning to cloud over, Ryder decided to press ahead.

On returning to the fleet, *Atherstone* once again took the gunboat in tow. As a result of the morning's activity, a sort of U-boat mania had gripped the small boats, and as Ryder records, 'Asdic reports of submarines to the right and to the left were being investigated by an ever-straggling line of MLs. I refused to be stampeded by shoals of fish and as we came up we acted as "Whipper in" and ordered them to rejoin.' By 1100 all was in order again and, under a growing pall of low cloud, the fleet resumed its steady progress eastwards.

Behind them they left an empty sea, the surface of which was not disturbed until Kelbling judged it safe to surface, if only temporarily, a little before 1400. Only at this time did he radio to Group Command West the sighting report that Ryder and Newman had feared so much. Stating that he had observed 'three destroyers and ten MTBs' at 0620 hours, in position 46° 52' north by 5° 48' west, he then went on to give their course as west, a conclusion based on his own considered opinion that they must have been a minelaying force withdrawing upon completion of a night's work off the French coast. Thus it was that the 'Chariot' force was done the very great favour of being reported leaving, and not approaching, its target. As a direct result of Kelbling's report the five destroyers of Schmidt's flotilla, which might otherwise have been in a position to affect the outcome of the enterprise, were instead sent out to patrol the usual approaches to the Loire. As they travelled seawards via the dredged Charpentiers channel, they would pass *U-593*, sailing surfaced for the estuary. Fortunately for all concerned, they would miss completely the elderly *Campbeltown* and her frail brood, sailing doggedly to the south of them, straight for the supposedly unnavigable estuary shallows.

Their solitude having first been disrupted by Kelbling, the force now found itself running towards a cluster of fishing vessels far too great in number to be dealt with by boarding or sinking. As a test of the theory that such vessels might be able to report their course and position, it was decided to board two that stood apart from the rest, one to port and one to starboard of the fleet.

At 1135 *Tynedale* was ordered to investigate the vessel to port, which transpired to be the French trawler *Nungesser et Coli*. Her crew were taken off and, her skipper having confirmed that it was not permitted for them to carry a wireless, she was sunk by gunfire a little after noon.

Tynedale having dealt with this ship, it was Curtis in the gunboat who embarked the crew of her companion to starboard, another French boat, named *Le Slack*. Having been thoroughly searched, and with the gunboat standing clear, *Atherstone* then put several rounds into the vessel's tough old hull. It was during this minor action that Curtis, having approached the trawler with all guns manned, received the unwelcome news that his after Rolls-Royce gun had gone U/S and could not be repaired outside a dockyard. This at a stroke robbed the gunboat of half her main armament, putting the gun's layer, Lofty Sadler, and trainer, Peter Ellingham, out of a job. Given Brens by Sergeant Steele, and never having fired this weapon before, they later took time out to practise while it was still possible for them to do so.

Returning to *Atherstone* to resume her tow, Curtis transferred his 'guests' to the destroyer. 'We had an expert interrogator with us who examined them all, ' writes Ryder, 'and likewise all papers and documents. Had we in fact been going for La Rochelle, the information would have been invaluable. As it was, we were reassured about the other trawlers and I decided to sink no more. We also obtained information about the presence of other fishing vessels, lights and swept channels.'

Passing through position 'D', Ryder brought the ships round a little more to the east. With the excitement of the morning behind them, the soldiers and sailors were now entering a period which for all too many would be their last hours of life and comradeship.

Adding to Ryder's growing sense of vulnerability, as they drove south of east along a course which it was hoped would convey to hostile observers an intention to make for La Rochelle, was news from Forbes that Schmidt's destroyers had been active. A signal received at 1240 confirmed a move to Nantes, a mere thirty miles upstream of St Nazaire, which must have taken place very shortly after they had been photographed on Wednesday the 25th. While berthed they would have posed one kind of threat, in that their guns could have been turned directly on the landed Commandos. On the move, however, they were altogether more dangerous, as they constituted a superior force which, if it was met at sea before the landings, could well put paid to all their months of careful preparation.

What galled Ryder more than anything was the fact that the existence of these ships in this general area was not fresh news. Already concerned about their possible impact on the raid, Forbes had tried his best to provide the force with additional destroyer escorts; but these, inexplicably, had been refused. Not only was this parsimony now directly threatening the success of 'Chariot', it had, in addition, led to a chance being missed, by which the raid itself might have been used as bait to lure these valuable German boats to their destruction.

Fortunately *Tynedale*'s encounter with Kelbling had thus far failed to lead the enemy to them. Perhaps he was late in reporting the attack; perhaps one might even dare to hope that he had been sunk. Either way the Germans still did not seem to know they were so near, which ignorance, bearing in mind the strength of the forces ranged at their disposal, would continue to remain the best protection of all.

Unburdened by such concerns as these, the men themselves ate, slept, played cards, checked and rechecked their equipment, talked, prayed or served their watches as was their wont or duty. Cards were a favourite pastime for many, although their concentration on the ebb and flow of fortune sometimes led men to pin their fates directly to their runs of luck. Occasionally these omens were borne out later by the facts: fortunately for most, however, more often they were not.

On board the old destroyer, her attenuated crew prepared for her final moments. Equipped with a total of four Normand boilers, arranged in pairs in forward and after boiler rooms, she was steaming on the power of the forward boilers only. The after boilers were kept topped up with steam should their extra power be needed in an emergency, in case of which the cut-down after funnels had been capped with deck-plates held in place by wing-nuts for quick and easy release. As it was critically important that she sink *in situ* immediately after ramming, measures were taken to let in water, over and above the charges placed for scuttling. To flood the machinery spaces, circulators, sea-cocks and condensers were all prepared beforehand, in the case of the big condenser doors by removing all unnecessary bolts and leaving those that remained only hand-tight, so they could be quickly spun off.

To lighten ship, bearing in mind the marginal nature of her draught, all unnecessary equipment and supplies went over the side, except for food and drink, of course, for which alternative billets were quickly found. So as not to suggest a voyage that was in any way out of the ordinary, the ship had been stored more or less as normal, all of which material would go up with her when she exploded.

Up on the bridge, Beattie and his officers sampled her sherry in company with the Commando officers, this being, as Montgomery recalls, 'probably the only time that a captain has entertained his guests on the bridge, while actually on service-duty'. In the spaces below, the men, having rapidly twigged that they need pay for nothing, continued to make merry with the contents of canteen, stores and NAAFI. Cigarettes and chocolate were secreted about their persons, sometimes waterproofed with condoms in case their new owners were forced to go over the side. 'We drank endless cups of "kye",' writes Lieutenant Corran Purdon of this period, 'and munched huge bully-beef sandwiches, delighting in the scrumptious, hot, soft, ship-baked bread, a real treat. Others made dreadful sandwiches containing such things as Brylcreem, shaving soap and toothpaste, and offered them to unsuspecting friends.'

An impromptu fancy-dress party followed the 'pillaging' of the stores. One of the leading artistes was Lieutenant Robert Burtinshaw, the tall, monocled officer of 5 Commando, who, sporting Beattie's naval cap, aped his brothers in the Senior Service. A hearty, but wholly capable officer, it is one of the many tragedies of the raid that he was not destined to survive it.

106

Across in ML 457, driving along on the port side of the arrowhead formation, it had been Tiger Watson's pleasure to come to know his naval host, Lieutenant Tom Collier, RNVR. Tom was a well-known yachtsman of whom Tiger writes, 'It would have been hard to find a more tolerant and hospitable man, and as it turned out a braver one ... During the two-day voyage we had plenty of time to talk together and in that tense atmosphere, charged with expectation, we quickly got to know more about each other than we ever would have in more conventional surroundings. Tom repeatedly assured us that whatever happened on shore he would not leave for home until we had re-embarked.' It was a promise not made lightly, as the night's events would all too ably show.

As they neared the point at which they would turn north and run straight for the estuary mouth, the character of each individual soldier and sailor was reflected in his assessment of and reaction to the danger that lay ahead. For Ordinary Seaman Frank Folkard, the easy-going nineteen-year-old after-Oerlikon gunner on ML 443, it was going to be an easy job, his breezy confidence being shared by many of the younger men, including Able Seaman Frank 'Smudger' Smith, the trainer of the gunboat's forward pom-pom. Reflecting the more measured view of the older men, however, Ordinary Telegraphist Stewart Burkimsher of ML 270 looked for support and comfort to his faith in God. A schoolteacher from Derbyshire with a wife and child, he recalls; 'To be told at the age of twenty-seven that your chances of coming back are very very low – it takes a lot of coming to terms with. I can't say that I was scared: I wasn't scared; but what worried me was the thought that they won't know what's happened to me and I should be leaving them and I didn't want to. And I just felt that I was letting them down. But I will say this – I prayed every spare minute I had, and long before we actually entered the river, I was quite at peace: I knew I should survive.'

Having made it through the long afternoon without further alarms, Ryder received an up-date from Forbes on the movements of Schmidt's destroyers. This took the form of a signal, timed at 1704 hours, warning that the one enemy surface force that could really do damage to 'Chariot' had returned from Nantes to St Nazaire and might well be encountered. With *Campbeltown* stripped of her heavy guns, there were only *Atherstone* and *Tynedale* to stand against these ships should a fight ensue. Worrying as this statistic was, Ryder could take heart from the fact that no enemy aircraft had come looking for them yet, which would seem to infer that the U-boat had, after all, failed to report their presence. Meanwhile Forbes was doing his best to protect them. Within two hours of his warning, he shot off another signal, this time confirming that the two additional destroyers, *Cleveland* and

Brocklesby, were being sent to reinforce 'Chariot', at their maximum speed of 27 knots. Although they might arrive in time to help pick up the pieces, they were being despatched far too late materially to affect the outcome of the raid. For Ryder this was a particularly irksome circumstance, since they might have achieved so much had they been sent sooner. Writing of the affair some months later, he made the comment that, 'If our humble efforts at St Nazaire have in any way helped to demonstrate the futility of sending reinforcement too late, then I feel we shall have greatly profited by it.'

At 2000 hours, with darkness falling, the force reached and stopped at position 'E', the stage of their journey where pretence was set aside and the ships began their run straight to the target. In a little more than 65 miles and just a handful of hours, they would be going right through the front door of a stronghold the enemy believed to be immune from attack. Had they but known it, both Ryder and Newman would have been highly amused to learn that none other than Admiral Dönitz himself had just visited the port and been assured by *Kapitänleutnant* Sohler, commanding the 7th U-Flotilla, that his grey wolves were in safe hands and that a British attack on the port was considered 'highly improbable'.

In wonderfully calm conditions the force shook itself out into its attack formation. *Campbeltown* slipped the MTB's tow and, having taken Ryder's and Newman's HQ parties on board, the gunboat growled free from *Atherstone*, her departure accompanied by cheers from the destroyer's crew. In a particularly poignant gesture, bearing in mind the parenting role his ship had played in her past associations with MGB 314, Jenks called out to them from the wing of his bridge 'Don't forget whose father I am!'

With the escorting destroyers moving to positions a mile apart from either flank, the MLs formed up into parallel columns, between the heads of which *Campbeltown* would sail to her rendezvous with history. The gunboat moved to the van, joining Irwin's and Boyd's MLs in the forward striking force. She was now the HQ ship carrying, in addition to her own crew and Holman the journalist, the naval party of Ryder, Green, O'Rourke and Leading Signalman Pike, and the military party of Newman, Day, Terry, Steele, Lance-Corporal Harrington and Privates Walker, Murdoch and Kelly, the latter two being Tommy-gunners charged with Newman's personal protection. Of these perhaps the most fortunate to be on board was Day, who had mistimed his jump from the destroyer and narrowly missed being squashed between it and the gunboat: he was lucky to get away with only a twisted leg. Newman records of his own move to the gunboat: 'One felt very much nearer the fighting and one's nerves instinctively became just that little bit tighter.'

To the rear of the columns the MTB kept station with the spare MLs, her three main engines now fully serviceable. As the Packard replaced by Lovegrove had been a wing engine, it was particularly fortunate that his efforts to get it up and running had been rewarded; for Wynn intended to use only the wing engines during his approach, as on any other combination of engines the MTB would have been even more difficult to handle than was already anticipated at the fleet's pedestrian speed.

Happy at last that all his ships were where they should be, Ryder signalled the advance to the north-east at a speed of 15 knots. No sooner had they set off, however, than Lady Luck, who had been their constant companion since leaving Falmouth, decided to desert them, her absence being marked by the unwelcome news that ML 341 was in difficulty and could not keep up. This was Lieutenant Douglas Briault's ML, second of the troop-carrying boats of the port column and with Bertie Hodgson's assault party 1E on board, as well as the first of the Commando doctors. Briault's port engine was unserviceable and would have to be repaired. Platt, in ML 447, as Senior Officer of the port column, overtook the gunboat to ask Ryder to reduce speed whilst the work was carried out; but at this particularly critical stage in the voyage, Ryder could do no such thing and he told Platt to act in accordance with existing instructions.

Having foreseen just such an eventuality, Ryder's orders clearly required that Briault put his troops on board one of the spare MLs. This he now did, transferring his Commandos and medical team to Lieutenant Falconar's ML 446. This operation took some time to complete and all the time the main force sailed further into the darkness ahead. While it was taking place, Sub-Lieutenant John May organized the draining of the deck fuel tanks, which were then filled with sea water. Such was the delay that there was now very little chance of Hodgson ever regaining his assigned landing position. This was a bitter blow, as it immediately reduced by 50% the number of assault troops available to take and hold the vital area around the Mole, and left no one to act in Birney's place should the lead assault party be prevented from landing. As ML 446 had been one of the four troop-free boats scheduled to go to *Campbeltown*'s aid should the destroyer become stuck on a sandbank, her new role effectively cut this rescue force by a quarter.

In spite of his very best efforts, Briault was unable to rejoin the main force and thus was left with no alternative but to return to England. Falconar meanwhile raced ahead, his progress being accompanied, as Sergeant Robbie Barron of 1 Troop well remembers, by 'sparks coming from the funnel which were quite visible in the dark'. After a two-hour stern chase, ML 446 would manage to catch up with the remainder of the fleet, but only in time to attach herself to the rear of the port column. She would therefore be well out of position, behind, rather than ahead of, the demolition parties who were relying on both Hodgson and Birney to clear the way for them.

While this little drama was being enacted well to the rear, Ryder 'continued on in, making *Campbeltown* the guide while we gave her the necessary orders as to course and speed. Green was pretty sure of our position; although we had been unable to get star sights, he had had frequent glimpses of the sun and the calm weather greatly helped. Communication was mainly by loud-hailer, and the fact that no one was keeping station on us gave us good freedom of movement. We could either drop back alongside *Campbeltown* to ask for deep soundings, or later on, when it got shallower, we could ourselves run out on one bow or the other with our echo-sounding machine, to locate shoals and check up on our position.'

Proceeding on a broad front through the darkness, with the destroyer escorts well out on either beam, and with the slight, reassuring figure of Green close by him, Ryder could be fairly confident of spotting the light put out for them by the partially submerged submarine *Sturgeon* lying at position 'Z'. A career naval officer who had decided to join the Navy after having read at a very young age '*When Beatty Kept the Seas*', Bill Green's shoulders were more than broad enough to carry the burden of being pilot of the fleet, responsible for bringing all these ships and men to the precise point in space and time where they might fulfil their destiny.

At 2200 hours, *Sturgeon*'s light flashed out of the distant darkness, directly ahead of the force and exactly where Green had predicted it would be. Here, right on the doorstep of the enemy, a British ship and British crew waited to impart to the lonely 'Charioteers' a last, lingering sense of belonging in this otherwise hostile and alien environment.

Captained by Lieutenant-Commander Mervyn Wingfield, RN, the 'S-class' boat *Sturgeon* had sailed from Plymouth on Wednesday the 25th, the same day Schmidt's destroyers had moved up to Nantes. In place a mere 40 sea miles from the target, Wingfield had taken great care to fix his position by means of bearings taken through the periscope. As required by his orders, he had surfaced to the point where only his conning tower was visible and begun flashing the letter 'M' towards the south-west. Trimmed heavy, so that she could quickly dive if need be, *Sturgeon* would be almost invisible to enemy radar, especially as in this case numerous fishing vessels were working the general area – a factor which might also help prevent the enemy from spotting the approaching fleet.

As the columns of darkened ships sailed by within hailing distance, Wingfield and his bridge crew exchanged greetings with their fellow countrymen, the familiar calls and accents ringing clear across the water. Watching the sub pass by along her port side, some of *Campbeltown*'s Commandos shouted, 'Put the kettle on for when we get home!' While from *Atherstone*, Jenks used a loud-hailer to demand of Wingfield, 'Hello, Mervyn; are you in the right place?' to which Wingfield replied, 'Yes; within a hundred yards, but don't make so much noise!'

Her duty ably done, *Sturgeon* doused her light and slipped beneath the waves to resume her patrol further to the north in the waters off Brest. As she slid from sight, she was used as a guide by the anxious Falconar. 'We almost ran into her, ' remembers John May, 'and the skipper said we would go and ask if she was on station or not. But she dived as we approached. I recall us leaning over the bridge and shouting, "Come up, you silly buggers!"'

For Tweedie in *Tynedale*, and Jenks in *Atherstone*, this was the point at which they would break away to establish a patrol-line across the course the surviving MLs were expected to follow as they made for rendezvous position 'T'. The loss of their guns left the fleet highly vulnerable to Schmidt's destroyers should these vessels be met between this position and the estuary proper.

Ryder and Newman could take a little comfort from the fact that they appeared to have made it this far, with the fleet still largely intact, and without their presence having been reported to the enemy; however, greater perils by far still lay ahead. Fate may have brought the two commanders safely to the theatre door, but the curtain had still to rise on the opening acts of what might yet transpire to be a tragedy.

10

Overture and Beginners

At 2300 hours, with *Sturgeon* an already fading memory, with nerves beginning to stretch tight and blood to run a little colder in the veins, the men prepared to take up their attack positions. With the naval guns' crews on the boats already closed up, it was time for the Commandos to crack a last joke and give packs and kit a final check.

The bright 'bomber's moon' had gone now, fate having chosen to draw a veil of cloud across the sky which, while it was a blessing to the little ships below, was to prove a menace to the bomb-aimers in the Whitleys and Wellingtons of the approaching diversionary force. A total of sixty-two aircraft, instead of the crushing force envisaged back in February, made up the stream which was timed to arrive overhead even as the 'Charioteers' slid unseen towards the estuary shallows. It was all a matter of priorities, and the priority of Bomber Command in the early spring of 1942, was to husband its resources for spectacular strategic raids, rather than see them frittered away in 'side-shows' in which the RAF would play only a supporting role to other Services.

Bearing in mind that the success of the whole enterprise was largely predicated on the bombers' ability to divert the enemy's attention away from the estuary approaches, the RAF's steadily dwindling interest had long been a source of concern at COHQ. As late as 22 March as few as thirty-five aircraft were being offered, with which to undertake a multi-phase support programme which included disruptive raids right through the hours of darkness. This derisory offer had prompted a chorus of protest, following which the number was increased to the only slightly less meagre, but immutable, sixty-two.

The heaviest phase of the bombing, whose purpose was to soften up the target area itself, was planned to cover the period from 2330 on the 27th to 0045 hours on the morning of Saturday the 28th; after which it had always been intended that the point of impact should move to the adjacent built-up areas. This secondary phase had, however, fallen foul of the politicians, with Churchill himself absolutely forbidding bombing which might result in civilian casualties: all of which meant that the most critical sorties of the whole raid would now be aimed not at the town where they might have offered invaluable support to the landings but at the docks and building slips far to the north, in which areas the effort would be essentially wasted.

Further inhibiting the effectiveness of the raids were Bomber Command's own operational orders, which strictly governed the behaviour of aircraft over the target, aircraft whose crews knew nothing of the details of 'Chariot', and were therefore unaware of the vital role they were expected to play in minimizing the casualty toll below. The bombers were to attack specified targets only, and were to identify these clearly before pressing ahead with their runs: they were to drop their bombs one at a time and not in salvoes, requiring the crews to make separate runs through the flak for each bomb dropped, and under no circumstances were they to stray below 6, 000 feet, irrespective of cloud-base. It was a very long way indeed from the punishing aerial contribution which had always been seen as the key that would open the door for Ryder and Newman, and in its final minimalist format was far more likely to fail than to succeed.

For the men who gazed skywards from the decks of the fleet, the first faint throb of the bombers' motors came out of the darkness towards 2330 hours. In response to the threat, the St Nazaire defences sprang to sudden and violent life, fracturing the night with their searchlight beams and causing the very horizon to dance and shiver to the tune and flash of many guns. To the watching 'Charioteers', for whom the aircraft were seen as courageous allies sweeping in from afar to clear the way, it was everything they had been promised and at this early, optimistic hour, it inspired them to believe they might yet make the passage of the estuary, safe beneath a flashing canopy of flak.

Seen from the other side of the gun-sights, the Germans were initially convinced that this raid would develop just like all the others sent against them. Having been attacked two nights earlier, they were quick to react to the traces revealed by their radar, with *Kapitän zur See* Mecke sounding the alert at 2320 hours – not long before Lieutenant Nigel Tibbits, RN, assisted by Able Seaman Demellweek, was due to set the long-delay fuses within *Campbeltown*'s explosive charge. As commander of all the flak defences, it was Mecke's responsibility to ensure such aircraft did not get through and, as he sent his barrage aloft, he could see nothing in their behaviour that would yet suggest a purpose beyond the ordinary.

For the aircrew droning high above these fears and expectations, this was but one more sortie to be got through. Drawn from numbers 51, 58, 77, 103 and 150 squadrons, some in the freezing bellies of the bombers had bearded this particular target before, and so knew they were in for a pasting. Their freedom of action already substantially restricted by their inflexible orders, they were therefore not best pleased to find that, because much of the target was obscured by cloud at 3, 000 feet, they would now be obliged to circle amid the flak while their bomb-aimers searched in vain for fugitive breaks.

Group-Captain Willetts himself was there, an observer who was perfectly placed to understand the danger to Ryder's ships that was inherent in the bombers' difficulties. Carried into action on board the Whitley of Pilot Officer Monro, a 51 Squadron aircraft which had flown out from Dishforth in Yorkshire, Willetts arrived over target to be greeted by what Brian Nation, the tail-gunner, recalls was 10/10th visibility with low clouds and medium to heavy rain. It could hardly have been worse, for having set the German defences alight, they could now do little more than prompt them to wonder why such an abundance of effort was being expended for so little apparent result. After wheeling through the tracer in a determined effort to make some sort of impact, Monro's aircraft would succeed in dropping a bomb or two before turning away for home; but it would be only one of a handful to do so, the majority being forced to quit the area with their bomb racks still full.

All across the town the civilians were puzzled as to why the Tommies had bothered to come at all. Young Jean Bouillant, sharing his family's basement with the anxious German patrol, remained convinced that only the imminent arrival of parachutists could explain such strange activity, and in this conclusion he was joined by Mecke, who saw it as the only possible reason why the Tommies did not press home the raid. Following his hunch, the flak commander put out a warning at midnight that all defenders should be on their guard against such unexpected developments. Thus it was that within a mere thirty minutes of its inception, and despite all the gunfire, the diversion upon which so many of COHQ's hopes had been pinned was already crumbling into dust.

Still some miles short of the estuary mouth, their faith in the bombers as yet undimmed, the 'Chariot' force ground steadily onwards. They had reached a position due west of the Ile de Noirmoutier and were watching out for the buoy which would confirm their entry point into the shallows. With the fuses set, which, if all the shorter mechanisms failed or were shot out, would guarantee an explosion during the early daylight hours of the 28th, *Campbeltown*'s fate was sealed and all that now remained was for her complement of Commandos to take up their action stations.

With midnight fast approaching, Major Copland called his officers together for a short, final conference in the destroyer's wardroom. It was a meeting of no little moment, in that it must necessarily be the last such gathering of friends and comrades before the inevitable toll of casualties bit deep into their ranks; however, its more sombre meaning was not overtly present in the 'calm, confident, cheerful gathering', described by Copland, who records that 'the atmosphere, outwardly at all events, far from seeming electric, was quite ordinary.' It was a gathering of gift and intellect of which any commander might justly be proud, the young 'tigers' 'all trusting in their troops, and their troops secure in them.' With the coming of the witching hour he despatched them to their posts. 'I gave the order "Action Stations, please Gentlemen."' he records, 'and we left the wardroom for our allocated stations.'

For Copland himself, the position in which he would make the final passage of the estuary was just forward of the bridge structure, where a steel screen mounted on the main deck would afford him some degree of shelter. To either side of this position were the port and starboard 3" mortar tubes, commanded by Lieutenant Johnny Proctor of Roy's party and No. 5 Troop, and crewed by Corporals Beardsell and Cheetham, of Copland's own small team, along with his Batman, Private Gerry Hannan, and Private Holland, who was of Roderick's assault party. Theirs were among the most exposed positions on the whole ship, bearing in mind that the armoured bridge, which towered above them, would attract more than its fair share of incoming fire.

Almost directly beneath Copland was the wardroom, a compartment which was reached by two flights of steps giving out onto the foremost portion of the well-deck. This was the space allocated to the demolition parties of Lieutenants Purdon and Brett of 12 Commando, and of Lieutenant Burtinshaw of 5 Commando. Purdon and Brett would remain below with their men until ordered to disembark. Burtinshaw, however, would make the final passage up on deck, liaising with his team through the resolute Sergeant Frank Carr, who was to position himself at the top of the companionway. The defences having hopefully been tamed beforehand, these parties would attack, respectively, the northern winding-house and the northern and southern caissons of the great dock.

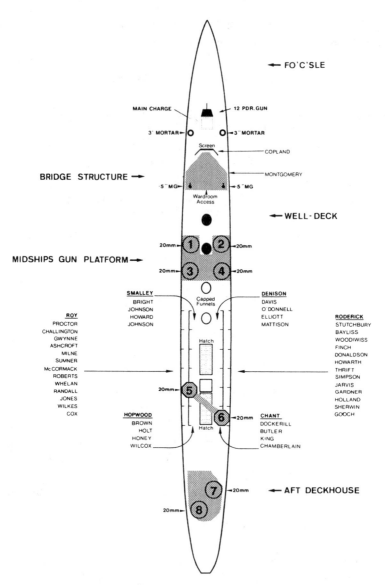

← FO'C'SLE

MAIN CHARGE ►   12 PDR. GUN

3" MORTAR ►   ◄ 3" MORTAR

Screen

COPLAND

BRIDGE STRUCTURE ►

MONTGOMERY

.5" MG ►   ◄ .5" MG

Wardroom Access

← WELL-DECK

20mm ► ① ② ◄ 20mm

MIDSHIPS GUN PLATFORM ►

20mm ► ③ ④ ◄ 20mm

Capped Funnels

SMALLEY
BRIGHT
JOHNSON
HOWARD
JOHNSON

DENISON
DAVIS
O'DONNELL
ELLIOTT
MATTISON

ROY
PROCTOR
CHALLINGTON
GWYNNE
ASHCROFT
MILNE
SUMNER
McCORMACK
ROBERTS
WHELAN
RANDALL
JONES
WILKES
COX

RODERICK
STUTCHBURY
BAYLISS
WOODIWISS
FINCH
DONALDSON
HOWARTH
THRIFT
SIMPSON
JARVIS
GARDNER
HOLLAND
SHERWIN
GOOCH

Hatch

20mm ► ⑤

HOPWOOD
BROWN
HOLT
HONEY
WILCOX

⑥ ◄ 20mm

CHANT
DOCKERILL
BUTLER
KING
CHAMBERLAIN

Hatch

⑦ ◄ 20mm   ← AFT DECKHOUSE

20mm ► ⑧

PARTIES STATIONED BELOW

BRETT
DEERY
FERGUSON
MOLLOY
WRIGHT
REEVES
BLOUNT
LEMON

BURTINSHAW
CARR
IDE
McKERR
FERGUSON
STOKES
EDWARDS
BEVERIDGE

PURDON
JOHNSON
CHUNG
HOYLE
CALLAWAY

SUPERSTRUCTURE: GUN- PLATFORMS _____

ARMOURED SCREENS _____

SCALE _____   0   20   40   60

J.C.D. 47

116

It was immediately aft of the midships gun platform that the majority of men would find their places, lying on their backs behind the four bullet-proof screens that had been attached to the deck, two on each side of the engine-room hatches. No more than 2 feet high, these would certainly shield the men from much of the fire coming in from the sides; but against shrapnel resulting from air bursts, or hits on the superstructure, they would offer no protection at all.

In respect of the positions assigned to the various parties, because of their absolute need to disembark first, the two large assault teams were to shelter behind the outer screens, Roderick's men to starboard and Roy's to port. The remainder of the deck parties, consisting of the protection squads of Lieutenants 'Bung' Denison and 'Hoppy' Hopwood and the demolition squads of Lieutenants Chris Smalley and Stuart Chant were to shelter behind the inner screens and disembark shortly thereafter.

To allow for effective liaison between Copland and Beattie, Bob Montgomery would remain at all times with the bridge crew. In the presence of both Sam Beattie and Nigel Tibbits, who at this stage was acting as Navigating Officer, the sapper Captain would be ideally placed to observe and admire the imperturbability of the very best kind of officers the Royal Navy could produce.

For the sailors the significance of midnight was that the men of the First Watch were replaced by those of the Middle Watch. Completing his four-hour stint was twenty-two-year-old Leading Stoker Frank Pritchard, who had joined the service in 1938. Frank had served in the battleship *Malaya* before commissioning *Campbeltown* in Liverpool the year before. He recalls that, while some of her machinery was quite technically advanced, it was also rather old, the result being that 'you never stopped, day and night, trying to keep the things at sea: because they were really clapped; they'd had it!' Normally Frank would have been looking forward to his bunk; however, as he made his way aft to the stokers' mess deck, he was too taken up with the significance of the occasion to think of sleep. Behind him he left the engine-room in the capable hands of Warrant Engineer Locke, and his stokers and throttle-watch keepers. Having already played a part in preparing the ship for scuttling, Frank would later return to help speed her demise.

Having shut his equipment down, the nineteen-year old cook, Walter Rainbird, joined the crew of the 12-pounder. A baker's apprentice from Nottingham, who had volunteered the previous May, Walter's job in action would be to load the shells while the Officers' Steward followed up with the separate cordite charges. The fire of the gun would be directed by the Gunner (T), Mr Hargreaves, RN.

Apart from the 12-pounder and the .50-calibre machine-guns mounted either side of the flag deck, the ship's only other weapons were her 20mm Oerlikon cannons, mounted four on the midships gun platform, two above the Commandos' armoured screens and two on the after deckhouse. While the majority of the bandstands would house only a gunner and loader, the elevated position on the port side above where Roy would lie would have a crew of three; for, joining the AB loader and the gunner, Petty Officer Bill Stocker, who was 'Chief Buffer', would be Petty Officer Frank Wherrell, *Campbeltown's* Ordnance Artificer. A qualified toolmaker, Frank had been with the ship since her commissioning in Liverpool, his duties involving the maintenance of the guns and fire-control systems. Not put off in the slightest by the prospect of Stocker's Oerlikon tearing the air asunder right next to him, Frank fully intended to fire a stripped-Lewis over the thin metal side of the tub.

As First Lieutenant it would be the duty of Lieutenant Gough, RN, to oversee the fire of all the Oerlikons once the signal to open up was received from Beattie. Waiting to pick up the pieces of the resulting engagement was the Canadian Medical Officer, Surgeon-Lieutenant W.J. Winthrope, RCNVR, of Saskatoon, Saskatchewan.

Out on board the MLs the story was the same, as soldiers and sailors took up the positions and duties that would carry them through to zero hour. On Billie Stephens' ML 192, his duties in the wireless room completed, Leading Telegraphist Jim Laurie moved to the darkened wheelhouse. As with all the 20th Flotilla boats, 192 had wheels both here, where the engine controls were, and on the bridge, from which position 192 would be conned during the passage of the estuary. Having had her wheelhouse windows padded against incoming fire, Jim, who would receive engine instructions from Stephens by means of a voice pipe, had just about enough light to see his instruments and keep an eye on the trace from the echo-sounder. A loud-speaker mounted on the bulkhead was connected up so that signals coming into the wireless room would automatically be relayed to him. With no view outside, he was to all intents and purposes trapped in his own private world.

Just a few feet forward of Jim's position was the Oerlikon of Able Seamen Davidson and Lapsley, who were gunner and loading number respectively. On the majority of MLs this would have been the foremost piece of arma-ment; however, 192 would go into action with an additional weapon right forward, in the shape of Ordinary Telegraphist George Davidson, a twenty-year-old rating from Kirkcudbright who, clad in a boiler suit and clutching a stripped-Lewis, was positioned right up on her bow. George was not a regular member of Stephens' crew. Having responded to a request for 'sparkers' to train as parachutists, he had been waiting for his draft to come through when posted as spare crew to the 20th. When the draft did finally arrive, Stephens had persuaded him to stay on, with the promise that there would soon be quite a party. Thus it was that he now found himself as exposed as the ornament atop the grille of a car, having volunteered to join a section which was to go ashore after landing and cause such local damage as it could.

Arranged mostly aft of the bridge were the 6 Troop boys of Captain Micky Burn's assault party. As they were friends more than mere subordinates, Micky took care to wish each one 'good luck' before taking up his own action station further forward, but within earshot of Stephens. Sharing command of this party was Micky's close friend and Section Officer, Lieutenant Tom Peyton, who had 'gasped with excitement' on the occasion of Newman's first briefing on the *PJC*. Stationed forward with Micky and one or two others was Lance-Sergeant Maurice Harrison, a twenty-year-old from London. Almost six feet tall, lithe, wiry and a fitness fanatic, he had joined the Queen's Westminsters at the tender age of sixteen, earning for himself the nickname 'Boy'. Educated at the Strand School, Maurice had left before his sixteenth birthday to join an advertising firm, after which there had been evening classes at Camberwell Art School for the purpose of furthering his career. Described by his sister as 'a charmer who could charm the birds off the trees – full of fun so there was always laughter in our house when he was around', his indomitable spirit and zest for life were so very typical of all the Commando soldiers.

Lying in wait for Micky, Tom, Maurice and all the rest, was drama enough for a lifetime, a fate which was to be shared by those on board the torpedo-armed ML 177, captained by Sub-Lieutenant Mark Rodier, RNVR, and positioned right at the tail of the starboard column. Described by his 'Jimmy', Acting Sub-Lieutenant Frank Arkle, as 'dark and good-looking in a very English way. Calm, sensible, decisive yet philosophical,' Rodier, had he survived the war, would probably have been 'something in the City'. Sub-Lieutenant Walter Heaven, a schoolmaster by profession who was newly arrived on the boat, completed the command team, although a fourth officer was also present in the shape of Stephens' Flotilla Engineer Officer, Sub-Lieutenant Toy. Along with C.P.O. Rafferty, Toy had embarked from Falmouth in Stephens' boat, only to transfer later to Rodier's, as it was better positioned to help MLs in need of repair. Making up her Commando complement, 177 had on board half of Hooper's Special Task Party, a fourteen-man group under the leadership of Troop Sergeant-Major George Haines.

Having passed by *Sturgeon*, Rodier made sure that his deck tanks were cleared of petrol and filled instead with sea water, a very necessary precaution, bearing in mind how explosive petroleum gases could be.

As they approached the estuary mouth Rodier went to great lengths to ensure that his First Officer knew of the location of all his personal effects, as he was quite certain he would not survive the action. It was a premonition of which Frank Arkle did his level best to disabuse his captain, but without success, for with the atmosphere on board, 'tense, very quiet, slightly unreal', it was all but impossible to ignore a growing sense of one's own mortality. Frank took up his action station forward, where his job was to control the fire of the 3-pounder, Walter Heaven taking up the corresponding position aft. In the fullness of time they would all come to realize that, disturbing though it might have seemed at the time, Rodier's conviction had been little more than the first breath of air, foretelling the storm to come.

At a little before 0030 hours on the morning of Saturday the 28th, the force passed the buoy that was their final marker for the estuary. They were one hour and eleven sea miles from the landing places, and in a matter of minutes would begin their perilous navigation of the shallows. Ahead of them the sky continued to dance and ripple reassuringly; however, coming into view on the port side was an altogether more portentous vision, whose stark promise was very much at odds with the psychological boost afforded by the faltering air raid.

Back in June, 1940, St Nazaire had been one of the bases through which the BEF had been evacuated following the French collapse; indeed Bob Montgomery had been among the thousands to pass through it. A number of ocean liners had been sent to carry troops away, one of which, the Cunarder *Lancastria*, had been bombed and sunk whilst packed with soldiers, airmen and fleeing civilians. Trapped within the ship herself, or caught in a sea of oil, more than 3,000 had died in a tragedy news of which it was thought best to suppress.

Sunk in waters too shallow to engulf what was left of her, *Lancastria*'s skeletal upperworks were still clearly visible. She held a special significance, having only a matter of days before her end been a safe and friendly refuge for men of the Independent Companies pulling out of Norway. One of these was Lance-Sergeant Dai Davis, a tall, slim, twenty-three-year-old former butcher who was now part of Denison's protection squad, having gone through the Norwegian campaign with Micky Burn. Sailing with Dai, and now with Micky's assault team, had been twenty-one year old Fusilier Fred Penfold, from Clapham who had also been in the butchering trade. Lance-

120

Corporal Stanley Stevenson, of Hooper's party on ML 156, was another who knew *Lancastria* of old, as did Sergeant Robbie Barron, who was now ensconced on the port side of Falconar's ML 446, a Boyes anti-tank rifle at the ready. Although Bob Montgomery had not himself sailed on that fateful voyage, two of his friends had taken passage in the old liner and had been lucky to survive.

Directly ahead of Falconar was Henderson's ML 306, which carried the demolition squad of the independently-minded Lieutenant Ronnie Swayne of 1 Commando. Tasked with destroying target group 'B', at the southern end of the New Entrance, Swayne had split his small force into two sub-teams, led by Sergeant Tom Durrant and Lance-Sergeant Des Chappell respectively. Of these, Durrant had particular reason to respond to the proximity of the old ship's carcass as his brother Jack had won the Military Medal for his actions during her loss. A twenty-three-year-old from Green Street Green in Kent, and, like his brother, a regular, Tom had come to the Commandos from the Royal Engineers, one of the relatively few career soldiers to flourish in Special Service. Of medium height, but very solidly built, swarthy of complexion, his face adorned by a pencil-thin moustache and an early version of 'designer stubble', Tom was a tough and demanding soldier.

At half-past midnight the first ships nudged into the estuary proper. This was the stage of the voyage that Ryder had particularly feared, lest patrol vessels sight them and raise the alarm. Should it come to a fight, there was little doubt that smaller German vessels could be easily dealt with by the forward striking force; however, the loss of surprise at this stage, allied to the inevitable loss of cohesion, would seriously jeopardize their chances of ever reaching the harbour.

Positioned on the bridge of the gunboat, Ryder had his work cut out in keeping the long, straggling columns of MLs together, while Green, diving in and out of the chart-room, checked and re-checked their position. Colonel Newman, his own turn still to come, was quite content to let the Navy boys get on with it. Calmly smoking his pipe, he saw to the needs of his own men, his humour and confidence an inspiration to all.

Ready to stand by Newman's side was Sergeant Ron Steele, adorned with all the equipment he would need to lug about on shore. 'When "dressed",' records Ron, 'my set, which was a walkie-talkie, was strapped across my chest, with the separate battery/charger unit slung on one side and field haversack on my back. With revolver in holster, grenades hung on webbing belt and all pockets crammed with spare revolver ammunition magazines, I was trussed rather like the proverbial chicken.' As he was of little value as a fighting unit thus 'dressed', Newman advised him 'to keep out of harm's way as far as possible, in order to obviate any damage to the wireless,' and, of course, to himself.

With the gunboat at 'action stations', and their after gun irretrievably lost to them, Able Seamen 'Lofty' Sadler and Peter Ellingham positioned themselves so as to make the best use of their newly acquired Brens. Peter chose to lie on the deck, port-side aft, resting his Bren on a depth-charge, while Lofty lay nearby, ready to fire from inside the Rolls emplacement itself. Manning the two twin .5" machine gun turrets mounted abaft the bridge were Ordinary Seaman Arthur Vallance to port and Ordinary Seaman Bill Whittle to starboard. Bill was the boat's 'senior hand', and a 'sea-daddy' to all, according to Able Seaman Frank Smith, who had only recently replaced him as trainer on the forward gun, when Bill's left hand was injured by a slamming hatch. Smith and his fellow 'Brummie' Bill Savage would serve the forward pom-pom with great distinction, the gun being under the overall control of Sub-Lieutenant Chris Worsley, as Gunnery Officer.

Approaching the point at which the bottom shelved steeply upwards, Ryder ordered speed reduced to 11 knots, so as to nullify the squat effect which caused *Campbeltown's* stern to dip at speed. As the strong set of the tide had carried them a little too far towards the left bank, a compensatory adjustment was made and the fleet settled on to its new course of 050°. Making the most of the gunboat's equipment and manoeuvrability, he from time to time ordered Curtis to leave the formation and take soundings and radar fixes off either bow of *Campbeltown*, 'both of which, ' he writes, 'were of great assistance in checking our position before leading the force over the shoals.'

In the region of the Banc du Chatelier, at about 0045 hours, Tiger Watson, having slept through both the formation change and the encounter with *Sturgeon*, chose to investigate the situation on the deck of Collier's ML 457. He came up while the air raid was still struggling to establish itself, and writes that 'Searchlights crisscrossed a sky spangled by flak bursts. We were now entering the estuary and moving steadily forward. It was time to get ready. I stationed myself behind the funnel with a spare Bren-gun and some 100-round magazines loaded with tracer bullets. One could sense the land close by and smell the mud and seaweed. Then through the hazy darkness the north bank could be discerned.'

Having bidden farewell to the warmth below, all fifteen of Collier's Commandos were now on deck, split into parties of five, each under the control of an officer. Charged with destroying the lift-bridge and lock-gates at the northern end of the New Entrance was the demolition party of

Lieutenant Philip Walton, Tiger's fellow section commander from 1 Troop of 2 Commando. Consisting of Lance-Sergeants Dick Bradley and Alf Searson, Corporal George Wheeler and Lance-Corporal Homer, Walton's party would be protected on shore by Tiger's boys – Lance-Sergeant 'Wicky' Wickson, Corporal Hooper, Lance-Corporal Field and Private Lawson. Carried also on Collier's boat, but not directly associated with the other two teams was the Demolition Control Party of Captain Bill Pritchard, whose job was to support and supervise all the demolition teams landing at the Mole. Comprising Corporals Jimmy Deanes, Bert Shipton and Ian Maclagan, all from 9 Commando, and Corporal Chetwynd from 12 Commando, this team had been confirmed as taking part only a matter of days before the off. Deanes and Shipton had originally travelled to Falmouth only to assist such teams as had already been earmarked for 'Chariot'. Maclagan, who as the possessor of a Tommy gun was the most lethally armed man in the party, was a later addition; Chetwynd had come to them last of all. They had been trained for no specific task: indeed Bert Shipton was not even sure of the form and function of all the charges he carried in his pack.

With the powerful Hall-Scotts thrusting them steadily onwards, it soon became clear to Tiger, to his men and to all the others who watched anxiously from the decks of the fleet that the air raid was running out of steam. As it spluttered to a premature and worrying close, the illusion of protection its noise and flare had afforded them all was replaced by a sense of foreboding. This was the time when the attacks of their aerial allies should have been mounting towards their crescendo; and the loss of their support prompted soldiers and sailors alike to wonder what now lay in wait on the other side of the silence.

As the nervous tension began to mount, Pritchard passed his hip-flask to the men clustered on 457's stern. He pushed it into Maclagan's hand and told him to have a pull and pass it on. Normally Maclagan detested rum; however, as he was later to recall, 'in this particular instance, although never having tasted nectar, it couldn't have tasted sweeter.'

Having been concerned right from the outset with *Campbeltown*'s draft, Ryder's worst fears were realized when, in the shallows close by the Banc du Chatelier, the destroyer hit bottom. In the manner of such contacts with clinging mud and sand, there was no sensation of impact, only a long, grinding shudder as her engines strove to push her through. Corporal Bob Wright, in the wardroom with the remainder of Gerard Brett's demolition party, recalls how 'we were conscious of a sudden slackening: it seemed a bit of grating or something: but I didn't know it was grounding. I should have had bloody kittens if I did!' Her struggle to free herself was most obvious to the boats out on either beam, as they suddenly found themselves shooting ahead. With Beattie noting her check in speed, she finally broke through into deeper water, only to ground again a matter of minutes later. In neither case was she brought to a dead stop and, thankfully, her second handshake with the bottom would be her last until such time as she was sent to meet it deliberately.

By 0100 the majority of the bombers were already embarked upon the long and dangerous flight back to their bases. It had been a frustrating and ultimately unproductive night's work, which at this early hour had yet to exact its full toll in losses. Whitley 'S-Sugar', of 51 Squadron, captained by Pilot-Officer Herne, was one of the aircraft to pay the ultimate price when she ditched in the channel off Portsmouth, her crew being picked up later by a minesweeper. Another was the Whitley of Flight-Sergeant Bray, also of 51 Squadron, whose fate was recorded in the log of Harold Reeder, her Wireless Operator/Air Gunner. Writing what was in effect an epitaph for a good idea sabotaged from the outset by a lack of command commitment and resolve, he recorded that they were 'unable to locate our target, after three-quarter-hour search at 7, 000 feet. A/C hit several times. Returned to base retaining bomb load. Crashed in hills above Ilkley at 0515 hours. Rescued at 0930 hours. Taken to Ilkley and Harrogate Hospitals.'

With the skies above all but clear, *Kapitän zur See* Mecke was not about to be fooled into believing that the incident was over and done with. Although he had ordered his guns to cease fire, he had not ordered their crews to stand down, which left the weapons manned and ready to resume their cannonade upon his order. The strangeness of the air raid having prompted him to consider British moves beyond the ordinary, he had in fact already instructed his troops to pay 'special attention' to the seaward approaches.

It was about this time that the leading elements of the 'Chariot' force were passing Le Vert beacon. This put them less than two sea miles south of the heavy coastal batteries clustered between the Pointe de Chémoulin, where Dieckmann's HQ was, and the Pointe de l'Eve, close to which was Mecke's HQ. They were now only five sea miles from the landing places and closing on them at a rate of one sea mile every six minutes.

Between the ships of the fleet and guns of the northern shore ran the deep-water channel, in which it was now possible for Ryder to make out the dim shape of a patrol vessel. In concluding that it had not seen them, he was, in fact, mistaken, for they had indeed been noticed; however, as the ship was not equipped with wireless it had no quick way of passing this vital intelligence to the shore. An attempt was made to attract attention by flashing her searchlight into the sky but without success; which allowed the strange vessels to pass unchallenged towards the Banc des Morées.

Further compounding the string of errors that were making 'Chariot' look more attainable by the minute was another unacknowledged sighting, made this time by none other than *Korvettenkapitän* Burhenne, the commander of Mecke's 809th Flak Battalion. Scanning the seaward approaches with his night glasses from his HQ between Le Pointeau and Pointe de Mindin, he saw a group of ships approaching, but his report to the headquarters of the Harbour Commander was dismissed out of hand. He then passed news of the sighting on to Mecke instead.

At 0115 a lookout on the northern shore alerted Dieckmann to the fact that an unidentified naval force was moving up the estuary. And at 0118 a member of Mecke's own staff inquired of the Harbour Commander if German ships were expected, and was told that they were not. The fleet had made a good three miles since first being seen by the patrol ship, and still the surrounding guns and searchlights remained inactive.

At 0120 Ryder passed about two cables to starboard of the disused Les Morées tower, which put the gunboat right in the narrows, and under a mile away from the flak positions of the 703rd Battalion, in and around Villès-Martin. Behind him the columns of the fleet stretched back some 2000 metres into the misty darkness.

On the fo'c'sle of the *Campbeltown*, which from this position on was free to act independently, Bill Copland calmly waited for the fireworks to begin. 'On we sailed in that hushed river, ' he records, 'no sound save the steady beat of our engines and our own murmured conversation. I had told the No. 1 of the gun-crew ahead of me to concentrate his fire on enemy searchlights when the action started and all the time I could see the crew ahead of me, dusky movements, alert for the first glimmer of light, but controlled, knowing they were not to open fire until orders were given.

'Suddenly a searchlight flashed out behind us and, looking back, I could see the whole of our little fleet outlined against the dazzling white beam parallel to the water – a breath-holding moment, and then relief – the light went out – they had just, but only just, missed us.'

The sudden appearance of the brilliant beam was a nerve-wrenching moment for all. It marked the moment of decision for the German defenders, who finally accepted the existence of the force and took immediate steps to forestall it should it prove to be the enemy. Just as Ryder was passing the tower, Mecke put out the general signal '*Landegefahr*', indicating the opening moves of the Battle of St Nazaire. It was a warning to all the elements of the port and estuary defences that there was an imminent danger of a landing being forced and an instruction that all guns which could depress sufficiently should prepare to engage naval targets. On its receipt all those forces with a primary or secondary role as infantry were brought to an immediate state of readiness in accordance with the area's overall defence plan.

At 0122 the cloak of darkness, which had shrouded the 'Charioteers' for much longer than anyone might reasonably have expected, was finally ripped away. Initiated by searchlight 'Blue 1', a little inland from the guns on the shore and at Villès-Martin, clusters of lights on both banks, a few of 150cm diameter, but most of 60cm, pierced the night to flood the narrow neck of water with their brilliance. 'From that moment, ' writes Ryder, 'the entire force was floodlit. Each boat with her silvery white bow and stern wave was clearly visible, with the *Campbeltown* astern of us rising up above all the others. The glare of a disturbed enemy was on us.'

With the columns of boats now picked out as clearly as beads strung out upon a leaden plate, it was apparent that their free run had abruptly been brought to an end. However, Ryder still had a trick or two up his sleeve, having long planned to use his knowledge of German recognition procedures to buy precious extra minutes. This was the subterfuge for which Leading Signalman Pike had been brought on board the gunboat. As Ryder recorded:

'He was what at that time was known as a "headache rating". He could send and receive the Morse code in German. This opened up possibilities, and I prepared during the voyage out a signal calculated to confuse the enemy and cause delay in their opening fire, in addition to which we hunted out the signal in the International Signal Book for forces being fired on by their own side, the letter 'M' flashed vertically with an Aldis lamp. We had also been provided by Naval Intelligence with the call signs of the five German torpedo boats that had recently appeared on the west coast of France, and finally, and this I hoped would be the "ace of trumps", we had the challenge and reply pyrotechnics for each three hours of the day. Having decentralized everything else, I kept this part of the operation under my personal control, and Leading Signalman Pike remained at my side throughout the action.'

At 0123 right on the heels of their sudden illumination, they were challenged from the shore, not by a single station as might have been expected, but by two stations simultaneously – from the observation post on top of the Port Authority Office and from one of the battery positions on their port beam. Churning doggedly onwards, Ryder and Pike set out to hoodwink both.

Following Ryder's instructions implicitly, Pike told the harbour station to wait and then set about responding to the battery, feeding them a bogus call sign and then weighing straight in with a long, uncoded signal which claimed, 'Two damaged ships in company – request permission to proceed in without delay.' On receipt of this a number of the searchlights went out; however, they were then again challenged from the harbour. 'We endeavoured to pass a similar message, ' writes Ryder. 'While this was in progress, however, the force was fired on by light flak from one position. Fortunately I had laid great stress when I briefed the Commanding Officers on the importance of not opening fire too hastily and, at this moment, everyone nobly held their fire. In the MGB we played our last card and made the enemy signal for "a vessel considering herself to be fired on by friendly forces". Who the enemy imagined we were, I don't know, but the fire stopped and we gained a few precious moments.'

It was a staggering achievement for the force to have made it this far in without being heavily engaged. The signalling duel had bought them five invaluable minutes during which the lead elements had broken through to the point where they were now knocking on the door of the harbour itself. But the storm had to break eventually and, with the Germans finally deciding that they were indeed hostile, the guns surrounding them opened up.

In a last vain attempt to win more time, Ryder got ready to fire the signal pyrotechnics of which he had such great hopes. 'Finally, ' he writes, 'the time came for the "ace of trumps". This was to be my personal contribution. I fired the Very pistol in the air, hopefully. Alas, instead of sailing up into the air for all to see, it dropped miserably into the sea. The fight was on. The signal cartridges obtained in great secrecy were for use from our aircraft firing downwards. No one was to know what we wanted them for. So much for my ace.'

It was 0128 and the 'Charioteers' were only one mile from their target. However, Mecke and Dieckmann and all the others they had so successfully duped would from this point on exact a bitter toll for every yard they made of it.

11

Trial by Fire

When the storm finally broke around them about half of the 'Chariot' formation had made it through to the very throat of the estuary, at this point little more than a sea-mile wide. This was Mecke's own water, a clearly delineated 'killing ground', every inch of which was dominated by the quick-firing cannon of his three battalions. Almost a dozen searchlights flooded it with brilliant light and, although it was out of range of some of Dieckmann's coastal batteries, those that would bear continued to add their heavy shells to the unremitting barrage.

With tracer pouring in from every side, Beattie took *Campbeltown* up to more than 18 knots so as to make her more manoeuvrable under fire. Machine-gun bullets sprayed across her bridge and funnels and a larger shell penetrated the ship's office, one deck below the radio and chart rooms. Stoker Petty Officer Archie Pitt, in charge of the Forward Fire Control Party, was wounded in the blast, his place being taken by Leading Stoker Baxter.

On the point of returning fire, Beattie ordered that the German colours be replaced by British battle ensigns. This was a moment of high emotion for the soldiers stretched out on the deck below, who saw a dirty, time-worn flag break out above their heads and be almost immediately illuminated by a searchlight. Its job now done, the German ensign was torn apart for souvenirs, Donald Roy's batman, Gunner Milne, cutting off a strip for his flamboyant officer to carry throughout the ensuing action.

All along the dipping, swaying columns of MLs, colours proudly broke to mastheads as guns' crews and Commandos itched for the signal that would let them make an even fight of it. That signal came from *Campbeltown*, whose

Oerlikons blasted into action, hurling streams of coloured tracer towards the enemy. Immediately forward of the bridge Copland yelled, 'Let her go!' to the mortar and 12-pounder crews; almost before he had finished shouting, the waiting gunners had sent their first rounds shorewards, their contribution helping transform the old ship into a spewing wildcat, her sides alive with stabs of flame.

Freed from restraint the guns of the little ships joined in. 'All hell was let loose, ' writes Watson. 'The air was suddenly full of the deceptively slow-seeming sparkling arcs of the shells ... They were coming at us at point-blank range.' Standing right amidships he saw ML 457's bow and stern Oerlikons spit out their shattering reply, much to the discomfort of the Commandos stretched out beneath the muzzle of the after gun. Firing his Bren from the hip Tiger joined in the Mêlée, directing his stream of tracer at the nearest searchlight. 'When, by "hosepiping" the Bren my tracers were almost on the light, it was hastily switched off, ' he writes. 'But no sooner had I selected another than the first one would switch on again. It was frustrating.'

Kneeling down to change magazines, he caught a glimpse of *Campbeltown* doggedly surging ahead. 'She was a memorable sight,' he writes. 'Ploughing along, brilliantly lit up by searchlights, the British battle ensign streaming over her stern, she was now heading for the dry dock at full speed, her sides alive with the flashes of the shells that were hitting her continuously. It was a sight that I shall never forget.' Rising to fire again, a stream of shells crashed into the boat, punching large holes in the funnel right next to him. But despite the danger, Tiger felt only elation as he stood his ground and fired back.

Steaming ahead of *Campbeltown*, the gunboat prepared to clear the way for Beattie. 'It is difficult to describe the full fury of the attack that was let loose on each side, ' writes Ryder. 'Owing to the air attack, the enemy had every gun, large and small, fully manned, and the night became one mass of red and green tracer.' Fully exposed on the open fo'c'sle, Gunners Savage and Smith, under Chris Worsley's direction, stood to their pom-pom with iron determination, their gallant efforts soon to be all that remained of the gunboat's firepower; for with the after gun already silent, it would shortly be the turn of the .5" machine-gun turrets to be disabled by hits which punctured and drained their hydraulic feed pipes. It was fortunate that the forward gun was operated by hand; otherwise it too would have failed, leaving the lead boat helpless.

A little way out on her port quarter, the Hotchkiss on the foredeck of Irwin's ML 270 was popping away at the searchlights in the port ahead and on the northern shore. Able Seaman Jack Elliott was the layer, assisted on the night by Able Seaman Wally Evans, and Stoker Andy Porter, a stocky, twenty-six-year-old Londoner who had been with the boat since commissioning. Andy had seen the ensign run up on *Campbeltown* and remembers well how after this, 'Jack looked at me, and he said, "Jesus Christ! There's going to be all hell let loose in a minute!"'

The action having begun, Irwin had no further need of a 'sparker', which freed Ordinary Telegraphist Stewart Burkimsher to join the 'bunting tosser', Signalman Len Kelley, behind the torpedo tubes. Both were armed with stripped-Lewis guns.

'Everything opened up simultaneously, ' remembers Stewart. 'There was a terrific noise. To begin with I had a wonderful view of these bullets criss-crossing, a tremendous picture of colour and noise, and I was very very impressed with the artistry of it all, until they started hitting the ship. You could see them, and hear them hitting the boat. And my first reaction then was to get flat. The First Lieutenant suggested that I went forward to bring some ammunition back, and I said, "I'm not going through that bloody lot!" But of course, later we did.'

In the same forward station at the head of the starboard column Lieutenant Tom Boyd's ML 160 was similarly engaged, her 'Jimmy', Sub-Lieutenant Tait, controlling the fire of Leading Seaman MacIver's little Hotchkiss. During the run in Tom had filled his deck petrol tank with sea-water, laid out his medical supplies in the wheelhouse and rigged the emergency tiller just in case his Lockheed hydraulic system was pierced and drained. He had been quite apprehensive then, but now felt absolutely calm. 'This is a queer do, ' he is recorded as having said to his coxswain, Acting Petty Officer Leonard Lamb, during their approach. 'It will soon be a bloody sight queerer, Sir!' had been the reply.

Next in line behind Boyd was Billie Stephens' ML 192, with those of Micky Burn's people who were suitably armed supporting the fire of the boat's own gunners. Micky himself, who was 'very excited, and not in the least frightened, ' had only a Colt .45, and so could not join in; however, right forward, Fusilier William 'Dingle' Bell fired out from the hatch to the messdeck, while close to the stern Lieutenant Tom Peyton fired a Bren from the equally dubious shelter of the wardroom companionway. Positioned amidships, Fusilier Fred Penfold prepared for landing. He had originally been detailed to the Bren of Corporal Fisher, but during the passage his orders had been changed and his place had been taken by Fusilier Lenny Goss. Penfold was not to know it yet, but he would eventually owe his life to this unexpected change of duty.

Trailing Stephens was Ted Burt's ML 262, her guns firing to port across the boats of the other column. Laying her forward Oerlikon was Able Seaman Sutherland, assisted by the loading numbers, Leading Seaman McKeown, and Able Seaman Tommy Hudson; directing its fire was the 'Jimmy', Sub-Lieutenant 'Robbie' Roberts, who, although on the reserve as a paymaster, had signed on as an ordinary seaman when his call-up papers failed to come through quickly enough. After running through two pans, the gun began to jam, a problem which was to afflict it throughout the action, ultimately with tragic results. Despite frequent clearing and re-cocking it would continue to misbehave, even though no specific cause of the malfunction could be found. Similarly mystified was Stoker Len Ball, who was firing the twin-Lewis on the coach deck, aft of the bridge. These guns also kept stopping and would eventually have to be abandoned.

While much of the initial hail of incoming fire had been directed at *Campbeltown*, the German gunners quickly became more organized in their choice of targets. Although stunned by the ferocity of the wooden warships' initial response, to the point where there was a perceptible, if only tempo-rary, slackening in their rate of fire, they soon found the range and began to inflict the kind of casualties to personnel and damage to structures that such a small and fragile fleet could not withstand for long. The 'Charioteers' simply had not been given the firepower to dominate their well-emplaced adversaries, a point which was later made by Curtis, who pointed out that, while the German gunners were willing to fire shot for shot with the MLs' Oerlikons, they proved far more vulnerable to the gunboat's pom-pom, fired with great accuracy by Savage and Smith. Had the force contained more gunboats, then the impact of their heavier armament might well have swayed the balance in the raiders' favour.

Entering the arena at a time when the hornet's nest had already been well and truly stirred, the rearmost MLs suffered accordingly. Lance-Corporal Stanley Stevenson, on Fenton's ML 156, who was acting as No. 2 to the Bren of Lance-Corporal George Ewens, records that, 'Some MLs were milling about, others were on fire and in places even the water around them was on fire; there was wreckage, smoke, tracer and exploding shells. I could hear and feel our own ML being hit time and time again.' Sheltering behind a depth-charge, George kept the Bren firing constantly at targets on the southern shore. His high rate of fire ate up ammunition at an alarming rate, requiring Stevenson to bring up new supplies from below. During his forays into the ML's interior, he would have a chance to see at first hand the human cost of the action, as the wounded were brought down for treatment.

Up on the bridge, Fenton was standing with Captain Hooper to his left and Troop Sergeant-Major Tom Sherman to the left of Hooper, when a burst of shells slammed into the structure, the resulting spray of splinters sending them all to the deck in a heap. Fenton and Hooper were badly hit and Sherman was peppered with fragments which shredded the heavy leather holster of the Very pistol slung round his neck and deformed his fighting knife, but were not enough to stop him from moving about. His first thought was to look to Hooper. However, fearing that the explosives in his haversack might have been activated by the blast, he judged it more urgent to pitch these over the side with some despatch. Hooper's wounds were to the leg and blood was beginning to seep from his boot. He was carried below by Guardsman 'Taff' Lloyd and Corporal Prescott, both of Micky Burn's 6 Troop. Fenton carried on as best he could, eventually being forced by the weight of fire to order the Hotchkiss crew back to such shelter as they could find amidships. At this stage no thought was given to abandoning their run for the shore.

Heavily hit also was Falconar's ML 446 which, having caught up with the tail of the port column, was now almost abeam of Fenton, and directly astern of Henderson's ML 306. Sheltering with Captain Mike Barling, RAMC, behind one of the deck petrol tanks, was Lance-Corporal John Webb, who, along with Barling and Private Tom Everitt, would help staff the medical post proposed for the base of the Mole. Not having been made aware of the plan to fill the deck-tanks with sea water before engaging the enemy, John's interest was quite naturally engaged by thoughts of what might happen were they to be hit.

It was fortunate indeed that the medical team were on hand, for within minutes of returning the German fire ML 446 took a direct hit amidships. According to John Webb:

'The enemy, having had practice on the craft preceding us, were shooting accurately by this time, and, as a result, we suffered badly in that first burst of fire. Lieutenant Oughtred was badly wounded in the neck; Tom Everitt went to his aid and had to apply manual pressure to an artery to prevent him bleeding to death. He hung on desperately until Captain Barling was free to give his attention . . . I was called to Captain Hodgson on the other side of the main deck. He was evidently badly wounded. I found it difficult to see what I was doing even though a searchlight was full on us. We were in the deep shadow of the bridge. I could detect neither pulse nor heartbeat and when, feeling for his wounds, I had found more than a dozen entrance holes in his body I realized that there was no hope. He must have been hit by a burst of machine-gun fire and killed instantly. I turned my attention elsewhere.'

At the time of the hit Sergeant Robbie Barron had been potting at search-lights from a position amidships with a .55 Boyes anti-tank rifle. As a result of the explosion, he was hit in the thigh and foot by shrapnel. Lance-Corporal 'Ginger' Freeman, lying next to him was also hit, although both carried on regardless. Robbie was brought the news of Hodgson's death by Lance-Corporal Ivor Bishop, who also informed him that Lieutenant Oughtred had been very badly wounded. With both the officers knocked out, the leadership of this all-important assault group automatically trans-ferred to Robbie, who was himself in no great state, and to his fellow section sergeant, Jimmy Bruce. Having already been thrown out of position, these losses were a punishing blow indeed, which did not augur well for the landing: for it was a long way still to the Mole, and it was clear that the German gunners were only just getting into their stride.

By the time the rearmost boats were clearing Les Morées tower, the gunboat, almost a mile ahead, was closing fast on the harbour itself and on the *Sperrbrecher*, which was moored right in the path of the approaching columns. 'In the MGB', writes Ryder, 'we were heading close past the bows of the guard ship, probably one of the German flak ships and not above 200 yards away. This was our target. She opened fire from the top of her bridge with some light automatic weapon; perhaps we were too low for her other guns to bear; anyhow she only fired one burst. Our pom-pom instantly scored a direct hit on the gun position and plastered the ship from end to end. This ship, with her light camouflage paint and high structure, stood out clear in the searchlights and was easily the most conspicuous ship in the river. As we looked back over our shoulders in her direction, we were glad to see the enemy shooting at her and hitting her all over the place.'

Some way behind the gunboat *Campbeltown*, too, was closing fast on the smoke-shrouded harbour. The exposed signal platform having been vacated, Beattie, Tibbits, the coxswain, the quartermaster and other essential ratings were now clustered behind the hardened steel plating which encased the wheelhouse. Montgomery was there too, keeping out of the way of the sailors, but ready to act as the link between Beattie and Copland. It was from this protected position that the coxswain, Chief Petty Officer Wellsted, was steering the ship, following Beattie's every instruction as the resolute commander peered out through the vision slit. With Copland describing the ship as being 'in the centre of a bowl into which was being poured a veri-table hailstorm of illuminated fire of all calibres, ' *Campbeltown* was being hit repeatedly, the noise of the strikes and explosions mingling with the crack and clamour of her own guns, and of the mortars and Brens of the Commandos. Blades of brilliant light swept her decks and poured in upon the wheelhouse, blinding Beattie who cursed them just as the captain of Montgomery's ML had cursed the lights of Plymouth during 'Vivid'.

In spite of the weight of shells directed against her, all of *Campbeltown*'s vitals survived the onslaught. Her bridge and funnels were particularly damaged and the engine/boiler-rooms amidships were penetrated by smaller calibre fire which, while it did not affect the machinery itself, posed a lethal threat to the crew on watch. Chief E.R.A. Howard and E.R.A. Reay were required to remain at the throttle-valves throughout; otherwise, Warrant Engineer Locke instructed his men to take shelter along the centre line of the ship, in the safety of the space between the turbines and condensers.

Out on the open deck and despite the armoured shields installed to protect their recumbent bodies, the Commandos of the first parties to storm ashore were dreadfully exposed and soon began to take casualties. Lying behind the inboard screen on the starboard side, Lieutenant Stuart Chant recalls that there was 'a large report rather like the noise of someone banging a steel door with a sledge-hammer'. A shell had burst right next to Stuart, who continues, 'It was then that I realized that my left leg was wet and sticky and my right arm was spurting blood down into my hand . . . but by some twist of fate there was no pain, just discomfort. As I passed my tongue over my lips I tasted small particles of dust and a powder-like substance which had a sweet, sickly flavour of almonds – nitroglycerine – so close had we been to the epicentre of the shell's explosion. I then realized that my hands, which had been shading my tin hat over my eyes were also covered in blood, but again there was no pain, only a new-found stiffness in my fingers and numerous pinpricks in my face.'

Lying just ahead of Stuart, Lance-Sergeant Dai Davis was with the small protection party of Lieutenant Bung Denison. Denison was one of the two section commanders of Johnny Roderick's 3 Troop, Roderick himself and the other section commander, Second Lieutenant John Stutchbury, heading up the assault party sheltering behind the outer screen on the starboard side. Dai was thrown against the engine-room hatch by the force of the exploding shell, losing a lot of blood from shrapnel wounds to his right foot, left leg and thigh. Of the three remaining members of Denison's squad, the Bren-gunner, Fusilier Bill Mattison, was hit in the neck and Corporal Don O'Donnell believed he had been blinded, until Dai was able to convince him that it was only blood in his eyes. Private A.J. Elliott was untouched.

Just a little to the right of Dai and Stuart the remaining members of 3 Troop lying, with Roderick, behind the outer screen, also took casualties. Dai is convinced that it was the shell which hit him that also mortally wounded Lance-Corporal Jock Donaldson, who, despite a premonition, had been determined to carry on regardless. Donaldson was one of the four Tommy-gunners spearheading Roderick's disembarkation, the remaining three being Corporal 'Buster' Woodiwiss, Corporal Nicky Finch and the ex-Guardsman Lance-Corporal Arnie Howarth. It is impossible to say for sure exactly what force was the agent of Donaldson's mortal wounds, but Private John Gardner, who had just turned nineteen and who had lied about his age in order to join the forces, recalls that 'stuff was whistling all over. You could see the tracer going over your head. You could hear them banging on the steel plating. So I reckon [Jock] looked up . . . and just was unlucky.'

Lying behind Chant were the four Lance-Sergeants of his demolition team, Arthur Dockerill, Ron Butler, Bill King and Bill Chamberlain, all from East Anglia and drawn from the various Troops of 1 Commando. Tasked with demolishing the all-important workings of the pump-house, they were lying on their backs, feet forward, and with their heavy packs of explosives and detonators at their heads. A baker by trade, born in Foulsham in Norfolk, Lance-Sergeant Ron Butler had been particularly moved by the hoisting of the battle ensign and had watched with admiration the sailors in the Oerlikon bandstands forward of his position, standing to their guns in the face of all the fire that was streaming overhead, and being hit and replaced in their turn by others. He did not know of Chant's wounds, and only realized that Chamberlain, behind him, had been wounded when Chamberlain crawled forward, hit Ron and bellowed in his ear that he had been hurt in the shoulder and now would be unable to carry his heavy pack. Crawling forward through the awful din, Ron bashed into Bill King, told him what had happened and the two agreed that they would somehow have to get Chamberlain's pack off in addition to their own, as every ounce of explosive counted.

Lying just on the other side of the engine-room hatches, Bombardier Johnny Johnson of 5 Commando sheltered behind the port inner screen, right next to his officer, Lieutenant Christopher Smalley. Clad in his pre-war service dress, as opposed to the battledress worn by most of his comrades, he was taken aback by the sheer weight of fire being exchanged across the waters of the port approaches, which seemed to dwarf even the heaviest of the barrages he had experienced with the B.E.F. in France.

Against the zipping red and green streams, the protection afforded by the thin steel screens was mostly illusory, especially as the German gunners were now firing at point-blank range. Describing the scene that night as a 'satanic son et lumière', Lance-Sergeant Don Randall, tucked behind the outer screen with the rest of Donald Roy's kilted assault team, recalls; 'At my feet as I lay, a Bren-gunner of our group had been firing bursts. The clatter of his Bren stopped suddenly; edging back, I found him unhurt, but the gun had been knocked out of his grip by a projectile passing through his port. He righted the gun and started firing again, and worming forward to my place, I saw the jagged hole in the inner line of protection plating left by the projectile after it had passed over my knees.'

Elsewhere on the open deck the demolition control party for the Group Three tasks suffered a setback when Lieutenant Etches, of 3 Commando, was hit and put out of action. A veteran of the Vaagso and 1st Lofoten raids, who had attended Sandhurst with Corran Purdon, Etches had been scheduled to oversee the work of both Corran and Gerard Brett, at the northern end of the dock. Sprayed with steel splinters by shells coming in from the south bank, he was wounded in several places, including both legs and his right arm. In considerable pain and only marginally mobile, there would be no question of him playing an active role on shore, which left Montgomery in sole charge of the destruction of all the dry-dock-related targets.

Standing to the rear of the wheelhouse, Montgomery himself was slightly wounded by spalling, due to repeated strikes on the plating outside. This was the moment when the old ship, riven by enemy fire but nonetheless still surging onward, was at her most vulnerable, when damage to steering or turbines, or a heavy hit upon the bridge, could so easily have undone all the hard work that had brought her to this point.

Through the glare and smoke, Beattie saw a lighthouse dead ahead and, imagining himself about to pass the tip of the Mole, had the alarm bells rung to prepare the men for ramming; but it quickly became clear that the ship, far from approaching her target, had in fact strayed a little too far west and was now closing fast on the narrow cleft of water between the two outstretched arms of the Avant Port. Ordering the wheel put hard-a-starboard, Beattie took her on to a new course of 055° and, as she began to clear the solid stone mass of the East Jetty, a German searchlight fell for a moment on the slim pillar of the Old Mole light, giving the helmsman a perfect beacon for which to steer. Chief Petty Officer Wellsted had by this time been killed at the wheel and replaced by the telegraphman who, hit in his turn, fell to the deck and attempted to continue steering from this position using a gyro compass repeater installed for the purpose. Standing close behind, Montgomery instinctively moved forward to take over, but much to his relief the imperturbable Tibbits stepped in and, with a calm, 'I'll take it, old boy, ' grasped the wheel and held the old ship on course.

Some distance ahead the MLs of Irwin and Boyd engaged the defences in

136

Campbeltown's path, while the gunboat, having herself cleared the Mole, hauled round to starboard in a 360° turn to leave the way ahead clear for Beattie. On the foredeck of ML 270 Elliott's Hotchkiss, firing under the direction of the Australian First Lieutenant Bill Wallach, managed to put out a searchlight that was shining dead on *Campbeltown*'s bridge, right when Beattie and Tibbits most needed clear vision ahead, while Boyd's Hotchkiss gunner, Leading-Seaman MacIver, succeeded in knocking out the 40mm gun position M10, which was one of the group of four clustered on the foreshore immediately to the right of the dry-dock entrance.

Clearing the Mole by half a cable, Beattie altered course to port, Tibbits' steady hand bringing the ship round to 350°. With only 500 metres to go, they would ram in less than one minute and in spite of the pounding they were taking, nothing could stop them now. Their duty complete, the crew of the 12-pounder, which might well suffer damage in the upcoming collision, were withdrawn aft, which was just as well since, shortly after they had abandoned it, the gun was knocked out when a projectile exploded on the fo'c'sle, leaving a jagged hole across two-thirds of its width, and starting a fire in the Chief Petty Officers mess below. A little way forward of the wardroom the CPOs' mess was directly above the upper portion of *Campbeltown*'s main charge, which made all the more crucial the swift and effective response of the Forward Fire Control Party, now under Leading Stoker Baxter, whose members quickly brought the blaze under control. Amidst the barrage of shells of every calibre striking all over the ship, it may well have been this explosion right next to the gun mounting that wounded Corporal Beardsell at his post with the mortars and all but severed the leg of Lieutenant Johnny Proctor, leaving him stretched out on the port side, racked with pain and his kilt smouldering.

With only yards to go now and everyone braced for the collision, the destroyer dug her stern in and tore through the torpedo net protecting the approaches to the caisson, which, as the planners had hoped, was found to be fixed in its closed position. It loomed right ahead, a solid mass, dark against the paler concrete of its retaining walls. As she was not quite aligned for its centre, and in order to clear a path astern for the MLs running into the Old Entrance, Beattie ordered 20° of port wheel at the very last minute, so as to kick her stern slightly to starboard. 'We hung on like grim death to any projection, ' writes Copland, 'expecting a terrific shock, and then IMPACT! A feeling as though one had applied super-powerful brakes to a very small car ... The débris from the shock of our own impact fell all about our bows, sparks, dirt and planks seemed to be flying everywhere and from our bows poured a dense white smoke cloud.'

The moment of her immolation keenly observed by Newman, who was on the bridge of the gunboat circling off to starboard, *Campbeltown* hit with such force and precision that her fo'c'sle ran right up and over the top of the caisson, giving the commandos a perfect platform from which to disembark. Her stem and the structure behind it crumpled back for some 35 feet, leaving the huge gate in intimate contact with the concrete structure surrounding her explosive charge.

Up in the armoured wheelhouse, and apparently very little impressed by such perfection, Sam Beattie's somewhat taciturn response was to announce, 'OK, we seem to be there, ' and then to look at his watch and add, 'Four minutes late.'

It was 0134 and Beattie and Tibbits and the rest of *Campbeltown*'s crew could not have done better had they been given a thousand chances. Yet, in the best traditions of the Silent Service, Beattie would never admit to the sense of drama surrounding this great and important achievement that so many around him felt. In later years, and when pressed to describe the moment of ramming itself, the most that could be drawn from this brave and self-effacing gentleman was a laconic aside to the effect that, 'I suppose one did experience a considerable jar.'

The lights having failed at the moment of impact, there was initial confusion among the engine-room staff who, having received no order from Beattie to stop engines, sought to keep steam up in case further motive power was required. Seeing that the pressure was falling, Warrant Engineer Locke moved to the forward boiler room where, with the assistance of Stoker Petty Officer Pyke, and working by the light of a pocket torch, he got the oil fuel pump running, only to have it put out of action by a shell which came in through the starboard side of the hull. Locke then went to the after boiler room and flashed up the boiler there, which, in anticipation of difficulties, was already prepared with a full head of steam.

With *Campbeltown* being hit repeatedly, the order to abandon ship was withheld for a time, both to speed the disembarkation of Copland's Commandos and to keep her Oerlikons firing steadily in their support. Until they could be knocked out by the assault teams, the guns in elevated positions to port and starboard effectively dominated the whole caisson area and would have wreaked havoc on the ship's open decks, had the gunners' attention not been so split between the destroyer and the approaching MLs that they failed to realize what rich pickings lay right beneath their barrels. Copland himself was later to remark, 'During all this time a large amount of tracer was used by the enemy, and remembering its volume, it still seems quite miraculous to me that casualties to Commando personnel were not much heavier.' As it was, his men had been very well served by the narrow steel barriers of the deck screens and, during the run-in, had suffered disproportionately fewer casualties than their naval counterparts, whose dead and wounded were strewn about the middle portion of the ship. Surgeon-Lieutenant Winthrope was even now doing his best for the many wounded while they waited for transfer to the small boats.

'Thank God for well prepared charges,' had been Copland's first thought on striking the caisson, mindful as he was of the several tons of explosive lying just beneath his feet.

'And then a flood of questions passed through my mind. "Where exactly had we hit?" and "Can we get off from the bows?" I dashed through the smoke, round that beastly hole in the deck and found, in the clear light of illumination from German searchlights that, not only had we hit the dock gate centrally, but that we were actually clean through it with our bow sticking out over the dry-dock interior. I found Gough and his party and, having seen that they were busy getting the big iron-runged ladder into position, dashed back amidships: through the narrow doors, gangways and well-deck covered with many wounded sailors, a job to get through, and I had to be rather rough in dragging them out of the way where they lay across the path for my chaps coming off. "Sorry to hurt you, mate, but my chaps MUST get through here" and "for Christ's sake leave this passage clear". Eventually to the main deck and issued orders "Roderick off – Roy off."'

After which he returned to the fo'c'sle to observe, instruct and, where necessary, assist, an unflappable figure who, seeming not to notice the zipping bullets and shells, guided his boys along the cratered, débris-strewn foredeck and urged them quickly over the side and onto the timber roadway that ran along the top of the caisson.

Moving swiftly forward along the starboard side of a deck now slippery with blood, Roderick's party prepared to storm the series of gun positions that ran along the foreshore to their right, the closest of which was only a few metres from the eastern end of the caisson. Having rejoined his unit at the end of his stint with the mortars, Private Bill Holland clearly remembers the dying Lance-Corporal Donaldson asking not to be left, and himself replying, 'Don't worry. They are coming for you.' There was nothing else to be done.

Reaching the fo'c'sle, and having been directed round the crater by Copland, Roderick and his men found their ladders damaged, and used ropes to speed their passage onto the caisson. Then, Tommy-gunners to the fore, they moved fast towards the sandbagged emplacement that was their immediate target. Rushing across the intervening space, Roderick was up with Woodiwiss and Finch, when Lance-Corporal Howarth, who was just behind, called out that he had been hit and was told to try and make it back to Newman's HQ. Recalling the attack on the position, Woodiwiss writes. 'I hurled stun grenades into the bunker, forced my way through the entrance and, after emptying my Tommy gun into the crew, I wrapped my plastic charge around the breech of the gun and left immediately. I laid down flat alongside the outside blast wall and in seconds the charge exploded and detonated the ammunition like a firework display.'

With three more guns as well as a searchlight position still to be overwhelmed before the area could be deemed secure, time was very much of the essence; however, such was the speed and polish of this tiny band of men that, buoyed up by their superior training and by the intimacy of comradeship that so characterized the whole Commando organization, no task could be deemed beyond their reach. 'As a team we used fire and movement to an art form, ' recalls Woodiwiss, 'never leaving cover the same way that you took it, never having to look back as your buddy looked after that.'

Gun number two, which was position M70, sat on top of a powerful concrete structure directly east of the landing place and with a field of fire encompassing both *Campbeltown* and the seaward approaches to the Old Entrance. Accessible only by means of a wooden external staircase, but devoid of overhead protection, it was vulnerable to well-aimed grenades. Covering each other, the team closed on the position and bombed it into submission. The gun captain, who tried to descend the outer staircase, was killed, as were a number of enemy discovered within the structure's interior.

Johnny Roderick now led the party on to gun three, only to find it already knocked out, this position, M10, having been the one successfully engaged by Leading-Seaman MacIver's Hotchkiss. The gun crew, who were still inside the bunker, were killed, as were numbers of other defenders discovered in nearby huts. Splitting his men into smaller parties so as to clear the area more quickly, Roderick sent Second Lieutenant Stutchbury and Private Holland to search round a Nissen hut, Holland recalling that, 'We dealt with two Germans and rejoined the party.' Private Gardner meanwhile remembers dropping a couple of grenades into the air vents of a shelter as he passed by. Such was the sense of urgency surrounding the whole attack that there was no time to be other than brutally efficient, a process which Roderick himself found 'very difficult because it was all or nothing, and it was either them or us, so they had to be destroyed, which is a thing that I've never felt happy about.'

Using grenades wherever possible to save ammunition, the men swept on to eliminate the fourth and last gun, and thus wipe the enemy from the whole of the southern portion of the neck of land immediately east of the dry dock. Now in control of a slice of enemy real estate whose size they were only beginning to fully appreciate, Roderick's steadily dwindling team was faced with the task of holding it until released by Newman's signal to withdraw. With Donaldson dead and Stutchbury and Lance-Corporal Simpson joining Howarth on the list of wounded, it was no mean task that lay ahead for the survivors of a team which had at full strength numbered barely more than a dozen.

Rushing forward to *Campbeltown*'s mangled bow in tandem with Roderick was the kilted assault team of Captain Roy, now the party's only officer, with Proctor lying badly wounded on the foredeck. Sergeant Colin Jones was another who had not survived the run-in unscathed, although, despite his hurt, he was being assisted off the ship by his fellow Cameron Highlanders. Further swelling the casualty list was Private Hughie Cox, who would be left behind and later evacuated on Copland's order to the gunboat. Greatly inspired, as were so many, by Copland's apparent immunity from enemy fire, Private Arthur Ashcroft, who had been Johnny Proctor's batman since their time together in the Liverpool Scottish, followed Lance-Corporal Harold 'Aggs' Roberts along the port side of the ship towards where Tibbits and Gough were struggling to secure the ladder. Arthur, having reasoned that bombs would be more useful for street-fighting, was carrying, in addition to his Smatchett and Tommy gun, two gasmask haversacks filled with grenades.

On reaching the shattered foredeck, he rushed to the side of Proctor to see what help he could offer, only to be briskly ordered by Copland to 'Get off, Ashcroft! I'll look after him!' Passing the knocked out 12-pounder on his way to the bow, and weighed down by his load of grenades, he then fell into the smoking crater on the fo'c'sle and was momentarily disorientated, avoiding the flames, but managing to lose both his tin hat and his Tommy-gun. As he hung there in the noise and confusion, he was intensely aware of being right above the ship's main charge, whose tons of live explosives might, for all Arthur knew, have been set to go off at any time.

Also struggling forward was Lance-Sergeant Don Randall, who, having volunteered to help Donald Roy scale the walls of the pump-house, was carrying, in addition to his rifle and demolition charges for the guns on its roof, a long bamboo ladder, a rather terrifying solution to the problem of getting men up to gun positions 64 and 65, the closer of which could be clearly seen firing down on the ship. On reaching the bow and finding that

141

there was a slight delay in the disembarkation to port, he used his own scaling ladder to climb down onto the caisson, after which he was ordered to get it quickly across the open quayside to where the target loomed high above them all. On reaching the pump-house, he placed it against the wall with the assistance of Private Johnny Gwynne; however, when Gwynne tried to climb it, several feet at the bottom end broke away, the bamboo having been shot through while being carried the short distance from the caisson.

At this point, Ashcroft having somehow managed to extricate himself and rejoin, Roy's party began to work round to the rear of the pump-house, where they discovered the guns' crews fleeing for their lives down an outside staircase. On Roy's order the Germans were fired upon and a couple brought down. Having lobbed grenades onto the roof to deal with any remaining enemy, and preceded by Gwynne, Roy and Randall then rushed up to prepare both guns for demolition, Roy dealing with position 65, which directly overlooked the ship, and Randall attaching his explosives to gun 64 at the northern end of the roof. Randall was aware of being for this brief period in one of the safest places in all of St Nazaire. 'There was, ' he recalls, 'an atmosphere of quite extraordinary serenity and detachment from the hurly-burly below and around. The crisscross streams of coloured tracer not far above our heads seemed only to emphasize and bear witness to unreality.'

Having been placed so precisely by Beattie, *Campbeltown* was now so securely pinned to the caisson that only the successful firing of her main charge lay between the 'Charioteers' and the denial of the Forme-Ecluse to the Reich's most dangerous warships. Watching his young Commandos dash from either bow, and hearing the gunfire and explosions that marked their rapid conquest of the nearby guns, Copland was therefore witness to a triumph in the making, which only required the destruction of the remaining Group Three targets to be complete. Preparing to send his demolition and protection squads out into the bridgehead so speedily secured for them by Roderick and Roy, he had no way of knowing that his success was being balanced out by abject failure at both the other landing places. Only on reaching Newman's HQ on his way to conduct the 'withdrawal' would he finally learn of the suffering of the small boats as they tried to reach the Mole and the Old Entrance in the face of withering enemy fire, and of the loss of so many young soldiers and sailors amidst the flames and despair of the river.

12

Not Without Honour

Having escorted Beattie all the way up to the caisson, Irwin's ML 270 now stood off to draw fire, while Boyd's ML 160 set off up the Loire in search of two 10, 000-ton tankers which were believed to be somewhere in the port.

Observing Boyd's departure, the crew of the gunboat, having almost completed their long turn to starboard, were now facing downstream to where considerable activity could be seen in the waters surrounding the Mole. The *Sperrbrecher*, in spite of her earlier pasting, had come to life again and was adding her contribution to a weight of enemy fire which was playing havoc with the Group One and Group Two MLs. Ryder's immediate response was to rush to the MLs' assistance, however, Newman was equally determined to be put ashore without delay, so that an HQ could be established before Copland's parties came streaming back across the bridge at 'G'.

Having been stress-free up to this point, the relationship between the two Force Commanders now fell foul of a dispute over whose immediate wishes should be granted precedence. With the gunboat's radio having failed, the only way for Ryder to neutralize the threat of the *Sperrbrecher* was to search out a 7th Flotilla ML and order her to torpedo the German ship, which action would keep Newman away from the fighting on land. Whereas, were they to run straight into the Old Entrance, then Ryder would be denied the opportunity to intervene at a point where he might well be able to tip the scales in the attackers' favour. After a hasty argument, Newman won his point and Curtis was ordered to effect a landing. At this stage Ryder was able to console himself with the belief that his diversion would only be a temporary one; however, once inside that narrow cleft of water, he would become so involved with *Campbeltown* that in the event he would not rejoin his ships until long after most had already been over-whelmed.

Altering course continually to avoid the enemy fire, Billie Stephens' ML 192 was the first boat of many to be hit and destroyed by guns which were largely impervious to the fire of the launches' puny Oerlikons. Close enough to be in the way of the hail of shot and shell that was missing the destroyer astern, she entered the port with all guns blazing and with Micky Burn's Commandos mostly spread about the deck amidships, primed and ready for landing. From his exposed position right up on the bow, Ordinary Telegraphist George Davidson was firing his heavy stripped-Lewis in bursts, despite being blinded by searchlights and almost deafened by the ear-splitting crack of the forward Oerlikon. Down in the darkened wheelhouse Leading Telegraphist Jim Laurie could only speculate on the boat's chances of survival as the noise outside grew steadily louder and louder. And up on the coachdeck those of the Commandos who were suitably armed, including Fisher and Goss on the Bren, added their staccato chatter to the swelling, enveloping cacophony.

Directed by Sub-Lieutenant Richard Collinson, the after Oerlikon had also been busy, putting out a searchlight on the jetty and then giving the *Sperrbrecher* a thorough battering as she was passed to starboard. Racing to clear the Mole, they managed to make a further 300 metres before being hit by a series of missiles which, within seconds, transformed what had been a living warship into a flaming wreck, her mid-section littered with dead and wounded. Richard remembers:

'We were hit on the waterline under the bridge, port side for'ard, by some-thing pretty big, which sort of rolled her over considerably and knocked her engines off beat for a second, and all the water splashed down on us on the after gun. Another shell landed plumb in line with us amidships and went off with a hell of a crump, about 50 yards short; then another one hit us on the port quarter and jolted us badly; and then the next thing was this one that hit us in the engine-room, and that was just one big woof, which stopped the engines – they were turned right off; it blew the port side of the engine-room out, and the deck off, and we started blazing furiously.'

In his position on the starboard side of the coachdeck Fusilier Fred Penfold was slightly injured in the buttock by splinters from the last shell; however, Fusilier Lenny Goss, who had replaced him on Corporal Fisher's Bren, was killed instantly, along with Fisher, when the deck was blown from beneath them.

M MTB 74, modified for attacking the battle-cruisers at Brest.

H The Director Tower of HMS *Tynedale* on the afternoon of 27 March, 1942.

43. St Nazaire, 1992: Survivors parading from the 'Chariot' memorial to the Hotel de Vill
1. Michael Burn, MC; 2. Col. T. Sherman, OBE, VRD, DL; 3. R. J. Barron; 4. Major
General C. W. B. Purdon, CBE, MC, CPM; 5. E. L. D. Chappell; 6 Lieut-Col. R. K.
Montgomery, MC; 7. W. C. Clibborn, TD; 8. W. Wallach, DSC, VRD.

Down in the wheelhouse Jim Laurie could see that the engines had stopped and shouted up the voice-pipe to the bridge, where Stephens was almost having to scream to make himself heard above the din. The steering had also gone, which meant that the ship, slewed sharply round to port by the force of the shells, but still maintaining a considerable forward velocity, was now running out of control towards the Old Mole and the narrow flight of stone steps which ran down beneath the lighthouse to the sea.

As they cut across the bow of Platt's ML 447, Micky Burn saw in the steps a chance to make a landfall. Ordering the Commandos on the foredeck to 'Follow me when I jump!' he waited until the blazing boat slid past the base of the steps and then thrust himself forward, splashing into the water some way short of his target. With the gap widening rapidly, Lance-Sergeant 'Boy' Harrison was denied the opportunity to jump; however, Lance-Corporal Arthur Young did make it to the steps where he was fortunately able to grasp the sinking Micky by the hair and pull him to the shore. Sitting there, totally unaware of being soaked to the skin, Micky saw the body of his good friend and section commander, Lieutenant Tom Peyton, come bobbing past in the water; however, no attempt was made to pull it in. Micky, who since the beginning of the action had been surprised by his own lack of emotion, remembers only 'having this extraordinary feeling of heartlessness when he came floating past us.'

Crashing into the Mole, ML 192's starboard side rode up the sheer stone wall before settling back and coming to rest below the pillbox. Though her bow was raised only momentarily, Able Seaman Lapsley and one other sailor, believed to be Ordinary Signalman Hale, somehow managed to scramble up the face of the Mole, Lapsley surviving to take shelter in the lighthouse, his companion unfortunately being killed.

In the moments before she began to drift away the boat listed slightly to starboard, causing her mast to cant over toward the stonework and presenting George Davidson with what looked like an opportunity to take a line ashore. 'I climbed the mast, ' he writes, 'to the point where I could see two Jerry heads peeping over the parapet of the flak tower. Since they did nothing about it I assumed they were as frightened as I was. I descended in a hurry, realizing that the list had been insufficient for my purpose.'

Watching George's antics, the Coxswain, Acting Petty Officer Hugh McPhail Bruce had been attempting to fight the fire with the boat's extinguishers, all of which had been damaged by shell fire. With something like 2000 gallons of petrol on board, it was only a matter of time before she blew up, and so, as she drifted along the line of the East Jetty, Stephens gave the order to abandon ship.

With the wounded put into Carley floats, the remaining men, with the exception of Collinson's party on the stern, took to the water and struck out for the quayside, about 70 metres away. Jim Laurie was momentarily trapped when he found the wheelhouse door jammed on trying to climb up to the bridge. And just before he got off over the bow Fusilier Penfold exchanged his last words ever with 'Boy' Harrison, who walked across the deck to him, said 'You all right, Penny?' and received the reply from Penfold, 'Yeah, I'm OK, Sarge, ' after which he was never seen again. Helping to launch the port Carley float, George Davidson also jumped over the bow, joining the struggling mass of survivors swimming for the shore.

Among the last to leave the doomed ML was Stephens himself, who stood right up on the bows and had a last swig of whisky from his flask, before lowering himself into the freezing river. After what seemed like an eternity he arrived with the others at a ramp up to the quayside. It was the 'Jimmy', Sub-Lieutenant Haighton who pulled him clear and, after a short period of rest, he was sufficiently recovered to lead the seven or eight survivors in an attempt to make contact with friendly forces ashore.

Having lost their weapons, the party were therefore incapable of resistance when confronted by a group of Germans. As they were marched away, Jim Laurie for one found it very hard to come to terms with the fact that he was now a POW – a new and undesirable status which George Davidson was determined to avoid. As they passed a clump of rolls of wire netting, standing on end, about two metres high, George slipped between them, his absence going unnoticed by their captors. So far, so good; however, as the conflict ebbed and flowed around him through the long, cold hours of darkness there would still be the problem of how and when he should make his solitary bid for freedom.

With Tom Peyton and so many others of 6 Troop dead or wounded, Micky Burn might have been forgiven for thinking that he could no longer make a useful contribution to operations far to the north of where Lance-Corporal Young had pulled him ashore. However, as an officer imbued with a strong sense of duty, not pain, nor loss, nor even the sheer impossibility of all that lay ahead was enough to dissuade him from pressing on, regardless of the odds. Young having been wounded in the foot and Micky armed with no more than a Colt and a hand-grenade, the latter therefore mounted the steps alone, dealt with a German he encountered on reaching the top and pressed shorewards, past the solid concrete masses of the two German pill-boxes. As he dodged past position 63, he was aware of being seen and of thinking that it was 'too easy' for the people in it and 'I'm a sitting duck'; nevertheless, despite being shot in the arm and upper thigh, he successfully made it into the gloom of the Group One area, the only man of his team to do so, and with the bulk of the dockyard still to negotiate before reaching the bridge at 'M'.

Micky having cleared the steps up to the lighthouse, they were quickly put to use by Sub-Lieutenant Collinson's small party, which included both the after Oerlikon gunner, Ordinary Seaman Hallett, and his loading number. Stationed on the after part of the blazing 192, this group had failed to pick up Stephens' order to abandon ship and, seeing no sign of life elsewhere on the boat, had decided to make for the tip of the Mole, about 20 metres north of the transom. Slipping into the icy water, they struck out for the steps only to find themselves under fire from their own MLs, which were plastering the stonework with gunfire. On reaching the steps Hallett was killed and Richard Collinson felt the shock of a bullet rush close past his head as he climbed.

At the top of the steps Collinson decided to remain for a time in the shelter of the space between the lighthouse and foremost pill box where, unseen by the Germans, he could watch the struggle of the Group One MLs, while his men joined Lapsley inside the lighthouse itself. Safe behind its stout walls an attempt could at last be made to tend the wounded, including Arthur Young, whose injured foot was dressed, and Able Seaman Burd, who had had a shell splinter go in through his buttock and pass right through his body to lodge under the skin of his groin.

With ML 192 destroyed, the force had all too quickly been deprived of both its Senior Officer MLs and such troops as had been detailed to support Pennington's and Jenkins' demolitions in the area of bridge 'M'. Following directly behind, Ted Burt suddenly found himself promoted to column leader and, carrying only the lightly armed demolition team of Lieutenant Mark Woodcock and his tiny protection squad under Lieutenant Dick Morgan, ML 262 now looked like being the first boat to attempt a landing in the Old Entrance.

Whereas, by virtue of seeking to put their men ashore so close to *Campbeltown*, the boats of this column might reasonably hope to find friendly forces already in control of the dockyard, no such luxury would be available to the MLs of Platt's flotilla, who right from the outset had been faced with the prospect of storming the Mole unsupported. Even allowing for the restrictions in numbers carried, an arrangement might have been included in the plan for the Group Two landings for some troops to move south to the Mole and assist Platt by attacking its defences from the rear; indeed Hooper's 'Special Task Party' was already under orders to check out possible gun positions on the foreshore immediately to the north of it; however, no such arrangement was ever made. In spite of the crucial importance of this powerful feature, its capture therefore lay entirely in the hands of the two small assault teams of Captains Birney and Hodgson, a meagre force at best whose impact had already been dramatically reduced by the transfer of Hodgson's party to ML 446, right at the tail of the line.

Carrying what was now the only party with the strength to seize and hold the Mole, Platt therefore entered the harbour at the head of his column, knowing full well that the four boats behind him carried only lightly armed troops, the success of whose demolitions depended almost entirely on his ability to put Birney's boys ashore. With Lieutenant Chambers controlling the fire of the for'ard Oerlikon and Sub-Lieutenant MacNaughton Baker, in charge of the after gun, he therefore took ML 447 towards her daunting target on a course that would leave the *Sperrbrecher* on their port side.

Being well-armed, Birney's boys were spread about the deck doing all they could to support the naval gunners. Numbering fourteen in all, and drawn from 2 Troop of 2 Commando, they were about as representative a cross-section of ages and backgrounds as could be found on any boat of the fleet. A much admired officer, formerly a solicitor, David Birney, in the command of this all-important team, was supported by Lieutenant Bill Clibborn. The senior NCO, Troop Sergeant-Major Ted Hewitt, was a window-dresser in civilian life. Sergeant Eldridge was an engineer and Lance-Sergeant Garland a furnace-man. Lance-Corporals Heather, O'Brien, Garrett and Patterson were, respectively a roundsman, a compressor driver from Eire, a wood-worker and a grocery assistant. Lance-Corporal Taylor's profession is not recorded. Private Rowe and Guardsman Bob Grose were carpenters. Guardsman Lewis was a salesman as was Guardsman Walton. Of these fourteen, only six would live until the coming dawn.

As one of the lead boats, ML 447 was a primary target for the enemy gunners, who, by the time she had hauled round to port to make for the slipway, had already knocked out both her Oerlikons, killed Chambers and killed or wounded most of Birney's Commandos. To all intents and purposes finished as a fighting ship, she nevertheless persisted in her attempts to come alongside, only to run aground even as MacNaughton Baker prepared to take a bow rope ashore. Under fire from Germans on the Mole itself, from the gun at the base of the Mole and from the cluster of guns to the east of *Campbeltown*, Platt decided to try and manoeuvre instead alongside the steps which led up to the lighthouse. Going full astern to pull the boat off, he had just rung down for full ahead when 447 was hit in the engine-room by a heavy shell which knocked out both engines and set the compartment ablaze. Helplessly drifting south with the tide and with all thoughts of landing

148

abandoned, Platt now turned his attention to saving his ship and those who remained of his and Birney's men, in an atmosphere which, in spite of their parlous state, was devoid of panic. With this one punishing blow the assault capability of the port column had effectively ceased to exist, and just as with the boats of the starboard column, the responsibility for effecting a landing now lay in the hands of troops neither trained nor equipped for the purpose.

Promoted to second in line by the earlier loss of Briault's boat, it was Collier's ML 457 that followed Platt into the harbour. Almost home now, her frail structure riven by hit after hit, she ran close by the *Sperrbrecher*, adding her personal contribution to the extensive damage already meted out by the lead boats. To Tiger Watson 'she seemed to be listing with great holes visible in her hull. There was also a small fire, and we were close enough to hear hoarse screams from her interior. I gave a couple of short bursts to the upper deck in case some ill-wisher up there fired down on us. Then we were past and heading for our landing at the Old Mole. I put down the Bren and prepared to land.'

Shielded by the bulk of the Mole from the piecemeal destruction of their column leader, Platt's failure to get Birney in went unobserved by the soldiers and sailors of Collier's boat, who therefore assumed their success, a conclusion which was reinforced by the perceived capitulation of German forces on the Mole itself. As they ran up to make their turn to port, Watson 'saw some German helmets bobbing along the skyline. I quickly reached for the Bren that was leaning against the funnel. I could not miss at that distance. I dropped it quicker than I picked it up as I had seized it by its red-hot barrel. Having retrieved it I now saw that the owners of the coal-scuttle helmets were running along the Mole towards the town in a ragged single-file with their arms raised.'

Reinforcing this suggestion of surrender was the sighting, as they themselves ran in towards the slipway, of Platt's ML 447 which, briefly glimpsed, gave the appearance of having backed away from the landing place after, presumably, landing her troops, all of which must surely mean that the Mole was safely in British hands. In the last hurried seconds Tiger had time only to be aware of more screams, this time coming from another ML which was blazing furiously some way off to starboard, and then, with a final surge from her Hall-Scotts, Collier brought them sweetly alongside the slipway.

A line was quickly taken ashore as the demolition men shouldered their heavy packs and shook themselves out into their landing order. One by one they passed by the bodies of Sub-Lieutenant Hampshire and the crew of the forward gun, and set foot on the shore of France, Watson's party first, followed by Walton, with Pritchard's men bringing up the rear. They were a mere fifteen out of the eighty-nine Commandos scheduled to land at this point, and perhaps for their peace of mind it was just as well they did not know they were alone and would remain so. Collier had solemnly promised to be waiting for them when their work was done; however, the sight of several burning hulks already drifting in the river did not seem to augur well for any prospect of a safe withdrawal.

With time so short, Tiger led the parties on to the Mole. Whatever may or may not have happened prior to this, the orders for every group were to ensure that the Mole was taken before pressing on into the dockyard. Convinced, however, that he had seen its defenders surrendering, his belief that it was already safe in British hands was only reinforced when he found it apparently deserted. Right above the slipway stood position No. 63, a pillbox which must have been only recently constructed if the smell of fresh cement was anything to go by. A ladder leaned against it, by means of which Tiger climbed up to the embrasure and fired a burst or two through it with his Tommy gun. A grenade tossed in for good measure might have been desirable, but just at that moment Pritchard shouted, 'What the hell are you up to, Tiger? For God's sake get on!'

Climbing hurriedly down and totally unaware that in moving forward he was returning the Mole to the control of a grateful enemy, Tiger therefore led the three teams towards the distant bridge at 'D'. It was here that the advancing soldiers were seen by Gérard Pelou who, making his way back toward the Santé Maritime, had only minutes earlier glimpsed *Campbeltown* scrape past the tip of the Mole. Ahead lay the coverless rectangle of the Old Town Square, separating the confusion of sheds and warehouses on their right side from the compact mass of the Old Town on their left. It was an area which should have been swept clean for them, but of the assault troops tasked with its clearance there was, perplexingly, no sign to be seen.

Faced with the prospect of working completely alone, the men therefore moved warily into the square, only to be met by a group of excited civilians. '*Dedans vite! C'est les Anglais!*' yelled Tiger; however, as his verbal exhortation seemed to have no effect, he attempted to make his point more clearly by firing a short burst over their heads. This demonstration was also ignored until underlined by a second burst, this time into the road at their feet; then they scattered quickly enough. 'I felt a brute,' recalls Tiger, 'when one youth who, in the uncertain light looked remarkably like my brother Bob, skipped away with a polite, "*Oui, oui, M'sieu!*"'

As well as scattering the well-meaning civilians, Tiger's bursts of fire encouraged one group of Germans to run out of sight down an alley. Pressing on, a second group were encountered who, when he ordered them to put

150

up their hands, responded instead with a tossed grenade. Tiger threw himself down; then 'another grenade exploded close to my left side, half-stunning me and setting my ears singing. "Two can play at that game!" I thought, for my British No. 36 Mills grenades were much more lethal than the German "potato mashers". But I was disconcerted to find that the last "potato masher" had burst open my haversack and scattered my bombs. I was also now being fired upon by a machine gun from somewhere behind me. I vainly scrabbled about, groping for those elusive grenades with my left hand, but this resulted in another burst of machine-gun fire clanging into a metal litter bin fixed to a lamp-post above me. The bullet holes stood out all too clearly in the light from something afire somewhere and were uncomfortably close to my head. Not wishing to be riddled like the litter bin, it seemed wise to withdraw.'

The advance having stalled at this point, Tiger ran quickly back. The empty expanse of the square was now being raked by several well-sited machine guns and it was only too clear that their chances of crossing it alive – especially where those weighed down by up to 75 lbs of explosives were concerned – were slim indeed. Lieutenant Philip Walton had already given it a go, although his team had not dared follow him. Seen to fall by Corporal George Wheeler, his imagined demise only served to reinforce the danger. Joining up with the remaining members of Walton's team behind the shelter of some railway trucks on the square's northern side, Tiger was dismayed to hear of the supposed fate of his friend. He called out Philip's name, but received in reply only another burst of machine-gun fire. He turned to speak to Lance-Sergeant Dick Bradley; however, Bradley, shot through the lung, fell to the ground badly wounded.

Free to operate quite independently of the other two teams, Pritchard's Demolition Control Party passed by at this point. In the flickering half-light, Corporal Bert Shipton came upon Bradley, lifted his head, checked for signs of life, assumed he was a goner and passed quickly on. Corporal Ian Maclagan later reported having seen two men *hors de combat* as he rushed by – more than likely Bradley being treated by Tiger who was injecting the stricken man with morphine from one of his tiny syrettes. The bullet had entered Bradley's chest, passed through his lungs and exited below the shoulder blade. He wrote of this episode, 'And so, with the effect of the injection and the enormous loss of blood, I gradually lost consciousness. My thoughts were with my mother rather than of dying.'

Watson, too, was hit. He was in the process of straightening up from the recumbent Bradley when he received a heavy blow on his left buttock. His bloodied trousers were warm and sticky, but at least he could still walk. Their present position was clearly untenable, yet a rush to better cover would mean leaving Bradley behind. Of course their orders had anticipated just such a quandary and resolved it in favour of the many. So Bradley was pulled beneath a truck, following which the others moved quickly into an alley on the north side, taking shelter there in the lee of a shed.

Pritchard's men, meanwhile, had managed to reach almost to the very edge of the New Entrance, at which point he and his four corporals sought shelter behind a small concrete hut just short of bridge 'D'. The firing was just about continuous now and the comforting shadows were being systematically ripped apart by brilliant avenues of light cast out by the oscillating searchlights. There was a urinal somewhere nearby and bullets could be heard pinging as they tore through its thin metal sheeting. Of the troops due to land from the other boats there was still no sign. They were five: they had made it and they were completely alone.

To their immediate left was the glimmering expanse of the Bassin de St Nazaire and in the corner formed by its junction with the New Entrance lay two small tugs moored against the quayside. Ill-armed though they were in a fighting sense, the men still carried their charges, and Pritchard was determined to make use of them. Along with Shipton and Maclagan, he ran to the boats, boarded them and hung charges below the waterline. The igniters were pulled and the three then ran back to the others. The charges went off with a roar shortly thereafter, the ensuing hissing inrush of water a satisfying advertisement to the thoroughness of the job they had done.

In the absence of support there was little more that could be achieved by this small team, and so Pritchard proposed to split his force into two. He and Maclagan would work south around the Old Town perimeter in a desperate search for any other teams, while Corporals Shipton, Deanes and Chetwynd would remain by the bridge and do such damage as they could to it with charges singularly ill-suited to the destruction of such a massive structure.

Back at the Mole, and having already shown great resolution in putting his three Commando parties ashore, Lieutenant Tom Collier was equally determined to be there to take them off again, just as he had promised during the voyage across.

Directly attacked by Germans who appeared after Watson's men had moved on, ML 457 quickly became the target of small-arms fire and tossed grenades, against which her crew could muster little in the way of an effective reply. A grenade landed inside the bridge itself, severely wounding Collier in the leg and killing or wounding nearby members of the crew, after which the ship was pushed off and steered into deeper if only marginally safer waters further up towards the Old Entrance. As she pulled away,

ML 457 was hailed by Richard Collinson who had seen the boat come in and disembark her Commandos. But his only reply was to be shot at, after which he allowed himself to be persuaded by his men that he would be much safer inside the lighthouse itself. As the survivors of ML 192 then settled down to await developments to the tune of glass shards tinkling down from above, Collier continued to manoeuvre his ship so as to be ready to meet his Commandos again, a courageous officer whom neither wounds nor danger could sway from keeping his word.

Next to attempt a landing, and the last boat in Platt's column to even come close to reinforcing Watson, Walton and Pritchard, was ML 307, with Lieutenant Norman Wallis, RANVR, in command, and Sub-Lieutenants Leo Clegg and John Williamson as First Lieutenant and Third Officer respectively.

Even more poorly equipped than Collier to mount an effective assault, Wallis carried only the small demolition party of Captain Bill Bradley, whose job was to destroy the centremost lock gate in the New Entrance. The childhood friend, whilst still in India, of Lieutenant Corran Purdon, Bradley, who was going into action with a cavalry trumpet on his back, had come to No. 3 Commando from the Royal Inniskilling Fusiliers. Supporting him were a mere six other ranks, four of whom were drawn from his own Commando; completing Wallis' passenger complement were Edward Gilling the journalist, and Captain David Paton, RAMC, who was packed and ready to help staff the aid post planned for the base of the Mole.

Approaching the structure at some 18 knots, Wallis could see Collier pulling off into deeper water, Stephens' boat burning to the waterline and Platt's 447 drifting southwards towards him past the tip of the Mole. On fire amidships, Platt's boat was clearly finished; indeed at that precise moment he was arranging to put his wounded off onto a Carley float, before ordering the remaining Commandos to swim to the shore, an order which only David Birney, Bill Clibborn and Troop Sergeant-Major Hewitt were in any fit state to obey. Having seen what was waiting, Platt attempted to warn Wallis as he sped past that a landing was now impossible; however, Wallis pressed on regardless towards the point where he could turn into the landing slip with every gun blazing, including all the light machine guns which, in anticipation of the danger posed by German bombers high up on the Mole itself, had been moved across to the port side.

His Asdic skills no longer required, Able Seaman Don Croft was acting as loading number to Able Seaman Bert Butterworth on the forward Oerlikon. Now, as Wallis began to nose toward the slipway, Don got ready to take a line ashore from the bow, only to feel the boat run aground just past the steps at the tip of the Mole, and just far enough out to make a landing attempt impossible. As 307 stuck there, her Asdic dome buried in the mud, a German soldier in a position close to the lighthouse began to bombard them with grenades, only to be engaged both by Captain Bradley and by Stoker Geordie Allen. From his position amidships, Captain Paton 'turned round to see what was going on and saw [Bradley] falling off someone's shoulders. He had been trying to get a Bren gun up to fire over the angle of the Mole by standing on a soldier's shoulders. He assured me that he had killed a man, but the recoil made him fall to the deck.' The bomber, whose missiles had fortunately missed, had indeed been killed, as were a number of his compatriots, falling from view behind the low stone wall which lined the whole upper surface of the Mole.

As Wallis attempted to back out of his predicament, the surge of 307's screws had the effect of swinging her stern in towards the landing steps, presenting Ordinary Seaman Stan Roberts with an opportunity to step ashore with a stern rope. However, with bullets hitting all around and chips of stone bouncing on to the ML's deck, his little corner of France proved less than welcoming. The Mole was still very obviously in enemy hands and Bradley possessed neither the numbers nor the weapons to take it. Not only that, but they were now also being closely engaged by gun position No. 62, which sat on top of the very building Paton had hoped to use as his aid post.

After a hurried consultation with Bradley, Wallis decided to clear the area before his boat also became a flaming hulk, and so Roberts was recalled and they began to pull away from the grip of the mud, the Asdic dome breaking off as they moved astern. One of Platt's Commandos was seen in the water and pulled on board with the help of Don Croft's line. Shortly thereafter a voice called out from the water, this belonging to David Birney, who had taken the plunge from Platt's boat together with Clibborn and Hewitt. Paton somehow managed to get hold of Birney's outstretched hand; however, just then 'the boat's propellers gave a great surge in reverse and our hands were torn apart because of the oily water.'

As Wallis cleared the danger area with the intention of engaging the lights and guns on the far side of the estuary, Don Croft returned to the forward gun, arriving just as a shell burst inside the bandstand. Don was wounded slightly in the back, though not sufficiently to prevent him taking full control of the Oerlikon after Bert Butterworth, who was hit in the leg by shrapnel, was taken below in terrible pain. Don would continue to act as forward gunner while 307 worked her way back towards the estuary mouth.

In the run-up to the Mole Sub-Lieutenant Leo Clegg had been wounded in the throat by shrapnel and had had his wound dressed by ratings not directly involved in fighting the boat, including the Telegraphist, Pat St G. Barry, who was helping load Oerlikon magazines down on the messdeck. Later it would be Pat's job to transmit, in plain language, a signal confirming that Wallis was leaving the estuary. In spite of all the action, the boat had sustained only two serious casualties, these being one of Bradley's Commandos shot through the right side of his chest, and Butterworth, whose wound was on his right thigh just above the knee. Having been treated by Paton, the wounded were put on Neil Robertson stretchers until such time as they could be moved to the more sophisticated facilities of the escort destroyers.

For David Birney, left astern in the freezing water, the struggle for life intensified as the strong pull of the receding tide kept him from reaching the shore and dragged him instead towards distant Villès-Martin. By the time he finally reached shallow water, he was in a bad state and died shortly thereafter from a combination of wounds and exhaustion.

Separated from David on taking to the water, Bill Clibborn also fell victim to the strength of the current, just as did Troop Sergeant-Major Hewitt and just as would so many other exhausted men during the remaining hours before daybreak. Already hit in the arm by shrapnel, Bill was in the water for at least 30 minutes before finding bottom and struggling up on to the Boulevard Président Wilson. With not a soul in sight he crossed over to where 'a little Frenchman' was peeking out. 'He soon twigged that I wasn't going to help his cause any more, ' recalls Bill, 'and I shot off in among some houses; I remember there was a stable. I didn't know what was happening at all. I was eventually rounded up by some German sea cadets and I thought they were going to shoot, but they didn't.'

Stripping himself of all his equipment, Hewitt struck out for the shore which, though tantalisingly close, seemed to come no closer in spite of all his efforts. A strong swimmer, he nevertheless found his strength fading fast, and, in extremis, was supported in his fight for life by a vision beside him of Christ walking upon the water. Guided and renewed by this experience, he began to swim again and eventually made it to the sheer concrete wall of a quayside. Hauling himself to the top by means of an iron ladder, he was captured immediately by a waiting group of the enemy.

Missing the Mole entirely was Platt's own ML 443, temporarily under the command of Lieutenant Horlock, RNVR. As a 'spare' Commanding Officer, he had been able neither to peruse the model of the port nor to become fully familiar with all the German defences. Unaware that the pill-box by the lighthouse contained a searchlight and blinded by the glare of other beams, he therefore confused the Mole with the eastern breakwater, a mistake which prompted him to believe he was much further south than was actually the case. Running right past his target, he therefore crossed the starboard column's line of approach and sailed on up the river until the gantries lining the dry dock were seen and recognized to port, in which direction he immediately turned, his intention still being to effect a landing as ordered. It was then that he and Lieutenant Verity saw the Mole silhouetted quite a long way to the south. It was a discovery that sparked some wry comment to the effect that their achievement thus far was little reward for all the effort that had gone into bringing them safely past the German guns.

Undamaged as yet, Horlock therefore set off along the reverse of his previous course. All his guns were still firing, with Sub-Lieutenant Peter Royal supervising the fire of Ordinary Seaman Frank Folkard's after Oerlikon and the Third Officer, the South African Lieutenant Shields, fulfilling the same role with Sam Hinks on the forward gun.

Immediately aft of the bridge wings, the twin-Lewis mountings were also in action, with Ordinary Seaman Joe Clayton in charge to starboard, and Ordinary Telegraphist Jim Hayhurst in charge to port. A twenty-two-year-old from Blackburn, Jim had earlier volunteered to take a gun up the mast in order to gain the height necessary to fire directly on to the Mole. Fortunately he would never be called upon to so expose himself to the enemy as, closing the Mole on his way back to the heart of the action, Horlock would soon find that, having missed his original chance to come alongside, a second was not about to present itself in a hurry.

With Group One's situation becoming more parlous by the minute, the fifth boat in line, which was Lieutenant Ian Henderson's ML 306, did actually manage to pick out the Mole and turn towards it; however, the approach was found to be blocked by the burning, drifting wreckage of his predecessors. With the demolition teams already queueing up below, Henderson then manoeuvred in the waters north of the Mole while he decided, in conjunction with Lieutenant Ronnie Swayne, whether another landing attempt should be made elsewhere. With his boat as yet undamaged, but with German fire thick in the air, the nearby Old Entrance seemed no more attainable than was the Mole. Desperately anxious to be put ashore, Swayne thought it might be possible to put the men off somewhere along the rocky foreshore which was now under the control, more or less, of Johnny Roderick's boys, but Henderson knew nothing at all of the navigational hazards involved and in the event the decision was taken to make a run for the open sea. With the boat still in every respect a fighting entity, this did not go down at all well with the Commandos, who, following their own belligerent agenda, were not so concerned as was Henderson with the operational responsibilities of his diminutive ship of war. As they turned away from the action Des Chappell records that, 'We were bloody annoyed about it. We knew what we had to do and we wanted to do it!' Even more galling was the fact that they could see behind them the flash of explosions on shore which showed that some at least were doing their jobs: 'And here *we* are, ' records Des with a bitterness half a century has not served to assuage, 'going bloody home!'

Last of the troop-carriers to try for the Mole, and far from emasculated by the loss of both her Commando officers, was Dick Falconar's ML 446: however, Falconar, just as had been the case with Horlock before him, failed to pick up the structure, with John May rushing to the bridge with the news that they had run right past it. Instead they pushed on up river to a position abeam of the dry dock, reversing course at this point with the intention of trying again. But Falconar too would return only to find the situation at the Mole so deteriorated as to make any landing impossible. This spelled the end of the Group One attempts to take the Mole and hold it as the point of later withdrawal. Only one boat and a mere fifteen Commandos had succeeded in coming alongside. It may well have been the displacement of Bertie Hodgson's fighting troops that finally tipped the balance away from success. But in a plan so fatally flawed from the outset, no cold calculation of military probability could ever have rated its chances as better than slim at best.

Sailing northwards through the firestorm, the boats of the starboard column were destined to fare little better as they fought to reach such shelter as the Old Entrance quaysides might provide. Passing to the right of the *Sperrbrecher* and seeing Stephens' boat burst into flame only half a cable in front of them, the men on board Lieutenant Ted Burt's ML 262 expected that they would now be first to try for the landing places. However, Burt was also quickly knocked off his course, firstly by being forced to starboard to avoid the *Campbeltown* as she suddenly altered to clear the tip of the Mole, and then, as he increased speed to close up the line, by having to take violent avoiding action to shake off the lights that were threatening to make a present of his ship to the same guns that had just put paid to ML 192. When he came back under control, it was to find that, primarily because of these manoeuvres, he had lost his station on *Campbeltown*, missed his turning and was now running northwards up the river itself. Reducing to 8 knots, Burt then nosed inshore, avoiding a dredger at anchor, until he was able to confirm his position, after which he turned short round and opened fire on ships on the stocks. The recalcitrant forward Oerlikon chose this point to jam yet again and, reporting to Burt on the bridge, Sub-Lieutenant Robbie Roberts

157

went aft to seek the assistance of Sub-Lieutenant Hills. Preparing to make his way south again, Burt then encountered the ML of Lieutenant Eric Beart, next in line in the starboard column, who had followed him up past the turning point. Replying to Beart's, 'Where the hell are we?' by loud hailer, Burt passed on their position, after which he took ML 262 up to 12 knots and set course for the mouth of the dry dock, still intending to put Woodcock's and Morgan's Commando parties ashore.

The lead having worked its way steadily down the line, the honour of being first to shape a course for the Old Entrance now devolved upon number four in the column, this being Lieutenant Bill Tillie's ML 268. Tillie's was the boat to which Petty Officer Sam Wallace had been assigned when the members of the Weymouth Base Staff were added to the force. She carried a party of seven additions to Newman's HQ reserve, and two parties of five briefed to operate up by bridge 'M'. Lieutenant Harry Pennington, with four other ranks, was directed to blow up the bridge itself, while Micky's Lieutenant Morgan Jenkins, plus four others from 6 Troop, were to provide them with cover.

Petty Officer Wallace had always believed that things would turn out badly, his thoughts being shared both by Harry Pennington and by Lance-Sergeant Bill Gibson, and their fears were quickly proved right when the boat was heavily hit and set ablaze some way short of *Campbeltown*'s stern. Her petrol tanks ruptured, she blew up shortly thereafter, killing half her crew and almost all of the Commandos she carried. Tillie survived, but not his 'Jimmy' or Third Officer, and nor was Sam Wallace listed among the handful to survive the conflagration. Pennington too was dead, along with all of his team. Morgan Jenkins, whose only fear was of the water, was reported as having said, 'Well, I suppose we're for the drink, ' before he was gone and with him all his boys from 6 Troop, including both Bill Gibson and his pal Peter Harkness. Of the seventeen soldiers only two, Lance-Sergeant Knowles and Lance-Corporal Parkes, managed to make it to shore.

With Tillie gone and Burt and Beart still up by the building slip, the unfortunate starboard column was suddenly down to boat number five, the already wounded bird that was Lieutenant Leslie Fenton's 156, and still no one had managed to penetrate into the landing place. Working her way past the Mole, she had continued to plough on in Tillie's wake. Guardsman 'Taff' Lloyd, returning to the upper deck with Prescott, after carrying the wounded Hooper below, got in the way of a burst of flak and collected some splinters in his leg as he pitched head first down the forward hatch. Able Seaman Harry Morgan who had begun the action as part of the Hotchkiss crew, but was now firing a stripped-Lewis from behind the shelter of one of the torpedo tubes, was another to be hit by splinters as the tube was struck.

Abreast of the Mole Fenton could see MLs from Platt's flotilla burst into flames. Then two of Platt's tail-enders crossed his bows and forced him to order 'hard a-starboard!' Increasing speed, he took his boat round fully 360° and ended up back on course for the Old Entrance, though with Rodier in ML 177 now off his port quarter, instead of some way astern as had been the case before. In the flickering light Rodier himself could be clearly seen standing on 177's bridge.

At this point a burning ML, which was probably Tillie's, exploded, and amidst the shell-bursts and flashing tracer, Fenton thought he saw the with-drawal pyrotechnics go up. In great pain he summoned Sub-Lieutenant Machin, his First Lieutenant, to the bridge and, as a landing seemed all but impossible, told him to take over and follow the other boats out, after which he collapsed and was made as comfortable as possible between the torpedo tubes. Having just assumed command, Machin almost immediately found himself in the middle of a furious crossfire. He gave the order to make smoke, right after which the steering was knocked out. Reducing speed in the hope of getting a torpedo shot at the *Sperrbrecher* which, newly active, was now the prime agent of his ML's undoing, both Hall-Scotts failed, leaving the boat adrift on the river with neither direction nor power.

Sending men aft to rig the hand-steering, Machin was then hit as he moved aft of the funnel. In spite of the pain, he nevertheless climbed down to the engine room to see what could be done there. Shrapnel having pierced the water-cooled exhaust pipes, the compartment was filled with steam, in the middle of which, despite splinter wounds in the eye and legs, Leading Stoker Thompson worked unflaggingly to get the least damaged engine back on line. Troop Sergeant-Major Tom Sherman was yet another who climbed down into the shambles to offer Thompson help. Tom recalls how one engine was completely covered in foam and how Thompson was working on the other one, the starter whirring impotently as it refused to light up. He also recalls thinking, 'Why doesn't he try cranking it?', an idea which did not survive the realization that each great motor put out a solid 600 horse-power. Thompson finally did succeed in bringing the starboard engine to life, although, in order to prevent it from stopping again, it had to be kept going full ahead. With the port motor finished, this arrangement, allied to the use of tiller steering, made the boat all but unmanageable.

Fenton, having regained consciousness, was taken below to have his wounds dressed and to be dosed up with morphine, and, after a hurried consultation with the wounded Hooper and Machin, the decision was taken to make for the open sea. The Germans had by this time decided that ML

159

156 was finished and had transferred their fire to other boats; however, when the smoke float was ditched to cover their withdrawal, the enemy gunners opened up on it. Fenton then relieved Machin for long enough to have the First Lieutenant's wounds dressed, returning below deck when Machin was in a fit state to take over once again.

Running through the gap between the East Jetty and the *Sperrbrecher*, Sub-Lieutenant Mark Rodier's ML 177, with Fenton pulling out of line to starboard, suddenly found herself promoted from last in line to first, at least in respect of making a straight run for the landing places. Thus far spared the toll of dead and wounded that was common coin amongst her fellow craft, she ran a little past the turning point, but then came quickly round to be the first ML in the starboard column to disembark her Commandos as planned. Coming alongside the southern quay at the full height of the tide, Troop Sergeant-Major George Haines and his thirteen men from assorted troops of 2 Commando were able to step ashore. First and foremost it was their job to check on the gun-sites, which it was believed might be in action along the seafront between their present position and the Old Mole; and it was in this direction that Haines now led off, his party trailing behind him in Indian file.

The catalogue of disasters that had thus far been the story of the starboard MLs having taken only a handful of minutes to enact, ML177 in fact entered the Old Entrance only shortly before Curtis completed his long swing out to starboard and came in to land Newman and his men. He placed the gunboat alongside a timber jetty on the narrow anchorage's southern face and, after a poignant handshake with Ryder, the Colonel was quickly over the side with the rest of his HQ team, his boots at last firmly planted on the soil of France.

Privates Murdoch and Kelly, their Tommy guns at the ready, were first ashore, followed, writes Newman, 'by Stan and I, with Sergeant Steele and the wireless set just behind, Terry, Walker and Harrington bringing up the rear.' This was the order in which they moved quickly up the road parallel with the Old Entrance lock, towards the tall building close by the southern end of bridge 'G' that had earlier been selected as the site of their HQ. 'There was no sign of any of our other troops,' the Colonel continues, 'but I fully expected RSM Moss and the reserve had safely settled themselves in and around the HQ building. We didn't take long in coming up to the building and I went round to try to find an entrance. I don't know who was the most surprised when on turning the corner of the building I literally bumped into a German. Before I realized who or what he was, his hands were up and he was jabbering fifteen to the dozen. I called up Tony Terry, who asked him

160

in German where he'd come from. He had just come out of this building, which was a German HQ. "Are there any more of you inside?" "Yes, " "Well, go in and tell them to come out with their hands up." In he went, but almost at once the entrance to the building became very unhealthy. A quick-firing gun from a vessel in the inner Bassin had seen us and was firing at point-blank range, something like seventy yards away. We had to beat a hasty retreat.'

Fired at by ships inside the Bassin de St Nazaire, by the guns on top of the U-boat pens and the 'Frigo' and by the batteries on the far side of the river, whose salvoes roared across to burst above their heads, the small HQ team could not survive for long without help from someone. Newman expected Alan Moss to be the agent of such deliverance; however, Moss and the reserve were still on board their ML, waiting for Lieutenant Beart to regain the Old Entrance, and in fact it was the unflappable Troop Sergeant-Major George Haines and his party, coming into HQ reserve after finding the seafront batteries to be non-existent, who saved the day. Haines had a two-inch mortar which he proceeded to set up in the open and, despite the miscellany of projectiles of all calibres stitching the air around him, used it to lob shells right onto the roof of the U-boat shelters opposite. Successful, at least temporarily, in silencing the enemy fire from that particular quarter, the HQ party were able to move forward again. After throwing a number of grenades inside their intended HQ, Newman then took up a position close to the base of bridge 'G', in which he could wait for the Group Three parties to come streaming back.

Crucial to the success of the whole withdrawal plan was the role of Sergeant Ron Steele, who had opened up his radio set on landing. Positioned close by his Colonel and oblivious to the movements and dangers surrounding him, he now set about trying to contact any outlying station, whether on land or on board the MLs, switching alternatively to 'call' and 'receive', and using the previously agreed call signal 'Biko' to 'Biko 1, 2, 3, etc'.

Having personally ensured that all sets had been netted whilst still in Falmouth, Ron was greatly disturbed by his failure to elicit a response. Despite his best efforts, he could not make contact with any other station, even including Fyfe. Range was certainly not a problem, particularly so in the case of the nearby gunboat, which led Ron to conclude that the primary factor contributing to the continued silence must be the failure to have included a sufficient number of expert operators in the force right from the start of training. The men had been available and, considering the number of extraneous personnel for whom places were found at the very last minute, there had certainly been room for them. However, with the exception of

Fyfe, none had been added, as a result of which parsimony Newman was now cut off completely from the rest of the force.

Isolated from both Ryder and Verity, the Military Commander therefore continued to believe that MLs would be available to ferry his men back home, when, had he but known of the failures at the Mole in time, he might have been able to prepare an alternative plan to save what he could of his retiring forces.

Continuing his attempts to make contact throughout the whole period of Newman's sojourn by bridge 'G', Ron Steele would enjoy no success whatever in ending the perplexing silence and the true situation affecting the Group One and Group Two landings would remain a mystery until such time as the Commandos' first sight of the blazing hulks on the river supplied them with answer enough. Fortunately, however, it did not require a wireless to hear of Major Bill's successes, for, clinging onto their tiny HQ perimeter, the crash and thunder of the Group Three demolitions came to Newman and his men from the north, echoing across the flame-reddened waters of the Old Entrance.

13

A Storm of Fine Men

By the time of Newman's arrival on the shore of France the pattern of the Group One and Group Two assaults had already settled itself into one of almost total failure, mitigated thus far only by the landings of Lieutenant Collier and Sub-Lieutenant Rodier.

Of the non troop-carrying boats, Tom Boyd was giving a good account of himself up by the building slips, while Irwin's ML 270 was currently circling out of control in midstream as her crew struggled to set up the tiller steering, her hydraulic system having just been drained by a hit on the stern. Almost the last boat in the formation, Bob Nock's ML 298 was running up past the dry dock to fulfil her secondary role of drawing fire and engaging enemy lights and guns in the river abeam of the oil tanks; while, bringing up the tail, Micky Wynn was making his way up towards the Old Entrance, eventually to come safely alongside Curtis's gunboat. During the final approach the courage and resolution of Chief Motor Mechanic Bill Lovegrove had been yet again put to the test when a shell bursting in the engine room had peppered his right leg with splinters and knocked out the centre Packard. With his stokers looking after both wing engines and in spite of great pain, he was now working tirelessly to make good the damage and restore for his Captain the full turn of speed which was MTB 74's only real defence against the enemy.

A sorry tale all round, the story of the small boats was punctuated by flames, smoke, shattered hulls and shattered bodies, presenting to all who could see a tableau of dramatic visual impact; however, Newman was out of sight of its despairing message and for Copland, the lurid scene was but a backdrop to the task in hand, partially glimpsed, but existing in a world apart from the clusters of crouching, stumbling, soldiers who passed by him *en route* to *Campbeltown*'s crumpled bow.

Making his way amidships after the successful disembarkation of Roderick's party and Roy's, Copland heard a voice call out, 'Major Bill! Major Bill!'; however, crossing the deck to where the gravely injured Proctor lay bleeding profusely, he could only say, 'Hang on, John, I can't stop now but I'll come back to you as soon as I can,' before it was time to call the remaining parties forward. Having got these moving, he ran into Bob Montgomery at the foot of the ladder to the bridge and, after quickly discussing the situation, the sapper Captain also went over the side, accompanied by his Tommy gun armed bodyguard, the Southern Rhodesian Sergeant Jameson of 9 Commando.

A total of seven parties rose up from the deck, or emerged from below, on Copland's command, with Lieutenant Denison's battered team at the head of the resolute men who quickly reached out from the destroyer to seize and hold the area surrounding the inner caisson. This party should have disembarked as a unit, but the wounds to Lance-Sergeant Dai Davis and Fusilier Bill Mattison meant that Denison and Private Elliott went over the side first, to be followed later by the others. 'We were busy sorting ourselves out, ' writes Dai. 'Pain and blood everywhere.' It took a few minutes to convince Don O'Donnell that he hadn't gone blind and wipe the blood from his face. 'I told him to catch up with Bung, ' continues Dai. 'Bill Mattison and I were in a pretty dazed state. I managed to get him going in front of me, and I was the last to leave. I managed to pick up the yoke of Bren magazines and encouraged Bill forward. Somehow we scrambled down the bamboo ladder. Thank God Mr Hopwood was holding the bottom. It was slipping and we would have gone in the drink.'

Pushing northwards, while to their left rear Donald Roy's men completed their destruction of the pump-house guns, Denison and Elliott met and quickly overcame the first direct challenge to their presence when they were fired upon from a rooftop. Employing both Tommy gun and grenade to lethal effect, they then swept on to overcome the more serious resistance presented by a group of enemy concealed in a trench, whose fire wounded Elliott in the leg before Denison could take them out. With Don O'Donnell by now rejoined, and Davis and Mattison struggling together in the rear, Denison then moved up to the caisson itself. It was here that the two wounded men finally caught up with their officer. While Denison, Elliott, O'Donnell and Mattison, retaining the Bren, set to securing the immediate area in preparation for the arrival of Purdon and Brett, and in spite of a jagged lump of steel embedded in his right instep, Dai then set off alone to search a group of huts close by bridge 'M'.

Having remained at the top of the companionway throughout the run-in, with an excellent view of the 'astonishing amount of metal' that was pouring in upon the *Campbeltown*, Sergeant Frank Carr, upon receipt of the signal to lead his men off, whistled Burtinshaw's party up from below deck, whence they emerged shouldering their heavy packs. Twenty-three-year-old Private Denis Edwards, a Dunkirk evacuee prior to joining 5 Commando and, along with Lance-Corporal Stokes, trained to enter the caisson by means of a manhole, found upon arriving on deck that it was 'raining bullets'. The amount of fire coming in was indescribable. He kept his head down and moved towards the bow through the 'sheer bedlam' of it all. Copland ordered him forward and forward he went, – past the wrecked 12-pounder and past the wretched Johnny Proctor who wished them 'all the best' as they went by.

Gerard Brett's and Corran Purdon's parties also emerged from the bowels of the ship into the actuality of a nightmare which until that moment had only been heard and felt.

Making their way up from the port side of the wardroom, and Corporal 'Cab' Callaway having come out from under the bookcase that had fallen upon him at the moment of ramming, Corran's four corporals found themselves surrounded by a dreadful cacophony that was underscored by multi-coloured streams of flashing tracer. Shouldering their packs, they too joined the stream of men making their way along the port side of the ship to where Tibbits and Gough, alternately laughing and swearing, struggled to keep the ladders in place. Corporal Bob Hoyle's reaction to the tumult was to wonder how anyone could survive a single minute, particularly Copland, whom Bob describes as 'marching up and down, giving orders out as though he was just on the parade ground'. Moving past Proctor, Bob was caught out by the ragged, downward turning edges of the crater on the bow, and fell partially into the smoking hole, only to be held up by his rucksack and hauled back onto the deck. Unknown to him at the time, he had picked up traces of phosphorus on his uniform trousers.

Emerging from the starboard side of the wardroom, the men of Brett's party had to make their way across the deck in order to get off the ship. Rounding the bridge structure, Corporal Bob Wright, a twenty-three-year-old Sapper from Binton in Staffordshire, saw a flash of light and felt a sledgehammer blow as a shell-splinter smashed into his knee and lodged beneath the patella. He dropped to the deck in great pain, breaking his blue recognition lamp in the process. In spite of what was a crippling wound, he nonetheless pressed on with his job, somehow hauling himself over the side and on to a bamboo ladder, which he went down 'hand over hand, because my leg was hurting like hell. And I sat on the deck immediately beyond the ladder and pulled out a field dressing because the blood was running down my trousers and sticking.' Sitting there he heard Brett calling his name and, making his way over, Bob ran into Jumbo Reeves, with whom he was supposed to enter the inner caisson's interior in order to place charges on the machinery inside. 'I just reported to Brett and said that I'd got hit and he said, "Are you all right?" I said, "Oh, yes", and Reeves said to me "Come on, then. We'll go!" '

Making their way into the shelter of the pump-house, Corran Purdon's team gathered breath before setting off for their winding hut. It was at this point that Cab Callaway said to Bob Hoyle, 'Your trousers are on fire' – an illusion provoked by the smouldering phosphorus Bob had collected on *Campbeltown*'s deck. Aware of a burning sensation, Bob took them off, preferring to go through the rest of the action trouserless. He did, however, have a long, blue knitted scarf that hung well down, adding a splash of colour to the white of his legs. When later taken prisoner and with no other solution presenting itself which might explain his strange appearance, the Germans would simply assume that Bob was Scottish.

Following behind Brett, Corran led his men at a trot along the western edge of the dry dock. All around them was the incessant din of cannon and machine-gun fire. To their right the vast dark cleft of the dry dock embosomed the tankers *Passat* and *Schledstadt*, whose crews would eventually work up the courage to fire on the Commandos from their rear; and to their left, starkly lit by the strobing flashes of explosions, loomed a disparate litter of buildings, whose narrow alleys harboured parties of the enemy. On the way north Corporal Johnson was hit quite severely; however, it was not enough to stop him and, dressing the wound himself, he continued with the others to the winding hut.

Of the teams disembarking to undertake operations around the outer caisson, Lieutenant Hopwood's party were over the side in time for Hopwood to be holding the ladder when Dai came down from the ship; the parties of Smalley and Chant were not far behind.

The five members of Smalley's team for the south winding hut went off in style; all, that is, except Bombardier Johnny Johnson, one of the three Johnsons working on the winding huts both north and south. Emulating both Ashcroft and Hoyle, Johnny was yet another who had problems negotiating the crater, slipping part way into it, yet somehow managing to extricate himself. He, too, remembers evidence of a phosphorous-like material on the steelwork. Climbing down a bamboo ladder which broke beneath his weight, he joined the remaining four members of his party on the caisson and off they went along the camber towards their target.

Struggling to his feet despite his wounds and shouldering his heavy pack, Lieutenant Stuart Chant led his men towards the bow, past the wounded in the midships section and past Johnny Proctor too, whose appeals for help had perforce to be ignored. Moving forwards Stuart also fell part-way into the crater, being saved from dropping further by the bulk of his pack. Dragged out by his men, he then led them down the vertical ladder to the caisson. With Chamberlain already wounded, Stuart's small party, in need of every man and every ounce of explosive to fully destroy the pumping machinery, had to manoeuvre both wounded man and pack across the deck, over the side and on to their target, but somehow they managed to do it. Moving ahead, Lance-Sergeant Ron Butler was encouraged by Copland, who 'put his hand on my shoulder as I was staggering past and said, "Just another scheme, lad?" And I said, "That's right."' Moving forward too was Lance-Sergeant Bill King, who looked upon this as one of the hardest parts of the whole operation; nevertheless he was not frightened, because "we'd been trained so well it was almost automatic. We did the job. You knew where you were intended to go; you got there and you did it. It's only afterwards you thought, "How the hell did I get out of that lot?"'

Brought along for the purpose of demolishing the outer caisson should *Campbeltown* somehow fail to get in, the party of Burtinshaw had rather been robbed of a purpose by the brilliance of Beattie's seamanship. With the ship so securely impaled, it was immediately obvious that the caisson's fate was sealed, in which case there was no point in Burtinshaw's full inventory of charges being attached to it. After a hurried consultation Montgomery therefore ordered Bertie to take his men to reinforce Brett. At this point Private Jimmy Brown, who had earlier been seconded to the sapper Captain from Bertie's party, was still full of hope that he might after all be allowed to see the raid through with his friends. But this was not to be, for on Montgomery's instructions he was instead given the task of blowing holes in the sides of the outer caisson – the reason being that, with the structure full of water, the violence of *Campbeltown*'s explosion would be greatly enhanced.

Following behind Purdon and Brett, sporting his usual monocle and still wearing Beattie's cap, Bertie, whom Corran clearly remembers humming, 'There'll always be an England' as he stood upon the dockside, therefore led his party north towards the place where destiny had decreed his life would end. Bringing up the rear, Denis Edwards and Lance-Corporal Stokes swapped last position. It was when he was last that Edwards was hit in the thigh by a bullet, a wound which did not prevent him from pressing on.

Up in the area of the inner caisson Burtinshaw's men would add some much-needed weight to a Commando representation already seriously weakened by the loss or capture of all the Group Two parties briefed to operate around bridge 'M'. With the loss of Tillie's ML, Pennington's demolition party had gone, as had Morgan Jenkins' protection team. And with the loss of Stephens' ML 192, all the assault troops needed to ward off German attempts to interfere with work on the caisson had also been killed or taken prisoner, save, of course, Micky Burn, who was even then wending his solitary way northwards, dodging in and out of the cover of buildings.

It was through the window of one such building that Micky saw a group of the enemy and decided to let them share a grenade, which he prepared by pulling out the pin, though for the time being retaining his grip on the lever. After a moment's reflection, he decided instead to let them pass and then move on to bridge 'M'. Only after a delay of some minutes and as he was walking along the dockside did he remember that the live grenade, kept from exploding only by the continued pressure of his grip, was still in his hand, and tossed it away into the nearby lock. Only too well acquainted with the fate of his own men, Micky knew nothing of the loss of either Pennington or Jenkins, and so arrived by the two tall flak towers in the expectation that their teams would appear eventually. The structures were surprisingly elaborate, built rather along the lines of guard towers, but also containing sleeping quarters. Fortunately they turned out to be unoccupied. He climbed up to the top of one and took away some uniforms just in case they might prove useful later; but with neither explosives nor incendiaries there was nothing he alone could do to destroy them, his attempts at setting them on fire proving futile. There was nothing for it but to wait and hope that Pennington and Jenkins would still arrive to save the day. Meanwhile Micky could not help but notice the potential of this isolated corner as a possible means of escape should things go badly for the attacking forces later.

Having held back the order to abandon ship until such time as Copland had completed his disembarkation, Beattie now instructed his crew to prepare the *Campbeltown* for scuttling, clear all below-deck spaces and make their way to the Old Entrance. Down in the engine-room, to which Leading Stoker Frank Pritchard had returned to assist the crew on watch, steam was finally shut off and water introduced into the ship's interior through the seacocks, condensers, circulators and any other means that could be found. To add to the weight of water already pouring in from these mechanical sources, the scuttling charges were also activated, the direction of this particular task

168

being the responsibility of Mr Hargreaves, the Gunner(T).

Leaving the bridge and making his way down to the main deck, Beattie decided that the wounded warranted a means of disembarkation that would be kinder to them than the route over the fo'c'sle and across the open quayside. Accordingly he tried to hail an ML to come alongside the stern just at the time when Ryder, similarly minded, ordered Curtis to take the gunboat alongside Rodier's ML 177, from which position, with the boats bridge-to-bridge, he instructed Rodier to take off as many as he could of *Campbeltown*'s crew and then make his way out to the open sea. As Rodier brought his ship around, Curtis was then instructed to put the gunboat alongside the northern quay, port-side-to, it still being Ryder's intention to go ashore and satisfy himself that all was well.

Positioning ML 177 alongside *Campbeltown*'s port quarter, Rodier took off some thirty men, including all of the destroyer's officers as well as a number of naval and Commando wounded, whose treatment was continued on board the ML by Surgeon-Lieutenant Winthrope. Nigel Tibbits was there, as was the First Lieutenant, Chris Gough, Mr Hargreaves the Gunner (T) and Warrant Engineer Locke. Helping in the transfer of the wounded was the Gunner's Mate, Petty Officer Newman, who had directed the fire of *Campbeltown*'s Oerlikons during the run-in. Beattie himself joined this party, having satisfied himself that his ship was clear, most of the remaining crew having by this time got off over the fo'c'sle.

Too occupied with warps and keeping the ML's propellers clear of the torpedo net to notice precisely how many men were crowding on to her deck, Sub-Lieutenant Frank Arkle recalls that the destroyer was still being fired upon during the transfer and that she was sinking by the stern. In spite of the enemy fire, ML 177 was, however, still substantially undamaged and at 0157 hours she began her run for the open sea, working up to close on 20 knots.

Still fully concerned with clearing the ship of his Commandos, including his own party of Corporals Jack Cheetham and John Beardsell, Lance-Corporal Jock Fyfe and Private Gerry Hannan, Copland quickly reached the stage where only the wounded were left. He was not aware of the disembarkation of *Campbeltown*'s officers on to Rodier's boat and so went looking for Beattie to tell him that all the troops were clear except the wounded. Of his abortive search he recalls:

'First to the main bridge – a shattered mass of twisted wreckage; up higher to the top bridge – no sign of Beattie. Down again and aft, calling his name. I ran into a party of sailors carrying more ladders for their own disembarkation, but could get no information from them concerning him. Time was flying and my job only half done, and I visualized troops returning to the Old Mole to re-embark, and I, whose second task was to organize and control the re-embarkation – missing, so I turned to searching the ship for wounded. I managed to get them, including John Proctor, over the side and sent them down with sailors to MLs loading up with the naval personnel near to the dock gate. John appeared to be badly hit in the thigh and had lost a good deal of blood. Fortunately I had tied some rubber tourniquets round my waist before the show and so was able to put one on his leg before literally throwing him over the side, all my efforts to carry him down our bent and battered ladders having failed.'

Accompanying Proctor, with clear instructions from Copland to make sure that he was put on board a boat, was Beardsell, who had been wounded whilst still on the destroyer. Lieutenant Bill Etches, meanwhile, was making his own painful way, not to the boats in the Old Entrance, but to the Old Mole, following the instructions of Copland to make his way back to the re-embarkation point if he could. Not content with such a pacific exit, he would, however, remain for a time with the party protecting the route of withdrawal across bridge 'G' to offer such help as he could.

Having left *Campbeltown* himself, Copland then organized his party for the long and dangerous journey to the Mole. He put Corporal Cheetham out in front, followed by himself, then Fyfe with the radio, and with Private Hannan bringing up the rear. Under orders to make straight for Newman's HQ, and then to press on to the re-embarkation point, 'avoiding whenever possible being involved in scrapping', he was instead persuaded by the noise of fighting along his chosen route to move to his right along the side of the dry dock. It was a diversion that would cause him to make a speedy circum-navigation of the whole Group Three operating area, before finally linking up with Newman.

Successfully making it to the inner caisson, Brett and his seven men of 12 Commando now found themselves in possession of a strip of decking upon which they would be dreadfully exposed to enemy fire. Directly ahead of them stretched the Penhoët Basin, its black waters winking with reflected light, its complement of ships adding their own spangled threads to the web of tracer already enmeshing the docks; to their left, inviolate on top of the Douaniers building, a nest of six Oerlikons spat streams of fire down upon caisson and winding hut alike; behind them in the dry dock the iron bulk of the two great tankers offered cover enough to those of the enemy who were brave enough to take advantage of it; while to their right an amorphous cluster of sheds and workshops gave perfect sanctuary to regrouping German forces.

With surprise for the moment still on their side, the men spread out along the full length of the caisson. Corporal Bob Wright, in spite of the splinter lodged painfully in his knee, was still up with the team, and he and Bombardier Jumbo Reeves immediately set to work on forcing open the hatch cover to which they had been assigned. Though outwardly similar to those on which they had trained in Britain, this access point to the caisson's interior transpired to be sufficiently different in a number of important respects to allow it to resist their very best efforts to free it, a problem shared by Corporal 'Fergie' Ferguson and Lance-Corporal Fred Lemon, both of the North Irish Horse, who had never imagined they would find their hatch cover locked.

Very much aware that time was getting shorter by the second, and that the men responsible for laying the ring main and external charges were making progress while he was not, Bob Wright decided that drastic measures were called for and shouted across to Brett that he was going to force his way in with limpet charges; however, these did not budge the cover an inch. Just then Bob's attention was diverted by the sight of two Germans coming out of the buildings to the party's right. So he warned Brett of their approach along a line which, but for the loss of ML 192, would have been blocked by Micky Burn's men and, after being told to deal with them, scrambled on to the eastern dockside with Jumbo, the two Commandos taking cover behind a capstan, their .45 Colts at the ready. Surprised at the Germans' apparent lack of concern, Bob records that 'They didn't seem to be aware that there were enemy on the caisson. They were going along at no more than a jog trot and they'd still got their rifles slung. And when I thought they were close enough I said, "*Now!*", and I fired two shots.' But Jumbo, for some reason hesitated until Bob shouted, 'Jumbo!', and then he fired at his man, who went down. 'And then, ' continues Bob, 'he said, "Sorry old chap, I'd got the safety catch on!" He always appeared unflappable, Jumbo did.'

With the Germans taken care of, Bob made his way back to report to Brett that no means of access could be found to the structure's interior. Finding his young officer hit, though he did not realize quite how badly, and propped up against a crane adjacent to the northern camber, Bob explained the problem and the decision was taken that he should instead explore the narrow space between the deck and caisson top, and look there for alternative spots to which his charges might profitably be attached.

While Brett's team, now reinforced by Burtinshaw's, strove valiantly on the caisson, Corran Purdon and his four Corporals were finding things much more straightforward at the winding hut. Very well ventilated, though also unarmed, his pistol and knife having gone along with his smouldering trousers, Bob Hoyle was aware of 'a hell of a lot of firepower' coming down around the area and was relieved to be able to dodge behind the blast wall that covered the approaches to the securely locked steel door. Corran had a go at shooting the lock off, cowboy style, but the bullet simply ricochetted over Bob Hoyle's head, after which Corporal Ron Chung, eschewing such risky practices, adopted the more direct solution of smashing the door open with a sledgehammer.

Climbing down into the hut's interior, Corran immediately set his men to work on preparing the winding machinery for demolition. 'Once inside,' he writes, 'following the drill we knew so well, we laid our made-up charges and connected them up. Corporal Johnny Johnson, in great pain, showed a wonderful example of fortitude, determination and efficiency. The other three, Corporals Ron Chung, Bob Hoyle and Cab Callaway, were as cool as ice and as cheerful as if on a holiday.'

Such was their skill that the whole job took a mere ten minutes, after which Corran sent Chung 'across to Gerard Brett's party to tell him we were ready when he was, and that once he and his team had completed their task and had passed safely through our area, we would blow up our winding house. Ron Chung ran across under intense fire ... He returned after successfully completing his mission, having found the area swept by a hail of bullets, and he himself being hit.'

Outside their hut, Corran's team put some distance between themselves and their handiwork, and waited for Brett's and Burtinshaw's parties to withdraw through their position. Although the general noise of fighting was continuous, they themselves were not always fired upon directly, a blessing which Corran puts down to the fact that the Germans may not have known they were there. If this was so, it was an oversight on the part of the enemy that most certainly did not apply to the men on the caisson itself.

With Brett having been relegated to the sidelines by wounds in both legs and one arm, the fortuitous reinforcement of his own team by Burtinshaw's meant that not only were more trained men now available to complete the work but there would also be an officer in a fit state to take charge. Of the several basic elements of their plan, the laying out of the cordtex 'ring main' and the planting in the water of the large external charges were proceeding as intended; however, the construction of the upper surfaces of this caisson was found to differ so fundamentally from the structures upon which they had trained as to prevent absolutely the placing of the all-important inner wreaths. Where they might have expected to gain access to the caisson by means of hatches which sat proud of the upper surface on towers which were vulnerable to their tools and explosives, the men instead found themselves baulked by the substantial timbers of a wooden roadway, supported on a frame of steel, whose tarmacadamed surface was flush with the hatch tops. Not only that, but the steel of which the hatches were made turned out to be far more sturdy than had been allowed for. Either way, it looked as though even the augmented team would have to rely on the firing of the external charges alone; and while these might well damage the gate, they would hardly be powerful enough to either destroy or unseat it, leaving a job half-done as reward for all their sacrifice and effort.

In the midst of all the noise, sweat and fear the men parties went about their business. Still refusing to give up on the inner chambers, Burtinshaw and Lance-Sergeant Deery struggled to force the middle hatch, even to the point, as had Bob Wright, of trying to blow it open. Having failed at that, Bob was even now crawling through the darkness below the roadway, seeking other targets, while, cool and capable as ever, Sergeant Frank Carr supervised the transformation of their complex assemblage of explosives, cords, fuses and igniters into the neatly integrated 'ring main' that would hopefully blow right through the caisson's northern face.

Calm and always professional, Frank Carr, who had joined the colours at the age of fourteen, was the sort of NCO to whom men in extremis turned for leadership and inspiration. Private Denis Edwards certainly had cause to be thankful for his presence then. Already nursing a thigh wound and weighed down by his heavy pack, he had had the misfortune to arrive at the caisson just as a projectile exploded in front of him. Shocked by its blast and believing momentarily that he had been blinded, Denis had fallen to his knees on the deck. It had taken him some moments to recover; with the slow return of his senses had come the vision before him on the caisson of the calm and solid Sergeant Carr, a sight to reassure any man.

With both sets of outer charges laid against the northern face, Frank reported to Burtinshaw just as the caisson parties came under fire from the closer of the two tankers in the dry dock. He had already known there were men on board this vessel. 'We saw them stick their heads out every now and again,' he recalls, 'but we didn't fire at them because it would let them know we only had pistols!' Eventually, however, the Germans plucked up the courage to start shooting, and the fire from their automatic weapons persuaded a number of the men, including both Burtinshaw and Carr, to seek temporary shelter underneath the caisson roadway. Already under fire from several other points, the Commandos' survival was clearly in jeopardy, in which case Burtinshaw decided they should rush the vessel itself and silence the opposition therein.

As the attack went in, supported by two of Lieutenant Denison's Tommy-gunners, a new threat appeared in their rear in the form of an enemy party thrusting forward from the maze of buildings west of the dry dock. Subjected then to what Sergeant Carr describes as a 'three-way hose-piping', the Commandos were obliged to deal with both hostile groups before they were able to resume their work on the caisson: and deal with them they did, though at a cost which unfortunately included Burtinshaw himself. Gravely hurt, he was carried to where several other casualties were sheltering, and it was here, according to Frank Carr, that this brave officer died.

Taking charge, Carr then moved out along the caisson to check for damage. 'With the amount of fire that had come in, ' he recalls, 'I had to check all the circuits to make sure that none of them had been cut; so I had to walk around the thing and check it. Luckily nothing had been damaged at all, and they were quite all right. Then we had another look at this wretched lid business, and it was a non-starter.'

Returning to talk to Brett again, Bob Wright came under fire and took shelter in the lee of a crane. 'Blount was there, ' he recalls, 'and he'd been hit and Burtinshaw had been wounded. I thought I must find Brett, and I found him. By this time Frank Carr was attaching the igniters to the fuse, and I believe one of our fellows was with him; and I went across, and he more or less said, "Bugger off; we've got this under control!"'

Out of time and out of options, Carr had decided to blow the underwater charges even though the job was but half done. They went up with a muffled bang, after which Frank went back to check for evidence of damage. Ignoring the danger from enemy fire, he 'walked round the deck to make sure something had been done. As you could see the water boiling away, I knew that there were holes down below. Then I could hear the water seeping around the sides and running, so I knew that the whole thing had been pushed off its bed and distorted in some way or other.'

With the charges blown it was time to begin the withdrawal to bridge 'G', and on Brett's orders all those who were still able to do so got to their feet and set off down the west side of the dry dock. Behind them they left the bodies of those of their comrades who had paid the price in full for even the partial measure of their success; of Burtinshaw, of Sergeant Ide, of Lance-Corporal Stokes, and of little Corporal Blount of the South Wales Borderers.

'I'd gone about ten or fifteen yards, ' remembers Bob Wright, 'and I turned round and saw Brett wasn't getting up. So I went back and I said, "Come on sir, we shall miss the boat!" and he was struggling to get to his feet and he said, "You know the orders, Wright! You'd better get back to the embarkation point." Well, the orders were to leave any seriously wounded, and I said, "Oh, come on; we shall get back"; and then we'd not gone very far when another man turned round and saw me supporting Brett. It was Corporal Ferguson and he got the other side, which made it much easier.'

With the caisson parties withdrawing, Corran Purdon could at last blow up his winding hut. 'The noise of firing was terrific, ' he writes, 'and the place continued to be lit up by searchlights and the fire of explosions. Gerard Brett's party came through us having suffered heavily. Gerard, badly wounded, was carried by Corporals Bob Wright and Ferguson. Once they were through and clear, from what we all hoped was a safe distance, I pulled the pins of our igniters. It was a memorable sight. The entire building seemed to rise several feet vertically before it exploded and disintegrated like a collapsed house of cards.'

In the absence of Pennington to blow bridge 'M', this final destructive act closed the Commandos' account at the northernmost extremity of their operational area. On a tally of profit and loss the balance was clearly in their favour, though not by as much as it might have been had a means of access been found to the caisson's interior. For, as the actions of the Germans would later prove, the blowing of the external charges alone had caused only minor damage to the massive structure, and certainly not enough to prevent it being used again.

Having suffered no casualties during their own disembarkation, the party of five whose target was the south winding hut were quickly along the outer caisson camber. Leading the team was Lieutenant Christopher Smalley of the Manchester Regiment, an officer of 5 Commando, from which unit were also drawn his four NCOs. In addition to Bombardier Johnny Johnson, these consisted of Lance-Sergeant Gerry Bright, who, by virtue of having come to Special Service from the Royal Armoured Corps, was known to all as 'Tanky'; Lance-Corporal Ron Howard, of the South Staffordshire Regiment, rather older than the general run of Commandos; and Corporal Johnson, also of the Manchester Regiment and known as 'Johnno'.

Arriving outside the hut's locked steel door, they found themselves faced with exactly the same problem as their sister team; as with Corran Purdon, they tried and failed to shoot the lock off with a slug from a Colt .45. Just then Gerry Bright spotted some narrow windows, through which he and the rest of the team managed to squeeze, without thinking too much about how they might get out again. Inside the hut the two huge winding wheels and their motors could be reached with ease; as with Corran's party, they set to placing and connecting up their charges without fear of interference from the enemy.

With even less distance to cover from *Campbeltown*'s bows, Stuart Chant's party made it to the pump-house even as Roy's assault troops were still clearing the area, and there met with the commander of their protection squad, Lieutenant Hopwood of the Essex Regiment, and Donald Roy's kilted 5 Troop. Hopwood had recently attended a fieldcraft course at Achnacarry Castle in the company of John Stutchbury and Tiger Watson, and Tiger has recorded his impressions of him as being that he 'was one of those delightful eccentrics that enrich the lives of those around them. Stocky, heavily moustached and bespectacled, he had a superficial resemblance to Groucho Marx.'

In the midst of all the noise, the two officers, as with Smalley and Purdon, found themselves shut out of their prize by high steel doors which no one seems to have imagined might be locked on the night. Momentarily fazed by this discovery, the irony of their situation was not lost on the members of Chant's team who, as part of an exhaustive training programme, had prepared for every conceivable eventuality, except perhaps the most obvious one.

Having dispensed with his responsibilities across at the caisson, Captain Bob Montgomery chose this most opportune moment to appear and offer as a solution to the problem, one of the small charges he carried with him for just such emergencies. Attaching the magnetic device to the lock, Stuart was invited to light its fuse, only to find that as a result of his wounds his hands were too shaky and sticky with blood for him to do it properly. Lest his men attribute his difficulties to fear, Stuart asked Bob to take over, which he did, setting the fuse alight. As they waited behind the blast wall for the charge to explode, Hopwood strayed a little too close to the door and had to be pulled back by Montgomery. Then the thing went off, the door swung open and they were in.

Having cleared the way for the pump-house parties, Montgomery was off again, this time to the dry dock itself with the idea that he and Jameson might get on board one of the tankers and do some damage there. They found the gangplanks enfiladed by machine-gun fire and, deciding to give it a go anyway, found that every attempt on their part invited another ripping burst. In the event it seemed wiser to desist, especially as the ships would be damaged anyway by *Campbeltown*'s explosion and the rushing torrent of water that would follow it; besides which it was Bob's responsibility to sanction all demolitions, for which duty he would need to remain within easy reach of the various parties.

Escorted by Hopwood, Chant's team entered the vast, echoing chamber of the pump-house, so very like its counterpart in Southampton. Standing in line before them were four large electric motors each of which was connected, by means of a vertical drive shaft descending through the floor, to an impeller pump installed on the lowest level, some forty feet below. The four pairs of motors and pumps were their primary targets, with attention being focused on the latter, whose special castings, it was believed, could not be replaced within a year; however, switchgear, transformers and subsidiary pumps were also on their hit list, the purpose being to render the whole facility inoperative.

Feeling ever more remote from the battle outside and guided by their feeble torches, the five men picked their way toward the iron-runged stairs that led down into the fathomless darkness of the pumping chamber. Already restricted by manpower shortages to the point where each man and each ounce of explosive was desperately needed, Chant nevertheless decided not to let the wounded Chamberlain attempt the tricky descent. Instead he was to remain behind and guard their rear, it being obvious that, working far below, the remaining members of the party would be particularly vulnerable to grenades dropped into the void. Chamberlain couldn't move his arm very well, so Ron Butler cocked his pistol for him before joining the others on the stairway.

With various galleries inviting them to stray off into a darkness so complete it had almost a physical presence, their descent was not an easy one. Chant was experiencing some difficulty because of his wounds, and in addition to helping him down, his men had also to carry the sixty-pound deadweight of Chamberlain's pack; nevertheless, they did finally make it to the bottom along a route which they would have to retrace speedily and accurately once the fuses on their charges had been lit.

On the floor of the chamber they were again on familiar ground, with the impeller pumps positioned just where they expected them to be. The long hours of training took over now, as with practised ease they began to place their explosives, one man to each pump, with the ancillary pumps included in the complex web of fuses. Their torches gave only a little light, but light was not a problem now that the drill could be followed undisturbed. According to Ron Butler, Lance-Sergeant Dockerill kept singing to himself as he worked, 'There'll be blue birds over the white cliffs of Dover – Hitler just you bloody wait and see!'

Far removed from the battles outside, Chant and his team were reminded of them by the distant thuds of explosions, which Chamberlain confirmed was only Roy and Randall blowing the guns on the roof, before moving swiftly to bridge 'G' and leaving Hopwood and his team of four to protect both Chant's and Smalley's parties as best they could.

With a less complex target to prepare for demolition, Smalley was ready first; however, when he attempted to fire his percussion igniters, having obtained permission from Montgomery to do so, they failed to initiate the expected explosion. In cases like this it was standard practice to wait for half an hour before returning to investigate the cause of any failure, but after reporting again to Montgomery, Smalley went right back into the winding house, re-set his fuses, pulled the igniters and was this time rewarded with a shattering blast, as the wheels and motors therein were totally destroyed.

Moving northwards up the edge of the dry dock after leaving *Campbeltown*, Copland and his team heard Smalley's triumph as a 'magnificent' explosion to their left rear. Next they came up to the pump-house itself where a quick word with Hopwood confirmed that all was well. Copland describes what happened.

'We moved on up the dock side and I noticed Fyfe rather heavily laden with rifle and wireless set, so took his rifle, my own having been blown to fragments on *Campbeltown*. Cheetham, ten yards ahead, stopped us and we stood in the shadow and watched the crews of the ships in the dry dock running aboard. All this time Fyfe was trying to contact HQ on his set. The call droned on and on, with pauses for Fyfe to say, "No reply sir; can't hear a sound." All through our movement Fyfe continued his efforts to establish communication and certainly it was through no fault of his that we failed to do so. Soon we reached the inner dry-dock gate and on to the bridge at "M" to see if I could get reports of progress. Fire of all sorts was pouring from the high buildings the other side of the basin and the dock roads seemed light as day. I saw a lone figure under a deserted wooden gun tower – Micky Burn. He reported that he alone of his force had managed to get ashore and asked me had I seen Morgan Jenkins with his protection and demolition party, who were to have blown this bridge. I knew nothing of their progress. Micky said, "I'll wait a little longer for them and then re-join." We pushed on toward the bridge at "G" and I took Cheetham's place in the lead. We tried to get along the dock road parallel with the St Nazaire Basin but every time we moved we were fired at by gunners on the ships in the Basin, so we doubled back and tried to get round the buildings. Twelve-foot walls barred our way and time was flying, so I decided to chance the Basin road again. Bunching together, we ran and dodged from cover to cover and managed always to keep one jump ahead of the machine-gunners on the ships. They always fired at the place we had just left.'

Deep within the bowels of the pump-house Chant and his men took about twenty minutes to fix their charges, after which all were connected and prepared for firing with duplicated sets of percussion igniters. Smalley might well have been able to go back to the winding house when his igniters failed first time, but a return to the depths of the pump-house should an explosion fail to ensue here was simply not to be contemplated. Sending Butler and King back up the stairs with instructions to remove themselves and Chamberlain from the building, Chant kept Dockerill with him and the two men waited for the others to call down that all was clear before pulling their igniters on the count of three. With only a ninety-second delay, there was barely time for them to make their way up to ground level, especially considering Chant's lack of mobility. But with the officer clinging on to the Sergeant's waistband, they made it through the maze of galleries and ran past the tall electric motors to savour at last the cool night air.

Having emerged from the depths of the earth, the explosives the men had left behind seemed much further away than was actually the case, and this feeling of detachment engendered a carelessness which prompted them to take shelter right outside the building, in the lee of the blast wall.

Fortunately for them the omnipresent Montgomery was at hand to order them away to safer cover, which they reached just before their charges exploded with a violence far greater than anyone had imagined, causing great blocks of stone to crash to earth exactly where they had been sheltering moments before. With the blowing of the pumps, one of the primary objectives of the raid had been achieved in style. Passing down the side of the Bassin, Bill Copland mentally added it to his growing list of triumphs.

With the remains of the winding hut blazing fiercely nearby, Smalley chose this moment to report his success to Montgomery and seek leave for himself and his team to retire immediately across bridge 'G'. Before moving off there was a mutual exchange of congratulations with Chant who still had to return to the pump-house to finish the job by doing to the motors on the main floor what had just been done to the pumps far below. In the company of Montgomery the team therefore retraced their steps through the débris, smoke and shattered glass, to find that part of the main floor had given way and allowed two of the heavy electric motors to tumble through into the depths below. With the remaining pair having obviously been damaged in the blast, there now seemed little purpose in demanding more of luck than luck could give, and, rather than risk his sergeants further, Chant decided to call it a day. Without planting extra charges, he simply set Bill King loose on the transformer pipes and switchgear, with a seven-pound sledgehammer which Bill wielded, according to Montgomery, with 'a sort of beatific smile on his face'. Having released an amount of oil, an abortive attempt was made to set light to it with incendiaries, after which Chant, with his three fit men helping Chamberlain along, followed Smalley's example in beginning a withdrawal to bridge 'G'.

His own work in this sector now complete, Montgomery too would join the general movement towards the shelter of Roy's bridgehead and thence to Newman's small HQ perimeter. Before leaving the pump-house, however, he saw a chance to add his personal contribution to the destruction around him by tossing an incendiary into a nearby shed, which went up with a most satisfying explosion of yellow fire.

14

Do You Want to Live For Ever?

During the whole period of the Group Three demolitions the area of water in and around the Old Entrance saw a considerable amount of naval activity as the gunboat was joined first by Wynn, and then by Lieutenants Burt and Beart in MLs 262 and 267 respectively.

No longer in contact with Newman, unsure of where Beattie was, and out of sight of the Mole, Ryder had taken the decision to concentrate fully on *Campbeltown*, the guarantee of this one ship's explosion clearly being the key to the raid's success; in response to his orders, Curtis had therefore turned the gunboat round and put her alongside the northern quay of the narrow anchorage, bows out, port-side-to.

As she berthed, she attracted like a magnet those of *Campbeltown*'s crew who had disembarked over her fo'c'sle. Walter Rainbird was there, as were Ordnance Artificer Frank Wherrell and the 'Chief Buffer', Bill Stocker, who had evacuated their Oerlikon tub on receipt of the belated order to abandon ship. Also seeking a berth was Leading Stoker Frank Pritchard who, with another sailor, was helping along a wounded commando sergeant they had rescued from *Campbeltown*'s deck. Many of the survivors had been hit, some, like Lieutenant Johnny Proctor, quite severely; even though little could be done for them in a medical sense, Curtis' crew did what they could to ease their suffering, finding space for them in the rapidly filling gunboat. Frank was instructed to take his man below and then find space for himself up top. By now very tired, he sat down amidships with his back to a hatch coaming, noticing very little of the drama unfolding around him.

Intent on learning what he could about Beattie, Ryder looked anxiously among the survivors for any of *Campbeltown*'s officers, but could find none.

He was even told that Beattie and Gough had been killed, but didn't believe it. As he climbed up on to the jetty to find out for himself, Wynn brought the torpedo boat in and secured against the gunboat's starboard side to ask for instructions now that his special torpedoes would not need to be fired at the inner caisson. 'I had in mind sending him to torpedo *Campbeltown* if plans there had appeared to miscarry, ' writes Ryder, 'and so told him to wait alongside.'

Accompanied by Leading Signalman Pike, Ryder came up the steps just as

'a grenade or fuse fell between the gunboat and the jetty and burst close to me. The decks were crowded and it wounded one or two men. There was a sinister burning smell and for a moment I was afraid that our ship was on fire. It soon cleared, however, and I continued on my way to *Campbeltown*.

'A challenge from a crouching figure with a Tommy-gun halted me abruptly. I gave the password which was my own name, and was permitted to continue. I reached the side of the dock entrance and hailed the *Campbeltown*, but all seemed quiet. There was a small fire burning still in the fo'c'sle mess-deck. The ML [177] we had sent alongside her had shoved off and there seemed to be no sign of life. I stepped forward and hailed again, but was greeted by a burst of fire which I imagined came from one of the ships in the dock. It struck the masonry of a small hut close by me. I dodged behind the hut and watched *Campbeltown* from there for what seemed to be a good five minutes. Then to my relief I saw a series of small explosions along her port side and it sounded as if there were others on the further side too. The ship had ridden over the torpedo net and was firmly held by the bow. However, she started to settle by the stern and so I decided that everything was going to plan there. My next task was to see how the other landings were getting on.

'A moment later, as I was returning to my ship, there was another explosion even nearer, in the hut containing the mechanism for withdrawing the outer lock gate. This explosion must have lifted a good bit of the roof as the débris pattered down around us for some time. Apart from this, we heard one explosion further up toward the other end of the big dock, which I took to be the mechanism for working the other gate, and there was a shed near the pumping-house which [Montgomery] had set on fire. It was now blazing furiously and casting a lurid light on the surrounding buildings and the black waters of the Loire.'

Returning to the gunboat and with 'Wynn's Weapons' now free to be used against other targets, Ryder gave the order for them to be fired against the nearby lock gates which gave access from the river directly into the Bassin de St Nazaire. This Wynn did, the hiss of the escaping compressed air making a big impression on Gordon Holman, who didn't know they were delayed-action devices, and therefore expected a sudden shattering explosion. Having heard them thud against the gates, Wynn then brought the torpedo boat around and took her back alongside the gunboat to make his report and share a congratulatory drink with Curtis. His sting having been drawn, there was little more that Wynn could usefully do, and so Ryder ordered him home with a contingent of *Campbeltown*'s survivors on board. Ordnance Artificer Frank Wherrell and the 'Chief Buffer', Bill Stocker, were among those to begin the journey home with Wynn, hoping that the little Vosper boat's great speed would soon see them safely away.

As Wynn powered into the river, Curtis prepared to follow him out, so that Ryder could at last see what had been happening down by the Mole. The gunboat had been lucky in that, during all of her time in the Old Entrance, she had somehow managed to avoid the worst of the enemy fire; however, this was an immunity not shared by either ML 262 or ML 267, whose belated attempts to land men elsewhere in the anchorage were met by an altogether more fearsome response.

In attempting to make good his error in having run up as far as the building slip, Burt had brought ML 262 back down river with the idea of running in under *Campbeltown*'s stern. Rodier's ML 177 was at this time still in the process of taking off his portion of *Campbeltown*'s crew and Micky Wynn had just come in to request new orders from Ryder.

Approaching the northern quayside, an enemy vessel, which Burt and Robbie Roberts took to be an 'R'-boat, attempted to ram ML 262's port side. However, Burt successfully avoided the attack, after which fire was directed at the German boat which, instead of pursuing the engagement, returned fire half-heartedly with a machine gun and disappeared upstream.

Resuming his course for the quayside, Burt then made fast in a bows-in position at about 0140 hours. As the parties of Woodcock and Morgan stepped ashore, the nearby winding house and pump-house exploded, causing debris to rain down across the general area, although fortunately without damage to either boat or personnel. At the time of their approach, Stoker Len Ball was still on the recalcitrant twin-Lewis, putting out of action a German position, before both guns jammed again and he abandoned them in favour of a single stripped-Lewis, fired over the port wing of the bridge.

Having just got all their men off, they then came under heavy fire when a harbour defence vessel, manoeuvring inside the Bassin de St Nazaire, engaged them over the top of the nearby lock gates. ML 262 replied with her forward Oerlikon as well as her stripped-Lewis guns, Len Ball, with an ammunition box at his feet, firing away at her superstructure oblivious to everything around him. The forward Oerlikon jammed again after about eighteen rounds, this time for good; however, it and the machine guns had twice managed to silence the light cannon mounted between the enemy vessel's bridge and funnel.

As had already been agreed with Woodcock, Burt then cast off with the intention of backing towards the lock gates, in case it should be necessary to tow them shut prior to demolition. No sooner had he cleared the quayside, however, than his own Commando parties were seen to be running back, a vision which prompted him to return, re-embark them and cast off for a second time, with Lieutenant Morgan giving as the reason for their early withdrawal the fact that the recall signal had been seen.

With all these manoeuvrings taking place so close to the area through which the retiring Group Three parties were passing *en route* to 'G', it was inevitable that some would see in her the prospect of a swifter and safer return to British shores than could be offered by the distant Mole. This was certainly the case with Lieutenant Chris Smalley and his men who made straight for her, climbing one by one over a fence whilst under fire, and then sprinting across the open dockside to the water's edge. Also attempting to reach ML 262 were Lance-Sergeant Ron Butler, of Chant's party, and Lieutenant Hopwood, who had come together during the pull-back from the pump-house. Rather further away from the boat than Smalley, they too were forced to negotiate a high, wire fence which had set into it a securely padlocked gate. With no means of forcing a passage, Ron climbed up and used his feet to push the top of the gate back sufficiently for Hopwood to crawl through, after which the latter did the same for Ron. It was at this point that Hopwood started to cough, and said to Ron, 'The buggers are using gas!' But it was, as Ron quickly assured him, no more than the smell of cordite from their own side's guns.

Keeping his propellers well clear of the torpedo net, Burt was making for open water when Smalley's party was seen running toward the boat. Without hesitation he went back for them too, after which, with the ship in the basin engaging him again, he pulled clear before Hopwood and Butler could get close enough to make their presence known. With the forward Oerlikon having by this time become as much of a danger to its own crew as it was to the enemy, Robbie Roberts now made its hopeless situation known to Burt, who ordered it secured.

Turning off *Campbeltown*'s stern, ML 262 was then hit several times in quick succession: in the funnel, shattering the exhaust pipes, at deck-level on the starboard side of the engine-room, starting a fire which was extinguished by sea water running out of the damaged starboard deck tank, at deck-level close to the after magazine, again starting a fire, which Stoker Hollands put out with hand extinguishers, and in the after Oerlikon position, knocking out the gun, killing the loading number, Able Seaman Walker, and severely wounding both Sub-Lieutenant Hills and the layer Able Seaman Martin. Up forward, and in spite of advice to the contrary, Chris Smalley attempted to bring the malfunctioning Oerlikon back into action, only to have it explode and kill him instantly.

Initially disappointed at having come so close to boarding her, Hopwood and Butler saw the flames erupt around the ML's deck and assumed that she was finished. However, the damage, in spite of looking bad, was only superficial; and with her engines and steering unaffected, Burt was still able to press ahead with his run for the freedom of the open sea.

Having followed Burt as far as the building slip, Lieutenant Beart, in ML 267, also came south again, running alongside a dredger and damaging it with grenades before making his own belated attempt to land the reserve party of RSM Alan Moss. Consisting of eleven men, everyone of whom, with the exception of Lance-Bombardier Jack Aspden, hailed from 2 Commando, this was the party which had been supposed to offer Newman at least a modicum of flexibility when it came to plugging the gaps which must inevitably appear in any such thinly manned enterprise. It included, in Armourer Sergeant Gerry Taylor, of the RAOC, one of the handful of men who should have accompanied the force no further than Falmouth. It also carried the 35-star red and green rockets which were to be fired from Newman's position as the signal to all the scattered parties to commence their withdrawal.

Approaching the south-eastern corner of the Old Entrance, Beart, who had brought along a rugby ball to help pass the time on the quayside, made an attempt to nose his boat directly on to the foreshore just below the landing stage. Lance-Bombardier Jack Aspden, who was a demolition expert from 9 Commando, recalls how he and a number of others jumped ashore over the bow, only to be recalled almost immediately. With the ML already beginning to back away, Jack took a flying leap and managed to grab a forward stanchion, hanging there and trying desperately to get a foothold on the curve of the hull, even as Beart began to manoeuvre. The ML was now under fire and suffering damage, but, dangling as he was beneath her bow, Jack was at least tucked away from the line of it.

Badly hit, the ML began to burn, and the order to abandon was given. As she started to settle, Jack dropped into the water, thankful now that he was a strong swimmer. There were numerous survivors milling about in a sea which was stitched by bursts of machine-gun fire. Jack for one stayed under the surface as much as he could, to avoid being hit. Alan Moss and a number of others managed to get onto a Carley float. Happening upon the very young Private Diamond, of 4 Troop, for whom there was not room, Moss slid without hesitation into the freezing water so that Diamond could climb up in his place. Continuing to move the float towards the shore, Moss was then shot and killed, Jack Aspden noticing his head jerk back as he was hit. Falling prey to both cold and exhaustion, Jack himself was tiring rapidly and would eventually pass out completely, remaining oblivious to everything until plucked from the water several hours later.

Of the crew of this ill-fated boat, Beart himself and ten others did not survive, the remaining two junior officers and three ratings becoming prisoners of war. Eight of the eleven Commandos were killed, including Lance-Corporal Ted Bryan of 4 Troop. Only three were taken prisoner, these being, in addition to Jack Aspden, Lance-Corporal Cockin and Private Jones, both of 4 Troop.

With the loss of ML 267, the account of the starboard column could now be closed, with only Mark Rodier having successfully landed his troops. As far as the group of vessels within the Old Entrance itself were concerned, Rodier had been first to quit the scene. Burt had followed him out with Woodcock's, Morgan's and Smalley's Commandos on board, and Wynn had powered away on his three great engines, fastest of all the boats to brave the waiting enemy guns. Curtis was last to leave, on his way to offer belated assistance at the Old Mole, leaving behind in the narrow anchorage only broken dreams and the wreckage of small boats, the dogged courage of whose crews had not been a match for the guns that were ranged against them. It was now 0230 hours and the focus of the naval battle had moved again into the shell-swept waters of the estuary.

With all the Commando parties operating west of the 'Normandie' dock having already begun to pull back, it now only remained for Johnny Roderick to begin his own withdrawal for the process of shrinkage to be fully enacted that would eventually bring all of Copland's boys back across bridge 'G'.

While successfully maintaining their block against attempts to oust them made by enemy parties moving down from the north, Roderick and his men had managed to attack the underground fuel dumps with incendiaries, though unfortunately without the expected results.

Operational orders had required them to hold their position until zero plus sixty minutes, at which time their immediate withdrawal was to have been signalled by the rockets fired from Newman's position. With bridge 'G' due to be blown at zero plus seventy-five minutes, this was a schedule which left little margin for error. As they were expecting to see the rockets go up, and as they could not possibly know of their loss with Moss's party, Roderick did not question the erroneous news given to him, more or less on time, that they had been seen. At about 0230, while Curtis was pulling the gunboat away from the Old Entrance quayside, he therefore began his withdrawal towards the now deserted hulk of the old destroyer. The route to bridge 'G' for most of his party would lie in crossing back over her smouldering bows; but not for all, as Private John Gardner and one or two others re-crossed the dry dock by means of the damaged inner caisson, leaving themselves with a long and dangerous passage southwards through the warehouses in order to reach the safety of Roy's bridgehead.

Roderick having satisfied himself that there was no one still to come, the main group climbed up and over *Campbeltown*'s fo'c'sle. Several of the men were struck by the eerie quiet of her now deserted decks as she lay pinned to the caisson, a haven of battered steel seemingly forgotten amidst a welter of flashing lights and raucous gunfire. Taking advantage of the pause, Rifleman Jarvis, not content to consign her to oblivion without securing a memento for himself, removed the chronometer from her bridge.

Moving quickly across the open dockside to the west of the ship, Private 'Dutch' Holland writes that he 'was running behind Roderick, and saw tracers behind him, and he was hit. A grenade or mortar bomb landed just then and blew me off my feet. But luckily I was not hit until later. A small wound was on my left arm, but no effects.'

Hit in the backside, Roderick was bowled over and fell to the ground, his Bren spinning out of his grasp. He managed to get behind the shelter of a stanchion for a short while before making another dash for safety. 'We hoped we knew where Charles Newman's party was, ' he recalls, 'and we made for that. I think by that time we must have all been fairly split up. But somehow we got there.'

Also moving to join up with Newman, but from the south this time, and inspired not so much by their orders as by pressure of circumstance, were the tiny parties of Walton, Watson and Pritchard.

Having left Corporals Shipton, Deanes and Chetwynd to work on the bridge at 'D', Captain Bill Pritchard had gone south with Corporal Maclagan along the side of the New Entrance lock. They passed each of the designated Commando targets in turn; however, the only troops in evidence were isolated parties of Germans, whose presence was betrayed by the echoing crunch of their boots. Corporal Maclagan, in describing what happened next, writes:

'We headed for the Power House, and as this part of the docks was full of tenement buildings, it meant going through small backyards, and in the back door and through the front of these tenements. We eventually reached the Power House, but again there was no sign of any of our men. We were retracing our steps and were trotting down a lane between these tenements, Captain Pritchard on the right hand side and myself on the left hand side, when quite unexpectedly Captain Pritchard reached a corner at the very moment that a German should turn the corner. The whole tragedy was over in a flash. In one second the two of them met, in the next Captain Pritchard had fallen backwards. I took a couple of paces towards the German and emptied the remainder of my Tommy-gun magazine into him. At this moment I was not aware of how Captain Pritchard had been struck, but on thinking of it later he could only have been bayonetted, as I am sure no shot was fired. I dropped down beside him to see what I could do. He was breathing terribly heavily. After a little he spoke and his words were, "That you, Mac? Get back and report to HQ. That's an order!" – he never spoke again.'

Alone in the middle of the Old Town, Maclagan decided to return to the bridge and re-establish contact with the remaining three members of his party; however, the whole area appeared to be deserted. With no time to waste, he pushed on up the side of the Bassin de St Nazaire and, surviving a grenade blast *en route*, made his report to Newman's HQ. He asked for help for Pritchard but, with so few men available, was told there was none to be given.

Left at bridge 'D', Corporals Shipton, Deanes and Chetwynd had enjoyed no greater success. Access to the lock gates was blocked by coils of barbed wire and the substantially girdered lift-bridge proved to be far too huge a target for their puny charges. Close by the side of the lock, Shipton could see what he took to be the figure of Philip Walton, who therefore could not have been killed while crossing the square, but any movement in his direction was deterred both by heavy enemy fire and by the incessant probing of the searchlights, which transmuted night into day and forced them to lie flat until the beams passed. They made for the cover of a cable drum of sufficient size to allow all three to shelter within its rim; but, as Bert Shipton was later to recall, 'We were right in the line of fire. And we'd no sooner got there than Jimmy got hit, and Chetwynd. I checked them out, and they made a funny little gurgling sound, and that was it. I was on my own.'

Still determined to get to Walton somehow, Bert went to run toward him, but was caught by a searchlight and, by the time he was free of it, Walton could no longer be seen. Trying then for the bridge, Bert crossed over to its west side, where the lifting mechanism was, by clambering through the girders supporting the roadway. A little way down the street opposite he could see an armoured car. There was clearly nothing that he could do alone, so he retraced his steps to the Old Town side. He even explored a little way along Pritchard and Maclagan's route, without seeing any sign of friendly forces. Then, ill-armed and apprehensive, and with German voices clearly audible, he wisely decided to abandon his lonely odyssey and retire northwards towards the HQ perimeter.

Sheltering on the north side of the Place de la Vieille Ville, Tiger Watson had meanwhile been intent on regaining the initiative after his party's initial reverses. With Bradley wounded and Pritchard's party gone on ahead, his small group numbered only eight, three of whom were armed with nothing better than Colts. If anything was to be achieved, they clearly must have more men, and Tiger therefore prepared to send up the flare which would advertise their urgent need of reinforcements. He tugged the Very pistol from his belt, pointed it skyward and pulled the trigger – but nothing happened; it had been damaged, possibly by splinters from the grenade that had exploded close by his side, and wouldn't fire.

> 'We were all rather shaken, but could not call it a day. I had by now got it firmly into my mind that we must destroy bridge 'D' at all costs, to prevent yet more Germans infiltrating the area. The Old Mole would have to be sorted out by somebody else ... We would try a different approach. George Wheeler was sent to find the Colonel's command post, inform him of the situation and bring back some help. The rest of us followed his route to the right until we came upon a passage leading west towards the Submarine Basin. We would take that way to the bridge.'

Had he been free to take it, Tiger's new route would have led him eventually to where Pritchard's men were at that time laying their charges on the two tugs. But it was to prove no safer than the square had been. There were German soldiers close by who could not be seen in the darkness, but who could be heard quite clearly. 'I still had one of my little stun bombs, ' writes Tiger, 'and, handing my Tommy-gun to Lawson, I lobbed it up the passage. It went off with a gratifying bang and a dramatic orange flash. But it provoked a much more violent response. We were suddenly enveloped in a cloud of dust as the small shells from a quick-firing gun, not forty yards away, crashed into the walls on each side, and behind us.'

The party had fallen victim to the guns of one of the ships in the Bassin de St Nazaire, directly ahead. Bill Lawson, who remained by Tiger's side through much of the action, was still there; but of the others there was no sign save a number of huddled shapes on the ground, which Tiger took to be all that remained of his party. Without more men they were finished; and as these could only come from Newman's reserve, it was in the direction of the Colonel's HQ that the two men now decided to head. They were travelling northwards, more or less parallel with the line of the quayside, and the ship, the pinging of whose telegraph could clearly be heard, kept pace with them, opening fire as they raced from cover to cover – fortunately without result.

Behind them in the gap between the sheds, the dust from the ship's bombardment slowly settled on the scattered bags of cement which, in the noise and confusion of the moment, Tiger had mistaken for his fallen comrades. The young officer had seen what he would have expected to see and had accepted it as such. In reality, however, his men were still safe, though not entirely unmarked by the sudden encounter.

With this route also closed to the survivors, Alf Searson, who had now lost contact with the group, dumped his heavy pack and attempted to find his own way through. Exploring the clutter of sheds and alleys, he found himself in an area which appeared to be used as a troops' canteen. He could hear chattering from the other side of the wall. Armed as he was with no more than a Colt and a Mills grenade, he debated whether it would be wiser to attack, or to 'wait for them to bugger off'. At length the chattering stopped. Anxious to know what had been going on, he went over the wall with a grenade at the ready, only to find his pal George Wheeler on the other side. The two men joined forces and made it back to the assembly area, in the relative safety of which poor Alf was destined to become a victim of 'friendly fire', one of several to do so on the night. Entering a building together, the two men set to searching it, George going one way and Alf the other. Alf heard German voices again, 'so I wasn't buggering about this time. I threw a couple of grenades over, stopped the sodding conversation, turned to come back and was immediately faced by a man with a Tommy gun and a little blue light, who was not at all friendly and shot me in the side!'

With the whole of the Old Town and much of the warehouse area clear at this time of British troops, the routes for German reinforcements were open and undisturbed. As time passed it was an area that would become steadily more dangerous to enter, and yet Tiger was bent on giving the Place de la Vieille Ville one last try. Short of men himself, the avuncular Newman let him have two Tommy-gunners, with whose comforting support Tiger then set off on his perilous mission. He knew it was 'tantamount to a death sentence, but nevertheless we had to try. It was with considerable relief that we bumped into Wickson with the rest of the party, who promptly turned about again to accompany us.'

En route to the square, Tiger, angry at what he saw to be the many failures of the night, strode down the middle of the road eschewing cover, while the others more prudently kept out of the way of snipers. Tiger in his present mood was not in awe of them. 'I dismissed the snipers with an unseemly epithet, ' he writes, 'and demanded angrily of my long-suffering companions, "Do you want to live forever!"' The phrase was singularly apt for the occasion and had just the desired effect. Dealing summarily with a group of the enemy who were foolish enough to bunch, they succeeded in reaching the square unscathed. But reaching it was one thing and crossing it another. Nerving themselves for the dash, they were relieved indeed when a runner arrived from HQ cancelling their little adventure and ordering them instead to assemble with the other parties for what most of the Commandos still believed would be their planned re-embarkation.

15

The Hard Way Home

In calling for the 'Chariot' force to remain in the area until 0330, the COHQ planners had assumed that the MLs could manage to survive for up to two hours in a neck of water wholly dominated by enemy gunners. Bearing in mind that the boats were only lightly armed and unarmoured, this was an assumption which blithely ignored the realities of firepower and ammunition supply, all of which stood so clearly in the enemy's favour as to suggest that an eventual safe withdrawal would be all but impossible.

Tucked away to the south of bridge 'G', Newman was, in the early stages of the action, no better placed than Ryder to know just how rapidly the situation out on the river was deteriorating. Fortunately, perhaps, this was also the case with most of his men who, struggling to survive in the sinister tangle of the dockyard, were spared the sight of the boats being knocked out one by one, which they therefore continued to believe would be waiting to whisk them home the minute their work was done. Down by the Mole, Corporal Bert Shipton's hopes had been dashed by the sight of Platt's and Stephens' boats in flames; while, laying his charges in the shadow of *Campbeltown*'s bow, Private Jimmy Brown's thoughts of salvation had died in the blazing pyre that was ML 268. But for most of the rest the realization that they were marooned without hope would not come until much later, as a chilling postscript to an action they had believed was all but complete.

With Stephens' boat blazing furiously and Tillie about to follow him into oblivion, with Platt's on fire and Fenton's all but dead in the water, it was clear within minutes of the little fleet's arrival in the port that it was not hours in which survival should be measured but in minutes and seconds.

At 0140 hours Lieutenant Irwin's ML 270 joined the growing list of casualties when she took a hit aft which drained her hydraulic system and knocked out her steering. From his position between the torpedo tubes, Acting Leading Seaman Fred Catton describes how 'I could hear our three-pounder gun on the bows firing away; then it happened. I felt a thud under my feet; the steering fuel lines had been shot away and we were out of control. I was ordered from the bridge to fit the deck tiller for hand steering, an eight-foot L-shaped length of pipe with a square end made to fit on top of the rudder shaft, which was situated under a metal plate on deck. I managed to unscrew it by the light of the searchlights. I was assisted by Able Seaman Walter Evans to fit the tiller and steer the boat', this being his duty for the next several frantic hours.

In the ten to fifteen minutes it took to recover control, ML 270 circled slowly in the waters between the underground fuel tanks and the tip of the Mole. Had Roderick's party not been so quick to knock out the guns directly to the east of *Campbeltown*, they would have made short work of her. As it was she was being regularly hit by small stuff, the strikes on her hull sounding to Stoker Andy Porter, with the three-pounder crew, for all the world 'like somebody walking by a wooden shed and hitting it with a hammer'. As the ML's only defence apart from her torpedoes, the little Hotchkiss kept popping away at targets on the shore, often directed by Irwin from the bridge.

Despite her lack of mobility, this boat led a charmed life as the work on her steering was carried out. Such was not the case, however, with other MLs nearby, as Ordinary Telegraphist Stewart Burkimsher found out to his horror when they drifted helplessly past a boat which had been mortally hit and was blazing fiercely. A lone sailor was standing on the stern and shouting to be rescued; yet without steering they were powerless to do anything but watch, and listen to the anguished calls of those like him who were trapped in the smoke and flames.

At about 0200, with the awkward, unwieldy tiller finally in place, Irwin regained a sort of control and turned the nose of his craft towards the open sea. Undamaged, and having brought to St Nazaire no Commandos of his own, he might have brought off forty men; as it was, however, he could do no more than limp away at 10 or so knots, passing his steering orders through the awful din along a voice-chain to the stern, and working both his engines as much to direct the boat as to give her motive power. As they made their way south of the Mole, Irwin saw a powerful explosion at the East Jetty, which the Hotchkiss crew attributed to a torpedo fired by Boyd's ML 160; however, it more than likely came from one of the pair of 'fish' loosed off by the withdrawing ML 177 which, having swung away from *Campbeltown's* stern, was even now beginning her own ill-starred bid for freedom.

As to ML 160's actual movements after steaming away from *Campbeltown*'s point of impact, Boyd had taken her swiftly northwards in search of the two tankers he would later learn had all the time been safely ensconced within the 'Normandie' dock. Taking constant avoiding action, he ran past the building slip upon which the searchlights were picking out the outline of the partially completed aircraft carrier *Joffre*, then, further north, towards the point at which the river began a slow turn to the east. Here, where the whole north shore was fringed by the Loire and Penhoët shipyards, he finally gave up the chase and turned back with the intention of offering such help as he could to *Campbeltown*.

Returning to the heart of the action, he noticed two light cannon mounted on top of a building by the northern shore, which were pumping out shells towards the flaming waters off the landing points. Recalling the events shortly after the war, Boyd was imprecise when it came to locating this particular battery; however, there is a strong case for believing it to have consisted of guns 37 and 38, which were 20mm pieces mounted on a building less than one sea mile NNE of *Campbeltown*.

Feeling 'quite at home' on the river, whose topography seemed familiar as a result of all the work they had done with the model, Tom brought his boat right inshore until he was within a cable of the guns and safely below their point of maximum depression. Here he stopped ship and, directing MacIver's fire through a megaphone, knocked the guns out with thirty rounds of HE and shrapnel, MacIver periodically exclaiming, 'Och! That's hit the bashtards again!'

Having silenced the battery and with the immediate area becoming rather too hot for comfort, they beat a hasty retreat. Out of concern for his Captain's safety, the coxswain, Acting Petty Officer Leonard Lamb, kept poking his head out of the wheelhouse door to see if Boyd was all right; but he was told not to worry. His tin hat having none of the spirit-boosting magic of his 'fighting hat', Boyd chose this moment to don this rather eccentric piece of headgear, which had been fashioned for him by his wife Barbara, and embellished with whimsical details of his own devising. It had begun as a knitted 'comfort', received by Tom when he was an Ordinary Seaman on HMS *Carlisle*. Originally a grey headband with cross-pieces over the top, Tom had prevailed upon Barbara to stitch pieces of sheepskin into the open spaces, after which he sewed his Royal Tank Corps badge on the front and a Royal Navy coat button on the top. 'The crew loved it,' recalls Barbara, 'and it was wonderful for morale.'

Resuming his course, Boyd then saw a ship and decided to torpedo it.

Although it was anchored, Boyd, in all the excitement, credited it with a speed of 10 knots when setting his torpedo sight. He fired one 'fish' at a range of 350 metres, and was relieved to see a column of water surge skyward from a hit amidships.

Held in the glare of the searchlights and constantly peppered with hits, the peril of ML 160's situation became very clear indeed when a large shell drove into the engine-room with a blinding crash and lots of smoke. Both engines cut out instantly, as did all the lights. Tom's immediate reaction was to say to himself, 'Well, this is it! What a bloody end.' But just then the engines cut in again as the engine-room crew of Motor Mechanic Cowan Walker, Leading Motor Mechanic Fred Morris and Acting Stoker Petty Officer Rice worked their magic below deck. Also hit a number of times was the petrol tank mounted on deck abaft the torpedo tubes which, had it not been filled earlier with sea water, would surely have gone up like a bomb. Lest his remaining torpedo be encouraged by a hit to do just this, Boyd turned and fired it in the general direction of the dockyards.

Alone and out of radio contact with the gunboat, Tom did finally make it to where *Campbeltown* was steadily settling by the stern. Off the tip of the Mole, an ML was clearly in trouble with a fire burning in her engine-room and Boyd immediately set off to go to her assistance. The crippled boat was Platt's ML 447, which at that very moment was in the process of being evacuated, Birney, Clibborn and Hewitt having already taken to the water and two wounded men having been lowered onto a Carley float. Ignoring heavy fire from both sides of the river, Boyd came right alongside, placing himself between Platt and the Mole, and began a hurried transfer of men, many of whom would otherwise not have survived.

Acting with considerable gallantry, Petty Officer Lamb was very much to the fore in carrying wounded men from the burning 447, a selfless mission in which he was assisted by the wounded Able Seaman Dennis Lambert of Platt's own crew, who among others got the mortally wounded Motor Mechanic Thomas Parker across to the 160. With the men in the Carley float also taken on board, the stricken 447 was methodically cleared until only the dead remained, at which point Platt himself stepped across to safety. Both of his junior officers had been lost, as had two of his crew, who were soon to be joined by Motor Mechanic Parker. Of David Birney's commandos the total to die would be eight, including Birney himself and Guardsman Bob Grose, the friend and billet-mate of Lance Corporal John Webb.

With some 2000 gallons of petrol still in her main tanks, it was clearly only a matter of minutes before ML 447 blew up, and this being the case Boyd was anxious to clear the area as quickly as possible. Manoeuvring away from the wreck, he had only just begun his run for the estuary mouth when he stopped again to pull three more survivors from the sea. Dead in the water, he presented the German gunners with a gift of a target and, just as he began to move for a second time, was hit in several parts of the boat, wounding a number of the rescued Commandos, starting a fire in the tiller flat, temporarily knocking out the port Hall-Scott and wounding Motor Mechanic Walker in the face. Forced by this damage to limp through waters where speed was their most appropriate defence, Boyd then had to take violent avoiding action to clear the huge water spouts thrown up by the shells of Dieckmann's heavy guns. Fortunately, however, at about 0330, with Walker, in spite of his wounds, having repaired the port engine, it was successfully fired up again, returning to the boat her full turn of speed.

Of the five MLs to sail north past the dry dock, Tom's was the only boat to do so intentionally, MLs 262, 267, 443 and 446 having strayed well past the landing places before returning to the heart of the action. Reversing their courses, Burt's ML 262 and Beart's ML 267 had succeeded, even if only temporarily, in putting their Commandos ashore at the Old Entrance, but, on approaching the Mole for the second time, Horlock's ML 443 and Falconar's ML 446 were to find this structure so resolutely held by the enemy that any attempt to come alongside would clearly be tantamount to suicide.

From his position abeam of the dry dock and with the Mole clearly silhouetted 800m to his rear, Lieutenant Kenneth Horlock did what he could to correct his mistake, running back through the tracer and shell bursts towards where the flaming hulks of his sister ships proclaimed the crushing superiority of the German guns. During all of his manoeuvres his stripped-Lewis guns and forward and after Oerlikons maintained a steady fire. At the after gun Ordinary Seaman George Rowlin, who was acting as loading number to the gunner, Ordinary Seaman Frank Folkard, was hit and sent down for treatment, carrying with him some empty Oerlikon drums for filling in the messdeck, where a number of Commandos were helping to grease and load each round. In order for this ammunition to feed correctly it was absolutely essential that it be carefully lubricated. When the cooper's grease ran out, the resourceful men broached a tub of butter and used this instead. With Rowlin gone, the 'Jimmy', Sub-Lieutenant Peter Royal, handed fresh drums to Frank as he needed them, the whole process of loading and firing dissolving into a blur of activity, smoke and shattering noise, sufficient to thrust aside all considerations of time and risk.

In the wheelhouse the coxswain, Leading Seaman Brady, stood to the wheel without regard to the bullets and splinters, while down in the gloom of the engine-room the irrepressible Petty Officer Motor Mechanic

Harry Bracewell responded instantly to every telegraph instruction.

Dropping down from the north, Horlock found Platt's blazing 447 blocking his approach to the slipway. As there was no sign of life on Platt's boat, Horlock's arrival must therefore have followed close upon the heels of Boyd's gallant rescue of 447's crew, as the stricken ship blew up shortly thereafter. In spite of the delay, which must have given other boats plenty of time in which to make their own attempts at gaining the slipway, no MLs were seen to be in place, and nor was there any evidence of British troops on shore. In fact all of the German positions seemed to be both intact and firing with impunity. With ammunition beginning to run short, Horlock was most unwilling to risk his ship further, so he consulted with Lieutenant Verity and the senior Commando officer, Lieutenant Joe Houghton, both of whom concurred with his assessment of the risk, before turning away and beginning his own bid for the open sea. As he sped southwards, he made smoke, the great white cloud putting the fear of God into Frank Folkard, whose first thought was that one of the shells that had been splashing all around the boat had finally put paid to their chances of making it home.

Following Horlock's example was Falconar's ML 446 which was in a considerably more parlous condition, owing to damage and casualties suffered earlier. At this precise moment all her guns were out of action, the bridge machine guns and the forward Oerlikon having jammed, and the after Oerlikon, courageously served by Ordinary Seaman Tew in spite of serious wounds, having been knocked out. Many of his own crew had been wounded and his Commando party had fared badly in the opening exchanges of fire, during which Bertie Hodgson had been killed. With its cannon still spitting fire, the Mole very obviously remained in German hands and a change of ownership did not look likely any time soon. It was painfully clear that any attempt to close further on the structure would probably result in the loss of his ship, and this being the case Falconar too judged it wiser to put his helm over and join the other battered survivors as they attempted to find a safe road through the rain of missiles. They made smoke, but this only served to attract more fire, with the result that the Third Officer, Sub-Lieutenant Hugh Arnold, was badly wounded.

Ignoring his own wounds, Sergeant Robbie Barron remained on deck until they were well clear of the harbour. He remembers 'telling one of our assault party on the way down the river, to go to the tiller flat and get some more ammunition for our small arms, but he came back saying he was unable to stay down there as the tracer was going straight through the hull of the ML at the time.' Only when they had passed through the worst of the danger did he go down to the messdeck, where the medical

197

party were doing what they could for the many wounded.

Having taken a wounded gunner below deck with the idea that it would be safer to treat him there, Lance-Corporal John Webb, whose preparation for the raid had been all but non-existent, had the shock of his life when 'there was a deafening bang and I saw a hole appear in the starboard side of the ML, and a corresponding hole appear in the port side: a shell had gone straight through the launch without exploding! The edges of the entrance hole were jagged splinters of wood. Our boats were made of wood! No wonder they burned so well. I had always thought that they were constructed of steel.'

Pushing off from *Campbeltown*'s port quarter at 0157 hours, Sub-Lieutenant Mark Rodier's ML 177 worked up to speed and began her own run for the estuary mouth, swerving through the lights and the fountains of salt spray thrust skyward by the many shells that plunged beneath the face of the sea.

Still substantially undamaged, she had on board a press of men equivalent to three times her normal complement, which left little room for Surgeon-Lieutenant Winthrope, assisted by Mr Hargreaves, to tend to the wounded. Fortunate indeed to enjoy the services of the destroyer's Canadian doctor, this ML was doubly blessed in that the skills of her own engine-room crew were supplemented by those of the two representatives of the Weymouth-base staff, the bespectacled Flotilla Engineer Officer, Sub-Lieutenant A.J. Toy, and Petty Officer Motor Mechanic John Rafferty.

Running southwards, a number of vessels were observed to be at anchor off the Avant Port. As it was safer for the boat at this critical point in the withdrawal to be free of both the danger and the topweight of her two torpe-does, Rodier fired them, although no evidence of hits was to be seen. With this being around the time that the crew of ML 270 were attributing a torpedo strike against the East Jetty to Tom Boyd's similarly armed ML 160, it is more than likely that what they actually saw was one of Rodier's 'fish', Boyd at this time still being some way up the river to the north.

Passing successfully out of the confines of the estuary throat, ML 177 next faced the hazard of the heavier coastal batteries whose shells, guided by radar, followed their every twist and turn. Their leaving signal having been made, they were a mere three miles from proving Mark Rodier wrong in the certainty of his conviction that he would not survive, when the 75mm guns of the Battery le Pointeau struck the first of the blows that would finish them.

Sub-Lieutenant Frank Arkle, having discussed with Mark the advisability of making smoke to cover their manoeuvres, was in the process of lighting the smoke float when a shell crashed into the engine room, stopping both

198

Hall-Scotts. Although the motors were dead, the boat was still moving fast through the water and, as Frank recalls, Commandos 'started launching the Carley floats from either side of the bridge. They did not secure the painters and the floats were out of sight with no one aboard before anyone could stop it.'

John Rafferty remembers:

'Down in the engine room I could hear the gunfire fading and I thought we were getting away with it. The next I knew I was lying on the engine-room deck almost submerged in water and in complete darkness. Struggling to the gang ladder I hoisted myself up, only to find that the hatch to the upper deck would not open. After a lot of banging and pushing it was eventually opened by a survivor who had been sitting on it. The scene I came upon was unbelievable, the deck was overflowing with dead and dying, and hardly anyone unscathed. We were still under merciless attack from several shore batteries, but amidst all this carnage, one of the crew was still at his post returning fire.

'Realizing that there was little I could do on deck, I decided to return to the engine room. I climbed down the steel ladder not knowing what to expect, but hoping that I could re-start the engines. The area was now bathed in blinding light from a searchlight streaming through a huge hole in the ship's side. As I contemplated the scene I heard calls for help from a Commando who came half-swimming, half-drifting through the hole. He was severely wounded and had lost an eye. With some difficulty I managed to push him up the ladder onto the deck. Returning down, I saw that the starboard engine was completely smashed, having taken a direct hit from probably a 75mm. The port engine was relatively unscathed, but all the electrics had gone and so had the hydraulics for the steering.'

With neither power nor direction, the boat was now an easy target. Toy went below decks to see what he could do, and in this move was fortunately followed by Beattie who was thus saved from being wounded or killed by the next hit, which slammed into the ML's superstructure. Frank Arkle was standing with Rodier a little astern of the bridge and he vividly remembers the funnel folding apart as if in slow motion. Rodier was between Frank and the blast and suffered terrible wounds. To some degree shielded by his Captain's body, Frank was nevertheless hit all down his left side. A large piece of shrapnel was blown into his left foot. Large pieces entered his left hip. His left thumb was broken and there were smaller pieces of metal in both hands and in his left leg and knee. Several pieces hit him in the face, one of them entering through his left eye socket. 'This eye,' he writes, 'was completely closed and I felt it hanging out on my cheek, so, as it seemed pretty useless, I plucked it out and threw it overboard. Some days later I was very pleased to learn that it was still there.'

Perhaps inevitably, the ML caught fire. 'Looking back now, ' John Rafferty recalls, 'I can't help laughing at our attempts to contain the fire, with me down in the sea filling a small wooden draw attached to a piece of string, and Beattie trying to reach it. After a few attempts we accepted the inevitable.'

With the engine room ablaze the boat was effectively divided into two. In spite of Warrant Engineer Locke's attempts to repair the compartment's damaged extinguisher mechanism, the flames soon became unstoppable, and ML 177 was finally abandoned at about 0500 hours. In a vain attempt to save his grievously wounded captain, Frank Arkle brought a drawer up from below decks to act as a float, and then climbed down into the freezing water. He had arranged with Beattie to hand Rodier down to him at this point, but Rodier died before the transfer could be made. 'After a while, ' writes Frank, 'I was joined in the water by two Commandos and we shared our bit of flotsam. We tried to swim toward the shore but tended to go round in circles. So I told them to keep moving their legs to keep warm.' In his hip pocket Frank had a flask of whisky, but to his very great frustration he was not able to liberate it, as his hands were by now far too numbed with cold to undo the button.

Standing on the stern with Beattie, John Rafferty was finding it more and more difficult to move his arms, his back having been showered with shrapnel at the time of the hit in the engine room. Recalling the final moments, he writes that the stern cocked up 'and Beattie said quietly, "That's it, time to go." We slid down the rudders and became parted. Fortunately we had our Mae Wests on. As I floated there I watched the bow and stern of 177 slide beneath the water, having resisted to the very end the most furious onslaught imaginable. The burning petrol was by now spreading and I could see a survivor getting encircled by it. I shouted to him to swim underneath it, but he responded that he could not swim. Another survivor and I managed to get to him, astonished to find him wearing two lifebelts, keeping him high in the water. Either myself or the other chap stabbed the one and pulled him as much under the flames as possible, until clear of the immediate danger. He did, however, receive severe burns to his scalp, but survived. His name was Alf Salter. Shortly afterwards exhaustion and the cold overcame me and I passed out.'

As no records were kept of the names of the ratings or Commandos who were taken off *Campbeltown* by this ML, it is impossible to state precisely how many of the men were lost. The names of the destroyer's officers are, however, known, and such mystery as there is surrounds the disappearance of Surgeon-Lieutenant Winthrope and Mr Hargreaves, the manner of whose deaths, just as was the case with Sub-Lieutenant Toy, went unrecorded. Beattie survived, as did Warrant Engineer Locke, but Nigel Tibbits, to whom so much was owed, was tragically cut down along with Chris Gough, when a burst of machine-gun fire caught them as they talked together, Beattie having moved away just moments earlier.

Similarly starred in respect of the treatment meted out to her by the German gunners was Ted Burt's ML 262, already bearing the scars of her near-fatal duel with the harbour-defence ship in the Bassin de St Nazaire. As she worked up to full speed, she was to all intents and purposes defence-less: both her Oerlikons were out of action and as the majority of her three Commando parties were demolition troops, they were in no position to supplement the thin streams of fire from the stripped-Lewis guns that now made up her meagre broadside.

Passing the Mole, Lieutenant Collier's ML 457 was seen to be on fire about a cable off. In spite of the very great risk, Burt decided to bring his own ship alongside and offer such help as he could, possibly even taking the crippled ML in tow. Himself grievously wounded, Collier had already ordered those who were left of his crew to abandon ship, although he refused to be taken off, instead urging Burt to move clear before his ML too was hit and destroyed. In time Collier would join his men in the numbing cold of the tidal stream that was sweeping men and wreckage alike towards the open sea. Of ML 457's total crew of fifteen, eight, including this officer, would not survive the night.

Ringing down for full speed, Burt had barely made half a cable when his ship was struck in the bridge, the engine room and the messdeck. At the time of the hit on the bridge, several Commandos, including Lieutenant Woodcock, were clustered in the area and Stoker Len Ball was maintaining a steady fire from the bridge wing with his stripped-Lewis gun. Len actually saw a hole appear in the structure right beside him, following which an exploding shell peppered his legs with splinters of steel and wounded Woodcock and a number of his companions. Reporting to the bridge at this point, Robbie Roberts, the First Lieutenant, enquired of Burt as to his well-being and was told by his skipper that his sole injury was 'just a bruised ass!', after which he invited Robbie to have a drink, holding out a bottle of gin, which was promptly shot from his hand.

The hits in the engine room had set the ship on fire and knocked out her engines and steering; nevertheless Burt thought it might still be possible to get out on the rapidly ebbing tide, in which case Robbie Roberts was ordered aft to organize the rigging of the clumsy tiller steering. Having by this time got the fire in the stern of the boat under control with hand extinguishers, Stoker Hollands reported this fact to the bridge. Anxious to have news of the situation in the engine room, Burt then sent him aft in an attempt to re-establish communication, but the whole upper deck was being raked by machine-gun fire and it is believed that he was killed by one of these close-range bursts.

In spite of the wounds to his legs, Len Ball was still more or less mobile. Ordered by Burt to move to the aft steering position, he withdrew, his left leg now numb. In order to reach the stern he had to cross over the top of one of the deck-mounted petrol tanks. Standing on top of it, lit up by the searchlights and flames, Len could not help but think of himself as 'target for tonight'. Moving on to where Able Seaman Don Walker's body could be seen lying in the Oerlikon gunpit, he did his best to undo the lashings on the tiller steering, but in the bad light and freezing cold it was almost impossible to make progress.

Down in the engine room the flames were soon burning out of control, the foamite fire extinguishers having been activated from the wheelhouse without effect. Leading Motor Mechanic Jack Pryde, who had only very recently joined the boat, remembers the hit as a hell of a bang followed by total darkness. He had instinctively thrown up his hands and was showered with small pieces of steel. As he had been standing close to the companion-way he was able to climb out of the darkness and smoke, only to find the boat adrift, on fire and the target of tracers which flashed towards them from positions all around the shore.

Hit also in the messdeck, a burst of fire had ripped through the crew spaces, just over the heads of Bombardier Johnny Johnson and Lance-Sergeant Gerry Bright who, having seen Smalley killed at the forward gun, had climbed down to the messdeck lobby to have a quiet smoke. It was a similar burst that caused fatal casualties only a matter of feet away in the coxswain's cabin, where Leading Seaman McKeown had taken station to help the wounded. He was killed, as was Able Seaman Martin, who had been severely wounded in the head and arm at the time the after gun was knocked out. Climbing up to the deck to find out what was happening, Johnny heard Burt give the order to abandon ship and returned to give the dread news to Gerry.

Some distance away on the stern, and with burning pools of petrol threatening to engulf them all, Len Ball thought it was high time he took to the water. He saw a Carley float go over the bow, which meant that someone up there was abandoning ship, and he decided 'Well, I'd better go, otherwise I'm going to get in the fire. So I took off my tin helmet, duffle coat and slippers – we wore slippers on the ships because of the petrol – and I dived in: and the water was freezing cold and the salt went for my legs, but that soon died off.' Striking out for the shore he found it all but impossible to make headway against the fast-retreating tide. But, steeling himself not to look, he did eventually make the quarter mile to the sea wall, where he was captured, as was Robbie Roberts, who, on hearing Burt's order, had followed Len over the side.

At about 0245, with 2000 gallons of petrol just waiting to go up, Burt had realized the end had come. Leading Seaman Leaney organized the lowering of the Carley floats and, with the help of Able Seaman Sutherland, got the wounded away from the boat. Sapper Hudspeth, of Woodcock's 3 Commando party, helped both Woodcock and Trooper Boyd over the side and into the water, although neither man survived. Jack Pryde, who had gathered with the others on the fo'c'sle, went over too, but hung onto a rope in the bitter cold as he could not swim. Eventually everyone disappeared except a fellow sailor who, like Jack, did not dare attempt to make it to the shore. Climbing back on board with the intention of finding something that would float, they cut away two of the splinter mats and tossed them over the side. Tying them together for safety, Jack lay on one and his companion on the other, and together they paddled away, eventually to come ashore on a beach, where German soldiers were waiting to take them prisoner.

Having told Gerry Bright that there was no longer any chance of a return to British shores, Johnny Johnson removed his boots, but decided to hold on to his pre-war tunic. The two then climbed up to the deck and went over the side to struggle and choke in the flame-licked water, along with a growing band of survivors. Johnny swam to a Carley float, but it was too full of men to take him. He had by now lost touch with Gerry; however, his namesake from Smalley's party, Corporal Johnson, was nearby and together they struck out for the opposite shore as for some reason Johnny was convinced it was part of unoccupied France. Confident of his swimming ability, Johnny intially saw no difficulty in the fact that they had more than a mile to go, but with the tide running so strongly, their progress was painfully slow. Deciding after all that they would be better to let it carry them along the shoreline to a point where a landfall might be made in safety, Johnny called out to his companion. Just then a searchlight caught the corporal and a machine gun spat out a burst, after which the swimming figure was nowhere to be seen. Assuming the worst, Johnny them swam downstream past the burning *Sperrbrecher*, at some point beyond which, in spite of repeating to himself, 'Keep your head up! keep your head up!', he succumbed to cold and exhaustion and gradually slipped out of consciousness. Drifting with the whim of the tide and to all intents and purposes finished, Johnny was eventually washed ashore some way down the estuary, from where his body, found rolling and tossing in the surf, was carried to a nearby German aid post. A German doctor in a last ditch attempt to revive him, injected adrenalin directly into his heart, which brought Johnny slowly back to consciousness. Awake at last, he saw Lance-Corporal Ron Howard sitting by the fire and wrapped in a blanket, his 5 Commando chum having come ashore at the same beach and been the first to spot Johnny being rolled along by a wave.

Also drifting downstream and slowly succumbing to the cold and strain was Ted Burt, who, having ditched his charts and burned his orders, had quit the burning wreck that once had been his proud command. Where so many souls were to die that night, lost and alone in the estuary, Ted was treated kindly by the tide, which carried him to Les Morées Tower, where the searching Germans would find him in the morning. Of his three Commando parties, and despite the fact that many men were suffering from wounds, the majority would survive, but of his own crew almost half had lost their lives, leaving of ML 262, which blew up shortly after she was abandoned, a mere nine sailors and a spreading stain of charred and formless wreckage.

Forced to make their bids for freedom one by one, the MLs stood little chance against the might of Dieckmann's batteries. Able to skim across the waves at 40 knots, however, the little MTB had the 3750 horse-power of her three great Packards to pit against the enemy gunners' skill, which meant that, as Wynn pulled away from the gunboat at about 0220, he was but a ten-minute sprint away from leaving the danger far behind.

Surging ahead of the heavy shells, Wynn had made a good five miles when two men on a Carley float rushed towards them out of the darkness. Having foreseen such a circumstance, the planners had included in the orders a strict instruction that commanding officers were not to stop. However, what might seem clear-cut as ink upon a sheet of paper, was considerably less so in the heat of battle and, judging that he must either stop or run the survivors down, Wynn chose to adopt the former course. Flying across the surface of the sea, he had held an advantage over the German gunners; but now this was gone: and even as the men were about to be hoisted aboard, two heavy shells crashed into MTB 74 and set her on fire, leaving the crew with no alternative but to take to the water.

About to go over the side with the others, Chief Motor Mechanic Lovegrove noticed that his Captain was nowhere to be seen and went back through the flames to look for him, eventually finding Wynn down in the wheelhouse where he had been blown by the force of a hit amidships. Barely conscious and wounded in one eye, Wynn was in no position to help himself, so Lovegrove pulled him up, guided him topside and jumped with him into the freezing water. Swimming to a Carley float around which many survivors were clustered, Lovegrove would watch over his Captain throughout a 12-hour period of drifting and despair, during which the bobbing, gasping survivors gave in one by one. When eventually discovered by a German boat, only Lovegrove, Wynn and Stoker Savage would remain of all the men who had gathered around the float, their solitude chillingly illustrating the size of the loss which was rooted in Wynn's decision to stop – a decision which in reality he could hardly have helped but make.

At the time of their discovery, which was early the following afternoon, there would be no evidence of other survivors. But some, though few in number, had won their personal battles with the numbing sea.

Seaman Torpedoman Len Denison, who during the run-in had closed up the port torpedo tube, while Able Seaman Eric Hargreaves had done the same to starboard, abandoned ship with Eric and swam with him to the Carley float. In spite of the dangers involved, the two then decided to try to swim to the shore, and so they eased away from the illusion of safety the float provided and struck out across the swiftly running tide. 'It was a cold, black night,' writes Len. 'Eric and I were talking about our situation and he just said to me, "See you, Len," and that was the last I saw of him. Swimming around, I felt a wire hawser and thought what the hell is this doing in the middle of the Loire? So I pulled myself along the hawser and came to a steel-runged ladder.'

Of all the developments a man in extremis might have imagined, this was perhaps the most unlikely, for Len had stumbled upon a disused navigation tower. Climbing free of the sea he took shelter in it, remaining high above the water until the Germans found and rescued him early on Saturday afternoon, the fourth and last of the torpedo boat's crew of ten to be so lucky.

Of the survivors Wynn had taken from *Campbeltown*, fate smiled or frowned upon them in much the same proportion. Only a handful made it through the night, these including both Frank Wherrell and Bill Stocker, who hopped over the side when MTB 74 was hit. Wearing their Mae Wests, they swam around until they came across a Carley float containing two survivors, one of whom was Stoker Petty Officer Archie Pitt, who had been in charge of the destroyer's Forward Fire Control Party until wounded early on. Climbing onto the tiny float they were carried westwards down the coast. Early on, they thought that if they could somehow remain unseen through all of Saturday, then there might be a chance of making it across to Spain; but Archie was deteriorating and, as the hours dragged by, they began to fear he might not last. Finally, early on Saturday afternoon the float was beached beneath a German gun position. Picked up immediately, they were taken into the office of a companionable senior NCO, who arranged to have their clothes dried, gave them a little Schnapps and asked them in English how they thought the war was going. He had once had a business in Liverpool and was married to an English girl. So much for getting to grips at last with 'the enemy'.

Last of the Old Entrance boats to leave, MGB 314 nosed away from the quayside at about 0230. His optimism already tainted by the distant sight of burning boats as Curtis had run in to put Newman ashore, Ryder was prepared to discover that Platt's attack had not gone to plan, hence his desire to offer assistance even at this late stage. What he did not expect, however, was to find that it had been an almost total failure, and that this all-important feature was still very securely in enemy hands; all of which meant that, as they moved out into the shell-tossed fairway, his reaction was one of deep shock when it was seen that every position was manned and intact.

Outside the shelter of their narrow anchorage, MGB 314 was immediately targeted by the guns which had already transformed so many MLs into flaming torches, whose smoke boiled and eddied across the surface of the sea. With the torpedo boat even now in the process of being abandoned, the number of total losses had already climbed to six out of fifteen, and would climb much further before the night was out. Four boats were limping away, minus steering, or engines, or both, this number including ML 262, which, as she worked her way out past the Mole, and with no frame of reference by which her real intentions might have been judged, Ryder took to be making a last desperate attempt to gain the slipway. A further four boats, all of which were troop-carriers from Platt's flotilla, were making their way out towards the rendezvous point. Collier's ML 457 was still manoeuvring north of the Mole, braving close-range fire in an attempt to hold position; and Bob Nock's ML 298 had still not broken away from her dogged circumnavigation of the buoys in the river out to the east of the fuel stores.

Grouped as they were between *Campbeltown*'s stern and the Mole defences, the gunboat and Burt's and Collier's MLs, were right in the centre of a web of fire. With such a weight of shells and bullets pressing in upon them, destruction for one or all was clearly only a matter of time and, as Curtis's crew looked on in horror, first Collier's boat was set on fire by shells from the pillbox on the Mole, and then, as Burt turned in to give assistance, he was likewise hit hard, this time by the guns on the other side of the Bassin, rivulets of flaming petrol pouring out of his ruptured tanks.

Having lost his after pom-pom and .5-inch turrets some time ago, Curtis had only one gun left with which he could attempt to diminish the German barrage, this being the pom-pom of gunners Savage and Smith, who stood dreadfully exposed on the fo'c'sle. Ordered to open fire on the Mole position which Tiger Watson had been investigating when urged away by Pritchard, the two men poured out a stream of shells, some of which were so accurately targeted by Savage that they passed right through the embrasure of the pill-box and burst inside among its crew.

Switching targets, Savage next did his best to knock out the roof-top guns and a searchlight which was shining dead along the Mole; but, firing as he was from such an inferior position, it proved impossible to engage these elevated targets effectively. Just then a party of Germans was seen to run into the Mole position and reactivate its gun, requiring Savage and Smith to engage and silence it for a second time.

Hit with ever more frequency, the gunboat was, however, going to have to move quickly, before she, too, was struck a mortal blow. In the absence of a floating reserve, the situation at the Mole was clearly beyond redemption. No other boats were seen in the searchlight beams or silhouetted by the glare of the flames; and with so many rescued men already on board, nothing could be done for the hapless Collier or Burt. In such an obviously hopeless situation, Ryder might well have been forgiven for breaking away. But with more than half an hour remaining during which Newman's survivors would still be making for the Mole, he chose instead to return to the Old Entrance, search for Colonel Charles and do his best to warn him that the fleet upon which all the Commandos' hopes were pinned was already all but destroyed.

For Ordinary Seaman Tom Milner, just turned twenty-one and formerly an apprentice carpet weaver in Durham, ML 298's passage along the right side of the *Sperrbrecher* had been his first real opportunity to fire his gun in anger. Tom was Bob Nock's forward Oerlikon gunner, a role in which he was assisted by Stoker Jim Mathers, his Scottish loading number.

As Bob manoeuvred in the fairway, Tom kept up a steady fire of red tracer at guns and lights on either side of the river, the incessant banging of his own Oerlikon being supplemented by the steady clatter of Ordinary Seaman Douglas Clear's after gun. In the early stages of the action it had been Tom's impression that the greater part of the punishment the boat was taking was being suffered by the after part, which made it all the more unfortunate when

Jim Mathers was struck and killed during one of his excursions to the ammunition lockers. Shrapnel also hit Tom in the face and back; nevertheless he continued to man the gun until it jammed, leaving Douglas Clear at the after gun solely responsible for maintaining the ML's bombardment.

With the coxswain, Petty Officer Robert Hambley, RN, skilfully following Bob's steering orders in the lightly armoured wheelhouse, ML 298 continued to draw fire during the whole period of the landing attempts. The noise was intense, so much so that Bob found his gun telephones to be ineffective and resorted to the use of a megaphone instead. As the attack developed it became clear that much of the enemy fire was being directed at the waters just off the Old Mole, so Bob engaged and silenced two guns that were firing on fixed bearings into the area from a position just east of the dry dock.

Mercifully spared the toll of casualties that had been the lot of so many of his contemporaries, Bob held on, with Ordinary Seaman Clear's voracious appetite for ammunition now being met by supplies from the forward gun until such time as he judged it appropriate to attempt to take off as many as he could of Newman's Commandos and then make for home. Breaking away, he ordered Hambley to steer a course for the Mole that would take them close enough to *Campbeltown*'s stern to be able to see if anyone was waiting there. In the immediate area of the landing points several hulks were burning to destruction; however, this chilling sight in no way affected Bob's conviction that men would be waiting somewhere to clamber on to his decks.

Passing close by the destroyer, which showed no signs of life, Bob attempted to close with the Mole, only to find its approaches blocked by burning remains. His aerial having been shot away, he was now on his own. Convinced that Newman's men must be waiting elsewhere, Bob therefore reversed his course and made instead for the Old Entrance, berthing against the outer segment of its southern quay. This area, in stark contrast to the waters around the Mole, proved to be eerily quiet.

After holding on for a few minutes, and with no one in sight either friendly or otherwise, Bob decided to cut his losses and make for the rendezvous point. Ringing down for full revolutions, he gave his steering orders to Hambley, the dip of the stern as they pulled away being a welcome signal to Tom Milner that they were on their way home at last. As they headed south towards the flames surrounding the Mole, the gunboat was seen driving north towards *Campbeltown*'s stern. She does not appear to have noticed ML 298 and, receiving no orders from her, Bob saw no reason to amend his chosen course of action.

On his way past the tip of the Mole, it was necessary for ML 298 to pass through a stretch of water littered with burning wreckage and pools of flame. Silhouetted by the fires, the decks were swept with shells and bullets at only a few hundred metres' range, causing many casualties among the crew. She also caught fire astern as burning petrol set her transom alight. In an attempt to put the German gunners off, Bob gave the order to make smoke; however, as they entered the estuary proper, and in spite of much manoeuvring, the enemy guns and lights continued to assail her, the beaconing flames aft having by this time grown to the point where the fire extinguishers were powerless to put them out; even the depth-charges were melting in the heat.

In spite of Ordinary Seaman Clear's best attempts to shoot out the search-lights, there was by this time very little doubt about the outcome. After a handful of near misses, she was hit several times by heavy shells, one of which exploded in the engine-room, knocking out both engines. Protected by its metal sheathing, the wheelhouse was still intact and Hambley was unhurt, but, apart from this, Bob had only a hazy idea about how high the casualty list was climbing. Douglas Clear was by now mortally wounded. His 'Jimmy', Sub-Lieutenant Spraggon, and his spare officer, Sub-Lieutenant Varden-Patten, were both dead somewhere out on the deck, and Bob himself was only marginally mobile, an earlier explosion having driven copper nails into his ankle.

Already past Les Morées Tower, ML 298 was by now drifting helplessly and Bob ordered the survivors of his crew, most of whom were wounded, to take to the two Carley floats. He remembers distinctly that he himself left the boat still adorned with his tin hat, binoculars, Colt pistol, duffel coat and sea-boots. Very much to the fore in clearing the ship, Hambley took care to search all the living and machinery spaces before he, too, went over the side.

Ordered off by Hambley, Tom Milner was moving towards the stern when he came across Stoker Leslie Charles Smith, known because of his initials as 'Elsie'. Elsie was lying on the deck covered in blood, swearing his head off and repeating over and over, 'They've got me, they've got me!' Tom picked him up, eased him over the side and went into the water right after him. Having been hit himself, Tom certainly knew about it when the salt got into his wounds. For the badly injured Elsie, however, the pain must have been truly unbearable, for instead of attempting to make a fight of it, he just put his arms up over his head and slid into the depths.

Striking out for a float containing four occupants, Tom was taken on board, bringing the total list of survivors from ML 298 up to six out of sixteen. With Bob Nock making his own way to the shore, this small float contained, in addition to Tom, his namesake Able Seaman Arthur Milner, Ordinary Telegraphist Kirk, the wounded Able Seaman Wood, and the indefatigable Petty Officer Hambley. In the fullness of time all six men would be carried shorewards by the tide and taken prisoner.

Whereas Bob Nock had found the Old Entrance a relatively tranquil place, the same pacific scene did not greet Curtis as he tried to bring the gunboat back inside. Describing their arrival, Ryder writes that, 'Matters were without doubt getting out of hand now. There was a fierce battle going on across the Old Entrance. It was impossible for us to go in. We were unable to join in this battle, as we were unable to see which was our own side. Somebody, presumably one of our own side, climbed back on board *Campbeltown* and poured a fierce fire from one of the Oerlikon guns into the general confusion. He was shot and fell from his gun. There seemed to be little that we could do here, we were loaded down with over forty men, mostly seriously wounded. We were floodlit by the blazing building close by, and lying stopped. Being the only ship left, we were attracting the individual attention of all hostile positions that could see us. Most of the tracer from close range passed low over our heads, but we must have also been clearly silhouetted to the batteries on the south bank, as they again opened up an unpleasantly accurate fire. We could see it coming straight at us, an unpleasant feeling. But they seemed to be shooting short, and it mostly struck the water and ricochetted over our heads. We lit and dropped a smoke float. While crouching on our bridge, I held a hurried council of war with Curtis and Green. The situation was undoubtedly deteriorating – in a few minutes we should inevitably be set on fire like the others. Both of the only landing places were in enemy hands, and sadly we realized that there was nothing we could do to help our gallant soldiers on shore. We had many wounded on board; our decks were crowded with them so that it was difficult to move. We must leave at once and save them.'

The decision having therefore been taken that they should quit the scene, the gunboat sped towards the south, still some minutes shy of 0300 hours. Unseen by the enemy, who continued to fire enthusiastically into the sparks and flames emitted by the smoke float, her majestic sweep past the tip of the Mole was somewhat ruefully observed by Ordinary Telegraphist George Davidson, still hiding among the rolls of wire netting, who saw her as 'the last bus', with all on board going home while he was not.

Keeping towards the south bank, they seemed at first to be getting away with it, but their luck could not last for ever, and eventually they were illuminated by the predatory beams, which seemed to act as silver pathways along which Mecke's brigades hurled streams of glowing flak. Approaching

Les Morées light, they overtook Fenton's crippled ML 156, which was instructed by signal to follow the gunboat out.

With something like thirty men on board who had been hit at least once, efforts to ease the suffering of those who crowded the deck and the spaces below continued throughout the withdrawal. Unlike MLs 446 and 307, both of which carried medically trained personnel, treatment on board the gunboat was very basic. Sub-Lieutenant Chris Worsley spent much of the run out applying dressings to wounds and using the boat's supply of tiny syrettes to inject those most in need with morphine. One or two of the men were suffering from phosphorous burns, for the treatment of which nothing could be done save to keep the burns moist.

'On one occasion, ' writes Worsley, 'I was bending over a commando who, because he had been wounded in the abdomen, was propped up against the starboard .5 turret, when a piece of shrapnel passed between the rim of my steel helmet and my forehead, to go into his abdomen. That, I felt, was a close call! On another occasion I found a sea-boot containing a torn-off leg, which I threw into the river, lying between the pom-pom and the forward ready-use locker. I looked around for the limb's former owner and found him lying on the deck near the site of my first action station. The leg had been ripped off obliquely downward from the inner side of the groin, leaving so short a stump that it was not possible to apply a tourniquet. To try and stop the bleeding I bound a field dressing on it as high and as tightly as I was able, then covered the rest of the wound with more field dressings. Except for injecting a syrette of morphine, there was nothing more I could do for him so I continued on my round.' At the time, and in the confusion of the action, Worsley was under the impression that the mortally wounded sailor was Frank Smith; however, it was not Frank but the forward pom-pom's loading number, Able Seaman Stephens, who lay dying on the bloodstained foredeck.

Sharing the grisly burden with Worsley were several other individuals, including the 'sparks', Ordinary Telegraphist Reynolds, the Coxswain, Leading Seaman McKee, and Gordon Holman, who marvelled at the courage of the men. Working largely by touch and by torchlight, within the gunboat's riddled hull, their contribution was critical in sustaining life-force during the long hours of waiting to rendezvous with *Atherstone* and *Tynedale*.

Passing by Les Morées tower, the gunboat entered that portion of the estuary controlled by Dieckmann's heavier coastal batteries. 'Whereas the tracer from the flak positions invariably passed astern of us, ' writes Ryder, 'the coastal artillery, on the other hand, must have over-estimated our speed, as their salvoes landed ahead. Great plumes of water rose up ahead of us, leaving a column of thin, misty vapour which must have helped to conceal us.'

Seen from Chris Worsley's point of view:

'Being straddled by the shells of heavy guns was very unpleasant, and though I do not recall them doing any damage to the boat, the huge water spouts which erupted a short distance ahead very sharply reminded us of the precariousness of our situation. A few moments later Dunstan ordered me to go down aft and turn on the Chemical Smoke Apparatus [CSA]. In order to avoid wasting any of the limited supply of compressed air, the three valves on the unit had to be opened in a particular order which, alas, I did not know. Then, because no smoke appeared within a couple of minutes, the First Lieutenant, Sub-Lieutenant Bill Brooker, came aft to give me a hand. He had no more success than I, and a little later our Navigating Officer, Lieutenant Bill Green, RN, came aft and joined us. While we were vainly manoeuvring the valves, I chanced to notice an Admiralty pattern smoke-float on the starboard end of the transom. I stood up and went over to the float, and though I knew it would put out a dense cloud of smoke, I forgot that there is no smoke without fire; for the float was set going by the friction of one chemical compound against a different compound, in the same way that a safety-match functions. The flame gave away our position and the enemy fired a burst from a large-calibre automatic weapon at us as soon as he saw where we were. The tracer going into the transom just under my left foot so startled and shook me that I picked up the float instinctively, without thinking of its weight, lifted it high over my head and threw it as far as I could over the stern. As the float bobbed up and down on the water, the flame continued to burn brightly, attracting the enemy's attention. He obviously thought he had set us on fire and had got us, for he now concentrated his fire on the flame.'

With the last plunging salvo from the shore batteries having been fired at a range of some four miles, the gunboat was to all intents and purposes clear of the estuary confines. Ryder was still alive to the threat posed by Schmidt's destroyers, but it seemed they were now sufficiently secure for speed to be reduced in the hope that Fenton's boat might catch up. Instead of Fenton nosing out of the darkness astern, however, the dim shape of what was taken to be another ML was seen ahead, and the gunboat altered towards her, only to discover that their friendly ML was, in fact, an enemy patrol vessel whose crew were very much on the alert. As the gunboat slewed violently to port in an attempt to open the range, the German ship began firing, holing the gunboat forward on the waterline and sending one long burst of tracer into

MGB 314's petrol compartment, though, as Ryder recalls, 'By the Grace of God we were not set on fire.'

Quickly working up to her full speed, the gunboat raced away, on this occasion sorely missing the firepower of her after pom-pom and powered machine guns. Up on the fo'c'sle gunners Savage and Smith had only seconds in which to train and fire their gun before the German ship drifted behind the shelter of the gunboat's stubby superstructure. 'It raked us from stem to stern, ' recalls Frank Smith, 'with small-arms fire, bullets and shrapnel flying around, pinging off guard rails and metal fittings, and dull thudding sounds as the bullets hit the splinter mats which were secured to the sides of the bridge. The action was sudden and unexpected; we were no more than a hundred yards away when she opened up on us. We only had time to fire a few rounds off before she was abaft the bridge, and the pom-pom couldn't bear.'

And then, almost as suddenly as it had begun, the brief but violent encounter was over. A small fire was visible on the enemy's deck, while the gunboat, sporting a new collection of holes, appeared to have got away with a clumsy encounter which could have spelled the end for all of them. The engines were all right, there was no vital damage to the structure, nor was there any evidence of fatal casualties. It was only when Frank Smith attempted to train the pom-pom fore and aft and found it would not budge that it was discovered that Bill Savage, deserted as ever by 'lady luck', lay slumped across the elevating wheel. Thinking at first that Bill had merely fainted, Frank was greatly distressed to learn that his fellow gunner, with whom every danger of the night had been shared in equal lots, was in fact dead. Hit by a small shell or by chunks of shrapnel, Bill had died instantly from a massive, open chest wound, during the very last throes of an action whose enviable list of honours would include a Victoria Cross in his name, in recognition of the courage displayed by so many of the ratings. Ordinary Seaman Bill Whittle fetched a blanket and covered Bill's body with it. Later Peter Ellingham and Ordinary Telegraphist Reynolds would be detailed to prepare the remains for an eventual transfer to a destroyer. With Bill dead and the loading number, Able Seaman Stephens, dying nearby, Frank was left alone on the gun until such time as Curtis could detail a relief.

Having already made one potentially fatal error in ship recognition, Ryder and Curtis were not about to make the same mistake again, so when another shape was seen ahead some ten minutes later, at around 0330 hours, rather greater care was taken in ensuring it was friendly. It was in fact Lieutenant Irwin's ML 270, still limping homewards at about 12 knots and steering by means of her long and awkward tiller. On her way out she had suffered an

213

engine fire, which had been extinguished by the prompt action of Stoker Leslie Holloway. Now all was chaos in the engine-room as the tired and protesting Hall-Scotts were used to help direct their progress, one motor even being reversed from time to time. This ML also had encountered the German ship and had engaged it with her tiny Hotchkiss. As with the gunboat, her crew were not inclined to be trusting, and when an unidentified ship was seen to be coming up rapidly from astern, all the guns that would bear were levelled upon the intruder, Ordinary Telegraphist Stewart Burkimsher, and the 'bunting tosser', Signalman Len Kelley, resting their Lewis guns on the starboard torpedo tube. But this time at least there was to be no final reckoning and when the two friends came together in a darkness which might well harbour other units of a vengeful enemy, Curtis reduced his speed to that of his damaged consort, and the two ships, bloodied but unbowed, continued their withdrawal in company.

16

Throwing For Sixes

The last vessel having now withdrawn from the harbour area, the action in and around St Nazaire itself ceased to be a joint affair and became instead the solitary province of the Commandos.

During the whole of the period of the dramas afloat, Newman's boys had been operating within a perimeter whose form was roughly that of a figure of eight, the north and south enclosures of which were connected by the bridge at 'G'. To the north of 'G' the parties landed from *Campbeltown* had begun their various moves towards the withdrawal point a little after two o'clock, while south of it the attenuated HQ group of Newman and Troop Sergeant-Major Haines, reinforced by those who were left of the Walton, Watson and Pritchard teams, waited patiently to receive them before starting a more general pull-back towards what was still assumed to be a bridgehead held by Birney at the Mole.

Recognizing that the bridge must be securely held until all the northern parties were brought out, the orders had been so arranged as to place no fewer than three Commando parties next to it. To prepare the bridge and the Old Entrance lock gates for destruction, the demolition team of Lieutenant Mark Woodcock and his protection party under Lieutenant Dick Morgan had been scheduled to storm ashore from Ted Burt's ML 262; while just a little to the north of their positions it was up to Donald Roy's assault group to secure a bridgehead until such time as Newman gave them leave to move away.

Totalling twenty-eight officers and men, this little force should have been more than capable of carrying out all the tasks entrusted to it. However, enemy fire had quickly beaten off both Woodcock and Morgan, and their failure to take the bridge had effectively left Donald Roy in sole charge of a position so devoid of cover that the eventual extermination of his men became a mathematical certainty, whose only variable element was time.

Moving forward upon completion of their pump-house tasks, this kilted party, whose numbers had already been reduced to twelve by the loss to wounds of Lieutenant Johnny Proctor and Private Hughie Cox, found itself in possession of a narrow isthmus surrounded on three sides by water. Facing them, and the object of their most immediate concern, lay the dockyard complex which took up all the ground between themselves and the unblown bridge at 'M'. From this ominous huddle of sheds and workshops, compounds and blind alleys, men might at any moment be expected to appear. But would they be retiring parties of their friends or the first probing squads of the enemy, sent forward to test the Tommies' strength and purpose?

Dreadfully exposed to German fire, save for the cover of a low wall in whose doubtful shelter most of Roy's party would choose to ride out the storm, the isthmus was overlooked by numerous enemy positions, against which no effective fire could be directed in return. And adding greatly to the weight of this already substantial cannonade, the warships in the Bassin, having earlier slipped their moorings, were now free to roam at will as mobile strong points. Of the four harbour defence vessels present, one had been scuttled by its commander lest it fall into British hands; however, three remained, in addition to whose guns the five large trawler-like vessels of the 16th minesweeping flotilla could bring both cannon and machine-gun fire to bear on any threatened portion of the dockyard.

Against such a weight of shot and shell Roy could do little save watch his boys succumb one by one to wounds. Working directly in his favour was the commendable speed with which the Group Three parties could be relied upon to place and blow their charges; however, what more than anything else prolonged his stand was German confusion as to the actual strength of the forces ranged against them in the docks. Had they but suspected just how small and isolated were the British parties, they could at any time have used their ships to carry troops across the Bassin and force the kind of landings that might well have won for them a speedy triumph.

Sergeant Colin Jones, who, though wounded on *Campbeltown*, had been helped ashore by his comrades, was first on a list of casualties which, over a period of almost ninety minutes, would grow to include Gunner Bob Milne, Lance-Corporals Frank Sumner and Harold Roberts, and Privates Johnny Gwynne, Tommy McCormack and Arthur Ashcroft, the last two suffering particularly badly. It was a harsh accounting; yet, in the absence of a direct assault, it still would not be enough to break the grip of 5 Troop on their few square metres of France.

Thus it was that when the survivors of all the northern parties began their dash for Newman's perimeter, Roy's men were there to ease the way for each and every one – guardians of the bridge, guardians of the only road that led to home.

First to emerge from the darkness and identify themselves to Roy by voice and light were the survivors of the demolition squads and their protectors.

Chant was first to make the crossing of the bridge, his team complete again now that Butler had rejoined. With Jimmy Brown having attached himself after completing his tasks on the outer caisson, this group crossed underneath the structure, swinging from girder to girder, the first of many to thus dip beneath the bursts of fire that swept above them. The wounded Chamberlain, with only one good arm, posed their only problem in that he had to be manoeuvred from grip to grip by the others. But he, too, finally made it to the 'home' side, allowing his young officer to report proudly to Newman, 'All tasks complete, sir; and all men present and correct'.

Following quickly upon the heels of Chant, the able-bodied members of the remaining teams also took their chances. Corran Purdon has recorded that his plan for crossing 'G' was simply to 'make a bolt of it, and trust to God!' – a straightforward throw of the dice in which he was joined by Sergeant Frank Carr and Lance-Corporal Fred Lemon. Well aware of the fact that he might soon become a POW, Fred took the precaution while making his own dash for the south side to toss his fighting knife away into the lock below.

Those who were wounded straggled in behind the rest. Some, such as Lance Sergeant Dai Davis, of Denison's party, hobbling painfully southwards with a lump of German steel embedded in his foot, were able to make progress under what remained of their own steam; but others, as was the case with Lieutenant Gerard Brett, could move only with the help of such friends who stayed behind to see them through.

Carried down the side of the dry dock by Bob Wright, himself in a deal of pain because of his wounded knee, and Fergie Ferguson, Brett's tail-end group received a welcome reinforcement, just as they approached the pump-house, in the shape of Corporal Joe Molloy of the Royal Ulster Rifles. But when they kinked sharp right to approach bridge 'G' itself, they found it so swept by fire that the decision was quickly taken to cross instead along the top of the outer set of Old Entrance lock gates, the very ones which were the target of Wynn's torpedoes.

'And I said to Joe Molloy, ' recalls Bob, ' "You go first". And he said,

"Yes." And I said to Fergie, "If you can get Brett across at the back, I'll go next, and if anybody comes up you can give us covering fire." Well, of course, just as Joe started there was a burst of fire and I saw Joe spin round and half-stagger, and I thought, "God! How the hell are we going to get across here!" ' However, Joe had not been badly hit and did after all manage to make it to the other side. A bullet had ripped across his back at shoulder height, laying open the flesh on either side of his spine; another half an inch and it might very well have crippled him.

Following close behind, with Brett half across his back and groaning with pain every time his wounded legs came into contact with the handrail, Bob was lucky in that not a shot came near him. Fergie was lucky too, which meant that all four men survived to be challenged by British forces. Carrying Brett across to make his report to Newman, Bob then left his young officer, with others who were wounded, in the shelter of a warehouse.

Moving south towards Roy, Bill Copland's push along the Bassin came to a temporary halt when his party reached the expanse of coverless ground they would somehow have to cross to get to 'G'. Describing what happened next, his words only hint at just how precarious was the Commandos' hold upon their ground and how easily they might have been driven from it by a force of equal skill and resolution to their own.

Copland recalls:

'We bunched up close and made a fast dash for it and again we were lucky. From the safe side of the gap I saw, about forty yards away, dim figures moving, and thought, "They should be Roy's party, so here goes", pressed my torch with its dim blue light, and called "Copland here". An answering blue pinpoint of light blinked back at me, and a voice called, "Roy here – come through". I stopped a few seconds with Donald, whose men were all disposed over what cover they could get from the heavy fire, and told him I was pushing on to the Old Mole. Motioning my party to move, I got half-way across the bridge when a burst of machine-gun fire cracked into the twelve-foot-high concrete walls at the side of the bridge. A strong hand pulled me to the ground, and an even stronger voice said, "Keep your bloody head down!" We lay on the roadway till the fire slackened, during which time I called out to my party to check their names. Cheetham, who had been with us at the last gap did not answer, so I crawled back to see him lying this side of the gap, about forty yards away. I arranged with Donald to have him sent down with one of his own wounded men, John Gwynne. Time was flying far too fast and I still had visions of fourteen beautifully empty MLs waiting at the Old Mole . . . so, collecting Hannan and Fyfe close behind me, we upped and made one final dash for the shelter of the buildings on the "home" side of the bridge at "G".'

Linking up with Newman, Copland was able to give the fullest detail yet of the sweep of successes encompassing the neutralization of the 'Normandie' dock, setting against these the failures at bridge 'M'. With the numbers on the 'home' side steadily building, it would soon be time to move towards the Mole, there to meet the boats that Steele, aided now by Fyfe, was still gamely trying to contact, the one transmitting constantly while the other stood by ready to receive.

Bill Etches having by now also made it to the south side, there was need for only a handful of individuals still to report, before the order could go out to the assault groups to pull back and complete the evacuation of the whole of the northern enclosure. In attempting to comply with Copland's request, Johnny Gwynne and Corporal Cheetham did cross over 'G' only to be taken prisoner by a group of enemy who disarmed them and then attempted to kill them both. Johnny was shot in the back; however, Cheetham managed somehow to escape. Making his own way down from 'M', Micky Burn, on passing through Roy's bridgehead and finding Roy 'unruffled', came upon the recumbent form of the very badly wounded Arthur Ashcroft. In spite of his admitted unpracticality, and only too aware that he was 'not the sort of person to trust with syringes, ' Micky administered morphine, using one of his tiny syrettes. In no condition to be moved as yet, Arthur would have to be left behind for the enemy to find and treat; however, there is little doubt that, but for Micky's impromptu administrations, young Cameron Highlander would not have made it through the night.

Among the very last to cross, Bob Montgomery and Sergeant Jameson had joined Roy not far in advance of the final pull-back. Still with some of his explosives left and finding a truck nearby, Bob decided to open the door and put a charge inside and see what happened; it blew apart most satisfactorily. Then it was on to the bridge itself, crossing as Chant had done by means of the girders underneath. On reaching the 'home' side, Montgomery was shocked to find that Jameson was no longer with him. As they had begun the crossing together, the only conclusion to be drawn was that he had either been killed or knocked to his death in the water below.

The arrival of the last few stragglers having confirmed that the northern area was clear, save for his bridgehead parties and the sightless shells of the dead, Newman was now anxious to pull both Roderick and Roy back as quickly as possible.

All the men had been briefed to watch out for the special 35-star rockets to be put up from the HQ position some time around 0230 hours, which would be their final signal to withdraw. But all the rockets had gone down with ML 267, which left Newman no alternative but to send a runner out across the fire-swept bridge. Lance Corporal Harrington, of the HQ party, was the luckless soul sent out, to find, no doubt to his great relief, that Johnny Roderick and his party, having mistakenly 'identified' the rockets amid the bursts of colour which everywhere lit up the night sky, were already almost home, leaving him only Roy to deal with. Writing later of Harrington's solitary dash, Newman would comment: 'To say that he went off at the double, delivered his message and rejoined us just as we were leaving the HQ building, needs special mention. He might well have been carrying a message during training at home.'

Together again, once the bridgehead parties had brought their much-needed weapons back within the fold, the role of the Commandos underwent a sea change, from that of doing their best to upset the enemy's applecart to that of getting clear before they found themselves run over by it. Numbering just below 100, many of whom, being demolition troops, were armed with nothing heavier than Colt .45s, the effectiveness of this group was further weakened by the fact that a substantial proportion were wounded. They occupied a loosely formed perimeter, which, as it filled with men, swelled slowly southwards towards the Mole. Under steadily increasing pressure from uncoordinated parties of the enemy working forward from the Old Town, this perimeter was not quite yet in mortal danger; however, nor was it by any means secure, as Micky Burn for one was soon to find when he was suddenly captured by three Germans while moving on alone. Able to speak his captors' language well, Micky was chillingly aware that they were debating whether or not to shoot him on the spot; so he did his best to sway their decision by assuring them that he would be a very important catch indeed if taken prisoner. All the time they talked, and having parted with his compass and his watch, Micky led them slowly back towards his own lines in the hope that his plight might be noticed by his friends. Effectively charming their fingers from their triggers, he succeeded in confusing them long enough for Troop Sergeant-Major George Haines to issue a challenge, at which point all three ran off into the darkness. Micky had been fortunate indeed. In similar situations arising elsewhere on the night, other threatened Commandos would have no 'Saint George' to sally forth so ably in their defence.

Having received so many encouraging reports of successes around the dry dock, Newman, who knew nothing of the destruction of Ryder's fleet, was at this stage in very fine fettle indeed. True there were no similar reports coming in from the southern area, but, as regards the withdrawal itself, he, along with most of his men, still confidently expected the Navy to be waiting to take them off. One or two of his men had noticed launches burning on the river, but as yet no coherent image had imprinted itself upon the minds of the Commandos as a whole that was dark enough to shade the glow of their achievements. Thus it was that when they set off through the roads and alleys their shock was all the greater when they saw that their pristine, cosy ships of recent memory were now a fleet of smoking wrecks, tossed across the surface of the river as by a giant, flaming hand which had at a stroke transmuted courage and defiance into chaos.

In Watson's words:

'When we saw the river before us we stopped, appalled. The surface of the water was lit up brightly by sheets of flaming petrol, while thick, oily black smoke rose above the flickering glow. A few blackened hulls, some still smouldering redly along the waterline, were all that remained of the MLs to take us home. We stood speechless. For a moment all seemed suddenly silent to me, despite the guns which were still firing down the river. Presumably shock had rendered me unconscious of sound for those few seconds. But there was no time for contemplation. Major Bill was already organizing a defensive perimeter.

'We got Wickson's Bren to bear on that thrice cursed gun on the Old Mole, which I had originally thought to be safely in our hands. Its crew were the very men who had been running with arms raised, and whose lives I had spared. They had crept back and done untold harm to my comrades since then. My indignation did not prevent a certain reluctance to open fire on a party of unsuspecting Germans who were, incredibly, standing at ease and, even more incredibly, smoking, as though they had knocked off for the night. But this was war; their recklessness cost them dearly.'

Realizing that, far from being able to get back home to his Patricia, he and his men would have to continue fighting throughout the night, Corran Purdon was later prompted to wonder just how different their situation might have been had their plan to use a second destroyer not fallen foul of the Navy. For the want of such a ship half their targets would survive the night intact and 100 good men were now pinned to the shore by the enemy. The half-measures taken to ensure their success looked to be yielding half the result that might otherwise have easily been within their grasp. It was a lesson proved in conflicts right throughout the ages from whose obvious conclusions military bureaucracy still appeared to be immune.

For Copland a succession of thoughts streamed quickly through his mind. 'Can we hold this position until all our troops get back again? What will Charles decide to do? We can't just give in without making a fight for it, whatever the odds against us are. Can we pinch a ship and get away?'

Setting to work with his usual speed and efficiency, he began to organize the men into some semblance of a defensible bridgehead. The area which they were to hold was a about 100 metres directly north of the Mole. With tail-enders still straggling in, its perimeter was fluid at best; in an attempt to keep the Germans from rolling it up, he put parties under Donald Roy and Troop Sergeant-Major Haines respectively out to either flank.

With more and stronger clusters of the enemy pushing ever northwards from the Old Town, the situation in this temporary holding area, as recalled by Watson, 'resembled a lethal game of cowboys and indians, with small groups of each side within yards of each other. It became even more like the Wild West when we pushed together some railway waggons and used them as cover.'

In the darkness both sides had problems identifying friend from foe, with death and wounds from friendly fire an almost inevitable consequence of such proximity. Lance-Sergeant Alf Searson already knew that bullets were blind to the subtleties of national identity and now Tiger himself was to witness just how easy it was for a man to be shot down by his own side:

> 'Out of the shadows where a moment before a group of Germans had been a figure leapt toward us. His right arm was upraised and he was shouting something that was lost in the din. Then he crumpled, shot down before he could hurl his supposed grenade. As he fell I was horrified to glimpse a patch of white. Could he be one of ours after all? I had to know. Calling to the nearest men to hold their fire, I scuttled out to the huddled figure on the ground. Yes, he was one of ours all right. He was wearing white scrubbed gaiters. He was still breathing, but tremors ran through him even as I knelt and gave him morphia. I think he was probably dying, but we will never know who he was, or to which group he had belonged. He had not used his blue pinpoint torch.'

Hurriedly assessing his options, Newman, who was sheltering along with Day, was in no more mood to compromise than were his men. He had already come to terms both with the fact that withdrawal by sea was now clearly impossible and with the consequences of the earlier failures at the Mole, which left all the southern bridges open to the enemy; but he was not encouraged by either of these reverses to be anything other than offensively minded, at one time even considering that his present force might still carry out the southern demolitions.

Surrender was not an option, and nor was the rather arrogant alternative of fighting it out for pride's sake in a position which gave him no room for manoeuvre. The Germans were brave enough; however, they did not possess the certainty in close-quarters fighting that the Commandos rightly regarded as their own special skill and it was in this small advantage, were it to be ruthlessly exploited before sheer weight of numbers told in the enemy's favour, that Newman's hopes of salvation lay. Rather than hang back, he would instead form his men into independent groups and attack the enemy across the very bridges they were using in an attempt to corner him. 'I considered, ' he later wrote 'that not only would such small parties, spread over a fairly wide area, be able to inflict on the enemy the greatest amount of casualties, but that they would have individually a better chance to filter through the town and make their getaway into the country beyond.'

Of the three bridges open to them, only the bridge at 'D' was in any real sense reachable, and even this, as it could not be approached directly, could be forced only after a detour through the roads and alleys the men had already negotiated once to reach the Mole. In effect Newman's hand was being forced by the failure of the radios to warn him in time of the débâcle involving Platt's flotilla, for had he but known earlier that withdrawal by sea was impossible, he could have taken his men to the north instead and into the vast maze of buildings out by Penhoët, through whose sheltering confines they would have had a very good chance indeed of reaching the countryside and pushing on for Spain.

As it was, the surviving Commandos were faced instead with a direct assault against the enemy's heart, along a front that was no more than a few yards wide. In assessing their chances it is impossible to imagine any circumstance short of a miracle that could see them across the lock in sufficient numbers to make their likely losses worth the sacrifice. In any cold calculation of probability they clearly faced the prospect of annihilation, and yet Newman's decision to hazard all came as a surprise to no one. It was all a question of perceived superiority, an emboldening amalgam of individual and collective pride which, tugging on the skirts of hubris, did not brook the concept of taking second place to anyone. The Commandos' blood was up. Those who had thus far tested the enemy had always seen his resistance crumble into dust. Giving up was simply not an option. If the enemy wished to stop them he must prove his blood the better, man to man.

Having decided to fight, Newman made his decision known to both Copland and Day, in a conflab next to one of the railway trucks. While they

223

were talking a German 'potato masher' grenade exploded at their feet. Not a man was scratched! Perhaps even miracles were not too much to hope for after all.

Newman remembers:

'By this time parties had become completely split up, so the only thing to do was to form groups of about twenty men in each, to set off out of the bridge-head towards the town, using "fire and movement", the old slogan, as their means of progress. Bill called up all group leaders and, whilst I was explaining the position to them and giving them orders, Bill was busy dividing the troops into groups. The scene at the bridgehead is difficult to describe . . . fires and smoke everywhere, and small-arms fire coming from most of the buildings around us. Stan dealt with some screaming Germans up an alley between two buildings close by us. Why do they scream so?

'Everyone was behaving magnificently and coolly returning the fire with ever-decreasing ammunition. When the group leaders reported, their salutes and bearing might well have been back in Scotland and the orders to fight inland were received with grins which reflected their delight at being able to continue the scrap.'

During the impromptu O-group Newman explained that, having broken through the German lines, their ultimate destination must be neutral Spain. As armed participants in the world conflict, they would certainly be detained there if caught. But as 'escaping POWs' they might just make it to Gibraltar and home. 'Then it's "*prisionero de guerra escapado*", sir?', observed Watson. 'That's the idea, Tiger, ' the Colonel confirmed.

With the men now loosely formed into groups, Copland made a last tour of the line. He was accompanied by Private Fahy of the King's Regiment who, armed with a Tommy-gun, opened up on a cluster of Germans rash enough to mount an attack. Then, on Newman's signal, it was time to disengage and shake out into the loosely structured column which would be their formation until such time as they arrived at 'D'.

Tipped with the steel of the assault and protection parties of Roy, Denison, Roderick, Hopwood, and, of course, Tiger Watson, the column moved off to the north a little after 0300 hours. Its centre portion contained the poorly armed demolition teams, the walking wounded and the HQ party, Steele and Fyfe having by this time dumped their radio sets; its tail was made up of a rearguard formed, on Roy's orders, by Lance-Sergeant Don Randall. Believed by Copland to be also in the van, Captain Micky Burn had in fact evolved his own plan to break out across bridge 'M' and, instead of turning short of 'G', pushed across it in the company of two of his own 6 Troop boys, Riflemen Paddy Bushe and Tommy Roach, both of whom had come ashore with Haines. They were entering an area which was by now wholly in the possession of the enemy and thus found it necessary to pass through blocks, which they managed to do successfully twice, but at the third attempt their bluff was called and they were obliged to turn back. In the ensuing confusion Tommy Roach became detached and was killed; however, Micky and Paddy found a hiding place in the engine-room of one of the merchant ships docked in the Bassin. They would wait there until such time as they saw an opportunity to make for Spain.

Pushing on through the complex of warehouses, the main body were assailed by enemy fire, seemingly coming at them from every direction. In spite of the time that had elapsed, the roads and passages were not yet blocked and such Germans as were hidden in the surrounding sheds seemed to be treating their adversaries with a respect the Commandos were keen to exploit.

'My group, ' writes Newman, 'paused for a while in a bomb-hole made by the RAF where a railway shed had once been, and then on we went towards the inner Bassin. In this advance to the bridge Donald Roy was magnificent, urging his men on and showing complete disregard for the ample amount of fire that was being directed at us. "Get on!" was the order of the day. The greater the distance between the six tons of explosive in the *Campbeltown*, yet to go off, and us, the happier I felt.'

'From Charles, ' says Copland of this same phase, 'came "get on; get on," amplified by my own voice.' At one point the spearhead was checked by enemy fire, and as he remembers, 'I called Haines up and told him to take his men forward, contact Donald Roy on the way, and then to crash ahead with all speed. "Any questions, Sergeant-Major?" "None, sir, " came the reply. It seemed just like an exercise with Haines as the perfect student, his conduct as ever just as though we were on parade. Haines pushed on and soon we began to move again.'

Pressing northwards from the bomb crater, Watson writes that 'Donald Roy, scorning concealment, strode along in the middle of the road, hurling grenades to right and left, his kilt swinging. It was a magnificent sight. The road joined another at right-angles, and on the corner a German rifleman would appear, fire a quick shot at us and bob back out of sight. I was keeping up with Donald on the right, using the shadow of a wall for concealment. I tried to give the sniper the benefit of a Tommy-gun burst, but because his corner was also on the right, the wall made the angle awkward.

'When he next bobbed into sight, Donald threw a grenade which seemed to explode right on the spot. I dashed forward as hard as I could to reach the corner and prevent anybody else commanding it. I was about fifteen yards from my goal when the muzzle of a rifle reappeared round the wall. The wretched fellow had managed to dodge the bomb burst. I squeezed the trigger of my Tommy gun, but the magazine was empty. It was too late to stop running. I had no clear idea of how I was going to tackle him when I got there but tackle him I must. As I ran I could see the rifle muzzle swing round until I was looking straight down the black "O" of the barrel. I felt nothing but a numb resignation. I only had time to think, "Well, this is it".'

The bullet broke Tiger's left arm just above the elbow. 'It was a neat "through and through", ' he writes. 'In fact it was the romantic wound of my boyhood fantasies and it stopped me in my tracks. I dropped my Tommy gun and sat down abruptly.'

Having cleared the corner it was Johnny Roderick who came back to see to Tiger. Unwilling to leave the wounded man behind, Johnny picked him up and would have carried him had not the pain of Tiger's broken bones proved too great. Back on the ground again, Tiger was injected with morphine, following which, with a hurried farewell, the assault group commander returned to the fray.

Next to appear was Hopwood, who, after purloining all of Tiger's spare Tommy gun magazines, made as though to go off with his Colt as well. This was really too much, for Tiger had already determined that he would sell his life dearly rather than be taken prisoner; nevertheless Hoppy persisted, and in removing the pistol probably saved Tiger's life. Then he too was gone, leaving Tiger to be trodden on by the parties following behind. 'We wished each other good luck, ' he writes 'as they stumbled over me and passed on.' And then, when the last were swallowed up by the darkness ahead, he was alone.

All along the struggling column many men fought such private battles as beckoning freedom drew from the tired and bleeding one final effort. With humour and high spirits lifting souls above the present danger, Corran Purdon, who was behind Stuart Chant, recalls how 'we charged on rather like a pack of rugger forwards. There was a certain amount of laughter, cursing and calls of encouragement, and every now and then someone was hit. Our Commando boots made little sound, the searchlights were no longer able to glare on us and we must have made a difficult target. However, a lot of us had some narrow squeaks and I vividly recall that when I tripped on a strand of wire and had fallen flat on my face, a German bullet struck the cobbles within inches of my head, throwing up sparks and chips of stone, one of which hit my face.'

Shortly thereafter, Chant himself was shot in the knee and brought to the ground. Wholly immobilized, there was no way he could make further progress without help. Arriving on the scene, Lance-Sergeant Ron Butler, one of his pump-house team, and Private Jimmy Brown together picked the wounded officer up and carried him towards the Bassin, with Sergeant Frank Carr covering them as they traversed the bad patches of ground. Realizing that all the time they carried him Butler's and Brown's own chances of making it across bridge 'D' were dwindling, Chant ordered them to leave him, which they did only with great reluctance. Watching them push south along the quayside of the Bassin, the chill of loneliness quickly descended upon him. At the time he was hit he had already been positioned towards the rear of the column, and now there were no more running, stumbling men to pass him by. Propped up against the side of a shed, and staring out across the water to the U-boat pens, he was caught between the enemy and *Campbeltown*'s huge explosive charge; there was absolutely nothing he could do, save wait and see which devil claimed him first.

Looping south towards the bridge, all of the parties had pushed along this open quayside, now thankfully clear of German vessels, which had moved away to guard the U-boat pens. With so many walking wounded, the integrity of the column had inevitably come under strain, the difficulties of keeping the men together exacerbated by the fire which dogged them every step of the way. The HQ party were attacked from the cover of a nearby warehouse. The column halted and Copland 'took a few chaps in and we dealt with it.' Pressing on, Bob Montgomery was hit by a grenade which exploded fairly close to him. 'I got a chunk of metal in my bottom, ' he recalls, 'and it was just like a rabbit being shot. I did a somersault and I thought to myself, "You're dead, " and then I found that I wasn't, and I got up and went on.'

With demonstrations of courage all about, the task of choosing names for special mention was not an easy one, but Newman recalls that in the final surge 'outstanding among them was Troop Sergeant-Major Haines, who was superb. He alone knocked out several pockets of enemy with Tommy-gun and Bren-gun fire. He always seemed to have a fresh weapon in his hands.' Donald Roy was the recipient of special praise in respect of his 'leadership and coolness'; also making a vivid impression were 'Bill's constant holding together of the groups, preventing what might have been easily formed splits in the party, and Stan dashing about as if he was on a rugger ground.'

Pushing on hard, the lead groups succeeded in reaching the southern end of the Bassin with their formation, in spite of casualties, still largely intact. Up to this point their left flank had been protected by the long run of sheds which ran parallel with the water's edge. But at the northern extremity of the fire-swept Place de la Vieille Ville, this cover ran out, requiring them to hold for as long as it took to assess the strength of the enemy positions whose fire must be braved during the run to the bridge itself.

'I could see heavy tracer fire coming from the main bridge ahead, ' writes Copland. 'Most of our party were in the shadow of the long warehouse alongside the road. I went forward and found ... heavy fire coming from the town side, and signs of a machine gun which was enfilading us. I came back down the column asking for a Bren-gun. Gradually my suspicions were more than confirmed, for a long burst of fire shot right down the centre of the road. I decided that discretion was indicated, so fell flat on my face. The firing ceased – wasted ammunition – no one was hit.'

Newman went forward with Roy and Haines to see for himself what the ground was like, which for seventy featureless metres his men would have to traverse to reach their target. There were guns in the houses of the Old Town immediately opposite and there were guns on the new town side of 'D', in particular a pill-box whose occupants quickly directed a stream of bullets at the Colonel's party. Viewed dispassionately, the Commandos' situation could hardly have been more hopeless, in that the price of admission to this killing ground must be surely be the loss of many men who would have better causes to die for than this. But neither Newman nor the potential victims of this last, desperate charge had come this far to give up now; and so, on receipt of his order to go for it anyway, they broke from their cover and surged ahead like a human tide, pitting their guts and tenacity against the will of an enemy they did not respect to stand in their way.

Corran Purdon:

'We all went for it like long dogs. I recall Donald Roy sweeping along the middle of the road, erect in his kilt, the cheerful Colonel Charles Newman, and the confidence-inspiring Major Bill Copland, who was a rock to us all. Other outstanding fire-eaters included Lieutenant Johnny Stutchbury, Troop Sergeant-Major George Haines and Sergeant Challington.

'A hail of enemy fire erupted as we crossed the bridge, projectiles slamming ... into its girders, bullets whining and ricochetting off them and from the cobbles. There was a roar of gunfire of varying calibres and the percussion of 'potato masher' grenades as we neared the far end. One of the latter burst at my feet and the explosion, combined with my own forward velocity, lifted me clean off the ground, wounding me in the left leg and shoulder. I remember landing on the back of the sturdy Stanley Day, No. 2 Commando's Adjutant. I could feel my left battledress trouser-leg wet with

228

blood, but, beyond a sense of numbness, my leg still worked and I quickly forgot about it.'

Already nursing his wounded knee, Corporal Bob Wright was hit again, and in the same leg, during his 'hell for leather' rush across the bridge. Fortunately it was only a flesh wound and, as with Corran, it was not enough to bring him down as he grabbed a Tommy gun from a fallen Sergeant and pushed on towards the German line.

Lance-Corporal Fred Lemon, whose .45 pistol posed little threat, was running behind one of the medical orderlies, Private Powell of 2 Commando, when he saw a hole appear in Powell's battledress as a bullet entered his back. In spite of his proximity to all this flying lead and steel, Fred himself made the other side unscathed.

Employing to good effect the massive girders on either side, Lance-Sergeant Bill King found them deep enough to protect even his large frame, as he and other members of the leading groups sought temporary cover. Sergeant Frank Carr was yet another to find solace in the lee of all this steel, as he began his passage over 'D' even as the Colonel's group prepared to burst through its defences at the farther end. Frank was with a party which included Private Jimmy Brown. During the crossing it would be Jimmy's misfortune to be downed by the explosion of some projectile and left on the bridge, dazed but otherwise unhurt, while all around him pressed on.

That the German fire did not exact a greater toll prompted Newman to conclude that they had forgotten to lower their sights. Whatever the reason, the German fire was so wild that many bullets spent themselves against the structure overhead. That the Commandos should have been stopped when forced to pass through such a narrow choke-point is a fact that positively leaps from the pages of every account of the action. That they were not reflects on both the competence of those on the German side who were responsible for giving the orders for the defence of the bridge and on the fighting abilities of the individual soldiers charged with carrying them out.

On reaching what should have been a solid German line the Commandos therefore swept through such defences as they found. As the surviving enemy beat a hasty retreat, Copland paused briefly to empty 'a magazine full of .45' into the pill-box slit, before rushing past and into the Place du Bassin, a mirror image of the deadly Place de la Vieille Ville, but which led directly into the heart of the new town.

Having broken free of the dockyard the men had freedom now, though only of a sort, as circumstances would quickly show them to have escaped from one cage only to enter another to which bars were being added steadily as more and better German units joined in the action. Units of the Wehrmacht had already entered the new town and their leading elements were moving swiftly to establish a *cordon sanitaire*. A motorcycle combination, complete with side-car-mounted machine gun came flying into view, only to be riddled with bullets before crashing headlong into a wall, but it was followed quickly by an armoured car, its guns spitting fire in every direction, which took station at a crossroads directly ahead. With the direct route to safety effectively blocked, the only option left to the cluster of hopeful *'évadées'* was to turn left into the built-up area which lay between their present position and the shoreline.

The integrity of the column had by now all but ceased to exist, as the men split up into groups of choice, or convenience, in pursuance of Newman's orders to follow the paths each individual leader deemed appropriate. Newman himself, along with Copland, Terry, Purdon, Denison, Montgomery and Etches, formed the core of a group which came together by the buildings on the south-east corner of the square, prior to melting away into the dark streets to their rear. There was a lorry parked nearby, which Copland tried to get started by hopping into the cab and trying all the switches in sight. But it proved to be a less then cooperative ally and, as Corran recalls, 'All he succeeded in doing was to switch on the headlights, illuminating, among others, the Charles Atlas figure of Bung Denison, our protection party commander, to cries of "put those bloody lights out!"'

Eschewing the potential convenience of the lorry, the party moved on up a side street to play hide and seek with nervous German patrols. Copland:

'We turned right at the first opportunity and, being fired on from our rear, dodged from cover to cover to the next crossroads and turned right again. We sheltered for a minute or two in an alley and then, having seen a church with a small, clear space around it, almost opposite us, we made a dash for it. Faced with a six-foot wall beyond the church we shinned up and over it, Hannan causing some amusement by falling into a hen coop, crossed a back garden, opened some good housewife's back door and found ourselves in a French kitchen.

'I went through the house to find the front door locked and the key missing, so back again and out, grabbing a drink from the kitchen tap on the way. Next door was locked up too, so we smashed in the kitchen windows with rifle butts, got in and ran through the house and down the front steps into the street beyond. We were greeted by machine-gun fire from both ends of the street and the approach, much too near, of a German tank. We went back to our desirable furnished residence again and let the firing continue. As they were all Germans firing at each other, it appeared to be a fairly sound policy.'

Newman takes up the story:

'By this time ammunition was short, and the wounded who had marvellously kept up with us were very weak and had lost a lot of blood. Poor Bill Etches had fought through the streets with us and was still going. He was nearly done, as were many others, and I felt that the time for a halt wasn't far away. Every crossroad by now seemed to be picketed with an enemy machine gun and movement was very difficult. In the street was a house with lights in it and the thought flashed through our minds to knock up the inhabitants to ask for a chance to hide till the following evening, but this was turned down and we got into a house opposite, in which we found a very convenient air-raid shelter, complete with mattresses, down into which we piled. As far as possible, wounds were dressed and well-earned cigarettes were smoked. A watch was kept at the stairhead, and I decided that here we should stay till night-time, when we should set out in pairs for the open country. I also decided that if we were found in the cellar I would surrender, as the wounded were in a pretty bad way and a single hand grenade flung down the stairs would see the lot off.'

Slipping off his equipment, Copland joined the others in giving such help as he could to those who were in need of it. Etches, who was afraid of being a drag on the rest, was injected with morphine, while someone dug a piece of shrapnel out of Bob Montgomery's bottom with a knife. There were about eighteen straw mattresses on the floor and some sixteen men left to make use of them, including, in addition to the officers, Sergeant Carr, Corporal Maclagan, Private Edwards and Sergeant Ron Steele, who stood first watch at the door. During the earlier stages of what Copland describes as 'this St Nazaire Obstacle Race', the party had been larger; however, a number of the men had become detached as the surging tide which had carried the bridge broke against the obstacle of the narrow streets into whorls and eddies, no single one of which had the power to force an escape.

Private Tom Hannan, who had remained with Copland throughout, sought cover with other men in a basement shelter containing French civilians. All were quickly captured, as were Fusilier John Cudby and the half-dozen others who had lost touch out in the street, when an armoured car rushed right past the main group and was fired on. Remaining with Newman and Copland to the point at which they broke through the houses,

Lance-Sergeant Ron Butler had then begun a solitary run for the country-side, very tired by this time, and armed only with a grenade. After successfully dodging a number of German patrols, he was captured in a police station, a fate which was shared by Donald Roy who, with a number of others, called at such a place by mistake while searching for water to give to the wounded. Lance-Corporal Fred Lemon and three other men sought to escape from a side street with patrols at both ends by dodging into an opening which led directly into 'the yard behind the bloody military barracks!' Lance-Sergeant Bill King was in a cellar, dressing the wounded leg of a young Commando who had asked if he could come along, when the Germans arrived to add them to their growing bag of prisoners.

Following a course of their own particular choosing were a party of six, consisting of Troop Sergeant-Major George Haines, Lance-Sergeant Challington, Corporal Bob Wright, Lance-Corporals Howarth and Douglas and Private Harding. As with the others, it was a case of up one street and down another and through this house and that house, until such time as Haines called a halt to check on their rapidly dwindling supply of ammo. Finding a bombed-out building with an intact cellar, they decided to hide there until such time as a suitable chance to escape presented itself. With his two leg wounds Bob Wright was really beginning to suffer by this time, but there were no medical supplies short of dressings with which to treat him. During the search of the town the Germans did in fact come as close as the top of the cellar steps before moving on, at which point they should by rights have tossed down a grenade. Otherwise it was just a matter of waiting and choosing who would try to escape with whom, Haines having decided that they should move out in pairs the following night.

Safest of all in respect of their choice of refuge, Corporal George Wheeler and Lance-Corporal Ronald Sims chose to hide first in the garden of a house, and then in the drain that ran underneath the dwelling itself. The drain was about twenty feet long by ten feet wide and just high enough to allow them both to crawl into it. Safely ensconced therein, the two Commandos settled down to see what new adventures the coming dawn would bring. Their actions of the night might have been fraught enough already to sate the taste for glory of any average man, but, as events would later prove, for them at least there was to be no ending here amid the cheerless structures of a country not their own.

While a majority of the men did in fact make it to the new town, a significant minority failed for one reason or another to make the crossing of the bridge, although two men, Corporal Bob Hoyle and Private Jimmy Brown, came within a whisker of success. Initially well up with Copland's group,

Bob was pinned down while moving along the right-hand side of the bridge and almost within reach of its western end. Unable to cross the road with the others, he instead climbed over the side and found refuge amid the tangle of girders supporting the roadway itself, a means of escape which was also adopted by Jimmy Brown who, recovering from the blast that had knocked him down and finding himself alone on the bridge, chose to climb over its left side. With each man intent on lying low, they settled to whiling away the rest of the night so quietly and inconspicuously that neither suspected the presence of the other. Only much later did they realize that they had in fact finished the raid together, mute within the same few cubic metres of space.

Halted well short of 'D' either because wounds or German fire precluded further progress, the remaining members of the column sought to hide themselves away before daylight came to rob their presence of its mystery. A party under Johnny Roderick, containing several wounded, sought shelter in a warehouse piled high with bags of cement. Bert Shipton teamed up with Dai Davis, by now barely able to move on his injured foot, the two finding a temporary nest beneath corrugated sheets in a warehouse stacked with cardboard. And at the very tail of the line, having lost touch with the main group because Corporal Johnson, who was nursing a painful wound, could go no further, Don Randall's tiny rearguard toyed with the idea of stealing a boat and sailing home in that.

Marooned in an area from which there was now no easy means of escape, these remnants of the column immediately became prey to the attentions of a whole confusion of German troops. Pushing up from the Old Town, and with no British troops save the parties of Walton, Watson and Pritchard to dispute their initial advance, these forces had been in position quickly enough to capture the first of the survivors to struggle ashore from the wrecked and burning MLs. With the exception of George Davidson and Richard Collinson's small party, this had certainly been the fate of most of the survivors of ML 192, who almost before they knew it were locked away within the massive structure of the U-boat pens; during the succeeding minutes and hours that was to be the fate of the survivors of almost all the other shattered boats.

In their haste to clear the Old Town for use as a base from which to push their fighting units northwards, the Germans had even pressed into service the civilian *Défense Passive*, whose presence on the streets unwittingly added to the problems of numbers later faced by those Commandos who chose to make their push for freedom here. Always acting under German guard, these volunteers' accounts help flesh out the story of the night's events, particularly in respect of the fates of individuals which otherwise might not have been recorded.

Having returned to the Santé Maritime, Alain Bizard and Gilles Chapelan were ordered out again at about 0245 to collect a wounded British sailor who had come ashore down by the East Jetty. The poor man had been forced to jump from his boat into water that was covered with flaming petrol and thus had sustained burns that were in need of urgent, expert attention. Carried back to the aid post, he received just this, as well as a sustaining cup of warm whisky, there being no tea available. Despite his wounds, he did his very best to warn his allies to avoid the battered hulk of *Campbeltown*, but his was a plea whose significance would not become clear until it was far too late to serve a useful purpose.

About two hours later Alain and Gilles were called upon to carry their patient across bridge 'B' and as far as the Sud 1 shelter, at which point, with Commando scares still erupting everywhere, they were blocked for a time from returning. While close to Sud 1 they were privileged to witness the stand of an unknown Tommy in the house of M. Lion, just opposite, who resisted for several hours all attempts to subdue him. He would eventually surrender at about 0700, but only when persuaded to do so by the arrival outside of a mobile quick-firing cannon.

Also acting as stretcher-bearers, young Gérard Pelou and another volunteer from the Santé team were ordered out in the middle of the night to recover the body of a soldier who had been shot dead whilst in the process of placing his charges on one of the New Entrance lock gates. This expedition, undertaken as it was at the height of the fighting in the warehouse area, is of particular interest because from Pelou's description of the scene there is a very good chance that the body was that of Lieutenant Philip Walton. Laid out on a stretcher, it too was carried towards Sud 1, in the area of which a search by German personnel yielded a fighting knife, a miniature slide-rule, a large chronometer and a grenade, this last item being carefully set on the ground before its finders beat a hasty retreat. As with Bizard and Chapelan, Pelou and his companion were also blocked from returning across bridge 'B', whose western end was by now heavily guarded. With no other employment immediately in sight, they moved on to the *Défense Passive* command post, on the Rue de l'Hôtel de Ville.

As the area under German control expanded steadily northwards, first the badly wounded Dick Bradley was found where he had been left beneath a railway truck on the northern edge of the square, and then Richard Collinson's party was added to the growing tally of prisoners.

His senses dimmed by morphine, Bradley had never had more than a minimal awareness of the movement of troops in his immediate area. Hit again as he lay helpless, this time in the thigh, the blow had been enough to lift him into a temporary form of consciousness sufficient for him to hear two passing Commandos conclude that he was a 'gonner', a statement with which he felt disinclined to argue. Drifting back into the pit, he did not become aware again until he heard two German soldiers discussing whether or not he was really dead. A fluent speaker of their language, he realized that one of them wanted to give him a bullet anyway, just in case. However, the other seemed happy to accept the fact that Bradley was no more, the result being that he was left in peace until such time as the German Medical Corps retrieved him and carried him to a café on the north-west corner of the Old Town. In the café, which was shared with civilians, his first-aid kit was found by some French women who bandaged his wounds as best they could. Dick remembers them being told off by a German for making more of a fuss of the English than of his own wounded countrymen.

Hiding away at the very tip of the Mole, the end had come for Collinson just as the firing outside seemed to be dying away, when a group of the enemy were heard approaching the lighthouse. As the only officer present, Richard felt it was his duty to go outside and surrender his men rather than risk them being suddenly stumbled upon. Presenting himself with his hands in the air, he discovered that his captors were a party of German sailors under the command of a petty officer, who pushed a Luger pistol into Richard's midriff with a hand that was visibly shaking. To Richard's surprise, the Germans addressed his party in French, but at least they treated their captives well, as they, too, were marched off to captivity in the U-boat pens. Within this massive building Richard was interested to note that the U-boats had been flooded down so that the Tommies could not get onto their casings to plant explosives. What with the German sailors all wearing helmets and armed with automatic weapons, he recalls that, more than anything else, it resembled a scene from the pages of *The Guns of Navarone*.

Having regained control of the southernmost portion of the warehouse complex, probing parties of Germans pushed into the vacuum left by Newman's withdrawal, always aware that every shadow might harbour a waiting Tommy. Left behind by the column, Watson was witness to the tentative nature of their advance, when he noticed one of their number peering cautiously round a corner.

Drifting into a state of 'pleasant lethargy' induced by his shot of morphine, Tiger had been preparing to try and catch up with his friends and put some distance between himself and the expected explosion of *Campbeltown* when he was discovered. 'I watched with interest as he came slowly into full view,' writes Tiger, 'and was followed by two companions. They approached cautiously, their rifles at the ready, but nearly jumped out of their skins when I addressed them. I was quite euphoric. "There's nothing to be afraid of, " I assured them in English. "I can't hurt you." They levelled their rifles but something in my tone of voice and seated attitude must have reassured them.'

Encouraged by Tiger, the three Germans helped him to his feet and began to search him, becoming quite angry when they discovered his fighting knife. Fortunately for him, a second group of the enemy then put in an appearance with the wounded Gerard Brett in tow, who defused what might well have become an ugly episode by explaining in German that there was in fact very little difference between the fighting knife and their own bayonets. He also impressed them by pointing out that both he and Tiger were due the respect habitually accorded to officers.

Supporting each other, Tiger and Gerard were then led to the café on the corner of the Old Town, where they found French civilians, German sailors and a number of British wounded already in residence. Dick Bradley was there, 'lying deathly pale on a stretcher'. Having received only very basic medical attention, which had plugged the hole in the front of his chest, he was still bleeding from the one in his back.

The newcomers were also given medical aid of a sort. A German medic noticed blood on Tiger's buttock and invited him to remove his battledress trousers. Tiger, however, refused, as he 'felt it would not be consistent with their British ally's dignity' to take his trousers off in front of the female civilians. Later an unconscious tribute to the courage of all the 'Charioteers' was paid by a German sailor who, noticing Tiger's rubber-soled boots, inquired if their owner was a parachutist. When no response was forthcoming, the sailor went on, 'Well, you couldn't have come up the river. You would have to be mad or very brave to do that!'

Also swept up by the German net was Lieutenant Stuart Chant. Sometime after he had been left by Butler and Brown he was joined by a boy from 2 Commando whom he did not know and whose name he did not ask. All around them the Germans could be heard searching the area for just such as they, but Chant's condition precluded an attempt to move away, nor were there any vessels nearby in which the two could have hidden.

Eventually three Germans arrived on the scene. They were dressed in black uniforms and carrying sub-machine guns, and were in an agitated and unpredictable state. They yelled for Chant and his companion to get up and put their hands in the air, which the young soldier did, against Chant's advice, only to be shot dead immediately. Unable to get up, Chant was saved when it finally dawned on the three that he was both wounded and an officer. Instead of killing him too, they therefore chose to drag him along to join Watson, Brett, Bradley and the rest in the rapidly filling café.

Last of the parties known to be loose in this area, Don Randall's rearguard did not succeed in finding the boat which he had rather desperately hoped might be their ticket home. Originally consisting of five men, four of whom only had pistols, this weak unit had been temporarily bolstered by the secondment to it of Private Peter Honey, whose Tommy-gun gave it some teeth; but Honey did not remain with the others for long, as his gun was soon needed at the front of the line. With Corporal Johnson unable to move further and with the unit under fire from several directions, Don now found himself in a quandary as he did not want to leave the wounded man behind. Under normal circumstances it would have been logical to assume that all the locks to the Bassin would be closed, making the theft of a boat rather pointless; however, the sight of Pritchard's sunken tugs lying askew, close to bridge 'D', prompted him to believe that the tide must be draining somehow. With this thought in mind Don had left the rest in hiding while he searched along the quayside. He had no sooner started back than the order 'Hände Hoch!' was barked at him out of the darkness. With the game clearly up, Don moved forward toward an enemy party which had been mirroring his own progress. When the others saw this they came out too, after which this latest catch was marched off to join the others in the U-boat pens.

With their units now in almost complete control of all the area south and east of the Bassin, the Germans set to searching its myriad nooks and crannies, any one of which might still harbour an enemy intent on escaping later. For the party of Johnny Roderick, even though most were suffering in some way from wounds, this was most certainly the intention, especially bearing in mind that their lair was quite ingeniously constructed and far more likely than most to escape detection. In addition to Johnny himself, and Alf Searson, who had been hit in the shoulder by friendly fire, this party included Private 'Dutch' Holland, and Sergeant Ben Brown of Hopwood's protection party. Joining it later was Private Bill Lawson who appeared in their midst with a grenade in his hand which was sans pin. In an attempt to preserve the silence that was their greatest ally, Bill was advised to push the bomb deep within the pile of bags, jam the spring so that it would not go off and withdraw his hand 'bloody quick'. It was a good idea, but it didn't quite work out as planned and the thing exploded anyway, blowing some shrapnel into Johnny Roderick's forehead.

High up at the very top of a pile of the bags, the men had managed to hollow out a small compartment within which they settled down to await developments. An attempt was made to patch up Alf's wound with field dressings; otherwise it was a matter of grabbing what little chance there was of rest before the coming dawn brought enemy search parties out in force.

At least with respect to the men and groups whose fates have been well documented, these final scenes all but bring the curtain down on the drama of Newman's impetuous charge towards the freedom of the countryside. British sources do not suggest a penetration much beyond the warehouse area and that portion of the new town accessed by the bridge at 'D'; however, contemporary French accounts would seem to indicate that a handful of Commandos, their identities unfortunately unknown, did seek shelter within the Old Town itself, there to secrete themselves away right where the enemy was strongest.

In the chill of their cellar beneath the old Hôtel Blanconnier, the civilians who had earlier been warned to stay put by Pelou were visited by a bloodstained German sailor who demanded to know if there were Tommies present. '*Nix Tommies!*' they replied, '*Ici Français!*'; even though they knew that a party of Newman's boys had just disappeared into a nearby alley and established a defensive position there, their actions having been observed through windows that were level with the street.

Deeper still within the Old Town, young Jean Bouillant came face to face with a group of 'Scots' whom he, his mother and his aunt did their very best to help. Having been left in peace by the German patrol which had taken refuge in their cellar shelter during the period of the air raid, there was a certain amount of alarm when movements were later heard again outside the cellar door. Thinking initially that it might be looters come to forage in the rubble of Loriot's bakery, the rear of which had been recently damaged by a British bomb, Jean set out to investigate, only to find himself faced by three kilted Tommies, one of whom was wounded and leaving a trail of blood behind him. They followed Jean inside, where he was able to put to good use the few words of English he had learned at the Collège Aristide Briand. Initially refusing an invitation to go upstairs to the family's flat, the soldiers changed their minds after a loud explosion was heard outside. In the flat, Jean asked the three if they were parachutists. 'No, ' they said, 'Commandos.' Then, with Jean's mother tending to the wounded, the Commandos settled down to eat, drink, smoke a cigarette and wait.

At daybreak, and with the Germans searching every house in the quarter, the Tommies decided to move on, but only after having asked if they might leave all their arms and equipment behind. Then Jean guided them to an empty house not far away, the owner of which, Hortense Chenay, had been killed in the raid that demolished the back of Loriot's. Leaving them there, Jean returned to help expunge all traces of them from the flat. With the exception of a few .45 rounds which he kept for himself as souvenirs, everything they had left behind was crammed inside a kit bag and tossed down a well, into which it stubbornly refused to sink as, in his haste, Jean had neglected to leave aside the men's Mae Wests.

Later still, and to Jean's chagrin, he saw their very own Commandos being marched away by the Germans. All his family's efforts had been in vain. Having spruced themselves up and, to Jean's mind, prepared themselves to meet their captors just as he and his elders had earlier prepared themselves to meet St Peter should the need arise, they presented to all who watched them pass a picture of dignity which could not fail to impress. For them as well as for the rest of Newman's men, whose strength and will had not been sapped by pain of wounds, their attitude was one of maintaining their superiority, even though all hope of breaking free had gone. Captured they may now be, but defeated never!

17

A Season of Fire and Ice

Having lost six of his ships within the harbour itself, the last of Ryder's eleven surviving units had cleared the port by the time of Newman's final push from the Mole. Within an hour a further three vessels had been mortally struck, leaving a mere eight out of the seventeen which had sailed so valiantly into the estuary to exit safely from it. By 0400 these were making for point 'Y', which was the first of the two positions at which retiring ships might come under the protection of *Tynedale*'s and *Atherstone*'s guns. A mere twenty miles from the estuary mouth, 'Y' would not be a healthy place in which to linger. Should it not be possible to rendezvous here, then individual MLs were to steam on to point 'T', a further 70 miles out along a course of 248°, where a turn could be made at last towards home.

After having detached themselves on meeting *Sturgeon*, the destroyers had been maintaining a patrol a few miles to the west of 'Y', reversing their north-west-south-east course at the conclusion of every hour. At 0300 they had turned southwards for the last time, under orders to maintain this final leg until 0420, only at which hour would they then be free to turn shorewards, aiming to reach 'Y' and turn to begin their long sweep out to 'T' at 0600.

In adhering to these timings, the two commanders were responding to instructions which had always assumed that MLs would not be leaving the Mole much before 0300. However, this timetable had by now been rendered all but meaningless, all of which meant that most of the boats they were sailing to protect were already far in advance of the positions where they might reasonably have expected to meet them.

With *Cleveland* and *Brocklesby* steaming fast to reinforce the fleet, a safe journey home could be all but guaranteed once contact was finally made.

However, as these ships had been sent so late, they were still too far away to be of assistance during the most perilous stages of the withdrawal. Not only that, but their guns were to be denied the British at a point in the exercise where they might have helped secure a victory of some note. For, sharing the sea with the remnants of Ryder's force were the five ships of *Korvettenkapitän* Schmidt's Fifth Flotilla, despatched the previous evening in response to Kelbling's belated sighting report. Recalled at 0250, these were now steaming at maximum speed towards the estuary mouth. Unfortunately for Ryder, their course was almost exactly the reverse of his own, which meant that at some stage a clash was inevitable: five destroyers against two, plus a handful of small boats, where, had *Cleveland* and *Brocklesby* only been sent a little sooner, the odds might instead have been to all intents and purposes equal.

Having been among the first of Ryder's boats to leave the harbour, Henderson's ML 306 had made such rapid progress that he was eventually forced to cut his speed rather than pass through 'Y' too early. In spite of this reduction he nevertheless arrived at the rendezvous well before anyone else and at a time when *Tynedale* and *Atherstone* were still plunging away from him on the last extended leg of their patrol. Rather than risk being surprised by German ships, Henderson therefore decided to make a run towards 'T' alone. A rendezvous with destroyers he would still make; however, they would be sailing under a darker flag than his and the eyes behind their gunsights would see in him a target, not a friend.

Also pushing west, though well astern of Henderson, Wallis's ML 307 had been joined by both Boyd's 160 and Horlock's 443. No more keen than Henderson to hang around at 'Y', they too decided to press on, trusting to the darkness and the space ahead of their bows to protect them.

Despite damage to her hull, ML 443 was still able to maintain her maximum cruising speed, 'tingles' having been used to patch the holes beneath her waterline. Freed from the need to serve his forward Oerlikon, Ordinary Seaman Sam Hinks went below to spend the remaining dark hours on the messdeck, helping reload Oerlikon drums. He was joined there by the after gunner, Ordinary Seaman Frank Folkard, who only realized after joining the others that he had been sprayed with shrapnel from hits on the gun pedestal, which he had been too excited to notice at the time. In terms of casualties, 443 had suffered far more lightly than most of Ryder's boats. Lance-Corporal Fowler of 2 Commando had been seriously wounded and was being cared for. Another Commando, believed to be Private Fred Peachey, had been hit during the attempt to reach the Mole, but had chosen to tell no one of his wounds.

241

Completing the straggling line of boats, the final four, three of them having sustained a fair degree of damage, were pressing seawards from positions even closer to the shore. Because they were likely to arrive at 'Y' much later, these were in the best position of all to be swept up by *Tynedale* and *Atherstone*. Falconar's ML 446 had come across the limping 156 during the early part of the withdrawal, the two proceeding in company for a time. In the same general area the gunboat was still tagging along with Irwin's ML 270, their speed restricted by Irwin's steering difficulties to 12 knots. With water pouring in through holes in 314's forepeak, this was not fast enough to lift the damaged portion of her bow above the level of the sea, as a consequence of which a bucket-brigade had to be organized in an attempt to bail her out.

Approaching 'Y' at close to 0430, with little idea of how many boats had managed to escape, or just where they might be in the enigmatical darkness, concerned at the extreme phosphorescence which was painting their bow waves a glaring white and nursing a very real fear of encountering Schmidt's destroyers Ryder was greatly heartened to see a large explosion light up the sky above the now distant port. It was impossible to be absolutely certain of its cause, but from its magnitude and timing there must be a good chance it was the *Campbeltown* rending herself asunder at last. Buoyed up by this thought, the gunboat and her consort then passed through 'Y' and came round to 248°, all eyes peeled for such subtle nuances in the surrounding pool of darkness as might all too quickly be transmuted into silhouettes of friendly ships – or foes.

Some dozen miles ahead and butting through the sea a little to the north of Ryder's course, ML 306 was easing further away from the zone of greatest risk with every mile that slipped beneath her keel. Fortunate indeed to have escaped the turmoil of the harbour with only superficial damage, she had suffered few casualties, with Durrant and Dark slightly wounded, the latter in the leg, and Swayne having inflicted upon himself a nasty burn when he carelessly attempted to change the red-hot barrel of a Bren. His leg now stiffening up, Dark had gone below at 'Y' to rest it. Below deck also were the majority of Swayne's and Vanderwerve's Commandos, although Sergeants Durrant and Chappell, Corporals Evans and Salisbury, and Private Bishop had remained on deck to load magazines for their four Brens, in anticipation of the enemy aircraft that must surely attack with the dawn.

In respect of her Commandos, this ML differed from all the rest only in that the parties of Ronnie Swayne and Johnny Vanderwerve had had a very uneventful raid thus far and were not a little angered by the twist of fate that had sent them scuttling home unbloodied and untried. Theirs had been the job of destroying the two most southerly lock-gates and the swing bridge in the New Entrance, Lance-Sergeant Chappell and Privates Hopkins, Bishop and Tomblin having been detailed to deal with the gates, while Sergeant Durrant and Corporals Evans, Salisbury and Llewellyn put paid to the bridge nearby. Responsible for their protection were Lance-Sergeant Gallagher, Corporal Sinnott and Privates Eckman and Preston, all of 4 Troop, 2 Commando, and in the charge of Lieutenant Vanderwerve, or, as Watson recalls, '"Randy Vandy", as the aspiring lady-killer was affectionately and probably quite erroneously known.'

Leading the demolition teams, Lieutenant Ronnie Swayne of the Herefordshire Regiment and 1 Commando, was himself a character of note, one of those strong men of independent mind who always stand above the rest and engender love and respect among those with whom they share their space. Tall and dark, a married man who loved music and had played rugby for Oxford, Swayne was frequently inclined to be forgetful and as Micky Burn recalls, 'was always leaving things about'. He had forgotten to load his revolver before storming ashore during an earlier raid on France and during his time on *PJC* had received an almighty rocket from Newman for having left his sheaf of highly confidential orders behind in the loo, where he had secreted himself in order to read them in peace.

At about 0530 Swayne was making sandwiches below when the call came for him to climb up to the bridge and join Henderson and Dark in peering out into the darkness beyond the forward gun. There, fine on the port bow, were to be seen the phosphorescent streaks of the bow-waves of several enemy destroyers bearing down upon them, the cold, pale glare of the disturbed water no colder than the chill the sight evoked within the blood of those who understood its fateful message. Bringing the ship quickly to action stations, Henderson cut his motors, the better to deny the enemy a sight of him, and waited. Thus far the darkness had seen them safely almost fifty miles toward home, but could it be relied upon to stand to their defence once more, or now, when needed most, would it turn its coat and betray their puny presence to the greater force?

Having been steaming fast toward the coast since 0250, Schmidt's powerful squadron, comprising the small destroyers *Seeadler*, *Jaguar*, *Iltis*, *Falke*, and *Kondor*, each of 800 tons and mounting three 4.1-inch guns, were a mere 45 miles from the estuary channel when a small shadow was sighted ahead and to port. Reducing to 15 knots, Schmidt in *Seeadler* led the others towards it until such time as it could be identified as a small boat, whereupon *Kapitänleutnant* Friedrich Paul in *Jaguar* was detached to chase it down while the others resumed their course. Passing by the object port-to-port,

Paul swung out of line and began to circle round behind it. He still could not precisely identify his adversary but assumed her to be an MGB. With all guns manned, he prepared to illuminate her with his searchlight, intending to force a quick capitulation.

Despite conceding more than 700 tons to his opponent, whose steel hull his sole remaining Oerlikon could barely bruise, Henderson had nevertheless determined to make a fight of it. He was not prepared to give up, but nor did his slower speed support a sudden dash for freedom. His forward gun was jammed; however, the after gun, which was the responsibility of the Australian, Sub-Lieutenant Landy, was still fully serviceable. Supporting this one pop-gun there was the boat's own twin-Lewis, mounted on the coach deck abaft the bridge, but apart from these the ML would have to rely on the Thompsons and Brens of the Commandos. Being mostly demolition troops, far too many of these were armed only with pistols. And being mostly demolition troops, there were still to be found on the messdeck, their heavy packs containing explosives and detonators together in intimate proximity. Should a lucky shot hit one of these, then Paul's diversion indeed would be shortlived.

Watching the German ship haul out of line, the Bren teams on the ML's deck waited to open fire the instant the order was given. In his place towards the stern Lance-Sergeant Des Chappell of the Royal Welch Fusiliers had specialized in the Bren before putting up his sergeant's stripes. The weapon had been his pride and joy then and at the conclusion of exercises it had not been unknown for his wife to strip and clean it for him.

Also hailing from the Royal Welch, and waiting beside his Bren amidships, twenty-five-year-old Corporal Glyn Salisbury, from Brymbo, was within hours of becoming a father. He had been so engrossed with loading magazines that he had missed entirely the drama of Paul's turn to port and, on finally sighting *Jaguar*, assumed the ship to be one of their own.

Circling astern of the almost stationary 306, on a course that was bringing him round on to Henderson's starboard side, Paul then switched on his searchlight, its beam entrapping the ML with an energy that was almost physical. Ordering 'slow ahead', Henderson began to move to starboard also, and on seeing the sudden churn of water beneath her transom, Paul gave the order to open fire, his intention at this stage being to ram the British boat. Moving swiftly abeam of the 306, his smaller calibre guns ripping into woodwork, metal and flesh, Paul then tightened his turn and began to close rapidly on the frail ML, his high steel bows more than capable of slicing through her with barely a shudder. At the very last moment Henderson somehow managed to turn away so that, instead of being hit full on, his ship was shunted to one side, the shock of the impact slewing her violently over and tossing a number of her complement out into the darkness. Vanderwerve disappeared over the side, as did Ordinary Seaman Rees and, among others, Corporals Salisbury and Sinnott, and Private Eckman. Vanderwerve would never be seen again, while Rees was badly injured in the foot by *Jaguar*'s screws. Sopping wet, but otherwise none the worse for wear, Salisbury managed to drag himself back on board. For the time being at least the rest would have to remain in the numbing sea.

Still under fire from Paul's light guns, whose rounds poured down upon them now from point-blank range, and in spite of her own defiant fusillade, the ML's list of casualties began to swell relentlessly. Durrant, firing back at the German ship with cold deliberation, was wounded a second time. Corporal Llewellyn, described by Glyn as 'a lovely lad', was killed, as was the Vaagso veteran, Private Tomblin. Lance-Sergeant Chappell, who later described *Jaguar*'s rearing bow as being like a huge carving knife poised above them, was hit in the left calf and right groin. With no feeling in his legs, which were hanging over the side of the ship, he began to slip towards the water but was pulled back by his mates and propped up against the funnel. From this position amidships he continued to fire his Bren until hit again, when a cannon shell exploding above him drove splinters right through the steel of his helmet. From this point on and fortunately for him, the oblivion caused by pain, shock and loss of blood would claim all but fleeting wisps of consciousness.

Greatly angered by the small boat's spirited response, Paul drew away to the point where all his guns could depress sufficiently for them to be able to engage the target. Ronnie Swayne, on going below to assess the situation there, saw Paul's machine guns stitch holes in the wooden hull, the fire that penetrated the living spaces killing a further two of the Commando team. On deck, and with their situation so obviously hopeless, Glyn Salisbury attempted to cut the dinghy free with his fighting knife but, failing at this, then set to tossing lines out to the men still in the water. He was pulling Corporal Sinnott in when forced to seek shelter from the renewed German barrage. At the point where Des Chappell was wounded by splinters resulting from the cannon strike on the funnel, Glyn was also sprayed with shards of steel all down his back and in his rear. Lying not far away, Ordinary Seaman Shepherd's leg was badly shattered. The after Oerlikon was knocked out, killing Ordinary Seaman Garner. Sub-Lieutenant Landy was hit, as was Leading Seaman Sargent at the wheel. Able Seaman Alder, whose preserve had been the exposed twin-Lewis mounting, was hit and replaced by Sergeant Durrant who, as a regular during the '30s, had been trained on just

245

such weapons. In spite of further wounds and once having stood to these guns, pain alone would not prove enough to drive him from them.

Continuing to move in a large circle around the 306, and from a position abeam and to port, the German boat then opened fire with her main armament, a fact which Paul later disputed, but which is claimed as true by survivors who were on the receiving end of his shells. A direct hit by some projectile on the ML's bridge killed the already wounded Sargent, blew Dark unconscious to the deck and mortally wounded Henderson. At this precise moment, with Landy hit and Vanderwerve lost to the waves, Swayne was therefore the only officer left of either service who was in a fit state to exercise control and respond to a surrender demand made by Paul, which now rang out across the intervening stretch of sea.

Drifting momentarily back into consciousness Des Chappell heard the call for them to cease firing immediately. He also heard the sudden chatter of the nearby twin-Lewis as Durrant, in spite of his wounds, replied with streams of lead. Paul's guns then resumed firing, their new onslaught only adding to the ML's already substantial tally of dead and wounded. A second surrender demand followed the first and again Durrant replied by squeezing his triggers, directing his fire toward the destroyer's bridge and continuing to engage until finally shot from the guns. His had been an heroic if ultimately futile stand, bearing in mind the destroyer's overwhelming superiority and the fact that the 306 only remained afloat because it was now Paul's preference to take her as a prize. And it finally brought to a close a paroxysm of firing during which death and destruction had threatened to sweep the ML's decks completely clear of life. At a little after 0600 hours, and with the first suggestions of dawn softening the horizon to the east, Swayne surrendered the ship and all those who remained alive on board her. As suddenly as it had begun it was over.

Sending his own men to board and search the British boat, Paul prepared to transfer her survivors to *Jaguar* and then tow his prize to port. At this point his intentions were not disturbed by thoughts that heavier British units might be somewhere in the area, otherwise his treatment of the ML might have been altogether more violent. In spite of all the firepower directed against her, the 306 was not terminally damaged and, unlike so many of her fellows, her fuel tanks had resisted the temptation to erupt in flame. One by one the wounded and the dying, which included Henderson, Durrant and Petty Officer Motor Mechanic Bennett, were transferred to the German ship where, in spite of all that had gone before, they were treated in an exemplary manner. The Germans themselves enjoyed no surfeit of medical comforts and had no doctor of their own; nevertheless, the scarce supplies were shared and Dark helped his enemies do what they could to ease the suffering of all. With the 306 now cleared of all but the dead, and having searched the surrounding waters for survivors, lines were attached and the long tow back to port began, at a speed hardly exceeding 3 knots.

Having detached *Jaguar* at 0530, Schmidt's four remaining destroyers had resumed their high-speed dash towards the threatened port, now sailing almost directly for 'Y', at precisely the time when *Tynedale* and *Atherstone*, having made their scheduled turn at this position, were beginning their seaward sweep along the withdrawal route.

Steaming abreast, each some two and a half miles to either side of the course the MLs would follow, the two British ships had made little more than a mile when they saw in the far distance the flashes of Paul's and Henderson's guns. Twenty-five minutes later and a mere four miles ahead, Schmidt's destroyers were sighted steering towards and already beginning to turn in line to starboard, Schmidt having seen the Hunts before he himself was spotted.

Ringing down for full speed, *Tynedale*, as the more northerly ship, altered immediately to port with the intention of closing on *Atherstone*; however, this ship, having received from her consort the signal 'enemy in sight to starboard', had herself hauled round to port and was now steaming south with the intention of drawing the enemy away from the escaping MLs. Because of this manoeuvre, instead of coming together the two British ships therefore remained apart and disposed toward the south in such a way that *Atherstone*, blocked by *Tynedale*'s bulk and smoke from engaging the enemy, was able to play no useful part in the coming action.

With the two formations now on a crossing course that was taking Schmidt's flotilla astern of *Tynedale*, Schmidt challenged the British ship by light. Replying in such a way as to forestall action until she had made to seaward of the enemy line, *Tynedale* gained a little time before Schmidt, now sure he was in the presence of the enemy, opened fire at 0631, his first shells straddling *Atherstone* at a range of seven miles and forcing her to discharge smoke as her only means of defence.

At 0635, remembers Sub-Lieutenant David Stogdon, who was *Tynedale*'s Gunnery Control Officer, his ship 'engaged *Seeadler*, as *Tynedale* came under heavy fire from all four destroyers, who were then on her port quarter at a range of 5, 500 yards.' Her forward mounting wooded, *Tynedale*'s reply was restricted to the fire of her after twin four-inch guns, meaning that she could engage only one German ship at a time, while all four of the enemy were free to rain shells down upon her.

Continuing to move away, *Tynedale* then shifted her fire to *Iltis* which, according to Stogdon 'appeared to be hit as a small fire between the funnels was observed burning for a few minutes. It was still dark enough for the enemy shells to glow red in the sky and, although the outline of the German destroyers was clear enough to get a reasonable inclination, observation of our own fall of shot was extremely difficult. We appeared to be in the middle of a cone of enemy fall of shot, rather than being straddled. The situation remained like this because of independent firing from each destroyer, and as there was no centralized control they were unable to move the fall of shot on to us. We sustained two hits, both high and well above deck level.'

Using their superior speed to place themselves in an advantageous position to fire torpedoes, *Seeadler* and *Iltis* both launched fans of three in *Tynedale*'s direction, but, as with most of the shells the Germans had fired, these also missed their target. Turning into her own smoke, and with the range then down to only 4000m, the British ship then disengaged, ceasing fire at 0644, having fired 52 rounds from her after gun – plus a contribution from her pom-pom – as against the 240 to 360 shells Stogdon estimates the enemy flotilla fired against him.

Why precisely the German ships failed to punish their single engaging adversary is not clear, although Stogdon attributes much of the credit for their survival to Lieutenant-Commander Tweedie's fine handling of his ship. And nor is it understood why they too were content to break off the action, instead of pursuing it to a conclusion which must inevitably have been in their favour. In justification of Schmidt's caution, Stogdon points out that *Tynedale*'s Yeoman of Signals made a play of flashing signals westward towards an imaginary back-up force. Far more likely to have influenced the German commander's decision, however, were the six equally imaginary additional British destroyers he would later claim to have been present during this sharp but inconclusive exchange, it being, one must suppose, more honourable to report having disengaged from numerous phantom ships than from such a paltry number of real ones. Either way, Schmidt broke off, turned to port and led his truncated flotilla back to St Nazaire, leaving *Tynedale* and *Atherstone* free to resume their sweep towards 'T'.

Not too many miles to the north-west of this encounter, Paul, on seeing muzzle flashes off his starboard bow, increased his speed only to have the tow lines to the ML part. Taking off his prize crew he then made away at speed to the north-east, leaving the 306 adrift with a smoke float nearby to mark her position. To the south in the dawn light it was now possible to see Tweedie and Jenks steaming west at high speed as they came back on to their earlier course of 248°, but, as no engagement ensued, *Jaguar* was left in peace to return to the estuary.

On board the steadily sinking gunboat, well to the west by this time and still in company with Irwin's ML 270, the flashes of gunfire from both engagements had been seen and noted, but while these implied an enemy surface presence somewhere in the area, their threat was no greater than that of the sea itself which was still pouring in through the many holes in her hull. Examining the damage, Able Seaman Peter Ellingham counted no fewer than fifty-two holes along the gunboat's starboard side, and, stripping off to go down through the foremost hatch, found several feet of water in the forward magazine.

With the coming of daylight Ryder ordered their speed reduced to 8 knots, and as the horizon opened out to either side, MLs 446 and 156 were seen, the former a little way off to the north and the latter still plugging valiantly towards them from the direction of land. His intention being at this point to bring all the craft together, Ryder had no sooner reversed the gunboat's course in order to close with Fenton when the joyous sight of the speeding *Tynedale* and *Atherstone*, still some miles astern, came to relieve them all of their most immediate fears of a chance encounter with the enemy.

At about 0720 the two groups came together and stopped, after which a hurried transfer of personnel was begun, with the wounded from Ryder's boats, plus any extraneous personnel, being taken on board the destroyers. Fortunately the weather was still their friend, the flat, calm sea aiding what might otherwise have been a very hazardous venture indeed. The casualties from Irwin's and Falconar's boats were taken on board *Tynedale*, as were Falconar's Commandos and medical team. In spite of his wounds, Sergeant Robbie Barron remained on board the 446 until such time as the last of his boys, along with all their weapons, had been taken off, after which he too boarded *Tynedale*, to be put in a cabin where he received a cursory medical examination. Later, he recalls, one of his own boys 'came in, a real Glaswegian and said, "You'll probably be able to use this when in hospital, " and of all things handed me a pound of butter. A great thought after all we'd been through and so unexpected.'

Coming up to the badly damaged ML 156, *Atherstone* set to clearing her of everyone before moving across to the gunboat. While it was still expected at this stage that 314, 270 and 446 would complete their passage home, Fenton's boat was clearly finished and the decision was taken to abandon her. In anticipation of the fact that she might eventually go down, Lance-Corporals Stanley Stevenson and George Ewens, who had survived their stint with George's Bren unscathed, had already removed their boots and hung them round their necks. Remembering how the transfer was made, Stan writes that: 'The *Atherstone* came alongside us with its nets down and, with our wounded, we all clambered aboard, leaving the ML to its watery fate. I still had all my personal weapons, including ammunition and grenades, intact. I think it was the only action I have ever been involved in without firing something. I handed over the Lewis to the Navy, as they like that sort of gun and they were very pleased to receive it.'

Not content with clearing the boat of its human crew, another rather smaller life was carried on board the destroyer when Guardsman Taff Lloyd, who was very fond of animals, scooped up a black cat which had been terrified by the gunfire and was now curled up on his bunk. It clung to the Commando's rollneck sweater as they climbed up the scrambling nets together.

Moving across to the gunboat, whose bloodied decks were littered with wounded and dead, Jenks was relieved to find Ryder still very much alive. In the case of the 314, the casualty list was so great that when all the men in need of care were taken off, the losses had to be made up with volunteers from Jenks' own crew. Making the transfer along with his personal staff, Ryder, too, climbed up to the destroyer. With so many wounded to be dealt with, the ship's wardroom was pressed into service as an impromptu operating theatre. Everywhere the response to the raiders was the same, as they were fussed over by a crew who could not do enough to please them. Carried down on to the messdeck and trussed up in a stretcher, having been wounded earlier by shrapnel, Leading Stoker Frank Pritchard was given a welcome cigarette by a sailor who lit it for him, placed it between his lips and then promptly moved away, not thinking that as Frank had no means of removing it himself, it must eventually burn right down to his lips.

During all of the time of the rendezvous manoeuvres the bucket brigade had maintained their efforts to keep down the level of flooding in the gunboat's forward spaces. So engrossed were they in their work that Chris Worsley for one knew nothing at all of their meeting with Jenks, nor of any transfers of personnel. The job of the struggling chain of men below deck was to remove the sea and return it whence it had come, and for a period of many hours that was all that mattered. So determined was Curtis to bring his boat home after all she had been through that he refused to allow Bill Savage's body to be taken on board the destroyer. For a sailor who had stood to his gun with such raw courage a burial at sea was not considered appropriate. So long as Curtis had anything to do with it Bill would be laid to rest in the soil of his birth, with his friends and family present.

After some thirty minutes the ships then formed up and made off towards the west again, leaving behind the sad sight of the foundering 156. Machin had made an attempt to scuttle his ship, but this had not succeeded and nor had *Atherstone*'s guns been able to put her under, the honour of the *coup de grace* falling to a twin-motored Heinkel float plane which put in an appearance shortly after the force moved off and wisely decided to bomb the one instead of the many before retiring from the fray shortly after 0800. At about 0815 a Beaufighter flew in from the north to give the ships at least a modicum of cover, it being a fairly safe bet that an enemy air attack in force must materialize sooner or later. At 0825 a solitary Junkers 88 did put in an appearance and was immediately engaged by the 'Beau', the two aircraft tussling so closely that a collision ensued, as a result of which both planes fell into the sea. *Tynedale* made a search for survivors, but sadly none was found.

At 0830 *Cleveland* and *Brocklesby* were seen to be steaming in from the west at high speed. On their way in from 'T', they had had an inconclusive meeting with MLs 160, 307 and 443, which were still working their way out to the open sea before turning north for home. At the sight of the two unidentified warships creaming through the water towards them, the captains of these small boats had quite naturally feared the worst and prepared themselves for it by, among other things tossing their charts and confidential papers overboard. All those who remember having sighted the two strange ships confirm that they were engaging aerial targets at the time. As the range very quickly came down, Ordinary Telegraphist Jim Hayhurst, on Horlock's 443, climbed as high as he could up on to the bridge and an exchange of signals took place during which identities were confirmed and the 443 was wished 'good luck' for her onward voyage. But with Schmidt posing such a threat in the east, no actual rendezvous took place during which the MLs might have received practical assistance from either of the Hunts.

Writing of the convergence as seen from the deck of Wallis's 307, Captain David Paton, RAMC, recalls; 'As the first greyness of dawn made itself felt, we saw ahead of us two major warships on the horizon, at full tilt, and all their guns firing. This is it, we all thought ... I went below to tell my wounded that they mustn't put too much air in their Mae Wests or I couldn't get them through the hatch. Then I heard an English voice on a loud hailer asking where the rest of us were. I was arranging to transfer my wounded when they just picked up speed and disappeared towards France and we were left alone in the Atlantic with no maps and no charts.'

At a little after 0900 *Cleveland*, *Brocklesby*, *Tynedale*, *Atherstone*, the gunboat and MLs 446 and 270 at last came together, making the withdrawing remnants of 'Chariot' a much stronger force than the initial fleet had ever been. As the captain of HMS *Cleveland*, Commander G.B. Sayer, RN, had seniority, this officer then took charge of the squadron, with Ryder at last relinquishing his responsibilities. Almost totally spent, he was now able to rest while the decisions were taken by somebody else.

Having seen for himself the spectacular results of Newman's actions on shore, and then what looked very much like the *Campbeltown*'s charge going up, Ryder had no reason to be other than convinced that the job which many had said could never be done had indeed been very well done. As a necessary corollary of such risky endeavours there must always be losses and, although these were hard to bear, given the enemy's crushing superiority in cannon they had not been quite so devastating as many feared who had claimed they would all be lost. The crew of ML 156 were safe on board; three of his boats were still sailing in company, and the new arrivals had reported a further three heading for home somewhere out to the north-west. If not exactly an occasion for joy – there were far too many ghosts in the air for that – Ryder could at least reflect with pride on the sheer guts with which his and Newman's flyweight forces had taken on and bloodied the nose of the current and thus far undefeated heavyweight champ. It was a sweet moment, but it would have been sweeter still had only Charles, Stan, Major Bill and all the others been there at his side to share it.

Having successfully avoided contact with *Tynedale* and *Atherstone*, *Kapitänleutnant* Paul had been plugging steadily eastwards during all of the various rendezvous which were bringing most of the remaining British ships together as a single force. Carrying with him his cargo of brave and bloodied men, he had made directly for St Nazaire even while the grievously wounded Durrant and Henderson had finally slipped away from life. As a mark of respect for his adversary's brave, if futile, fight, he had at one point gone so far as to invite Ronnie Swayne to share a glass of brandy in his cabin, so that he might personally express his admiration for their courage.

As she approached the deep-water channel through the estuary shoals, *Jaguar* was running in upon a stretch of water which other German boats had been patiently quartering since daybreak in their search for survivors numbed with cold, whose desperation was by now turning minutes into small eternities, for bodies burned and oil-soaked, rolling lazily with the swell, which once had been young men sailing out of Falmouth with all their lives before them.

A number of the shipwrecked 'Charioteers', including Johnny Johnson and Ron Howard of ML 262, Bob Nock, Tom Milner and the handful of others who had got away from the wreck of ML 298, had been carried by the ebbing tide to an early landfall on the northern shore; while, having been sunk so close to the estuary mouth, this same sweep of water was pushing

Micky Wynn and the steadily dwindling number of the MTB's survivors out towards the Bay of Biscay. For most of the bobbing, gasping men, however, this was the time, with dawn slowly lifting the horizon to the east, when salvation finally came, at the hands of the very enemy they had been trying so hard to kill just hours before.

Ted Burt was picked up by a German boat, as was Lance-Bombardier Jack Aspden who, having passed out in the water, was only dimly aware of being plucked from its icy grip in the half-light of the new day. Drifting along on a Carley float, to which the gravely injured Collier had clung until such time as the struggle overwhelmed him and he tragically slipped beneath the waves, the pitifully few survivors of his ML 457 were also found, as were Sam Beattie, John Rafferty, Frank Arkle, Alf Salter and the other numbed and half-drowned remnants of the body of men who had sped away from the harbour on board ML 177.

Having long since given up trying to get at the whisky flask in his pocket, Sub-Lieutenant Frank Arkle saw in the arrival of a German trawler a chance at last to get a taste of the revivifying liquid. Recalling his own dawn rescue, he writes of how he 'lay on the deck on the port side of the bridge, after struggling up the clambering nets over the trawler's side. A sailor was very decent to me, bandaged my foot and hand and brought me some German acorn coffee. At this time I did not know I was wounded in the hip, and I was convinced I had lost my left eye ... Another sailor came along. I indicated that I wanted something from my hip pocket, the button of which I had not been able to undo as my fingers were too cold. He took out my flask of whisky, said "Ach – Schnapps!" and walked off with it. Probably the most disappointing moment of my life!'

As it was in the estuary so it was in the town, where the Germans were bending to their search for Newman's men with a will that was reinforced by the coming of the light. Gone now were the sinister shadows and tortured proportions of the dark hours, to be replaced by a grey ordinariness that was no more than an empty shell which might bear the scars of their experience, but was by now all but empty of the heat of it. Where before the Commandos, as a consequence of surprise, aggression and ignorance on the part of the enemy, had held the initiative, now their struggle was diminished by the selfish need to survive to that of simply hiding out until the cloak of night became their ally once again.

Throughout the small hours those who had been caught on land, such as the parties of John Cudby and Tom Hannan, and those who had been pulled from the sea, such as Robbie Roberts and Len Ball, had been moved to the large concrete shelters built by the Germans, whose space they would share for several hours with anxious French civilians. As Len Ball remembers, when he was put inside what was probably the 'Sud 1' shelter, all the French were moved to one end while he was installed at the other. A female German doctor tended to his wounds. All his clothes were taken away and he was given a single blanket in which to wrap his freezing body. Seeing his distress, the female doctor arranged a second blanket for him and a cigarette. Small acts of human kindness perhaps, but nonetheless a surprise to Len, who had always been brought up to to think the very worst of the Germans.

Down in their cellar the larger party of Newman, Copland, Montgomery, Purdon et al had hardly settled to their wait when the start of a noisy and systematic search of the building above them ended their hopes of hiding out till Saturday night. Originally Ron Steele had been their sentry at the stairhead, but now it was the multilingual Tony Terry who stood duty at the door. Copland was still working with the wounded when, as he writes:

'I heard the noise of heavy footsteps above me, then voices, then loud German shouting. I expected a hand grenade in our midst at any moment but, providentially, it was not to be. Instead Germans, literally bristling with grenades and Tommy guns, appeared in the doorway. Calling out, "These men are wounded; do you understand – blessés?" I dropped what I was doing at the behest of one of our visitors and joined the procession of those who could walk, up the stairs, across the street and, to our utter astonishment and amusement, into the house which had been illuminated and which we had thought might shelter us. It was the German Headquarters!

'During our crossing of the street a few French civilians, young men, appeared, but were quickly and roughly pushed out of the way by our hosts. We were taken upstairs, searched, questioned, vainly, and left for a while under a numerous guard. A little grey Feldwebel stayed with us and was quite pleasant, a last-war soldier. Our interrogation was continued, this time by an apparently decent young officer who did not seem unduly surprised or disappointed when he found he was to learn nothing but only said, "I did not expect to get any information from British Officers." For an hour or two we were left in a bedroom where we dozed on the floor.'

Most of the survivors of Billie Stephens' crew having been moved to the U-boat pens some hours before, Ordinary Telegraphist George Davidson's sojourn amidst his rolls of wire on the quayside had been both lonely and interminably long. At about 0300 he had seen the gunboat speed by and, after that, he writes, 'I lost track of time. I was very cold and my right arm felt numb because of a small splinter-wound. I tried a couple of times to look for a better hiding place, but sporadic small-arms firing in the dock area made me think again. Eventually, just at daybreak, in desperation I broke cover and ran head-on into a number of German troops.'

Having been so quickly taken prisoner, Davidson was walked the short distance to the base of the Mole, searched for weapons and made to stand with his back to the low wall that ran along the structure's edge.

'I thought that I was about to be shot. In desperation I told them in French that I was Scottish, because I realized that my unmarked overalls led them to think that I was French. The officer in charge immediately asked me in very good English why I was not in uniform. I lied to him that I had been working in the engine-room when we were hit. After some consideration he had me escorted to a private house, still in the dock area. I was taken into a small room where an army officer stood behind a desk with an armed escort. One of our Commandos was there when I arrived. We were asked to turn out our pockets. I had nothing at all, but my colleague laid a hand grenade on the desk!'

Elsewhere in the docks the arrival of daylight prompted the move to the pavement outside their café prison of Tiger Watson, Stuart Chant, Gerard Brett and Dick Bradley. Making their number up to five was Private McCormack, a kilted member of the squad of Donald Roy, which had held on so well just north of bridge 'G'. A grenade had exploded in his face, mutilating him. As he sat on the cold stone with his bloodied head in his hands, making, as Stuart Chant records, 'the most horrible gurgling noises', he epitomized the futility and stupidity of the periodic human madnesses during which it becomes heroic to do such things to men.

Sitting right next to McCormack, and with Gerard Brett on his other side, Tiger recalls of this sad and deflating period that 'We were stared at by curious Germans. Some U-boat men came up. One spoke some English, and told us that he had been in the merchant navy before the war, and had a girlfriend in Hull. "Ah, you're lucky! For you the war is over!" he added wistfully.'

And then the photographers came and, on top of everything else, the group were forced to endure the wartime version of a modern media 'blitz', with German propaganda teams filming and photographing the crushed invaders the better to persuade the neutrals of the Axis' worth. 'We tried with mixed success to look both defiant and indifferent, ' recalls Watson. 'They moved about us and clambered over us to get the best pictures, as though we were a collection of inanimate objects in a still-life study arranged for their benefit. They were particularly intrigued with McCormack, who sat unaware with his head bowed forward. As we subsequently learned, they even photographed him when, legs apart, they discovered that he was wearing nothing under his kilt. That cold, unfeeling picture of a suffering human being was derisively published in a German Forces magazine. The suppression of humanity and decency for propaganda purposes is one of the vilest manifestations of war.'

In one or two of the German photos Stuart Chant can be seen still sporting his steel helmet, even though, by this late hour, one might have thought the need of it long gone. In fact he was only being practical in recognizing the danger posed by *Campbeltown*'s hulk which, contrary to Ryder's supposition, was still intact and jammed in the caisson not above 500 metres away. Had her short-delay fuses worked as planned, she would have gone up many hours ago, providing for them all the crashing evidence of success that Ryder, far out at sea, had taken the explosion at 0425 to be. But these had all too obviously failed, leaving those who understood such things to hope and pray that the unreliable long-delay fuses would not suffer the same fate. These were already fast approaching the farthest extension of the envelope of time during which they had been expected to set off the charge, and still nothing had happened. Likely to work best at warmer temperatures, there was no sure way of predicting how they might have been affected by the extremes of temperature within the stricken ship; nor was it possible to know what damage might have been done to the charge as a whole by the many shells which had struck the forward part of the hull, or by the impact of the ramming itself. Also, and anything but a pleasant thought, there was the chance that the enemy might somehow have been able to interfere with the mechanisms in such a way as to successfully disarm it. Whatever the reasons, the pain of silence where instead there should have been smoke and thunder was felt by all the men. Their brave old ship had not gone up yet and with every passing minute the likelihood of her ever doing so seemed all the less.

After about an hour the five men were loaded on to the back of an open lorry with other wounded, including Arthur Ashcroft, and driven out of St Nazaire. Their destination was the town of La Baule, a handful of miles to the west and a safe haven where the valuable crews of the U-boats were billeted when not on duty.

'This journey turned out to be a nightmare for me, ' recalls Dick Bradley, 'and from the very second I was lifted from the ground my wounds front and back started bleeding again. Every time the lorry went over a bump in the road, and there were hundreds of them, I could feel the warm blood running from the wounds again. After all this loss of blood, I never expected to be alive at the end of the journey.'

For those such as Dick who were in urgent need of medical attention, 'the end of the journey' in fact turned out to be the imposing Hotel l'Hermitage, right on the esplanade, requisitioned by the Germans and now a naval hospital of sorts. 'Laid out, ' as Watson recalls, 'on a deep-pile carpet in an enormous room festooned with imposing crystal chandeliers, ' it would quickly become clear to all that the quality of the establishment's decor far outstripped that of its healing facilities. Lying closely packed on mattresses placed on the floor and constantly watched by armed guards, the men would eventually be taken to 'operating theatres', there to find that the Germans were critically short of some rather basic supplies. While some were given anaesthetics to ease their pain, many others were not, the crucial drugs being rationed in a manner which seemed to bear no relation to the seriousness of the surgeries being carried out.

Of the 100 or so wounded who would eventually be brought to l'Hermitage, most would remain for several days before being moved away from La Baule. In the case of the able prisoners, however, this sleepy resort was to prove no more than a staging post in which they would be held for only a matter of hours before being shipped to a POW camp in Rennes. Their 'holding tank' was a café which was already known to Bob Montgomery, who had enjoyed a meal there in May, 1940, before being evacuated to England. His unit at the time had been stationed in nearby Pornichet. Carried out of St Nazaire by lorry in the hours preceding noon, both soldiers and sailors were uplifted by the sympathetic response of the French who watched them pass. 'All along the route, ' writes Copland of his own excursion later in the morning, 'people gave us concealed "V" signs and shook hands with themselves in joy – concealed because Germans always stood near them. At La Baule we parked our rather tired bodies in a café with a more numerous guard than ever, and always with Tommy guns pointed at us and looking very grim. Soon the café really seemed like a café, for we received some ersatz coffee and dry bread. Parties of our chaps, Commando and naval, kept joining us, and as stories were swapped the atmosphere became merrier and merrier.'

Fuelled by relief at having made it through the maelstrom, and by reunions with friends and comrades whose fates till then had not been known, the men's spirits could not help but rise. In the case of the early arrivals, all that was needed to make their victory over adversity complete was to hear the distant thunder of *Campbeltown* taking her caisson off to kingdom come. Amid the confusion of questions and responses, laughter and ribald comments made at the expense of their uneasy captors, Robbie Roberts was overjoyed to see that his captain, Ted Burt, had after all been saved. Along with a number of others, Richard Collinson filled out a spurious Red Cross form, the real purpose of which was to elicit personal details for later use in propaganda broadcasts. With his father, also a serving naval officer, having been captured by the Japanese during the collapse of Hong Kong just three months earlier, it would be Richard's mother's misfortune to learn eventually from Lord Haw Haw, that her son was also a prisoner. In one corner of the café stood a pool table, on which Buster Woodiwiss and Nicky Finch, newly united after having become separated during the fighting, began to play. This sort of behaviour being considered not at all appropriate to their new and lowly status, one of the guards swiftly confiscated the cues.

Within St Nazaire itself the Germans, intent on scouring every structure in the port until they could proclaim it clear of the contagion of Newman's men, began to put pressure on the civilian population. Within their homes any hiding places that might conceivably harbour a Tommy were searched by soldiers and sailors who saw a threat in every twitch and shadow. The families who had left their homes to hide within the bunkers were not allowed to leave until the occupiers had cleared away the German dead, leaving only British corpses to help imply a greater loss to the raiders than the price paid by their own men. Even when finally cleared to leave, the French were required to have their papers checked before being permitted to pass into the light of the new day.

Freed at last to return to the Santé Maritime, Alain Bizard and Gilles Chapelan set off to tour once more the area they had been patrolling when the bombers came. Close to the Mole there was visible the burnt-out shell of one of the British boats and out across the ash-coloured water, the wreck of the *Campbeltown* could be clearly seen, dashed against the massive caisson as though a child had tried to crack it open with a flimsy toy. Moving across the Place towards Bridge 'D', they saw the bodies of Deanes and Chetwynd lying among their scattered kit, with two German soldiers standing guard over their ghosts. To the young men's right the tugs sunk by Pritchard, Maclagan and Shipton lay askew in the waters of the Bassin and on the other side of the bridge sat the forlorn hulk of a Red Cross ambulance, doors wide open, tyres punctured, its bodywork pierced by bullet holes.

Although the town was mostly quiet by now, reinforcements were still moving in, tired and dusty columns marching along the arterial highways which led directly to the port. A cordon of steel was slowly being established which would eventually turn St Nazaire into a territory foreign even to those who lived there. And all the time the search went on, street by street, house by house, as the last of the hopeful *évadées* were prised one by one from their hiding places.

Micky Burn and Paddy Bushe were hustled out of the engine-room of the ship in which they had taken refuge. With the Germans' reaction impossible to predict, Micky placed his own body in such a way as to shield his companion from harm. Out in the morning air they were marched away with bayonets at their backs, hands up, and very conscious of the fact that their capture was being filmed for propaganda purposes. In the hope that the resulting images might eventually be seen by, or reported to, British Intelligence, Micky formed the fingers of both hands into V-signs, with the aim of advertising the raid's success.

In the event the film was to become part of a newsreel seen in a theatre in Arnhem by a pre-war friend of Micky's who had contacts in the Dutch resistance. With the connivance of the theatre owner, several frames were removed from the reel of film and sent off to Britain, via Stockholm. On seeing it Brigadier Haydon would correctly interpret its message, whereas on first noticing the odd configuration of Micky's fingers his parents would take it as meaning only that their son had been wounded in the hands.

High up in their nest atop the stacked bags of cement, Johnny Roderick's small party might well have made it through until nightfall, had their weakened condition not limited their efforts to build a concealing parapet around their nest. With the Germans searching every corner of the warehouses, they were therefore spotted around mid-morning, made to climb down from their perch and taken to a nearby German ship, upon whose deck they were held for a time under guard. In the same general area it would soon be the turn of Bert Shipton and 'Dai' Davis to be routed out from their hiding place by a group of Germans, one of whom was particularly aggressive. They too were marched away at bayonet point, with the slightly built Shipton half-carrying his taller, hobbling companion. With prying eyes seemingly penetrating even the most unlikely of spaces, Bob Hoyle was discovered among the girders supporting bridge 'D'. With no trousers on, he was assumed to be Scottish, and, having long since lost both his Colt and his commando knife, was not treated quite so badly as he feared might otherwise have been the case. As with so many others, he was bitterly disappointed at having achieved so much but without being able to enjoy 'the icing on the cake of getting away'. Later, Jimmy Brown too would be prised from his hiding place deep within the girders and encouraged at rifle point to join the throng of men collecting in the U-boat pens.

Within the harbour itself, as the forenoon wore on, German ships continued to arrive with bodies, wreckage and survivors to add to the forlorn harvest being slowly gathered in from all along the estuary shores.

At a little after 1100 local time the trawler carrying the survivors of

Rodier's ML sailed up the river to be greeted, as Frank Arkle recalls, 'by dozens of faces peering over the jetty. It was now low tide, and there was a very long metal ladder up to the quayside. Somehow I managed the climb and walked to where the rest of the wounded and captured were standing. A German who spoke English fluently then turned up with a microphone and started talking to us with the object presumably of information and propaganda. At this time I thought I had done enough walking, so I became a stretcher case!'

Still lying on the deck of the trawler, intensely cold despite being covered by a blanket, and with a German sentry standing guard over him, John Rafferty saw a few survivors in a group, one of whom was Jock Bruce, the coxswain of Billie Stephens' ML 192. They had worked together over a period of six months preceding the raid and knew each other very well; yet when Rafferty called out 'Glad you made it, ' Bruce was unable to recognize him.

Also climbing up on to the quayside, cold, barefoot and naked except for the ubiquitous blanket, Beattie's mood was not improved by the sight of his battered command still stuck fast against the caisson. Passing close to the hulk as he was led off to be questioned, he happened upon Micky Burn, who was equally puzzled as to why she was still in a single piece when by rights she should have long since been reduced to many thousands.

About two and a half cables short of *Campbeltown*'s stern the process was by this time well in hand of transferring the wounded from the anchored *Jaguar* on to a barge. The tide was well out and so it was necessary for the men either to climb up to the quayside by themselves or to be lifted on to it. Glyn Salisbury had just begun the climb when, as though she had finally tired of all the waiting, the old ship at last gave up her soul in a sudden thundering explosion, the concussion from which seared across both town and harbour. Glyn has described it as the sort of 'cutting' crack that accompanies the very worst forms of lightning. So devastating was the shock that even the sea itself was thrust aside, causing the barge to bottom momentarily.

Below deck on the German ship Swayne was conversing with Paul when the noise and vibration brought them running up to find débris falling all around and a pall of smoke where once the massive caisson, apparently inviolate, had stretched across the entrance to the 'Normandie' dock. The men already on *Jaguar*'s deck, on board the trawler or spread along the nearby quayside, were stunned by the old ship's immolation, so long expected and yet so shocking in both its suddenness and its intensity.

Lying on the deck of the trawler, John Rafferty remembers the sight of one of *Campbeltown*'s funnels shooting up into the sky. Alf Searson, on the deck of the ship in the Bassin with the rest of Johnny Roderick's small group, was impressed, though fortunately not physically so, by one of the destroyer's iron gratings which fell much too close for comfort. Alain Bizard recalls a fragment of the hull, weighing more than forty kilos, coming down in the garden of the Santé Maritime and Joseph le Pehun records that a twisted fragment more than six metres long crashed onto the Place du Bassin. Still hiding in their drain and keeping their strength up by munching on chocolate, George Wheeler and Ronald Sims heard the bang, the shock of which knocked plaster from the walls of the cellar where George Haines, Bob Wright and the remaining four of their group were patiently waiting out the day. Colonel Charles and Major Bill, not yet moved to La Baule, received the signal of their collective success with glee, as did all the men already in the café by the Loire who, much to the annoyance of their guards, put up a rousing cheer. In l'Hermitage, Watson, having earlier fallen into an exhausted sleep, learned of the explosion when he was awakened by the noise of 'a small German petty officer' who was 'positively screaming with rage'. Perhaps the most dramatic scene of all was that where Beattie, exhausted and cold, was being questioned by an English-speaking officer and lectured on the futility of using so slight a ship to attempt to destroy so great a dock at the very moment when *Campbeltown*'s explosion blew the office windows in.

As a demonstration of the raid's success the men of Chariot could have hoped for none better because the caisson could surely never have survived a blast of such cataclysmic proportions. It proved their worth and its echo rang across the town like a volley fired in salute over the graves of Nigel Tibbits and all the other brave men who had been robbed by death of the chance to see their dream fulfilled.

18

Ashes of Innocence

If the thunderclap which rocked the town came as a shock to the waiting British, the discharge of almost 10, 000 lbs of ammonal was to the Germans, who were only now beginning to feel themselves free of the trauma of the night, a blast straight from hell, which cut through steel and flesh alike, and caused such devastation as would turn the stomach of even the most hardened warrior.

Sitting in a café in the rue de Prieuré, which, a little before noon local time, shook to the sudden concussion, Pierre Brosseau was dismayed by the thought that, with so many civilians now moving about the streets, the blast might have taken the lives of some of his countrymen: however, he and his friends would shortly learn that it was not the French whose bodies had been ripped and shredded by the hurricane of burning air and flying steel, but the hundreds of German sightseers who had flocked to the hulk from far and wide to parade about the broken ship.

Where one moment there had been crowds of soldiers and sailors, and even a handful of female friends and companions, either on the ship itself or in transit to or from it, now there was only the charnel wreckage of their bodies strewn about the quays in bloody fragments.

With the passage of the morning and the failure to find her hidden charge, the belief had grown among the Germans that the old ship was not a threat, that she was no more than a sad and lonely manifestation of the Tommies' failure to understand the magnitude of the task before them. They had sought to batter down the massive caisson with a light destroyer, whose plates had simply torn and buckled with the impact. Experts had toured the decks and hull, and delivered themselves of their opinions, firstly that she was not mined, and secondly that, sunk as she was by the stern and on a falling tide, she would not prove easy to tow away in the short term.

A cordon was established to keep the gawpers and souvenir hunters out, but was either not enforced or not observed as the curious of all ranks poured in upon the dock to claim by physical association with this impressive relic their own connection with the night's events. They walked the decks and marvelled at the screens of steel behind which the Tommies had sheltered. They climbed up to the bridge and looked out as Beattie had looked out through its armoured vision slits. They toured the cabins and spaces below, finding souvenirs aplenty in the food, kit and cigarettes that lay scattered about. They exerted by their presence the sovereignty of the victorious and they died in the single, shattering blast that was the product of both their arrogance and their miscalculation.

At the very moment she went up Herr Klaus Ehrhardt, a Fleet Engineer Officer attached to the seventh U-Flotilla, was but 100 metres away along the quayside. Billeted out in La Baule, Klaus had made for the U-boat pens immediately the action had started, and when the shooting was over had followed everyone else in making for *Campbeltown*'s crumpled bow, never imagining for a moment that the twisted, blackened steel contained a charge. In no particular hurry to move away, his life was saved by his driver who suggested that, with noon approaching, perhaps it was time for lunch. Similarly fortunate in having moved away just minutes before the whole forward part of the ship disintegrated were seamen Heinz Grossmann and Heinz Hunke, of Minesweeper 1601, moored at the start of the action within sight of Pritchard's attack on the tugs by bridge 'D'. They had just reached Newman's old HQ position when the earth suddenly danced and shook beneath their feet, and they found themselves assailed by blast and débris as a rain of steel crashed to earth all around them. Protected from the worst of the shock by a warehouse wall, they managed somehow to survive, but two others of their crew did not, these unfortunates being numbered among the three to four hundred other souls consigned to the winds in this, their exclusive holocaust.

Blown off its seat and thrust inwards by the pressure of the sea, the outer caisson folded back against the western wall of the dry dock. Freed from its restraint, a raging torrent swept toward the inner caisson, carrying with it the shattered remains of *Campbeltown* and damaging both *Schledstadt* and *Passat*. Having been incompletely blown, and in spite of all the forces directed against it, the inner caisson held and, in fact, would eventually be repaired and floated down to replace the outer gate. But when added to the demolitions of Chant, Purdon and Smalley, the destruction of the one would be more than enough to transform this great dock into little more than an impressively chambered ditch, of no strategic use to any force.

Removed from danger by their distance from the scene, the clusters of prisoners by the Avant Port could see in this act only the denouement which finally put to rest their fears of failure. For them the raid was over, the battle demonstrably won. But for the Germans, who had come to believe that the Tommies were beaten and the killing finished, it was a nightmare reborn which stretched their nerves to breaking point and left them angry and afraid. Within the toll of dead were numbered many officers whose loss significantly strained the chain of command by means of which guidance and discipline could be imposed upon the troops. In succeeding days their loss would be especially felt as soldiers and sailors, motivated by fear, turned upon those in whom they saw a threat. With the British gone by this time to camps and hospitals well outside the town, only the French would remain to bear the weight of these assaults, and it is a regrettable, if unforeesable, consequence of 'Chariot' that so many innocent civilians died because of it.

While the Germans began to assess the loss and damage, to attempt to divine the degree of threat that other such devices planted by the British must now surely pose, and to make more rigorous still their search of port and town, the remaining British POWs were driven off to La Baule. Whereas for most the journey was made directly from the major holding areas, in the case of Johnny Roderick's small group, who had originally been placed on board the German ship, they were first lined up against a wall and then held for a time in a café before joining the others in their uncomfortable trek to the west.

Joining up on shore with the remnants of other crews and Commando teams, Ronnie Swayne and the men of 306 now found their treatment to be very different indeed from that which they had enjoyed on board *Jaguar*. While on the German ship a state of mutual respect had existed, which, at the point where his prisoners were preparing to disembark, had prompted Paul to call his ship's company to attention and Swayne, in return, to make a gift of his Commando dagger to Paul. But now this détente was swept aside as shouts, threats and physical intimidation confirmed to them all that from this day forward they were no more than trophies of an enemy whose control over their lives would be absolute.

They were left for a time on the quayside without food, drink or medical assistance, while the inevitable photographers sought to catch on film a record of their suffering and loss of presence. Only after this, the first of many degradations, were they taken to l'Hermitage, or to the café on the seafront. In the café, having already heard the mighty blast, the early captives were

264

ready with eager queries as to what exactly their old ship's finale had achieved, and when Beattie, wrapped in his blanket, joined the excited throng to add his story to the whole, the bearded warrior who had conned his 'Trojan Horse' with such precision won a terrific cheer from all.

While the news of their success gave cause for celebration in La Baule, the coming of noon was to offer no such joy to their compatriots out at sea, who, believing the job already done, were coming to terms with a decision made by Sayer which was to dash the hopes of the crews who had brought their boats so bravely away from St Nazaire.

Having come together at 0900, the seven ships had been pushing west all morning in an effort to put as many miles as possible between themselves and the German airfields. But with 314 taking on water forward and 270 being erratically directed by what Stewart Burkimsher refers to as her 'handraulic' steering, their speed was less than half of that which the destroyers could make alone.

With the passage of the hours, the new Senior Officer had become more and more concerned at their lack of progress. They were still little more than 100 miles from the enemy coast; the clouded sky was a perfect haven for enemy planes, which had already made two attacks on the force for the loss of a Ju 88 shot down by *Brocklesby*; three other MLs, which for safety's sake should be brought within the fold as soon as possible, were somewhere out in the wastes of the sea and the wounded were suffering, some of whose lives could only be saved by bringing them quickly to a hospital.

While a strong sentimental attachment might exist between the small boats which were so obviously holding them back and the crews they had served so well, Sayer was unaffected by such a bond and was determined to base his decisions on practicality alone. Against the wishes of Ryder, Curtis, Irwin and Falconar, whose sense of loyalty fuelled a strong desire to bring their charges safely home, he therefore ordered all three crews to board the destroyers, following which the 314, 270, and 446 would be sunk by gunfire.

At the time of Sayer's decision, the bucket brigade was still going strong on the gunboat. When the news came down that they were to abandon, it struck Chris Worsley that it might be an idea to save the haul of cigarettes which were stored in the wardroom, so he stuffed them into a kitbag before boarding *Brocklesby* with the rest of the crew. With her people taken off, the battered and bloody Fairmile was sunk by *Brocklesby*'s guns. Having been brought this far, the body of gunner Savage was placed in the destroyer's wardroom bath to await preparation of the canvas shroud in which he would be buried at sea. However, Curtis again intervened and won his case for having the body returned for burial in British soil.

Of the evacuation of Irwin's ML 270, Stewart Burkimsher writes that, as she 'manoeuvred alongside the *Brocklesby*, nets were lowered and eager hands reached downwards to grasp the even more eager upstretched ones as we balanced on the deck, bollards and torpedo cover. The swell caused the deck levels to vary by many feet, making the transfer a very hazardous operation.'

On board the destroyer the men were treated kindly and given tots of rum. But as he stood on the deck to watch their abandoned boat drop rapidly astern, Stewart sums up the sentiment felt by them all when he writes: 'It filled me with grief to see 270 dejectedly abandoned and treated so after serving us so well. I could have wept.'

Freed at last of their burdensome brood, the four destroyers positively leapt ahead, surging off to westward at 1350 hours, in the hope of sweeping up the three remaining Fairmiles as they made their run for home at 25 knots. Having set out to follow their orders, which, if acting independently, were to make for a position 46° north by 7° west, and then to follow the 7° meridian to the north and home, these three boats were now engaged in an attempt to ease the suffering of their wounded by transferring Doctor David Paton from one to the other. They had, thanks to the combined fire of all the guns that would bear, already shot down a Heinkel III, which had come in low that morning, dropped its bombs harmlessly into the sea and then been destroyed when it hit the water. Now the gunners, tired and short of ammunition, anxiously searched the clouds for the specks that would next roar in to threaten them.

At about noon the 307 slowed, Horlock came alongside and David leapt across, to be followed by stretchers which were tossed onto ML 443's deck. Without the facilities of the destroyers upon whose supplies and equipment he had been relying, David was hard pressed to deal with the worst of the wounds; however, his ministrations were infinitely better than any of the men might otherwise have hoped for. Having dealt with the worst of Horlock's casualties, David next transferred to Boyd's boat, where he found Tom most aggrieved by the lack of any but the most basic medical supplies. Having taken survivors off the 447 and then plucked still more from the waters off the Mole, Boyd had a total of eight in need of attention, one of whom, a Commando with a huge splinter wound in his chest, was in extremis. His wounds having bled badly, he could not survive without blood, and of blood there was none. With a transfusion of any sort being out of the question, he would die that night.

With no charts to guide them, the three continued to press westwards, eventually turning north at 1700 in the hope of running into something solid – Ireland perhaps, but preferably the English coast. Platt having transferred from Boyd's boat to his own 443, he had now displaced Horlock as her captain, returning the latter to his early status as a 'spare'.

Completely unaware of all that had transpired elsewhere, they pressed their case for freedom with a dogged persistence such as Curtis, Irwin and Falconar would have been happy to display had only Sayer allowed them to run for home themselves. At 1850 hours, having intercepted their signals to England, Sayer decided to split his force, sending *Tynedale* and *Atherstone* with the wounded directly to Plymouth, while *Cleveland* and *Brocklesby* searched fruitlessly for the three lost sheep.

During the long afternoon which followed *Campbeltown*'s explosion, the painful process of inquiry began by means of which the disaster might be explained to an angry and vengeful Berlin. That the Führer would not be best pleased to learn of the attack was a foregone conclusion; however, Hitler's was not the only wrath to fear, for having only the previous afternoon assured Dönitz that his 'grey wolves' were safe from assault, the commander of the 7th U-Flotilla, *Kapitänleutnant* Herbert Sohler, now found himself in the invidious position of having to explain why they were not.

In the shadow, first of the raid itself and then of the noonday blast, the most common reaction, apart from fear, was of confusion: confusion among the Germans who, believing the primary value of the port to lie in its U-boat base, were puzzled as to exactly what it was the British had come to achieve; confusion among the French themselves, many of whom had believed the night's events to herald the start of an invasion. Reacting passionately to this expectation, a number of civilians, displaying more fervency than judgement, had joined in the fighting, seeing in it a chance to snipe at the enemy with such pitiful weapons as at that time made up their armoury. But with organized resistance as yet little more than a dream, their passionate contribution was ill-fated from the start. For most of the men and women of the town, who had wisely spent the night in hiding, the lesson of the new day was that they should bow to the additional restrictions without demur. Until such time as they might come to understand all that was happening around them and why, it could serve no useful purpose to stand in the way of an enemy who was shocked, embittered, and everywhere.

With the survivors of MTB 74 at last plucked from water and shore, and with the exception of the few hopeful *évadées* still determinedly holding out for nightfall, the port and estuary were by early afternoon all but clear of the British. Having gathered all the able-bodied prisoners in the café in La Baule, where a number had already been subjected to a mild interrogation, it was considered prudent to move such 'desperadoes' on as quickly as possible to the first of the several POW camps of which they would have experience over the next several years; and so, at about 1400 hours, they were again herded into trucks and driven off under the eagle eyes of the uncompromising *Feldgendarmerie*.

After what Bill Copland recalls was 'a nightmare drive of some seven hours', the men finally arrived in the Breton town of Rennes. Describing their arrival at the very basic Front Stalag 133, which had been designed to house French colonials made prisoner during the débâcle of 1940, he writes:

> 'We climbed stiffly from our trucks and to our astonishment found ourselves almost surrounded by French coloured troops, prisoners also, laughing, shouting and throwing cigarettes to us. All attempts by the Germans to prevent this welcome and the kindly generosity accompanying it were in vain. I shall never forget that welcome. As at every other halt during our progress, shoals of photographers arrived, all in uniform and all determined to photograph the savage British Commandos.
>
> 'Now we were herded into the filthiest huts I have ever seen, broken concrete floors, dirty, evil-smelling mattresses, one indescribably filthy blanket per man and a foul stench everywhere. That evening, in spite of everything, including the spotlights and machine guns which were continually trained on us, we had a sing-song at which Ted Burt . . . was the star turn, and later talked ourselves to sleep with Bung Denison as the chief contributor. His cheerful nonsense did much to keep our spirits up.'

If the new arrivals in the Stalag were not best pleased with their conditions, at least they would be spared the medical horrors even now being inflicted upon their friends at l'Hermitage, where the process of operating on the worst of the wounded was already well underway. Spirits here, dragged down by shock and pain, were rather less buoyant than in Rennes, as men watched their friends being carried away to the 'theatre', and waited with justifiable apprehension to be strapped to the tables themselves. 'It was the most depressing time of my life,' remembers Corran Purdon, who lay with Micky Wynn on one side and Dick Bradley on the other. 'The realization that we were prisoners of war, that we would not be quickly rejoining our loved ones and friends, coupled with the squalor of our condition and the unpleasantness of our captors, came in massive contrast to the excitement and elation of the operation.'

Toward the end of the queue for the chop, Watson had plenty of time to watch the German surgeon select those to be taken away and think of how it would be when the next on the list was himself. 'He looked like a proper Prussian,' writes Tiger. 'He was a big man with closely cropped hair on a large, square head. He would enter the room still wearing his blood-streaked rubber operating apron and gloves. He then stalked slowly along the lines of wounded and would stop by some unfortunate. There would be a short colloquy with his assistants and then a brief exam. The victim of this barbaric priest was then borne away to be sacrificed or so it seemed to my over-wrought imagination.'

The 'theatre', for want of a better word, was a high-ceilinged room in which stretcher cases and walking wounded were transferred to one of the several tables upon which men, more often than not writhing about and groaning or shouting with pain, were cut, probed, stitched, bandaged and then moved aside quickly to make room for the next. Des Chappell, who regained consciousness only to find himself face down upon one of the tables with his arms securely strapped and someone holding on to his legs, realized that his head was being probed for splinters with little or any anaesthetic having been administered. Stuart Chant was given ether – but it didn't take, the failure consigning him to a prolonged period of 'unmitigated horror and pain', as his right arm, left leg and right knee were probed for bullets and shrapnel. Dai Davis was strapped down but given no anaesthetic whatever, as the surgeon dug deep into his instep where a bone had been broken by a chunk of shell.

Micky Wynn's eye was removed without benefit of any painkillers, and nor was Dick Bradley sedated when it was time to deal with his thigh wound by the simple expedient of cutting away large pieces of flesh. However, in stark contrast to this barbarity, Frank Arkle, who had been subject to fears of all sorts when he too was strapped down, was given a general anaesthetic, from the comfortable oblivion of which he woke to find his side dressed, his hand put in plaster and his injured foot encased in a splint which ran up to the knee. The following day he would be considerably 'bucked' to learn that he had not after all lost the eye he believed he had chucked over the side of the burning 177. Bill Clibborn, too, was put to sleep while they worked on him, though Johnny Roderick recalls that, having been instructed to strip down completely and climb on to one of the tables in the presence of several German nurses, 'They just stuck probes in to feel for metal and pulled out what they thought was necessary, and we got no anaesthesia at all!' In Tiger's case, when his turn did finally come, his arm was painfully manipulated into the position in which a splint could be attached. With this done and his burned right hand also heavily bandaged, he was returned to the ward unable to do a single thing to help himself.

In contrast to the bustle and perturbation of the prisoners' day, Saturday, as far as the handful of men still free were concerned, was but an irksome slog of seconds passing into minutes, passing into endless hours of waiting.

Entirely ignorant of events as they concerned their comrades, the world of which they had certain knowledge did not extend beyond the boundaries of their hiding places. They had heard, or hoped they had heard, *Campbeltown* go up. There had been the disquieting noise of Germans searching, and the odd, distant crack of a shot; but apart from these few clues, they were to remain perplexed by the mystery of what they would find outside, until such time as nightfall came to draw them from their lairs.

Having already divided into three pairs who would try for freedom independently, the party of Troop Sergeant-Major George Haines made sure that all arms and ammunition were left behind in the dusty cellar before braving the street above. Haines and Lance-Sergeant Challington went out together, as did Lance-Corporal Douglas and Private Harding, but when it came to the last of the six, Corporal Bob Wright had to tell his intended partner, Lance-Corporal Arnie Howarth, that he should go out on his own, as in his present, barely mobile state Bob would only hold the Guardsman up.

Assuming that he would have little choice but to surrender, Bob left the cellar last. Once in the street, however, he found that he could move more freely than he had anticipated and decided to give it a go after all. An open German Volkswagen drove right past without appearing to notice, but then a French teenager appeared and warned Bob that if he did not get under cover quickly he would inevitably be shot. Responding to Bob's request that he be taken to a doctor or a hospital, the boy guided him to a German-staffed aid station, which had medical orderlies and *Feldgendarmerie* in attendance. Here he was searched and, after a great deal of shouting, given preliminary medical aid. In the fullness of time he too would be shipped to l'Hermitage.

In the case of Corporal George Wheeler and his Canadian companion, Lance-Corporal Sims, the arrival of the witching hour was their signal to leave the drain which had been their cramped home for the day. It was only on leaving their refuge that they discovered that it was right next door to the *Kommandantur*! Successful in finding a safe route through the streets, they broke out into the country, without maps of any kind, but under a bright moon which helped them find their way before daybreak to the nearby village of l'Immaculée Conception. With movement by day too risky to contemplate, they spent most of Sunday in a chamber within a haystack, before being discovered by the locals at 7 in the evening. Given food, wine and advice by the farmer, they were fitted out in civilian clothes and given some money, in return for which they left their Colt.45s behind for the farmer's use. With the friendly darkness upon them once more, they set off for Spain at 1130, with George, who was only recently married, recording that, 'My only interest in all of this business was to get back to my wife.' This sentiment was, he unashamedly affirms, 'my driving force'.

On the morning of Palm Sunday St Nazaire could at last begin its slow return to those conditions of life which in wartime pass for normality. As nothing of any significance had occurred since the explosion of the previous day hopes inevitably began to rise with the passage of the morning that the nightmare was now at an end. The Tommies had gone and with them, please God, the threat of further violence and loss of life.

While the fears of the townspeople began to ease, such a relaxation of vigilance was wholly alien to the three groups of ships whose often exhausted crews were still beating northward on the second morning of their long and dangerous withdrawal to British ports. Dawn for them had meant nothing more than yet another return to 'action stations', as they anxiously scanned both sea and sky and dreamed of sleep far beyond the malignant grasp of the enemy.

Having survived a further bombing sortie at dusk on Saturday, the three 'lost' Fairmiles of Platt, Boyd and Wallis had made excellent progress during the night; indeed, as three tiny specks alone on the face of the sparkling sea, their greatest concern on Sunday morning was that they could only guess at their position, such uncertainty leading to fears that they might be so far west as to miss the coast of England altogether.

With some of the wounded in need of treatment right away, radio silence was broken to request that ambulances be made ready on the Scilly Isles, as it was more than possible they might make their landfall here. However, they need never have worried on this score, as an early encounter with a coastal convoy confirmed they were making more or less directly for Falmouth. At 1000 hours the Lizard was sighted ahead, this feature being not entirely unknown to Tom Boyd who, in 1940, as a Sub-Lieutenant and Navigating Officer with the 7th Flotilla, had run aground there while returning from patrol in thick fog, thus earning for himself the soubriquet 'Lizard' Boyd.

Approaching the harbour at about noon, with little more than vapour remaining in their fuel tanks, a signal was received which required that the Commandos remain below decks and out of sight of the many faces waiting to hail their triumphant return. The charade of naval independence from the Commando presence in Falmouth was being maintained to the last, thus robbing the soldier survivors of 'Chariot' of the recognition they very rightly felt was their due.

Led in by ML 443, the 'lucky thirteen', whose survival had greatly impressed the triskaidekaphobics among her crew, the three MLs quickly discharged their wounded into waiting RAF ambulances, whose crews, David Paton records, were booed by some of the men who harboured less than happy memories of the part played by their bomber allies. Now it was time to become used again to the alien priorities of those who only fought their battles in offices, and whose chosen weapons were regulations and the rigid observance of accepted social norms. Having been ordered not to shave so as to conserve water, David was carrying a three-day growth of beard. So as to satisfy the 'niceties', a 'crisply starched and very officious VAD girl' immediately took him aside and reprovingly observed, 'Doctor, you haven't shaved!'

With the wounded taken off, the boats came alongside the *PJC*, whose crew lined the rails and cheered their approach. Thus the handful of Commandos who had made it back were transferred to the ship from which so many had left only three days ago. On board *PJC*, soldiers and sailors alike were fêted, with Lance-Corporal Joe Rogers recalling that 'the Navy treated us like lords and gave us a wonderful meal.'

Also returning to Falmouth that afternoon were the destroyers *Cleveland* and *Brocklesby*. On arrival in port, Dunstan Curtis directed Chris Worsley to go ashore with the body of Bill Savage, which had been placed on a piece of plywood, secured with lines, and covered with a Union flag. It was ferried ashore on a little 'puffer' and placed on the flat rear deck of a van, to be carried slowly to the mortuary, with Chris marching behind it as it passed by the silent crowds that lined the streets.

As the two ships carried a number of men taken from the torpedo-armed ML 270, whose base was Dartmouth, these linked up with their friends on Boyd's ML 160, on which they were then carried home, just about all in and wanting nothing more than a long and dreamless sleep.

In the case of the long-suffering *Tynedale* and *Atherstone*, their port of arrival was Plymouth, where Ryder too was quickly made aware that his independent existence was now at an end. He was standing on the jetty in Devonport, watching the wounded being taken off and wondering what the reaction would be to the raid at home, when a Wren dispatch-rider roared up. She handed him a small, buff-coloured envelope which Ryder thought might be a congratulatory note from either Forbes or Mountbatten. But its contents were not quite so encouraging. It was, in fact, the Admiralty's delayed reply to the letter of rebuttal he had submitted some time ago concerning their criticisms of his activities during the loss of HMS *Prince Philippe*; and it confirmed that even after everything that had happened since, the award of their Lordships' displeasure would not be withdrawn.

Exhausted, and feeling personally responsible for the failure to re-embark his comrades from the Mole, this was the last thing Ryder needed to hear. Their Lordships' pursuit of his culpability seemed, he writes, 'rather inconsequential at that moment'.

On this National Day of Prayer, whose respectful sentiments seemed aptly suited to the occasion, the wounded were transferred into Stonehouse Naval Hospital where their visitors, among others, included both Ann Dvorak, the beautiful actress wife of Leslie Fenton, and Lady Astor, the local Member of Parliament. As far as the able Commandos were concerned, their temporary base, before returning to Scotland, would be Seaton Barracks, where men under the command of Lieutenant-Colonel Lucy, of the Royal Ulster Rifles, were waiting to welcome them home.

As there had been no way of predicting how many returnees they would be called upon to feed, the men in the barracks had erred substantially on the side of optimism when making their provisions, leading to a situation in which the men who did arrive to be fed were humbled by the emptiness surrounding them. As Lance-Corporal Stanley Stevenson movingly records, 'One of my most vivid recollections is on entering the dining hall, seeing the rows of tables laid for many meals. We were just a small group and occupied one end of one table. It dawned on us at that moment that we had lost many comrades and that we were extremely lucky to have returned. There was also a feeling of guilt, that we should not have been there and that we should have been with our missing comrades. It was a very quiet meal.'

If the atmosphere was sombre already, the mood of the men was not improved by a saffron-kilted piper who insisted on playing laments until Ronnie Mitchell, who was in Plymouth to collect the remnants of the force, asked the duty officer to stop him forthwith!

That evening, recalls Lance-Corporal John Webb, 'I was not the only one who, in bed that first night, wept away the tension until sleep finally obliterated thoughts of our comrades lost in the small boats, or ashore in a hell ten times worse than the one we had been through. We were home and they were not, and we wept for them.'

On Monday the 30th, with the sailors about to depart on their well-deserved survivors' leave, the funerals of the dead took place in Falmouth. At a ceremony attended by his shipmates and by his brother Roland, Bill Savage was laid to rest with full honours. It was the end of this quiet, modest man's life, but the beginning of a legend in which this lone sailor's courage, just as was the case with Sergeant Tommy Durrant, would come to stand as a symbol of the resolution and fortitude of ordinary men, qualities which are all that ever really shield us from tyranny.

As far as the few Commandos who had landed at Falmouth were concerned, their first move was to Plymouth to join the other members of their units. Here they were collectively interviewed by three officers from London, whose approach, at an understandably emotional time, was less than subtle. 'The only question they asked, ' writes John Webb, 'was, "did any of you land?" Of course, none of us had landed. The senior officer turned to the others and said, "These are no use to us." Then they turned and walked out. There was silence for a few minutes and then we gave vent to our outrage.' The men were justifiably hurt by this unwarranted display of indifference, 'not only for ourselves, ' adds John, 'but for the wounded we had brought back with us, and the dead, such as Captain Hodgson, we had not.' In the circumstances it was a cruel, if unintentional snub to men who had every right to believe that they had given of their best.

19

Echoes

As the men went on leave, recuperated in hospital or returned to their units, their exit from the scene effectively signalled the end of 'Chariot', at least as far as the British soldiers and sailors were concerned.

In St Nazaire, too, the confused and anxious civil population might have been forgiven for believing that their term of trial had also come to an end. However, just as had been the case with *Campbeltown*'s charge, the delayed-action torpedoes fired off by Micky Wynn had failed to explode as planned, which meant that, even as the town eased slowly back towards normality, their two special warheads were still ticking their way to destruction.

As the macabre task of recovering bodies continued throughout Monday, French workers were again permitted to return to the docks, where the Germans made little or no attempt to conceal from their sight the full effects of the destruction wrought by the Commandos. In the 'Normandie' dock there was little to be seen of the old destroyer save formless wreckage, but in the areas once held by Roderick and Roy the human refuse of Saturday's blast was still being cleared by working parties who distractedly shovelled the bits together and laid down sand to cover the blood.

On the surface Germans and French alike seemed to be accepting as permanent the uneasy truce which had existed between them since Saturday's tragedies. But in fact this was merely a façade behind which were concealed seeds of unease and mistrust, which finally blossomed into outright hostility when, at just a little after 4 o'clock, the first of Wynn's 'fish' exploded. Where one moment the surface of the river had been undisturbed, now there shot high into the air a column of dirty water which carried away both the outer caisson of the Old Entrance lock and the last vestiges of German composure.

As urgent steps were taken to identify the cause of this new terror, suspicion naturally fell upon the French and measures were put in hand which would renew and enhance the restrictions placed upon their movements after *Campbeltown* blew up. And then, at a little after 5 o'clock, the second torpedo detonated, its concussion snapping nerves which had been stressed to breaking point and ushering in a period of senseless and random violence which would leave many civilians dead.

Having been allowed back into the docks, whose workshops and facilities were seen by the Germans as the natural focus of sabotage, the civilian workers now sought to flee as rapidly as they could, running for bridge 'M'; among them were khaki-clad members of the Todt Organization. Seeing them approach and confusing the German workers' uniforms with those of the British, the sentries at the bridge opened fire, their panic response being taken up by others of their comrades who imagined the French to be rising against them. Fearing for their lives, groups of soldiers and sailors, many of whose officers had been swept from existence on Saturday, now began to shoot indiscriminately, seeing enemies in every doorway, alley and window, and often engaging each other.

Across in the new town where they were doing some work for the Delapré family, Gérard Pelou and his father heard both the crash of the torpedo explosions and the dread crackle of musketry which followed them. Much of the firing seemed now to be coming from the direction of Old St Nazaire and, as Mme Pelou was in that quarter all on her own, the two men decided to go to her right away. With movement through the streets neither speedy nor safe, they finally reached the Old Town just as it was being cleared of its inhabitants by parties of trigger-happy German troops. As a hiding place for Tommies and those who would challenge the authority of the Reich, this untidy jumble of buildings was ideally suited and it had accordingly been ordered evacuated. During their search for Mme Pelou the two men were challenged. M. Pelou was arrested but Gérard managed to lose himself amid the throngs of frightened civilians and return to the Delapré's, in whose house he would be obliged to hide until such time as the worst of the danger had passed.

When they had been routed out of their homes, the civilians were herded like cattle into the cold and dirty blockhouses where they would remain under guard through all of Monday night. Among the men, women and children crammed into 'Sud 1', were the Bouillants, who were uniquely disturbed by this turn of events as young Jean, who had planned to retrieve a Tommy-gun from the kitbag which had been flung down the well and which had refused to sink, had his pockets filled with bullets. Needless to say, if these were found, the prospects for the family were grim indeed, and so, over the course of the night his mother and aunt had to make frequent trips outside to perform their natural functions, which the women were permitted to do unguarded, each time carrying with them two or three of the offending articles until all at last were gone.

Early on Tuesday morning the population of the remainder of the town awoke to find notices prominently displayed which carried the signature of the mayor, M. Toscer. Prepared during the night under duress, these warned that further acts of aggression against the Germans would result in hostages being taken and shot. While this threat was being digested, coaches arrived by the blockhouses to take all the Old Town residents away to a camp on Savenay racecourse which had formerly housed Senegalese prisoners, where all fifteen hundred or so would be held while their homes were meticulously searched and their unprotected belongings often looted or damaged. On their return towards the end of the week, they were given a mere twenty-four hours to leave, after which every building in the Old Town not commandeered for German use was razed to the ground.

With this act of vandalism, the 'living' areas of the town were effectively separated from the most vulnerable portions of the docks, and until such time as these vital facilities were confirmed as clear of both saboteurs and hidden explosives even the civilian workers were kept away from their jobs. It was an attack on an innocent population which was almost Roman in its scale and it was quite at odds with the punctilious observation of the military niceties which by and large governed German behaviour towards the soldiers and sailors who had brought violence to the town in the first place.

As he could speak French well, and as he was fit enough to undertake this disagreeable task, Corran Purdon was taken to the morgue for the purpose of identifying those that he could of the British dead. Then, on Wednesday, all the recovered bodies were buried in a field at Escoublac, just outside La Baule. In a moving ceremony attended by a British party of twenty officers and men, the coffins were lowered into the ground, after which the party passed by in single file and the Germans fired three volleys in salute. In spite of their own very substantial losses, the Germans were nothing if not correct when it came to bidding farewell even to the dead of their enemy. It was a blood-bond, forged in conflict, which exclusive camaraderie unfortunately did not encompass civilians.

Although they were already confused by the turmoil which had burst in upon their lives in a physical sense, the Nazairiens were also having to cope with a barrage of disinformation put out by the Germans, the purpose of which was to convince both the occupied peoples and the neutrals that the

British assault had been a costly and humiliating failure. Within the port itself there was, of course, the very visible evidence of the destruction wrought in the area of the dry dock. However, everyone knew that the real value of St Nazaire to the Axis was its U-boat base and this had not been disrupted at all, which meant that, until such time as the British got round to explaining what it was they had really come all this way to do, a vacuum of understanding would continue to exist, which could be ruthlessly exploited by the highly effective Nazi propaganda machine.

Based on Ryder's mistaken assumption that the explosion at 0425 on Saturday, as seen from the deck of the withdrawing gunboat, had indeed been *Campbeltown*'s charge going up, initial British reports had been prompted to claim the destruction of the caisson as a matter of fact. A communiqué issued by COHQ on the evening of Sunday the 29th expanded a little on this theme. However, with almost all the landed Commandos having failed to return, absolute confirmation of the full results of the raid would have to wait until such time as the weather was clear enough for PRU sorties to come up with pictorial evidence.

In the absence of such certainties, British applause in the immediate aftermath of 'Chariot' was therefore muted, a condition which most certainly did not apply to the other side, whose streams of denials and distortions began to flood the media almost while the smoke of *Campbeltown*'s blast still hung above the site of her triumph. Operating on the general principle that a lie, once voiced, can never be completely unvoiced, because, whatever efforts are made to expunge it, traces will always remain to fester within the body of the truth, the Germans produced reports that were designed to corrode and belittle subsequent British claims. Describing the raid in 'Zeebrugge' terms, as a failed assault on a U-boat base, while also characterizing it as an abortive attempt to open a second front at the specific behest of the Bolsheviks, they stated that the attacking forces had been all but annihilated, that *Campbeltown* herself had been hit and sunk in the estuary, that such few soldiers as did somehow manage to scramble ashore had been captured almost immediately and that, at dawn, Schmidt and his five torpedo boats had succeeded in driving off a superior force of Royal Navy destroyers.

Against such a persuasive assault, the British were eventually able to mount a strong rebuttal, based on aerial photographs which clearly showed the outer caisson to have been driven to one side. However, even these were proclaimed as fakes, this new doubt only adding to the damage already done to the mind sets of all those whose trust of British statements was neither absolute nor automatic.

As the primary aim of the raid had been to render the 'Normandie' dock inoperative, with a considerable extra effort having been put into the destruction of associated dockyard facilities, it was quite natural for both sides to judge its success or failure primarily in physical terms. However, to reduce its achievements to a mere accounting of broken metal and bricks was to miss its real and enduring value to the successful prosecution of the war, which was to show to the world that the British were far from finished and to demonstrate just how insecure was the German hold on the long and vulnerable coastline of the new Reich.

Having been driven from France so ignominiously scarcely two years before, the British had won a reputation for perfidy which 'Chariot' was the perfect vehicle to help dispel. And at a time when many Frenchmen and women could not decide whether to fight the invader or to be practical and learn to live with him, a return of khaki in force, not just to the mainland of Europe, but to one of the very ports through which the Tommies had earlier been forced to flee, offered a potentially huge boost to recruitment within the new and struggling resistance movements. It was therefore as a physical demonstration of the rekindling of Britain's offensive boldness and creativity that the raid should have been trumpeted, and trumpeted without delay, to an impressionable world – a demonstration in deeds, not words, that the occupied peoples were not after all alone, a downpayment on the promise that freedom would be bought for them one day.

While this battle for hearts and minds was being fought out in print, and over the airwaves, a much less public, though no less bitter, struggle was taking place behind the scenes, as efforts were made to apportion blame for this blow to German prestige. Already a long-standing feature of German military affairs, the dispute between the Nazi Party machine and the Wehrmacht was excited by this incursion into an important U-boat base, to the point where Hitler became personally involved in the search to identify those responsible for such apparent incompetence.

On Sunday the 29th the Führer ordered Field Marshal von Rundstedt, as Commander-in-Chief West, to conduct an immediate personal inquiry, which event took place on the following Tuesday, even as the population of the Old Town were being bussed away to Savenay. After looking in detail at the manner in which the raid was carried out, and at the actions taken to forestall such events by the defenders of the port, von Rundstedt concluded that the best had been done that could have been done in the circumstances, and that no one specifically was to blame. On receipt of von Rundstedt's 'whitewash' report, Hitler was far from content to let the matter drop and on 3 April General Jodl, as Chief of Staff of the armed forces High Command, was instructed to pursue the attribution of blame, his contribution only serving to open a rift between Berlin and Grand Admiral Raeder, who felt that the finger of blame was being unjustly pointed in the direction of the Kriegsmarine.

In the event all that would happen as a result of these contradictory interventions was that the demand for heads to roll would become lost in a welter of accusation and counter-accusation, which would only serve to enhance the moral and physical achievements of 'Chariot'. Only in a practical sense were measures taken that could be construed as productive. In an immediate response to the raid, Dönitz ordered that the U-boat HQ be moved away from Lorient to the safety of Paris, and, in an attempt to make such embarrassing adventures impossible in the future, instructions were given for locks to be protected by bomb-proof shelters, for all port approaches to be protected by boom defences and ground mines, for extra patrol vessels to be made available and for the procedures governing ship identification to be considerably revised and improved. Army units were to be stationed closer to threatened ports, defences were to be strengthened and garrisons significantly augmented. And, Hitler having already expressed his fears of British landings in his Directive No. 40, discussions would begin in May with representatives of the Todt Organization, which would result in the construction of the hugely expensive and wasteful Atlantic Wall.

For the British, too, there were lessons to be learned from 'Chariot', not all of which, unfortunately, were quickly taken to heart. As all future attacks, large and small, against the territory of the Greater Reich were likely to be sea-borne affairs, St Nazaire served to highlight the pressing need for the design and construction of specialized amphibious vehicles such as could put a company of men ashore, or an army complete with all its heavy weapons and supplies. This need was addressed with the help of the Americans, whose campaigns in the Pacific would be largely amphibious in nature, and the result of the collaboration between the Allies would be the triumph of 'Overlord', two years into the future.

Whilst physical needs could be quantified with relative ease, when it came to the principle of separate armed services working together in concert, employing common strategies to reach a common goal, solutions were not, however, always so simple to reach. As the Army, Navy, and Air Force each had separate identities, separate histories, separate staffs, and, in the case of 'Bomber' Harris, separate agendas, it was inevitable that there would be friction and suspicion whenever the need arose for them to work hand-in-hand. In the case of 'Chariot', which was a combined operation only in name, with the Navy withholding its ships, and Harris withholding his aircraft, such interservice rivalries most certainly put at risk the success of the whole, and they made it painfully clear that there was an urgent need to seek commonality of thought and purpose before a large-scale assault on the mainland could even be contemplated.

In respect of such large-scale assaults, the 'Chariot' experience should have caused warning bells to ring loud and clear where thoughts were harboured that future direct assaults on enemy ports might be successful. That this particular attack did actually succeed in penetrating the estuary mouth unseen and unharmed was almost entirely due to a fortunate succession of lucky breaks, allied to the existence of the shoals which had offered the possibility of a surprise approach in the first place. The weather during the crossing of the Bay of Biscay had been uncharacteristically benign; signals intelligence had allowed the fleet to be routed clear of enemy reconnaisance and weather flights; *Kapitänleutnant* Kelbling of U-593 had wrongly reported their course, leading to the departure from the scene of Schmidt's powerful squadron of destroyers; the guardships in the estuary had either not seen them at all, or had failed to communicate their presence to the shore; there had been no mines and no boom defences; radar had failed to spot their approach and, when finally seen and reported, intelligence had again come to their aid in the form of ships' morse-names which were familiar to the port's defenders. Having thus got as far as the port itself, Beattie had been guided to his target by the fortuitous illumination of the Old Mole light, and on reaching the caisson this was luckily found to be in its closed position, which was the ideal set-up for ramming.

Taken altogether and even allowing for the RAF's failure to perform any task other than the alerting of the German defences, fortune had smiled on this raid to an extent which not even the most optimistic planner could hope would be repeated in the future; and yet, within a mere five months, during which the enemy, alerted by 'Chariot', must surely have tightened both his procedures and his defences, a large-scale attack would be mounted against the port of Dieppe, with tragic consequences both for the men involved and to the reputation for potency of Commonwealth arms worldwide.

Having favoured the 'Charioteers' during their approach, fortune had been no less kind when it came to protecting the handful of surviving ships during their return to British shores. However, within the estuary itself she had been powerless to prevent a course of events being acted out which had been invited all those weeks before, when MLs had been foisted upon the planners of the raid in place of the second destroyer everyone but the Admiralty had seemed to recognize was needed from the start.

As ordered to sea, the fleet had, in effect, consisted of two quite separate raiding forces whose instructions required them to act in concert, but whose targets and chances of survival were quite distinct. On the one hand there was *Campbeltown*, a strong, steel ship, armoured as necessary, capable of defeating the lighter enemy guns and able to protect the majority of her Commando passengers, whose target was the strategically important 'Normandie' dock; on the other hand there were the little ships, singularly ill-suited to the task in hand, too lightly armed to engage and defeat the defences, unarmoured and highly flammable, whose troops by and large were to be directed against targets of nuisance value only.

In the event the success of the night was almost entirely *Campbeltown*'s. She rammed her caisson exactly as planned, she disgorged her troops in good order, she was scuttled in place, and then she exploded – eventually. Once over her bows, Copland's parties were all but unstoppable, just as the parties from the MLs would have been had it only been possible to land them too; but, as so many had predicted, these small craft were shot to pieces almost immediately. Where a second destoyer might well have been able to put troops ashore in force and hold for an eventual withdrawal, the little ships had never really come close to seizing either of their intended landing places. Had they been able to carry a higher proportion of 'fighting' troops, it is just possible that the story might have been different; as might also have been the case had the force been augmented by a couple of additional gunboats, acting to provide local fire superiority where dictated by events. But in reality, having trained so hard and travelled so far to do a job which they had all been led to believe could affect the course of the war at sea, 'might have beens' simply were not good enough. As originally envisaged by Hughes-Hallett and the COHQ planning team, the raid had required two specially lightened destroyers to work as intended. Anything less was a compromise, and in combat compromises invariably cost lives and put at risk the chances of achieving anything at all.

As put into practice, this particular compromise cost the lives of 169 of the 611 soldiers and sailors who actually took part in the action, the majority of these being lost on board MLs which were attempting either to land their men or to withdraw from the river, often with the survivors of other boats on board. In the main these fatal casualties were due to shell or gunshot wounds or burns; however, among those who drowned, there is a strong possibility that some, at least, succumbed to the depressive after-effects of the Benzedrine which a proportion of the men had taken earlier to enhance their alertness.

In addition to this high loss of life, a further 200 young men, the majority of whom were hurt to one degree or another, were destined to see the war out as prisoners. Having been treated initially at l'Hermitage, the wounded were moved, after just one week in La Baule, to join their comrades in Rennes, in their case not in the Stalag itself, but in the nearby St Vincent's Hospital, where operations would continue, in some cases, for many months to come, and where Tommy McCormack was finally destined to die. By this time many had been interrogated, their inquisitors including Paul Schmidt, who had been Hitler's personal and trusted interpreter since the mid-1930s: but the procedures had not been pressed in the face of universal obduracy.

From Rennes, initially for the able prisoners, but later for the wounded, too, the next move was into Northern Germany, to a camp by the name of Marlag und Milag Nord, which complex had been designed to hold both Royal Navy and Merchant Navy detainees. While some would remain here till the end of the war, others would eventually be moved on to Colditz and Spangenberg Castles, or to the universally hated Stalag VIIIB at Lamsdorf. Over a period of years, and despite the apparent hopelessness of all their situations, many officers and men would devote themselves to the task of engineering escapes and among those to finally succeed in bidding adieu to their captors would be Billie Stephens, Dick Bradley, Alf Searson and Jimmy Brown.

Of the total force barely more than one third had therefore been able to stage a successful withdrawal to Falmouth and Plymouth, accompanied by only three of the fifteen MLs which had been at the heart of the action. Of these three, the gallant 160 was not destined to survive her companions drawn from the 7th Torpedo Flotilla for long, as, shortly thereafter, she was bombed and sunk while under repair in Brixham. Tom Boyd having been invited to join Chief E.R.A. Howard in a War Bonds tour of the USA, this long-suffering ML was, at the time of her loss, the new command of Lieutenant Bill Wallach, latterly the 'Jimmy' of ML 270. With the destruction of this ship only the 307 and the 443 were left afloat of the MLs which had come under fire in the estuary. In July, 1942, as part of a reconstituted 28th Flotilla, they would sail for the Med with Platt in command, and in the company of the 341, which was the only other ML of the original force to survive. Having been 'lucky 13' at St Nazaire, the 443 had the privilege of being present during the surrender of the bulk of the Italian fleet, before she too was sunk, eventually succumbing to a mine, off Vada, in Italy.

For most of the sailors who made it back their fate was to be posted to ships or shore stations elsewhere in the fleet, although, in the case of the crew of the gunboat, Curtis was able to take Frank Smith, Bill Whittle, Fred McKee and Bill Reynolds with him to his new command, which was MGB

501. For the Commandos it was simply a matter of returning to their units and settling down once more to the task of getting on with the war. Where 2 Commando were concerned, with so many killed or taken prisoner, the immediate priority was to rebuild under the very able tutelage of their new CO, Lieutenant-Colonel Jack Churchill. In the summer of 1943 this unit would also sail for the Med and there be decimated for the second time in the mincing machine that was Salerno.

Having done their level best to avoid capture during the German sweeps of the town which had begun on the morning of the 28th, only the seven hopeful *évadées* who had slid quietly from their hiding places later that first night remain to be accounted for. Of the group in the cellar T.S.M. Haines and Lance-Sergeant Challington had the misfortune to be captured just as they reached the open countryside; however, Lance-Corporal Douglas and Private Harding did finally succeed in making it all the way to Marseilles and thence to Britain, a feat which Lance-Corporal Howarth would match, if rather more slowly.

Having been wounded in the fighting, Howarth was initially cared for by the family of Dr Etienne Baratte, who was the headmaster of the Collège Aristide Briand, before being passed on into the unoccupied zone. Here he was caught and imprisoned by the Vichy police, eventually helping to lead an escape from the Fort la Revere in Nice, so that he could complete his own return to Blighty. Of the second group, both Corporal George Wheeler and Lance-Corporal Sims would succeed in their bids to cross the Pyrenees and break through all the way to Gibraltar. Celebrating George's arrival home on 21 May, Mountbatten wrote to Ryder of the 'grand story' the resourceful corporal had to tell, an assessment of George's record of scrapes and adventures which no one would wish to dispute. And a grand story indeed it is; however, as with the equally colourful tales of all the others who were never caught or who later escaped, a full recounting will have to wait until another day.

In recognition of their bravery and determination, all five successful *évadées* received awards, the Mention in Dispatches for Howarth being only one of fifty-one MIDs to be recorded in the aftermath of the raid, and the MMs for Wheeler, Douglas, Harding and Sims being a mere four out of the astonishing total of eighty-five medals awarded to 'Charioteers'. Ryder and Newman, as leaders of the raid, and Beattie, as captain of the *Campbeltown*, all received Victoria Crosses, as did Tommy Durrant, in recognition of his stand against the *Jaguar*, and Bill Savage, as a statement of the debt of gratitude owed to all the men of Coastal Forces. Surprisingly, and bearing in mind both his pivotal role in the training of the Commandos, and his fearless leadership under fire, Bill Copland was not thought deserving of his country's highest accolade. In company with Tom Boyd, Douglas Platt and Donald Roy, Major Bill's award was a DSO.

And so, with the ritual distribution of honours and the loss, capture, or dispersal of all the men who had shared in the pain and pride of this first great raid on the coast of France, Operation 'Chariot' passed into history.

Against all the odds, in the face of official mistrust, and with such poor tools to hand as those with which the British war machine had seen fit to equip them, the men of the Army Commandos and of the littlest ships of the Navy had succeeded in penetrating one of the most heavily defended ports in Europe. And, as a result of their multi-pronged attack on the 'Normandie' dock, this important facility was effectively removed from strategic consideration for the remaining years of the war. The Germans did attempt to repair it by, among other things, floating down the inner caisson to replace the damaged outer one; but by the time such work might have begun its value to the Axis had been so diminished by their waning fortunes at sea that its renewal ceased to be worth the time and effort involved. Ironically when the dock was finally put back into service, it would be for the benefit of the long-suffering inhabitants of the port of St Nazaire, and the first ship to be re-fitted in it, arriving on 11 November, 1947, would be an ex-German liner, sailing under her new name *Liberté*.

It is only as a military exercise whose objective had been to thwart, or discourage, the dispatch against the Atlantic convoys of the battleship *Tirpitz*, that the raid was not a success, specifically because the Germans themselves had already come to understand the enormous risk to their prestige that was involved in such a venture; indeed, even by the early months of 1942, though it would not become fully clear until later, the era of the big-gun warship had already almost drawn to a close in the face of the development of increasingly sophisticated bombers and submersibles. *Tirpitz*, her every movement constrained by political as well as by economic and strategic prohibitions, was never to venture beyond the confines of the North Sea, although, in a demonstration of her continued potency there, she would cause convoy PQ17 to scatter in July, as a result of which precipitate response to the mere threat of her guns, the lumbering merchantmen would be decimated by U-boats and by the Luftwaffe.

Taken in concert with the failure of the raiders to fire the fuel stores, or to render the Bassin de St Nazaire tidal, the incorrect appreciation of the value to the Germans of the 'Normandie' dock would, on the face of it, seem to indicate that the raiders' material effect on the German war effort was minimal. However, their achievements were in fact far more complex and long-lasting than this simple accounting of temporary physical damage might suggest. At a period when Britain was experiencing defeat in almost every theatre of war, and when a considerable gulf in time remained between the Americans' decision to wage war on the Germans and their actual arrival in the field, the raiders showed a sceptical world that the Tommies still had fire in their guts. They boosted the morale of the French and, at a time when German arms were ascendant, they delivered a slap in the face to the Führer which was both embarrassing militarily, and very costly indeed in respect of all the men and material the coming years would swallow in the folly of his attempt to gird Europe with a fortress wall.

In respect of Combined Operations, 'Chariot', as well as making for all time the reputation for drive and courage of the Commando soldier, pointed clearly to the techniques which would have to be learned, and the equipment which must be developed, before an invasion could be mounted which would stand more than an even chance of success. It was not due to any failure of the 'Charioteers' making that the highly trained Commandos were rarely ever used again in the role which had proved so effective in the Lofotens, at Vaagso and at St Nazaire. And nor do the raiders bear any responsibility for the decision to try too soon to emulate their success, which crashed headlong into reality on the foreshore of Dieppe.

As a wartime event, it is natural that any assessment of 'Chariot's' achievements should be based primarily on an appreciation of what the operation did, or did not, do to assist in the ultimate defeat of the Reich. But because of the way it was constructed, because of the comradeship, the innocence and the unashamed patriotism of the young men involved, at a stage when thoughts of fighting had not yet been completely debased by genocide and by the mass extinctions of civilian populations from the air, because of their willingness to die for a cause which they firmly believed to be right and because of the guts and unquenchable determination that saw them through to success in the face of every kind of adversity, 'Chariot' sends out a message which extends beyond war and which speaks to every man, even today, of just what can be achieved by the power of human will alone.

In a speech to Commando and naval survivors, made on the occasion of the fiftieth anniversary of the raid, Micky Burn spoke of this about as well as any man could when he made the observation, 'What I think we all did, all of us, had a spiritual as well as technical and tactical importance. What it comes to is that we did the impossible. So whenever some great project is afoot, national or international, or even some private individual act is in mind which could be ennobling, and have good results and give heart, and when people mock at it and say, "Oh, it's impossible, it can't be done", we have a certain right, indeed a certain joy in contradicting, because one week and half-a-century ago we managed to achieve it.'

His is an edifying conviction, particularly so when set within the context of an increasingly cynical and self-indulgent society, and to its underlying sentiment one can but respond, 'Amen to that'.

Bibliography

Command Attack, Gordon Holman: 1942 (Hodder & Stoughton)

The Little Ships, Gordon Holman: 1943 (Hodder & Stoughton)

The Greatest Raid of All, C.E. Lucas Phillips: 1958 (William Heinemann)

Raid on St. Nazaire, David Mason: 1970 (Ballantine Books)

The Attack on St. Nazaire, Robert Ryder: 1947 (John Murray)

List the Bugle, Corran Purdon: 1993 (Greystone Books)

St. Nazaire Commando, Stuart Chant-Sempill: 1985 (John Murray)

British Special Forces, William Seymour: 1985 (Sidgwick & Jackson)

The Commandos: 1940–46, Charles Messenger: 1991 (Grafton Books)

The Raiders: The Army Commandos 1940–46, Robin Neillands: 1989 (Weidenfeld & Nicolson)

Churchill's Private Armies, Eric Morris: 1986 (Hutchinson)

Commandos in Action, Graeme Cook: 1973 (Hart-Davis MacGibbon)

The Secret Forces of WWII, Philip Warner: 1985 (Granada)

The Green Beret: The Story of The Commandos 1940–45, Hilary St George Saunders: 1949 (Michael Joseph)

The Battle of The Narrow Seas, Peter Scott: 1945 (Country Life)

Destroyers at War, Gregory Haines: 1982 (Ian Allan)

Allied Coastal Forces of WWII, John Lambert and Al Ross: (Conway Maritime Press)

    Vol 1: *Fairmile Designs And U.S. Submarine Chasers* 1990

    Vol II: *Vosper MTBs And U.S. ELCOs* 1993

Anatomy of The Ship: The Destroyer Campbeltown, Al Ross: 1990 (Conway Maritime Press)

Night Action, Peter Dickens: 1974 (Peter Davies)

Fast Attack Craft, Keiren Phelan & Martin Brice: 1977 (Macdonald & Jane's)

Inshore Heroes, Wilfred Granville & Robin Kelly: 1961 (W.H. Allen)

Able Seaman RNVR, Herbert Messer: 1989 (Merlin Books)

Hitler's Naval War, Cajus Bekker: 1974 (Doubleday)

Ultra at Sea, John Winton: 1988 (Leo Cooper)
The War at Sea, 1939–1945, Vols I & II, Stephen Roskill: 1954 (HMSO)
Menace, Ludovic Kennedy: 1979 (Sidgwick & Jackson)
Sink the Tirpitz, Léonce Peillard: 1968 (Jonathan Cape)
Churchill and The Admirals, Stephen Roskill: 1977 (Collins)
Pursuit: The Sinking of The Bismarck, Ludovic Kennedy: 1974 (Collins)
Make Another Signal, Jack Broome: 1973 (Kimber)
Hitler's Strategy, F.H. Hinsley: 1951 (Cambridge University Press)
The Special Operations Executive 1940–46, M.R.D. Foot: 1985 (BBC)
Hitler's Atlantic Wall, Colin Partridge: 1976 (D.I. Publications, Guernsey)
British Intelligence in The Second World War, Vol. II, F.H. Hinsley and others: 1981 (HMSO)
Bomber Command, Max Hastings: 1979 (Michael Joseph)
"Bomber" Harris and The Strategic Bombing Offensive, 1939–1945, Charles Messenger: 1984 (Arms and Armour Press)
Hitler's War Directives, 1939–1945, H.R. Trevor-Roper: 1964 (Sidgwick & Jackson)
The Second World War, Winston S. Churchill: 1950 (Houghton Mifflin)
  Vol 3: *The Grand Alliance*
  Vol 4: *The Hinge of Fate*
St. Nazaire 1939–1945, Daniel Sicard: 1994 (Editions Ouest-France)

Articles/Pamplets/Documents

After the Battle No 59, 1988 (Battle of Britain Prints International Ltd)
Starshell, Vol IV, No 15: October 1992
Warship Profile 5: HMS Campbeltown *(USS* Buchanan*)*, John Wingate: 1971 (Profile Publications)
Orders, Instructions And A Selection Of Action Reports, Narratives And Letters, Courtesy of the Imperial War Museum
Booklet 60: Association Préhistorique et Historique de la Région Nazairienne
Souvenance *Booklets 1 and 2:* Memoire et Savoir Nazairiens

Index

299